By Corinna Lindon Smith

Rising Above the Ruins in France
(New York, G. P. Putnam's Sons, 1920)

Tombs, Temples, and Ancient Art, with Joseph Lindon Smith
(Norman, University of Oklahoma Press, 1956)

Interesting People: Eighty Years with the Great and Near-Great
(Norman, University of Oklahoma Press, 1962)

Library of Congress Catalog Card Number: 62-11273

Copyright 1962 by the University of Oklahoma Press,
Publishing Division of the University,
Composed and printed at Norman, Oklahoma, U.S.A.,
by the University of Oklahoma Press.
First edition.

Interesting People

Eighty Years with the Great and Near-Great

By Corinna Lindon Smith

NORMAN

UNIVERSITY OF OKLAHOMA PRESS

INTERESTING PEOPLE

Corinna Lindon Smith, aetat. 82.
Pencil sketch by her daughter Rebecca.

To my granddaughter Jessie,
her husband Reverend Samuel W. Hale, Jr.,
and their children Billy, Betsy, Whitney,
Jessie, Joseph Lindon, and Dan.

PREFACE

THERE MUST BE a substantial reason for writing an autobiography. My father, George Haven Putnam, suggested it when I was a child. He was speaking of history, as he often did to me.

"How is history made?" I asked him.

"By the thoughts, words, and actions of people every day," he replied.

"Then," I said, "we should be very careful to do good things, shouldn't we?"

He nodded and I set about doing the things I considered important because my parents did. In my mature years I had the opportunity to choose courses of action which seemed valuable, and in so doing I have perhaps had some part in that process by which history is made. My record in this book is of events with which I have been personally associated during more than eighty years, some of them of historical significance, some merely interesting or amusing.

It is a book about people: Thomas Hardy, Henry James, Lewis Carroll, Lord Cromer, Frank Crowninshield, Theodore Roosevelt, John J. Pershing, Ignace Paderewski, Isabella Stewart Gardner, Margot Asquith, Evangeline Booth, Will Rogers, Mark Twain, Alexis Carrell, George A. Reisner, Amelia Earhart, and Lewis Lawes, among others—and about me.

If I have a point of view about people, events, and progress, it is that I have considered it a rare privilege to have lived my early life at the close of the Victorian era, my middle years in the period of fateful realignment of the world's populations, and my later years when, as Shane Leslie once remarked, "reticence had been abolished" and only reality, harshly viewed, seemed of a piece with human endeavor. Not all of these things have I liked, but you may

vii

be sure that witnessing them has evoked in me a sensitivity to history which may not be altogether ordinary.

From my earliest years until the present moment, I have thoroughly enjoyed myself, and most when in the presence of my contemporaries, little and big, in many lands—England, Europe, the Near East, the Far East, and our own country. The kinds of people not obsessed with the gadgetry and conveniences that beset our every waking hour nowadays: these have made the era in which we live what it is; these have given me much happiness.

My contemporaries have found their way daily into my personal journals, the keeping of which has been with me a lifelong habit. These records have given me the privilege of renewing not only my own life but the lives of those whom I have admired.

If I describe a New York which no one now living can recognize, or an English countryside which no longer remains as it once was, it will have to be remembered that I have lived in "times not our own," to borrow a phrase from Walter Savage Landor. We speak glibly of the abolishment of time and space, but only those who, like me, have actually witnessed the process of abolishment can understand what has happened to our world in somewhat less than a century.

Lest there be any misgivings about my favoring the past unduly, let me say that I consider the past valuable as a book of reference, to be consulted often before decisions are made which will affect the present or the future.

This notion of the advisability of evaluating change by balancing it against experience, I once heard expounded by an elderly Navaho in a blanket and braided hair. The way he put it was that white man had not yet learned that "not all change is progress."

My effort has been to be tolerant but just; to assess the past for what it was, not what it might have seemed; to think twice before rejecting what is valid, from a younger person's perspective, in the new; to enjoy the long wave of the present as it is borne to us by the restless seas of human striving—a wiser age yet a puzzling age, beset by problems which not even its own technology can solve, exhibiting wealth and poverty, intellectual faith and moral despair, a questioning of its goals and a certainty about the essential worth of man. In short, it is an age like many another in the history of human kind.

In what follows, I do not expect to set values straight. I wish merely to recount the times and the thoughts of my contemporaries, who will help me tell you what life was like from Victoria's day to our own.

I wish to thank Viola Rajaniemi for arranging my files consisting of rough notes and journals; and Carol Davison, Peggy Cockroft, and Janet Cartwright for typing the manuscript.

Most of all to express my appreciation to members of the staff of the University of Oklahoma Press for making me feel at home in publishing surroundings similar to those of G. P. Putnam's Sons, where I was brought up.

Corinna Lindon Smith

New York City
January 3, 1962

CONTENTS

INTERESTING PEOPLE

I

THE HOUSE OF PUTNAM,
AND THE SHEPARDS, TOO

IF ANYTHING I have done in my life remains durable, it is, I believe, because of what the Putnams and the Shepards gave me and because of what the society in which they lived gave them. Both my father's and my mother's ancestors were of English origin and migrated to Massachusetts at about the same time. For the past three centuries there has been in my inheritance a New England background of just and honorable men and women, cautious about their judgments but, having decided on their rightness, acting upon them with all persistence. They were steadfast and stubborn, but mostly in the interest of good causes. A goodly heritage this, based on a strict code of ethics and behavior, and frugal living, with no place for self-seeking and opportunism.

The earliest known ancestor in the house of Putnam was Nicholas Puttnam or Puttenhem, born at Penne in the county of Buckinghamshire in 1523. Eventually the original homestead was to come again into the ownership of the family, purchased by a young English collateral, and a large estate of farmland useful in raising crops in World War I.

I can trace the direct influence on my own career of General Israel Putnam, of Bunker Hill fame, and of his cousin, General Rufus Putnam, a leader in the settlement of Ohio—Israel for a quality of obstinacy transmuted to my refusal to be licked by anything important once undertaken and a determination never to be afraid; and Rufus for my fondness for the West and my administrative bent (according to my father)

3

Since my childhood I have tried hard to emulate the discretion of the wife of another general in the family, General Joseph Palmer. Mrs. Palmer, on recognizing her husband's eyes in a group of supposed Indians in her kitchen, never asked him why the strange costume nor what he was about to do in it. The disguised Indians were planning to commit the first act of the American Revolution as leaders of the "Boston Tea Party."

I am also indebted to several of the Putnam women who handed down to the younger generation their intellectual aspirations and a gift for learning languages, more particularly to my father's mother, Victorine Haven Putnam.

My grandfather, George Palmer Putnam, had no easy childhood, as a consequence of the complete breakdown in his father's health, which brought to an abrupt end in 1810 the promising career of the senior Putnam as a lawyer in Boston. Fortunately, G. P. Putnam's mother Catherine had more of an education than was usually given to girls in the early part of the nineteenth century, and was, moreover, a woman of energy and resources. She supported the family by opening a school in Brunswick, Maine, a town in country surroundings. When, in 1829, the building was destroyed by fire, she opened a second successful school in New York. But my grandfather, the youngest of the four children, started off on his own at the age of eleven to earn a living in Boston. For four years he was an apprentice in a business that sold carpets.

When he was fifteen, he joined his family in New York and, as he put it, "the book trade and I were introduced to each other," when he had succeeded in finding a job at a small book and stationery store on Broadway near Maiden Lane.

By 1833 G. P. Putnam had entered the employ of Wiley and Long, publishers and booksellers, and in 1840 the firm of Wiley and Putnam was formed by John Wiley, only a year older than my grandfather, who took him into partnership, thus giving him his start as a publisher.

My grandfather was impressed with the possibilities of building up a business through the importation into New York of British books, and in arranging with English publishers for editions of

4

American books. In pursuit of this enterprise, he migrated to London and, in 1841, established a branch of Wiley and Putnam in Paternoster Row. Later the firm moved to Waterloo Place and soon became a center for American residents and for a small group of Englishmen who were interesting themselves in American affairs.

John Wiley, from the start, had been lukewarm on the subject of extending the book trade to include England, and by 1848 he decided to withdraw from the London venture. On this issue the partnership of Wiley and Putnam was dissolved. My grandfather was the first American to publish on both sides of the Atlantic, and he was also the first and only American publisher who paid royalties on English and foreign books published by American firms years before these authors were protected by international copyright. He conceived the principle of international copyright in 1837 and by 1852 the text was drafted for legislation. The copyright bill did not become law however until 1891 upon the initiative of his eldest son (my father), George Haven Putnam.

In 1857 a junior member of my grandfather's firm was dismissed on the discovery that he had been using its resources in speculations. As a result, in the business panic of that year, Putnam's went through bankruptcy. My grandmother Putnam insisted on having the Yonkers home, which she owned, sold for the benefit of the creditors. The family, consisting of seven children, moved to a small house. Although she had not much of an education, her mind was active and receptive.

Therefore, when all the personal assets of the family were lost, she, following in the footsteps of her mother-in-law, opened a successful school in New York. But within a few years the firm of Putnam's was once again a flourishing concern, thanks to the confidence of friends and authors in my grandfather. Among the latter was Washington Irving, who declared he would withdraw his books from the market unless Putnam's continued to publish them. It seems incredible that the sale of Washington Irving's many books in large part supported the Putnam family during those lean years, to be followed by the critical period of the Civil War.

Putnam's became Putnam and Son when Papa was only fifteen

and was teaching Greek and Latin at the MacMullen School, New York City, managing to keep himself, through home study, just a few lessons ahead of his pupils. The next year he was a student at Göttingen University, Germany.

He did not reach the age of enlistment, which was eighteen, until the third year of the Civil War. But in Germany, as a youngster, he had distributed pamphlets in Göttingen and other cities, written by his father, explaining the cause of the North. He did the same thing in England, getting to see men of importance as his father's son.

When he was mustered out with the 176th New York Regiment in April, 1865, after two years of service, his father persuaded him to give up an ambition to teach history. Instead, he rejoined his father in publishing and promised to become head of the firm after his father's death.

The other three in a family of ten who also had outstanding careers were the eldest, Mary Corinna, a pioneer in the field of women medical doctors, and the two youngest, Ruth as a historian, and Herbert, who won great distinction as librarian of Congress.

Mary, or Minnie, as she was called, informed her father that she intended to become a doctor. He declared that medical science was a "repulsive pursuit" for a woman, but with his customary philosophy he accepted the inevitable. In September, 1866, she sailed for France, where she went into residence with a French family in Paris. Soon she spoke the language fluently and was able to write it correctly in articles she published to supplement her meager funds.

A personal introduction to the American ambassador from her father resulted in her being recommended to attend some of the smaller clinics in Paris, also to work in hospitals. A letter to her parents written in September, 1868, described the achievement of her purpose in coming to France. She wrote:

"For the first time since its foundation, several centuries ago, a woman's petticoat, worn by your daughter, was seen in the august amphitheatre of the École de Médecine."

It was not until June, 1869, that Minnie found time for a brief visit home in order to be at her brother Haven's wedding to Rebecca Kettel Shepard of Dorchester (my parents). She was short of money

6

and therefore made the three weeks' voyage to New York traveling
steerage on a sailing vessel.

On her return to France, the conferring of her degree was interrupted by the Franco-Prussian War. She refused her only opportunity to leave before the siege of Paris in 1870, and continued her
studies during it. It was not until the summer of 1871 that normal
conditions had been restored. She then passed her thesis and became *docteur en Médecine de la Faculté de Paris.* A large and distinguished professional audience gathered in the Court of the École
saw her receive for her thesis a *parfaitement satisfait* (perfectly satisfactory), which is the highest degree ever awarded.

She was deeply touched by the spontaneous ovation of the male
students present and considered the general acclaim given her in
the American, as well as the French, press significant as recognition
of the fact that a woman could speak with the voice of authority on
scientific medicine. This she proceeded to do immediately on her
arrival in New York, where she opened an office for private practice.

In 1873, her marriage to Dr. Abraham Jacobi, who had left Germany after the revolution of 1848 with Carl Schurz to make his
home in America, ably seconded her successful career. Together they
brought brilliant scientific thinking to bear on the solution of medical problems then current.

Ruth, after her graduation from Cornell, on discovering that
much additional source material on the history of Holland was
available since John Motley had produced his monumental volumes,
decided to write the life of William the Silent. She spent several
years in research and the resulting publication was well received by
scholars, including those of Holland, where the government had
the life translated into Dutch for use as a textbook in the public
schools. For the remainder of her life Ruth counted many Dutch
friends among her intimates, and any Putnam received a warm welcome in Holland for her sake.

As for Herbert, he had started his distinguished career by being
in charge of the Library in Minneapolis, later going to the Boston
Public Library, before he was appointed by President Woodrow
Wilson to be head of the Congressional Library in Washington.

7

There he remained for more than thirty years, achieving the extraordinary record of never having had a political appointment urged by a member of Congress nor an appropriation refused to carry out the development of an unique national library.

One of his many special contributions was the constantly improved program for "feeding" suggestive information to branch libraries all over the United States to guide purchases, a service that was reflected in the higher selection standards for the benefit of local reading publics.

These three learned Putnams were to mean much in my adult life. Aunt Minnie, for whom I was named, got over her disappointment at my refusal to be trained as a doctor. She was understandably pleased when I pursued a career in public health as a volunteer.

As for Uncle Herbert, he became a life-long friend of Joe's and mine and several times joined us abroad. And twice he used his wonderful library system in furthering projects of mine.

Aunt Ruth's friendship with Dutch families in Holland was to add greatly to the interest of my visit to our American ambassador at The Hague. And in Java, through her introductions, I met many Javanese married to Dutchmen.

The home to which my grandfather, Otis Shepard, brought my grandmother, Ann Pope Shepard, on their marriage in 1823, played an important role in my childhood memories. It was built on a plateau at the top of a very steep street, called High. There was a long, narrow, casual garden of fruit trees and plants to the rear, facing the First Church of Dorchester on the summit of Meeting House Hill, only a few moments' walk away.

The location of the house, close by the church, resulted in my grandmother Shepard's sharing intimately in the activities of various pastors. Even more so, it helped to develop a strong religious faith and moral principles that were outstanding in her important characteristics and fortified her in the uncomplaining acceptance of suffering in her family, and other trials, until her death in 1886. Furthermore, she had strong ancestral ties not only with Dorchester but with Meeting House Hill.

8

Her ancestor, William Blake, born in 1594, was the first generation of the Blake family in New England. The Dorchester Town
records of 1637 state that he was one of one hundred and four
settlers among whom the "land of the neck was divided." He became selectman and "freeman" of Dorchester, a requisite for this
latter position being membership in the First Church. He was active
on the Committee appointed in 1645 to build it. The plan was ambitious, calling for an enormous square building with an elaborate
façade and a very tall steeple that would tower above the countryside. Two hundred and fifty pounds, a large sum in those early
days, was raised for the purpose. The parish house, attached to
the back of the church, and an adjacent school were of slightly
later construction.

Both her grandparents and parents had moved to Dorchester
from Stoughton. My grandfather Shepard had also in his early
manhood left Stoughton, where he was born, to live on Meeting
House Hill. He became town clerk of Dorchester and later taught
in the school attached to the church.

Dorchester was an important settlement that straggled over a
vast area to Dorchester Heights, which was behind commercial
South Boston, and overlooked the harbor in a wide sweep. Beyond,
near the bridge leading to Quincy, was Pope Hill, named for one
of the family. Everywhere, from Meeting House Hill as a center,
and including Pope Hill, intermingled with homesteads were imposing mansions separated from neighbors by plenty of space and
having the charm of privacy.

It was a self-regulated, restricted district where well-known families of the early pre-Civil War period made their homes, to an
even greater extent than in the region bordering the Boston Common. Later both were to be superseded by Back Bay. What a sight
it must have been on Sabbath morning to see the sombre-garbed,
respectable occupants emerge from their houses to enter carriages,
and in slow processions converge toward Meeting House Hill. As
a period scene, the conveyances and fine horse flesh gathered on the
green surrounding the famous church rivaled in interest the distinguished appearance of the congregation.

In those days there was no thought of planned parenthood, and Ann Pope Shepard had not fewer than ninety first and second cousins. In her genealogy were listed such Boston names as Lowell, Lyman, Cushing, Tappan, among the predominating Blakes, Popes, and Pierces.

Her grandfather, John Pierce, was a lover of church music, an appreciation he handed down to many of his descendants. The choir of the First Church of Dorchester contained nine members of his family. An anecdote is told of one very stormy Sabbath when so few people arrived for the service that the congregation met in the vestry. The choir was led as usual by his daughter, Mrs. Pope, then in her eighty-second year, who stood and sang assisted by her children, grandchildren, grandnieces, and grandnephews—*and no one else!*

This Pierce family taste for music has persisted into the present generation, and conspicuously in a great-great grandson, Edward Burlingame Hill. For twenty years he was head of the Music Department at Harvard University, a famous composer of symphonic works, and a recognized music critic at home and abroad.

John Pierce, D. D., a son of the music lover, was born in 1773, graduated from Harvard twenty years later, and was ordained at Brookline as Pastor of the church, an appointment he was to hold for the next fifty years. He died in the year of his retirement. "The Pierces have been a godly race," was a remark he made when praised for some special sermon. He also meant to imply his pride in having his people a part of a social tradition of worthy citizens who gathered together in one another's homes to discuss topics of the day. A youngster of six evaluated this tradition with amazing acumen. He was Frank, the son of William Lloyd Garrison, the abolitionist. A guest found the boy in the Garrison home sobbing in a dark corner beyond the dining room, from which he had been excluded while a group of Garrison's friends were being served a formal meal.

"What's the matter?" little Frank was asked. "Didn't they give you any of the good food?" To which he replied, "Yes, a lot, but I am *missing the conversation.*"

From all accounts, Grandfather Shepard was strikingly handsome, with a low brow, wavy, light brown hair, unusually fine eyes, and classic features enhanced by a clear complexion. He was intelligent and well educated, and had a remarkable memory, with a passion for the plays of Shakespeare, which he knew from cover to cover. On the slightest encouragement, he would recite long passages in a ringing voice that carried far—and sometimes disturbed the neighbors.

Grandfather Shepard gave up a teaching career, which was a mistake since his capacity for business proved to be limited. Admittedly he had serious shortcomings in character, in addition to being a poor provider for a wife and eleven children (seven of them girls) who lived to adulthood of the thirteen born.

All this granted, his appearance and intellect were useful legacies to his family. His daughters were called the "lovely Shepard sisters."

Also it was unquestionably his intellectual interests that inspired three of his daughters to go to Antioch College at a time when higher education for women was rare: Aunt Lucy, who married Thomas Hill, the president of Harvard; Aunt Addie, who had many happy years in Rome with the Nathaniel Hawthorne family (supposedly Hawthorne had her in mind in creating the character of Hilda in *The Marble Faun*, and during her stay in Rome she became a friend of Elizabeth Barrett Browning's); and my mother, who entered Antioch but resigned during her sophomore year to nurse in a Northern military hospital at Baltimore. Aunt Kate, the eldest, devoted her life to assisting her mother in the care of the family.

None of the four sons had much schooling, but fortunately the eldest, Otis, born in 1827, acquired a financial genius that was only equalled by his devotion to his family, which led him to support his mother and educate and otherwise care for his sisters after Grandfather Shepard's death in 1859. Otis's favorite maxim was, "If you have something to do, then do it at once, and with all your might." This philosophy he followed consistently throughout a spectacular career. He began to work at the age of sixteen in a grocery store, but soon left, since he saw no opportunity to make the amount of money he considered desirable. In his early twenties, he had started a lumber business on his own. The firm soon became Shepard and Morse and prospered, as did the other varied business ventures he went into, even coming through panics unscathed.

As the Civil War approached, and during it, Otis and his younger brother Horace were stirred to fever pitch by coming in contact with the cause of the slaves, through stories told them by Uncle Alexander Pope, their mother's brother. He had dedicated himself to the "underground," and, aided and abetted by his wife Charlotte Cushing, was engaged in planning the escape of slaves and looking after them upon their safe arrival on the soil of Massachusetts. Learning from Uncle Alexander of the number of apparently decent citizens of their own state who had profited by the importation of slaves from Africa, they were both shocked, and Horace enlisted promptly in a Massachusetts regiment.

Otis found himself on the horns of a dilemma. He had married in 1854 and had two small sons, his mother and sisters needed him, and his financial responsibilities were heavy in important business transactions that would go to pieces without his creative imagination and personal supervision. He left the decision to Massachusetts Governor Andrews. Without a moment's hesitation the Governor said, "The sinews of war can only be carried on by men like you. Stay at home." Otis did, although he was just as anxious to be among the men fighting at the front as was his brother Horace.

This protective attitude towards his family was to benefit many future generations of Shepards, since in his will he set up a trust for members of the family who needed assistance for education, illness, or any other emergencies. It is still being administered by his youngest son.

Grandmother Shepard's daughters never outgrew the need for her sympathy and a tenderness combined with strength and wisdom. Her unobstrusive goodness towards those whose lives were bound to her by close ties was felt not only by her immediate family but by neighbors. She retained until the end the spontaneity of youth and an energy that defied her increasing years.

She was tall and thin and very erect, with a narrow, wrinkled face, a nose too long for beauty, and rather small faded blue eyes set close together, and a firm chin. In later years she wore a white cap trimmed with bits of ribbons and lace, as was the frill softening the lines of a stiff bodice and a full skirt.

I am thankful that I am old enough to have my own memories of Grannie, as her grandchildren called her, to supplement later descriptions of her character and appearance. I had seen for myself the expression in her eyes and the smile that spread over her face, giving it something more than beauty, and a laugh that was contagious.

My first recollection of her in her home was when I was a very small child. My mother was cross with me because she had told me to keep out of the garden and be quiet, and I had disobeyed. Grannie was seated with her arms outstretched. She gathered me into her lap for a comforting cuddle, after I had begun to feel very tired from running madly about in the garden, and she said my mother was not to mention my muddy shoes nor the tear in a new dress. In other words, she was the kind of nice, old-fashioned grandmother whom no child would forget.

Her birthday on October 5, which from sentiment she had chosen for her marriage, was an event she looked forward to and planned far in advance. Her daughters and the neighbors considered its simple celebration a very special occasion for which Mama always came from New York. In 1885, when I was nine, I persuaded her to take me to stay with Grannie for two weeks preceding the birthday, while she made a round of visits to some of her girlhood friends.

I believe the reason for every detail of this visit reaching out to me from the shadows of long ago was that Grannie's home and she herself were so entirely different from anything I was used to. It began when I stood beside her inside the entrance gate. Mama stepped into a carriage and said for me to be "good." Grannie called back, "Ask her to be happy with me: that's more important." And she and I were laughing like children when we waved goodbye to Mama.

The sole architectural feature of the house was a portico, but only large enough to hold three rockers. It had the usual arrangement of unpretentious homes of the period, small rooms with low ceilings, and consisting downstairs of a front and back parlor with the dining room and kitchen behind. When Grannie took me to neighbors, including relatives next door named Swan, I noticed that the curtains were down and the front parlor was dark. She told me that the Swans only used it for company, but she felt anyone who entered her house was company.

The floor of her front parlor was flecked with spots of sunlight, and was bright and cheerful like every other room, with a carpet I liked. It had a small flower pattern and was hand-woven, Grannie told me with pride. The idea that she considered all visitors company made me once invite the milkman, much to his embarrassment, to sit down in the front parlor with me.

In the dining room was a massive sideboard that left very little space for a table and chairs, and often, when many of the family came to meals, Grannie said some of them had to eat in the back parlor, where she usually sat when sewing or doing needle-point as relaxation from household duties.

It was a very late autumn, but much was still in bloom, and Grannie and I spent many happy hours in an old-time rambling garden, where I helped her fill with flowers a large basket slung over her arm. She had a "green thumb," and every plant she put in the ground herself, and tilled and watered with unfailing constancy, blossomed. Her lilies of the valley were famous in the neighborhood, also the blue amaryllis were unusually beautiful.

Near the kitchen was a grape arbor and we climbed on tall steps and gathered bunches of Isabella grapes that I helped her prepare for making jelly. Often she was over the stove making cake or cookies, and Annie, the maid, would take most of them with her, tied in neat parcels, to deliver to friends of Grannie's.

At the time, I was too young to appreciate her unselfish industry, which made duty a pleasure and gave her joy in her work, so much of it for others.

She had a sense of humor and chuckled as she described how she had dealt with boys caught red-handed on the branches of a large cherry tree on her place and also in trees that bore sickle pears. In her hand was a large bowl, which she handed one of them and said, "Keep what you want for yourselves, boys, and bring the rest into the kitchen." From this time on, hers was the only garden where fruit was never stolen. Her insight into human nature was also shown in her handling of adults.

During my visit a woman came in with red eyes, and she and Grannie sat a long time together in the front parlor, the woman doing most of the talking. Finally, as she rose to go, I heard Grannie say, "Do not parade your sorrows." I asked her later what that remark meant, and she said it was to keep your sorrows to yourself, as everyone had them. She lived up to this philosophy, as I was to learn after I was grown up. She never became bitter facing tragedy and sadness in her own family.

Grannie had prepared me for something exciting when she tied on her bonnet and I got into my best dress, but we only walked to the back of the church, where Grannie took me on Sundays, and up some stairs into a schoolroom that was empty except for several teachers. "Your mama was in this same room her first year at school," one of them said. Then another pointed to some letters in a square on the wall and told me that was a record of the fact that Rebecca Shepard had been awarded a special prize for reading aloud and knitting at the same time at the age of six. The women were all peering into my face, expecting me to say something. I was frightened of them and hung my head, clinging to Grannie's hand in silence.

She talked a little, and then we left without my saying a proper goodbye. "It was my fault," she said. "I should have told you beforehand what the teachers were going to do and how to talk to them." At Grannie's words and a comforting pat, I felt consoled for having been shy and stupid.

I was allowed to be present at the birthday festivities. The rooms were crowded, everyone helping themselves to food and talking at once, except Grannie, who sat in her rocker smiling happily but saying very little. When the old house was again quiet, she asked me what I would remember about her party. I replied, "That your hands were folded and you did nothing."

2

HIGH BRIDGE, LOW ROBBERY

I saw the light of day in a house at 31 West Sixty-ninth Street on September 27, 1876, but narrowly escaped being born on a tug that my parents had boarded to escort their friends the Bayard Taylors to quarantine on a voyage to Europe.

My earliest recollection is at the age of four. I was walking on a bridge over a river, and laughing as gusts of wind blew me about while clouds rushed past in the sky. I darted ahead of Mama and Papa and in chasing my hat I saw some very small openings in a stone fence. After a few hard bumps, I wriggled through one of these openings and stood on the edge of a narrow granite slab that jutted out over the river. It was exciting to look down at the water far below. I called out, "Mama, watch me jump down and float!"

But, as Papa's wild leaps towards me, and his loud shouting to "turn back," confused me, I swayed, teetering with no rail to hold on to, the water now looking black. I was crying and no longer wanted to float.

Then I heard Mama's voice, "Haven, stop talking!" Instantly I forgot my terror, in wondering what he would do on hearing said to *him* words he often used to me. When she told me not to try to turn around, but to back slowly towards the opening I had crawled through, I stopped crying and obeyed.

Even after eighty years, I can feel the firm grip of Mama's outstretched hands dragging me into her comforting arms. To this day, on entering or leaving New York by train from the Grand Central Terminal, I look up at this so-called High Bridge. Its stone arches still span the East River but now are flanked on both sides by a number of taller, less picturesque bridges of modern steel and concrete construction. A reminiscent shiver of terror yields to a feeling of amazement that my body was ever small enough to squeeze through so narrow an opening in a stone fence.

Soon after this high-bridge adventure, my childish instinct warned me that something was very wrong when I had watched my baby sister, carried out of the house in a box, and a strange woman instead of Mama gave me supper. I refused to eat. She got my clothes off and forced me into my crib; she tied me in, when I climbed out, and shut the door with a bang. I cried myself to sleep.

Early next morning I ran into Mama's room. She was in bed, her eyes were open, but she did not smile at me. A tall, thin creature with a big nose, dressed all in white, with something white on her head, jumped up from an armchair. Her rustling skirts and fierce eyes scared me, and I tried to get to Mama's bed, but the creature dragged me away and carried me into the hall. I was glad I had kicked and bitten her.

Papa came and told me to stop screaming, and with him was the woman who had put me to bed. He called her "Nurse" and said I was to stay with her and could not see Mama. After that "Nurse" always found me when I hid from her, and if I got through Mama's door, the creature in white pushed me out of the room. In my utter despair I decided to run away.

Seizing my doll, I wrapped her in a large handkerchief and tore down the back stairs into the street without a coat. Shadows were dreadfully scary. I hurried along in the darkness and at the sound of following footsteps I ran faster. But a man with bright gold buttons on his coat caught up with me. "Where are you going?" he asked, walking beside me. "I am running away," I told him, and looking up into his face I recognized him as someone who came into our kitchen, whom Cook called "the policeman on our beat," whatever that might be. And I told him my troubles.

I was so cold and hungry I did not mind his carrying me on his shoulder back to Cook and the kitchen.

"Get Mr. Putnam, and be quick about it," he said. The policeman kept talking to Papa, just as Mama had on the bridge. "Don't ever run away again—Mama and I need you with us all the time."

"Will you tell Nurse to let me into Mama's room?" I asked.

"Nurse won't be here tomorrow to keep you out. From now on Mama and I will take care of you."

The last thing I remember, I was in Mama's bed, and she held me tight while Papa fed me ice cream. This way of handling my running away was to influence my relations with my parents throughout important formative years. Wherever we lived, I continued to sleep in some kind of alcove, or in a small bedroom near theirs and no nurse ever again looked after me. Half asleep, I would listen to my father asking my mother's advice about public affairs and things connected with publishing. A retentive memory made me able to absorb information far beyond my age. Another reason for a special intimacy was that my mother always had breakfast in bed, brought in at 7:30, and until I went to college I ate mine with her.

Although my father's publishing business was on West Twenty-third Street, by the time I was four we had moved to a district known as Washington Heights, considered very far out of town in those days. Our house was on 152nd Street in a rural community comprising one general store and having its own self-contained social contacts and amusements (very simple ones). Everyone knew everyone else, including the local merchants such as the butcher, the baker, and the candlestick maker, and the children all played together.

The postman brought the news and delivered the morning paper. Watching the lamplighter set his ladder against the line of lamp posts one after another, turn on the gas, and with his long torch light the street lamps, was an excitement no child willingly missed. Gas was used in all homes, and in the entrance halls and living and dining rooms a glaring acetylene lamp was hung in the center.

In those days, the elevated road did not go above 125th Street and it was Papa's custom to walk to and from that station to reach his office. The morning of the great blizzard of 1888, he left the house before six and managed to get the only train that ran on the elevated that day. All public conveyances were at a standstill, there was no telephone and the telegraph wires were down. He was afraid the family would worry if he did not get back and he managed the trip of nearly seven miles on foot, buffeted by the wind and fighting

General Israel Putnam.
Courtesy his great great granddaughter
Mrs. Harry W. Kidder.

George Palmer Putnam, founder of the publishing firm
which, after his death in 1872, became G. P. Putnam's Sons.

George Haven Putnam, my father,
from a sketch by Sir William Orpen, "after port."

At this age, Lewis Carroll doubted
that I could still enjoy make-believe,
but who could deny the White Rabbit?

the blinding snow. Incidentally, he was the *only* husband who did get back to Washington Heights from downtown that night.

His adventure made headlines in the press, and his daughters Ethel and Corinna were also mentioned. Late in the afternoon we discovered our cat was missing and, inadequately clothed, we rushed out, with the blizzard at its height, to hunt for her. After a terrific struggle, we reached the country store half-frozen. We had joined a group gathered around the stove when several policemen entered. We heard them say that they had just come from the sad duty of telling Mrs. Putnam her girls could not be found, whereupon Ethel and I exclaimed in unison that we were the "lost Putnams." The policemen, tied together by a rope, carried us back home on their shoulders just as the cat was coming down the front stairs lazily yawning after a long nap.

Bertha, who was sixteen, went downtown to school, but Ethel and I attended a local one for boys and girls, run by two daughters of John James Audubon, the naturalist, and called the Audubon School. The elder, Miss Eliza, with stern features and black side curls, was formidable in both appearance and actions. At one school entertainment for parents, she went to the side of a mother seated in a group and, without a word, produced a pair of scissors and snipped off a small bird with spread wings ornamenting the woman's hat, walking away with it.

This was an effective method of proving that her father's ideas against using birds for adornment would be enforced within the precincts of the Audubon School. Miss Eliza managed to instil in every one of the pupils, girls and boys, this principle of bird protection.

The great excitement of fall and late spring would be the descent of the Pumpelly family for a few days' stay with us on their way to and from a plantation in Georgia. Aunt Eliza, Mrs. Raphael Pumpelly, who was one of my mother's older sisters, could have posed for Venus de Milo. She was superbly beautiful. Uncle Raphael had a striking personality and a reddish beard that reached almost to his waist.

Their romance was breathtaking for the young to dwell on. Clarence King, who was temporarily in Boston, dropped in on his old friend, Raphael Pumpelly, in a hired carriage with a fast pair of horses to give him a word of greeting before he (King) went out to Dorchester to take Eliza Shepard for a drive, which was the purpose of this trip from New York.

Pumpelly was so fascinated by King's description of Eliza's charms that he asked to go along just for a glimpse. He fell madly in love with her at sight, with the result that Clarence King walked back from Dorchester to Boston, and it was Pumpelly who took Eliza for a drive and refused to bring her home until she had promised to marry him.

Houses in those days were somehow elastic and could accommodate many guests at a time. One bathroom sufficed. The elders took to sofas, giving up their bedrooms, and children lay about on the floor in odd corners. Possibly it was this early training in being turned out of my bed often that made sleeping on the hard desert sands, or on the bedrock of tombs, no hardship in later life.

Uncle Raphael always took the whole tribe of youngsters to the theatre, four children of his own and three Putnams. Once when it was to *Uncle Tom's Cabin*, we all shrieked with terror when the bloodhounds chased little colored Eliza across the ice. To the usher's protest at this disturbance to the audience, Uncle Raphael replied, "It's too realistic; I am almost crying myself."

He bought Aunt Eliza's gowns for her, also hats, which were then bonnets with ribbons tied under the chin. On one visit he let me go with him to the most fashionable milliner on Fifth Avenue. He deliberately put onto his own head one bonnet after another, studying it in mirrors from every angle; so great was his dignity and concentration that not even a cash girl giggled at the unusual sight of a long bearded man with a bonnet kept in place on top of his head by velvet ribbons under his chin.

The move to 140th Street came about because Mama was fascinated at sight with a great rambling house for rent or sale. It was situated in the midst of extensive grounds, with several barns and outbuildings belonging to the days when it had been a chicken farm. The entrance driveway faced a broad avenue shaded by attractive trees.

The house, on inspection, was in a poor state of repair, but had much charm inside and out. Soon after the blizzard, we were settled in ideal surroundings for happy-go-lucky youngsters.

The room I occupied had been originally an elaborate dressing room, with a frilled table across a long window. This was off the main bedroom where my parents slept. One morning, when Papa got up at his usual early hour, it was to find the pockets of his trousers laid over a chair rifled. In the center of the dressing table in my room was a bright ten cent piece on top of a note pinned to a cushion with the words scribbled in pencil, "For your fare downtown."

To Papa, this consideration on the part of a burglar seemed to compensate for the loss of an unusually large amount of cash he had happened to have, Mama's jewels, all the flat and other household silver, none of which was ever recovered. It is my memory that, from then on, the family did not again have solid silver for the table to replace the inherited silver which was stolen.

A second burglary occurred during the summer when we were at Lake George and Papa was living in the house as a temporary bachelor. One morning at about 10 o'clock, a furniture van drove up to the front door. Two men got out and entered the house with a key. They began to remove many pieces of furniture. O. Henry, the writer of short stories, who was a nearby neighbor, dropped in to see what was going on. He was informed that Mrs. Putnam had decided she needed additional furniture for the recently built house at Lake George. She had sent the key, and they were taking what she wanted over the road in the van. O. Henry chatted with the men while they ate a picnic lunch on the front steps, and he assisted them in carrying out a heavy sideboard that was an heirloom and several other antique pieces of value bought in London, the men joking about what women thought they needed in a country house.

Their last words were, "I wonder why Mr. Putnam puts up with such foolishness!"

Papa's surprise at returning from his office to find the downstairs pretty well denuded of furniture can be imagined. He stepped across to O. Henry's house to find out if he had chanced to be there and seen what had happened. O. Henry's account took Papa to the police station, but the van and its contents had disappeared into thin air, and no trace of the furniture ever turned up. Mama used to say that these two burglaries had made the problem of frequent moves easier for her.

From that time on, O. Henry was in and out of the house and was a general favorite, particularly of mine. He would invite Ethel and me to supper with him, and later, seated in an armchair, would pull away at his pipe and tell us stories that kids of today get in the Lone Ranger programs.

Almost every Saturday evening, two men arrived at our house and would be taken by Papa into his study. I had heard my father refer to them as fellow Mugwumps. When some of the boys with whom I played said their fathers called Papa a "no-good Mugwump," I became much perturbed and confided in O. Henry, who told me that a Mugwump meant being a "mighty fine citizen."

On a Saturday evening when R. R. Bowker, one of Papa's fellow Mugwumps, had not gotten a message from Papa telling him the meeting was called off, he arrived only to have the maid tell him that both Mr. and Mrs. Putnam were out. He started to go away, but I rushed up to him impulsively and said, "Aren't you proud to be a Mugwump with Papa?" From that moment we were friends. He often brought me a present, such as a plant or a book, and a small brooch that had belonged to his mother, which remained a cherished possession.

R. R. Bowker became to me a subject for hero worship. Thick lensed glasses did not hide the kindness of his face and the charm of his rare personality. Rather shy and inarticulate (except in leadership), he had a quality of earnestness and conviction in the opinions he expressed with great simplicity that made a lasting impression on even the rather mature girl of twelve that I was.

He would talk to me about good citizenship in terms I understood, which appealed to my imagination. I remember his saying it was easy to have a splendid life like my father's and yet witness what he believed in forgotten, but that would not happen if young people followed his example. Even a girl like me, he said, could make others feel it was a fine thing to work for better city government than New

York politicians gave. I was so enthusiastic that I started a Mugwump Club at school and got as president one of the boys whose father thought Papa was a "no-good Mugwump."

It was at about this time that O. Henry termed one of my performances, which I had casually mentioned to him, "cornering the market." This was it: the girls and boys in the neighborhood were still playing marbles in the first days of spring when I decided to begin the craze for tops. I had saved up my allowance and bought all the available tops in the stock of our general store: eight tops that spun after being wound up with a string, costing but five cents each; and sixteen small straight ones which went by being lashed with a whip of cotton strips attached to a short stick, at a price of one cent apiece.

I hired my sister Ethel and a number of other girls to make the whips and start the craze. This they did, acting under my instructions, invading the avenue in a noisy gang, and having a wonderful time, whipping and spinning tops. Immediately all those playing marbles lost interest and ran to the store to buy tops, only to discover there were none to be had.

I produced my supply and offered to sell both kinds of tops at my price, which was ten cents for a spinning top and five cents for the others, including a whip. After a stampede home by the youngsters to appeal to parents for money, I was sold out.

Ethel and my other employees went on strike when I gave them only one cent on each transaction, thereby keeping a tidy profit for myself. Their claim was based on the fact that they made the whips and also started the craze that had brought me the trade. I refused to give them more, declaring that as the idea was mine, I deserved the money.

O. Henry listened attentively to my recital, then said disapprovingly that this example of unfair practice in "big business" was unworthy of the daughter of a Mugwump fighting to make a more perfect world.

His rebuke caused me to feel so utterly miserable that I redivided the profits between my employees and the consumers, keeping only the allowance I had invested. But my conscience was not satisfied until I put into the Sunday School plate all my allowance money, thereby ending my venture into high finance, with neither a penny left nor a top with which to enjoy a game for which my initiative had been responsible.

My next business activities were concerned with families of French Canadian Indians, who lived in shacks across a field from our Lake George place. They supported themselves by the weaving of straw baskets. I liked the company of these Indians better than that of my sisters' friends, and I was often in their camp among adults and half-grown youngsters like myself.

My work competed successfully with that of the adults and surpassed that of the younger Indians, perhaps because I was far more industrious. Also I proved to be an unshy saleswoman, and was entrusted with selling to tourists on semi-weekly excursion boats.

Once a photographer turned up, accompanying a writer who was to do a feature article about the camp for an illustrated popular magazine. After taking shots of several groups in which I was included, I was asked by the photographer to pose alone. The photograph was one of those reproduced in the article with the caption, "An Indian girl who looks almost as bright as a child of educated white parents."

I have no recollection that any of us children were required to do anything helpful in the home. There was always a good-natured cook and a maid-of-all-work who did what cook didn't—both cheerfully providing food to the many friends we brought home. This implies a different procedure from modern housekeeping.

Bertha ruled Ethel and me with a rod of iron, and we avoided her as much as possible. She was a Spartan with herself and at the age of ten gave up playing with dolls because she considered herself grown up. She was very studious and seldom without a book in her hand, usually a Greek grammar. She had persuaded Mama to teach her Greek at this early age.

Bertha kept chickens in the chicken houses already prepared and named them for letters of the Greek alphabet. The sounds so fascinated me that soon I learned the alphabet from her. This gave me an early interest in the Greek language that was to persist.

24

Animals were an important part of my life at that period. I had the usual dogs and cats, but one really extraordinary animal in his performances was a light brown rabbit, so large that I suppose he should have been classified as a hare. Papa was so regular in his habits that one could keep time by him. Every morning at seven sharp, Cook took up a pitcher of boiling water for his shaving. The rabbit would come inside from his hutch in the back yard and follow Cook up the basement stairs and two other flights to Papa's bathroom, then solemnly enter and watch him shave. That event finished, he returned to what the back yard offered him in the way of amusement.

But when Papa returned from Colorado Springs after an illness, it was with a beard that he never removed. The rabbit seemed to lose heart when his daily trips upstairs no longer had a special objective, and he finally gave them up. Soon after, he burrowed his way out into the avenue and was killed by a dog. A squirrel and sparrow I had tamed and carried about in a pocket paid for their over-confidence in believing the best, even of cats, and were both devoured by one.

The fifth (and final child) named Dorothy was very frail and cried a lot. Apparently, the only way to stop her crying spasms was to make a louder noise. Being very strong as a child, I was delegated to beat the tin cover of the open grate in the nursery with a poker. This made such an infernal racket that the baby could not compete with her cries and gave up the attempt. I would sometimes be aroused from sleep in the middle of the night, to go into action, when everyone was being kept awake.

I don't believe modern psychiatry would approve of this method of quieting the nerves of a delicate baby, even though it gave everyone a chance for undisturbed sleep, including the baby.

3

GRACIOUS LIVING

IT WAS A BLOW to be told that we were to move to a new development on the west side of the city proper, starting at Seventy-second
Street, near Riverside Drive on the Hudson River. The house at
245 West Seventy-fifth Street, Mama explained, was in a locality
that would make it much easier for Papa to reach his office. I accepted the decision without protest, but Mama, reading utter dismay
in the expression of my face, said she realized I would miss the space
and freedom that a broad avenue and side streets without much traffic permitted in playing running games with children of neighbors.
Then she reminded me that I was now almost fifteen and the city
would offer equal attractions even to a tomboy like myself.

I felt inconsolable as there flashed through my mind what I was
about to lose in the way of amusement. Within city limits there
would be no coasting down steep lanes, nor "punning" (hitching
sleds to delivery carts on runners). And in the fall and spring the
even greater fun of a ride on the seat beside a good-natured driver
of a heavy wagon loaded with food supplies, or several of us crowded
inside, in the dark, between packages and large sides of beef and
mutton.

The excitement was keen in being jolted over paved streets, with
the driver noisily grinding the brakes to ease the horse on a down-
hill stretch. There was the interest of stopping at homes when the
mistress or cook came out to the wagon and collected what had been
ordered in the way of dry groceries. I liked to watch the selection of
vegetables and fruit, and most of all to see the beef or mutton being
cut, and unlike the method of the butcher of today, much of the
waste fat and bones were removed *before* weighing.

26

Often we children would assist in carrying supplies into the house and be given a cookie or piece of candy, and then the wagon, creaking into motion, would continue on its way to the next customer. Ice wagons appealed, but no one ventured to sit inside because of the chill produced by great blocks of ice covered with sawdust. I never ceased to marvel at the skill of the iceman, who would sling a block, held by steel tongs, over the end of the wagon and, with a sharp blade, cut a cake to the size desired by the waiting householder. Because of its weight, he himself took it inside and placed it in the ice chest. Today's refrigerator ice has not the same flavor as that which came from a cake, chipped by a pick, in the middle of the family box, around which the food was stacked.

What seemed the most overwhelming calamity was the loss of delightful all-day Sunday trips into the real country, usually with both parents, but at times with Papa alone. First, quite a long walk to reach a trolley line, the unforgetable elegance of the cars with wicker upholstered seats, curtains at the windows, and a wilton carpet on the floor. As a matter of course, everyone carefully wiped his feet before entering. This luxurious transportation was an expensive treat, as Papa sometimes mentioned when taking out his black wallet. He handed three crisp one-dollar bills to the genial conductor, who leisurely collected the fares and paused to pass the time of day with his passengers. If Mama was along, Papa only got a fifty-cent piece back in change.

After getting out, walking again, or occasionally riding in a long buckboard to some charming site in a grove of trees, with a stream nearby from which to fill a canteen with fresh cold water, we had our picnic.

Gone long since are the wide-spreading trees, and nothing remains of the view now as motorcars rush past row after row of houses with the sameness of a seaport town—entirely without charm.

Mama was right in her suggestion to me that by now (1891) I was ready for a different kind of life. In retrospect, I realize how fortunate for me it was that, as an impressionable, fast-maturing girl, I knew New York in the early eighteen-nineties. The graciousness of the slow tempo symbolized by Fifth Avenue on Sunday after church and in holiday parades, when "society" was out in force, made a strong appeal to my imagination.

In my ears would be the clip-clop of the hoofs of high-stepping horses between the shafts of stately open carriages, vying with one another in attracting my delighted attention. The occupants were beautifully groomed ladies wrapped in costly furs and flashing jewels, and wearing unbelievable hats with fantastic ribbon trimmings or long feathers. To me, the dandified men in top hats and stiff coats were romantic heroes. Domesticity was evidenced at times, as, when facing an elegant couple, subdued children sat on a narrow seat, boys in velvet suits and lace collars, and girls self-conscious and motionless in frills and furbelows. Even the coachmen fitted into the charming picture, with rosettes on stiff black hats, liveried coats, white breeches, and well-polished boots.

There was no traffic overcrowding, since vans were few and far between, and respectable in themselves, with dignified drivers. Therefore the eye missed none of the details of each carriage at a passing glance.

The sidewalks offered equal drama. Speed was out of the question in the kinds of costumes worn by reigning belles and women of every age. All moved with difficulty in trailing tight skirts that stirred up the dust on the pavement and swept it along with them. They wore bodices, sharply drawn in at the waist, with collars kept in place by tall whalebones. This fashionable attire was completed by a small hat or a narrow-brimmed sailor perched well above the forehead on a pompadour hairdo. The pace of their escorts was equally controlled by boiled shirts and stiff collars, frock coats, tight trousers, and high buttoned kid boots. A man's head was surmounted by a tall silk or grey cloth hat.

An accommodating kaleidoscope has preserved several scenes to be recaptured as though by the twist of a hand. One took place on an Easter Sunday when I had just turned sixteen. I had persuaded my mother to let me wear a trailing skirt to walk down the Avenue with a beau who, incidentally, was far too old and sophisticated for me. Unexpectedly I saw my father's youngest brother Herbert. He

28

met my eager eyes without a sign of recognition. In spite of my long skirt, I managed to turn quickly and hurried after him, "Uncle Herbert, it's Corinna," I called out breathlessly. To which he replied, "A niece who uses her skirt to clean the sidewalk is a person I intended to ignore," and walked on. All my pride in my long skirt evaporated, and against the protests of my young man, I insisted on going home, and alone, as fast as a cab could take me.

Long intervening years of close friendship as an adult with Uncle Herbert, travels abroad together with him and Joe after my marriage, and frequent meetings with him as librarian of the Library of Congress, have not dimmed my horror at the way he looked straight through me on that Easter parade.

The other incident involved the most frustrated male I have ever seen throughout my long life in many and varied countries. He was an exquisite creature, tall and graceful, walking on Fifth Avenue with a seductive young woman. I watched him lean towards her to whisper something in her ear. She blushed becomingly, and at that moment a gust of wind caught his hat and lifted it off his head. It flew before him down the sidewalk, just beyond any speed he could muster as he futilely jabbed after it with a silver-headed cane.

The dignified magnificence of mansions on the Avenue was in character with the outward appearance of the people who occupied them. None were more so than the residences built by William H. Vanderbilt for himself and his daughters as they married. These massive square structures, representing stability and a feeling of permanence, were of brownstone, protected from the public by tall iron grilles. They dominated the buildings in their vicinity.

The several I saw inside provided a bewildering experience for a young girl brought up by a publisher father, whose accent was on books in every room. Here was imposing furniture in vast rooms and halls, wide marble stairways, amazing rugs of intricate pattern, huge tapestries, statues casually placed about, and paintings by old masters.

They did not seem to me *homes*, and I found it difficult to visualize family life going on in them. But I was mistaken. It did.

Velvet suits and lace collars and girls dressed up like fancy dolls were seen not only in carriages on Fifth Avenue but at Dodsworth, a very select dancing school. The classes began for youngsters at about the age of eight and were carried on until fifteen or sixteen. Many New Yorkers, later distinguished in business, the professions, or government posts, learned manners, the correct movement of the body, how to walk, bow, and many other old-fashioned graces, at Dodsworth. The two years I went through that stern training stood me in good stead, for they produced in me a feeling of being at ease at great functions at home and abroad.

Once, many years later, when the president of a New York bank was presented to me at a reception, his movements, the courtesy of his demeanor, and a slightly formal bow made me exclaim, "Were you ever at Dodsworth?" "Yes," he replied, "and you too!" We both laughed, but it was a friendly, comradely laugh because of something important we had had in common.

The times from which we come are often more apparent to others than to ourselves. In the early nineteen twenties, I was on a New York vacation from my children, at a time when we were living in Boston. As I strolled slowly along Fifth Avenue my curiosity was aroused by the number of people who turned to give me a second glance in passing. In an attempt to find out what was unusual about my appearance from a New York point of view, I stopped and asked the question of a respectable middle-aged man who had noticeably stared at me.

"You are the only person I've seen in New York who is not in a hurry," was his reply.

4

THE INFLUENCE OF WOMEN

Mama had definite views about leading life in her own way in New York, and succeeded in upholding them. For instance, at a time when women went around aimlessly leaving cards at the homes of friends or on hostesses who had entertained them, she refused to make calls. She saw people, including intimate friends, only by appointment in her home or theirs. She liked uninterrupted hours so she could be with her children, and quiet evenings with her husband, or time to read.

Having been brought up in Boston, she found constant surprises in New York, one of them being that people did not read Greek and Latin for amusement. She herself, before she was twenty, had taught both languages to boys in the Worcester High School. When I first went to Boston to live as a bride, quite a few men approaching middle age recalled to me that they had once been my mother's pupils in Worcester, and remembered her as a remarkably inspiring teacher.

The slums of lower New York appalled her, and the sight of young children with no place to play except in dark alleys and streets, with disaster threatening them from the traffic, aroused her deepest sympathy. My father had kept in close touch with Grover Cleveland since he had supported his first candidacy for president, and when we moved to Seventy-fifth Street, the Clevelands were living further downtown in a large house.

My mother was no Don Quixote charging at windmills and did what she termed "collecting assets" before she embarked on any much-needed reform. Intuitively she turned to Mrs. Cleveland to enlist her active support in the campaign to get kindergartens introduced into the New York school system. She considered, and rightly, that if Mrs. Cleveland was interested, other women would follow enthusiastically. I was thrilled when I accompanied my mother for an informal discussion of the subject with Mrs. Cleveland. She had the rare quality of making everyone feel at ease in her presence, and gladly undertook anything she considered worthwhile. She took fire at once on the kindergarten project, and under the auspices of this, the most civic-minded women in the city, it was adopted.

Another joint enterprise carried through was the establishment of a standard of decency for salesgirls in department stores. Sales people stood behind counters those days almost twelve hours. No rest rooms or chairs were provided, not even a peg to hang their outer garments on. A meeting of the same well-known, civic-minded women was called to discuss action. The majority agreed to the principle of putting on a black list the stores that refused to accept adequate working conditions for their female employees, and to get women to refuse to trade at them, stating the reason.

It was my mother who suggested the opposite approach, that of placing on a "white list" the stores which adopted the regulations. The amendment was immediately accepted, and within two years practically every store in New York advertised widely in the press that it was on this "white list."

I liked to go with Mama for her interviews with politicians. She handled these men so tactfully that they never realized they were agreeing on an impulse of the moment to do far better than they had intended, and she made them feel proud of themselves. She was the kind of woman for whom a promise, once made, was not to be forgotten.

The things I had seen on a tour through slum areas with my mother made a lasting impression on me, and aroused an unspoken determination on my part to help when I was old enough.

My Aunt Minnie (Dr. Mary Putnam Jacobi) was a pioneer in establishing a woman's infirmary and adequate facilities for the care of sick children. By taking me with her to clinics and on visits to bedfast youngsters, she laid a foundation that, years later, was to lead to my accepting responsibility for furthering health administration and preventive medicine.

32

I was proud of my mother as a hostess. She was lovely to look at and had such a good time with her guests that they could hardly fail to have an equally good time. There was much entertaining of my father's many friends and visiting authors. He liked to have informal gatherings at dinners in his home, and they went off well. The only complaint my father made was that Mama was so attractive the men would not go home.

We continued to have a cook and one general maid, and when there was company, instead of getting in extra help, as most households did, my family used me. I found it fun to put on a uniform with a neat cap and apron. At times I would get so absorbed in listening to the conversation between my father and the guests that I would stand stock still with a platter in my hand.

"Teddy," as Papa called Theodore Roosevelt, would drop in for a family meal unannounced, on his infrequent trips from his ranch in the West, where he was living for his health. He never got over teasing me about a *faux pas* of mine. The maid was ill and I was serving. I had just brought into the dining room a large ham and was about to set it down for Papa to carve, when Teddy told such a funny story that the platter tipped and the ham rolled over the carpet. With the quickness of an experienced hostess, my mother said to me, "Bring in the other ham!" She didn't get away with it, because Teddy, turning to me, interpolated her instructions, saying, "She means for you to pick up the ham, walk into the pantry, and return with it."

His anecdotes of life in the West gave me my first desire to go beyond the Mississippi. One very special and unforgettable incident occurred when Teddy dropped in to Sunday dinner at a time he was supposed to be at his ranch. As he sat down to table, he announced he had a "grievance" against my father. This was its basis:

Soon after graduating from college, he had a little money to invest, a legacy from a relative. He was going West to live but first came to see my father, saying that he knew his own impulsiveness sometimes led to indiscretions in a business way. Consequently, while away, he would be at the mercy of people who might urge him to put money into wildcat ventures. His only protection would be that he had no available funds. "Haven," he said earnestly, "no matter how urgent the appeals I send you for this money, which I now entrust to you for safekeeping, hold on to it."

Sure enough, after about six months, Teddy wrote asking to have the money withdrawn, inasmuch as he had a wonderful investment prospect for it, with large dividends in store. Papa ignored the request. Altogether he received about six letters, each succeeding one more insistent than the last. Finally, a telegram came which read, "After all, Haven, the money is mine. Kindly withdraw it immediately and send it along."

This my father had done. At the family dinner Teddy burst into violent vituperation of Papa's action. "Didn't I tell you never to send me that money, no matter how urgent my demands?" he thundered. "Now I've lost every penny and it's your fault!"

An incident concerning Joseph H. Choate was also unforgettable. This occurred at rather a large dinner for an English author at which Andrew Carnegie and Heber Newton (an odd combination) were present. Choate was talking to Papa *sotto voce*, but I remained within earshot. He was complaining at his boredom at not being able to avoid attending certain political dinners (a particularly dull one had recently occurred in Westchester County in honor of a local favorite son). Choate said that the chairman, in introducing the speaker, had gone on and on with praise until finally, reaching a climax, he said, "He has the urbanity of a Chesterfield." Whereupon Choate confided to my father, he had not been able to resist murmuring to his neighbor, "He's wrong, it's only the suburbanity of a Westchesterfield."

Mrs. Kate Douglas Wiggin was an intimate friend of Mama's for whom I developed a girlish crush at the age of sixteen. She was far too generous-minded to accept such a relationship, and when on her visits to New York, I would help her by serving tea, she always made a point of introducing me to her guests and drawing me into the conversation. In those days, a group of friends would sit quietly together for several hours, not merely drifting in for a restless moment.

34

Once when a cake Mrs. Wiggin had ordered failed of delivery, I took matters into my own hands and decided to make gingerbread. I had neither an aptitude for cooking nor the necessary training, but went at the job with enthusiasm. I set down a piece of gingerbread on a plate before Mrs. Wiggin and each of her guests. I noticed that she looked rather startled after a bite, then, with determination, she managed to get down a few sizable mouthfuls, announcing that her friend Corinna Putnam had made the gingerbread for this occasion. At this cue, most of the guests with a labored effort did fairly well. When they had left, I said to Mrs. Wiggin, almost in tears, "My gingerbread was a failure." I will never forget her reply, "It was almost good enough to eat, and I would not permit my guests to let you down, when you had tried so hard, dear child."

I am deeply grateful to Mrs. Wiggin, because it was owing to her persuasiveness that I got to know Bonnemama, as Papa's mother wanted her grandchildren to call her. I had told Mrs. Wiggin frankly that Bonnemama never seemed aware of our presence at family gatherings.

Her sister, on the contrary, great Aunt Corinna Bishop, was very different, and I loved visiting her at Pigeon Cove in my childhood. No one would have suspected her age from her coal-black hair. Her features were sharp, and she was eccentric in her clothes, with a taste for the bizarre in color effects. On her trips to New York, she brought with her a shivering small black dog, but at the expense of great physical discomfort to herself, as her railroad trip from Massachusetts had to be made seated on a trunk in the baggage van, dogs being forbidden in the parlor car.

The sisters were very unlike in other respects. Bonnemama was always immaculately and suitably dressed, with her gray hair well arranged. She was still beautiful and very conventional in her appearance and actions.

One afternoon I went to see Bonnemama at the Navarro Flats, facing Central Park on Fifty-ninth Street. I told her I thought it time we were acquainted. She agreed smilingly and seemed pleased at my coming. In the course of an intimate conversation I asked her

35

what she was like as a girl. She replied she had never had any girl-hood, since she was married at sixteen and had three children before she was twenty. "Didn't you have any fun?" I persisted.

At this she gave a reminiscent chuckle and told me that she had had plenty, beginning on her honeymoon.

She and my grandfather, she said, were visiting John Motley in Holland, and the night of their arrival he was giving an official dinner, as the American ambassador. She was only sixteen and the long bannister rail was too tempting to resist, so she slid down it into a great hall where the guests were assembled.

"And," she added, "your shy, dignified grandfather rose nobly to the occasion. With a quick movement, he managed to leap across the room and caught me as I landed. 'Let me introduce my wife,' he said composedly."

5

GROWING UP

WITH GIBBONS SCHOOL

ETHEL AND I both went to the Gibbons School, which was located downtown. In the long walk there and back, through Central Park most of the way, I learned more than in the classroom, with Papa as our companion, since the hours fitted his office day. What a contrast this procedure was to the school bus of today, and businessmen rushing to the subway to save time.

Our park route was by a winding dirt footpath to Fifth Avenue, along which we listened to the singing of a variety of birds from spring until late fall and beginning again in March. Papa, as he walked at a quick pace, told us on the early morning trip of current events at home and abroad. On the return he talked about history. He began far back in time and described what was going on in different countries at the same period. What he said was based on a manual written by his father which had first interested him in history as a young boy. Gradually, a picture formed in my mind of nations and the people comprising them. Many years later, Wendell Willkie was to call this "one world."

Papa had known the Park since his early boyhood, and occasionally on the walk home he took us on a detour. One such was to locate a path, on the East Side near the present reservoir, extending to the back of the Metropolitan Museum of Art. At the age of fourteen, as foreman of a gang, he had supervised a cutting through impenetrable growth to make this path. He was working on a plan given him by Frederick Law Olmsted, a friend of his father's, who was responsible both for the idea of this great park for the people of the city and for carrying it into effect. Except for the widening of all paths and the surfacing of them with asphalt, and a few intersections of traffic tunnels from east to west, Central Park has remained unchanged.

Whenever possible I hurried through the allotted work of the afternoon session at school and rushed downtown to have half an hour in Papa's office before walking back home with him. He sat at a massive, awkward, roller-top desk used by his father before him. Eventually I was to be the proud possessor of the desk, which father and son had used consecutively at Putnam's for almost one hundred years.

The premises occupied by my father's publishing house had fascinated me since childhood. My first recollection was being there with him at the age of six and watching printing being done at the rear of the retail store. I saw large sheets of white paper held by steel arms reaching out from huge machines. A frightening thud caused me to clutch Papa's hand for protection, and then, to my amazement, black marks, which I knew as words, covered the paper.

Papa often quoted the comment I had made to him after watching this phase of bookmaking: "Some one did a lot of thinking before the press knew what to do."

The firm had become G. P. Putnam's Sons after grandfather died in 1872. Papa was the head as publisher, Uncle Irving was in charge of the retail store, and Uncle Bishop was responsible for the manu-

37

facture of the books. (In later years, manufacture was to be done in the Knickerbocker Press Building at New Rochelle, after Putnam's moved from Twenty-third Street to West Forty-fifth Street, at the time considered too far uptown for a business concern.)

In these school-day visits, Papa always seemed to find time to recall incidents of grandfather's contacts with his authors, as well as some of his own with interesting personalities. My favorite anecdote connected with grandfather, who was rather timid and spoke with a stammer, was about Edgar Allan Poe at the time he was writing a serial for *Putnam's Magazine*. The first installment was already printed and the next issue was being held up for the second, because Poe had disappeared on a bender. Papa's vivid description made me visualize my grandfather, who always wore a long coat and top hat and was the essence of respectability, going from one low dive to another looking for his author, picking up good-natured vagabonds in each dive who might offer assistance in his search. When he finally found Poe, he locked himself in a room with his author so he could not escape. He patiently served Poe coffee and food until he could hold a pen and write the needed second installment.

Another story that appealed to me concerned Susan Warner, the author of *The Wide, Wide World*. Grandfather's mother, Catherine, was a woman of determined character and very religious. Her son had already lost much money on her interpretation of the Old Testament, which he had published in three volumes, when she brought him this manuscript from her friend. Grandfather glanced through the text and gave his verdict that it would have no sale. His mother insisted on his publishing it, declaring that "Providence would see to it that all God-fearing folk read it."

Reluctantly he yielded, the Sunday schools in the town of Providence gave the first order for copies of *The Wide, Wide World*, an example followed by churches of every denomination throughout the United States, and the sales in succeeding years eventually surpassed even those of the works of Washington Irving.

Papa retained so vivid an impression of Thackeray's coming to his father's Sixteenth Street home that I needed no photograph to picture his tall, lank figure, large snub nose, and unusually round spectacles. Dickens was also a guest on one of his American visits, and presented Papa with an autographed copy of *David Copperfield*.

My father, as a boy, was introduced to a picturesque American by his father in the following way: "Remember this gentleman, Haven," his father said. "He has discovered a new people in the East of whom, in the course of the next half century, I believe we will hear much." The tall, good-looking man was Commodore Perry, who had recently been received by the Tycoon of Japan, and at the audience secured permission for commerce with the United States, a favor that thus far had not been accorded any other nation.

I also found intriguing the occasion, related by Papa, of Tom Thumb, at the height of his fame, sitting in a child's chair in the middle of the nursery table while the Putnam children were eating supper.

When Papa was busy, I spent the time reading files of my grandfather's, either contracts with authors, written in his beautiful script, or correspondence. A characterization of Carlyle's in a letter to Emerson has stuck in my mind. He referred to grandfather as an "intelligent, modest and respectable looking fellow," who wished to do something about publishing his (Carlyle's) books in America, and said he was inclined to let him do so. Also, an extract in a letter from Emerson to Carlyle (May 31, 1846), "I am heartily glad you put me in direct communication with these really energetic booksellers, Wiley and Putnam," and he advised his friend Carlyle by all means to "close with Putnam of the good mind."

I also liked framed, unpaid I.O.U.'s above my father's desk from some of Grandfather's principal authors. Among these documents of more than family interest was one signed by Washington Irving for $350 in connection with a trip to Japan. Another bore the signature of William Cullen Bryant.

Being with my father in his office gave me a feel of the publishing business that I was never to lose, and it added to the comradeship between us.

During a lively girlhood, not all my interests and activities were centered in authors and publishers. I was athletic, and skating at Van Cortland Park was at the time the rage for young people, who went in groups (accompanied by a chaperone). It was a gay scene, with shirtwaists and short coats of bright colors, and contrasting brilliant tam o'shanters worn at a jaunty angle. But long skirts were worn for skating. This absurdity, restricting freedom of movement, once almost cost me my life. I had fallen through a break in the ice and while rescuers were attempting to reach me through the narrow opening, my skirt clung to my arms, making any assistance on my part impossible.

In Ethel's and my school days, dances for juniors were given in large private homes. Printed dance cards were furnished, cutting in was not allowed, and a popular girl would have no vacancy in the list of scheduled dances shortly after her arrival. The climax of the evening was supper, served to girls and their partners seated on the stairs.

At one such party, a man from Boston was introduced to me. He took my card and wrote on it, "Supper—W. Cameron Forbes." I found him different from New York boys of my acquaintance as I listened to his conversation with rapt attention. That dance took place more than sixty-five years ago. Cameron Forbes, after a subsequent long and distinguished career as governor general of the Philippines, ambassador to Japan, and in other government posts, remained different from New Yorkers, and I continued to find him worth listening to until his death in 1959.

The streets had much of interest to offer. For instance, the sight of the fire engines pulled by three galloping horses, with the bell clanging loudly and black helmeted men in fire-fighting garments clinging to the engine wherever there was a foothold. I happened to be on Fifth Avenue when I saw a police patrolman turn in an alarm. "The Windsor Hotel, Fifth Avenue!" I heard him say. "Get out everything!" I was among the first to reach the scene. The blaze was already beyond control. Within a short time a large crowd had collected, and I was prevented from escaping from the horrible sight of people jumping from the hotel windows with agonizing shrieks, to become mangled corpses lying on the streets.

There was one heroic rescue I remembered after the horrors I saw had faded. A dancing class of fashionable children under eight was being held on the fourth floor. One of several teachers, smelling smoke, went into the hall to find the elevator shaft in flames. With great presence of mind, the teacher stopped the music and quietly told the children they were going to play a new game. Hand in hand, they were to move slowly down the stairway, step by step, through the mist of clouds. No one was to speak or cease going forward. The thirty children, with a teacher in front, another behind, and one in the middle, managed to reach the lobby uninjured. They were carried into a side street by rescuing firemen, to be delivered into the safekeeping of half-distracted parents who had been forbidden to enter the building.

One of my favorite pastimes was to stand across the street on Twenty-third Street from the very narrow triangle between Fifth Avenue and Fourth Avenue, where the Flatiron Building was of recent construction. The interest lay in watching crowds of businessmen at noon on a day when the wind was blowing in strong gusts.

The cautious made a detour, to avoid possible disaster to limb or life, on the theory the building might tip over from the strain to the underpinnings, which were supporting a structure of great height— all of twenty stories. Only daredevils ventured to walk along the sidewalk directly underneath. The visible tension of pedestrians, displayed in anxious upward glances and a pride in their courage, provided an amusing combination.

The Flatiron Building was also notable as being among the first to have above the roof an advertisement in electric lights. It called the public's attention to Heinz 57 Varieties.

Soon thereafter the Singer edifice was underway. The outer framework had been completed when the sound of the riveting of steel, heard at a distance, decided me to investigate at close quarters. I even induced the foreman to take me to the top in an empty car during the workmen's lunch hour. He warned me not to look down for fear of becoming dizzy, as we were about to mount to the unheard of height of *forty stories*, and he saw to it that I clutched the protecting hand rail.

The car stopped with a jerk and he led me out on to a small platform. I was conscious of a vast expanse of sky, the harbor and the

East River, and on a level far below us were roofs of buildings built on intersecting streets and avenues. I felt I was standing at the very top of the world. This was my introduction to the potentialities of the skyscraper, long since realized in the Empire State Building.

So far, this chapter has said little about school. The Gibbons School was run by the unmarried daughter of James Gibbons, the abolitionist who organized the underground railway for slaves escaping to the safety of northern soil and arranged for their care after arrival. His widow, an old lady of over ninety, sweet faced and very frail, who wore a white lace fichu and a becoming cap, lived in the apartment reserved for the family above the school floors. Pupils were served a noon lunch before the afternoon session.

It was considered a rare privilege to be invited to spend a short time with this remarkable woman. The privilege was accorded only by a special summons from her. Fortunately for me, never more than several weeks went by without her inviting me to eat lunch in her quiet retreat, where she sat in a rocker surrounded by cherished relics of an all but forgotten past.

My interest in the Civil War, thanks to Papa and his experiences in Danville and Libby prisons, intrigued her, while the details of individual slaves in hair-breadth escapes through the underground enthralled me. Mrs. Gibbons shared my father's enthusiasm for Albert, the Prince Consort, who guided Queen Victoria well and often against the advice of her ministers, as in the instance of preventing recognition of the South for the advantage of cotton interests in England.

She listened attentively when I told her how Papa's life had been saved, when he was very ill in Libby Prison, by a southern woman, who took him into her home in Richmond on parole and with her daughter nursed him back to health.

I will never forget this marvelous old crusader of Quaker stock, seated, gently rocking, telling, with flashing eyes and ringing words, the iniquities of slave owners and her part in circumventing them, quietly remarking, "Such an act by gentle women prohibits hatred, which is the worst evil of all."

Francis W. Crowninshield, or Frank, as he was to be known, was some years my senior when he became my mentor. It was during my first year at Gibbons and he was in his first job, which was in Putnam's Retail Store.

In retrospect, I attribute his cynical attitude towards life, which was to persist, to factors that affected his sensitive nature in his extreme youth. He resented not having had a college education because his father insisted upon his supporting himself after leaving high school.

It hurt his pride to be in a store, even though he was devoted to my father. After being promoted to my father's publishing department for a while, he was successfully tempted to leave by Frank Munsey, who offered him a large salary. And his pride was again wounded on discovering it was Frank's social position that Mr. Munsey thought would be useful to him.

Later years of worldly success in a publishing career, and great personal popularity in the inner circles of society, failed to dissipate the melancholy of his boyhood.

In his youth, it was Frank's capacity for gaiety that appealed to me. But I found him restless in spirit and he seemed to enjoy being depressed. Some of my most vivid girlhood recollections are of being made desperately miserable by him as he read aloud passages of Schopenhauer, at that time a prophet for many besides Frank.

The following incident took place in what is now Harlem, which was then a falling off place beyond the confines of Central Park, a dreary spot indeed, with piles of debris and goats meandering about, ill-kempt and forlorn. It was a perfect setting, squatting atop a mound of rubbish, for accepting the pessimism of Schopenhauer.

After a while, my attention was distracted by a goat who, in an aimless and vain search for something to eat, compromised on a tin can which he was doing his best to devour, though in an attitude of utter dejection. To me, the goat's pessimism was Schopenhauer's in another form, "Tin cans are not meant for food, any more than the world is a place in which to be unhappy, which is Schopenhauer's teaching."

At my unexpected interruption, Frank's eyes followed mine and saw what the goat was doing, and he began to laugh. His gaiety was always contagious and in his irresistible change of mood, we ended by going to Weber and Field's Variety Show. How dated and harmless those two really funny comedians would be considered today, but our going was incredibly unconventional and Papa was shocked beyond words.

In another reaction from sadness, when Frank and I attended a matinée of *The Black Crook*, even Mama reproved me. "Women in tights on the stage are expected to be seen by men alone," she said sternly.

6

BRYN MAWR AS INTERLUDE

IT WAS OBVIOUS from my sister Bertha's childhood that she would become a scholar, and equally obvious that neither Ethel nor I would. Bertha graduated from Bryn Mawr in 1893 *magna cum laude*. An inherent interest in labor, intensified by a course in sociology and economics, caused her to investigate the machinery which enforced the Statute of Labourers, enacted by Parliament under Edward III, 1349–1359, as a preliminary to a Ph.D. dissertation at Columbia University.

When she came to the Public Record Office in London to gather her material, it had long been accepted that no records of justice of the peace proceedings earlier than the sixteenth century were extant, and the official guide gave her no help in finding her way through the mass of unidentified or incorrectly described rolls of judicial proceedings included in the two classes known as Assize Rolls and Ancient Indictments.

But with a Putnam quality of obstinacy, referred to by George Washington in a letter about Israel Putnam, whom he described as "honest, courageous, but never open to conviction," she continued her excavations in the Public Record Office. She had discovered some seventeen rolls of proceedings before justices of labourers in fourteen counties for the years 1349–59, mostly in the Assize Rolls, but a few among the Ancient Indictments. In an article of that year in the *English Historical Review*, she established the complementary relation of the Ordinance and the Statute of Labourers as constituting the code administered by the justices—at first the *ad hoc* justices of labourers, later the more generally commissioned justices of the peace. By 1908 the field of her lifework had opened up: she was to be the historian of the early J.P., treading scholarly ground complementary to that of the great historian of English law, Frederic William Maitland.

Two of her many scholarly achievements impressed me the most, one being *Proceedings before the Justices of the Peace, Edward III to Richard III*, published by the Harvard Law School, containing records from eleven counties, with a magisterial introduction by herself and a legal commentary from Professor Plucknett.

The other resulted when, not content with her successful attack on the Public Record Office files, she found her way into the kitchen of the House of Lords, on a personal permission from the Lord Chancellor. She was following a hunch that the seventeenth century rolls of the deputy of the peace during the reign of Cromwell might be there, and strange to say, *they were*.

In addition to her research for seven books on medieval English legal history, she taught for thirty years medieval European history, English economic history, and, for good measure, a course in economic expansion of Europe into India at Mount Holyoke College.

Needless to say, she had needed Bryn Mawr, where she had received her undergraduate education.

Ethel was far more creative and imaginative than I was, and, while we were still at the Audubon School, was editor of a small magazine in which she wrote extraordinary serials. Among them was one entitled *The Missing Link*, which told of this creature's adventures after he became a man, as he wandered about the world, and she described with wit and surprising acumen the strange things (to his way of thinking) his fellow men were doing. She was a conscientious student, but once told my mother she preferred to write her own stories rather than study books by others. Psychologically, it was inadvisable for her sake that we be in the same class at school, since I was two years younger. Instead of going to college, she learned typewriting and shorthand, at both of which she became expert. For years to come, she sat daily, hour after hour, typing the manuscripts she had taken in shorthand from our father's dictation, until the ten books he managed to write during his leisure hours at home were put in final form for printing.

How well I remember my passionate pleadings with Mama to persuade Papa to let me go to boarding school, preferably Farmington. "He has decided on Bryn Mawr for you," she said in a voice I knew was final. I had one year at the Brearley School in preparation for passing the entrance examinations for Bryn Mawr, and was lucky in having the principal, James Croswell, alone in Greek. He was not only a born teacher but a great philosopher, and many of the precepts he taught me bore fruit in my later life. He constantly expressed disappointment that I was not a "serious" student. Once he said to me, "It will be difficult for you to get an education, because you will never fail an examination and never deserve to pass one." This was a prophetic summary of what was to happen in a brief college interlude.

I entered Bryn Mawr with the class of 1897. I had the sort of physical stamina, inherited from my father, that was based on a determination not to accept defeat, rather than on bodily strength. In basketball and tennis, I instinctively practiced the Japanese "*jiu jitsu*," the art of turning the opponent's strength to his own destruction.

When young women were playing a long, powerful stroke from the base line, I saved my strength by the half volley. I was a fast jumper and anything that I could not get overhand from the center of the court was out. Also I played net. I was captain of our class athletic team, which held every athletic record during my stay at college. I introduced strict training and persuaded several of the lesser coaches in athletics at Yale and Harvard, whom I knew, to come to Bryn Mawr and instruct my various teams. One of the procedures recommended was a frequent two-mile jog trot, which I led over the countryside.

In my freshman year I was at Merion Hall, where most of the graduate students roomed. I was grateful to those among them who welcomed me as Bertha's sister. Despite the intellectual stimulus offered in daily companionship with them, and the excellent example set me by my roommate, Mary M. Campbell, our class president, who was a serious student, my scholarship was casual. I had chosen haphazardly courses in such ill-assorted subjects as biblical literature, biology, economics, and Latin.

Greek I took to naturally, and English literature under President Thomas I found exciting because of her brilliant mind and her positive tastes in literature, presented with great originality and decision.

My curiosity for experiments was great. I soon created a campus tempest in a teapot by dressing up as a flower peddler and selling violets from door to door in Philadelphia. This performance inadvertently reached the press and I was summoned to the Deanery for questioning by Miss Thomas about an undignified escapade, in which I had persuaded my classmate Gertrude Frost to join me.

I managed to win her support in overcoming official disapproval by explaining that I had yielded to an irresistible urge to drop out of my protected class and discover how people would treat me when they did not know I belonged to a good family. I gave her a description of contrasts in treatment I encountered, having doors shut in my face and the threats of dogs "sicked" on me, to acts of kindness and sympathy. The latter behavior reached a climax when a family friend opened the door. His inquiring whether I "was hungry" or "needed assistance" caused me to beat a hasty retreat before I was recognized.

This was my first experience with the President alone, and her striking personality, brown hair brushed smooth from her forehead, keen dark eyes and handsome features, fascinated me. Her handling of me in this adventure, listening to my motives with close attention, had an influence on me that was immediate and lasting. She continued to be consistently friendly to me, which I appreciated, even though it did not serve to arouse ambition in me to study.

47

We had a common bond in athletics, and a number of times she personally asked me to arrange a basketball game, on some special occasion when visitors would be present.

I bluffed my way to a high mark in an essay labeled "Shelley," for which I had mistakenly prepared by reading Keats. Fortunately for me, I merely indulged in ecstatic poetical flights without mentioning the name of Keats or one of his verses.

I was equally lucky in an examination on Elizabethan plays. I had selected six of Shakespeare's, and as the day for the written test was all but on me, I put into effect a plan which made it technically possible for me to sign a statement that I had completed the required reading, though actually I had not opened even one of the volumes. I had persuaded six of my friends to come to my room and read the plays aloud, all at the same time. Incredible as it may seem, I was able, with intense concentration, to catch the most important scenes, on which I made a few notes, in the midst of a bedlam of voices.

Incidentally, many years later, when the entire Koran was being recited in a Mosque at Luxor for my benefit, as I had to learn it to insure my safety in Cairo during mob outrages, four *sheikhs* followed the same procedure, and with the same results—I got the pertinent verses in each *sura* (chapter).

But to return to the examination. On the day set for it, I was pretty ill in the college infirmary with a broken right arm. Miss Thomas considerately agreed to give the test to me orally, propped up in bed. Upon her entrance to the sick room, there was some delay because the doctor was rebandaging my arm.

During the rather lengthy process, I seized the fortuitous opportunity to tell her of my interest in the plays of Shakespeare, inherited from my grandfather Shepard. On seeing I was holding her attention, I mentioned my mother's having known William J. Rolfe (the great Shakespearean scholar), and that he had been impressed by her versatility at a small gathering where he was present, in doing equal justice in reading aloud two such different parts as Hamlet, on the one hand, and Shylock from the *Merchant of Venice*, on the other. When the doctor left, we were having such a cozy chat that Miss Thomas almost forgot the purpose of her visit. With her amazing enthusiasm and capacity for throwing herself wholeheartedly into anything she undertook, she proceeded quite unconsciously to amplify my uninspired answers to her questions. A good time was had by us both, but it was she not I, who should have received the mark of "high credit."

But the aftermath of the oral examination is worth recording. Thirty-five years later, when I went to an Arizona sanatorium for a month, I took with me my mother's Friendly Edition of Shakespeare, edited by Rolfe, with his prolific notes and comments. Constantly, as the plot of the play developed, something Miss Thomas had explained so many years ago gave me an understanding of characters and events, as, with complete absorption, I devoured Shakespeare's entire works.

In reading the sonnets, I remembered her statement that he had been in an entirely different mood when he composed them, but even so some of his special characteristics would identify them as his.

Another reference to Shakespeare's mood when writing the sonnets seems pertinent to mention here. It occurred after the Arizona experience. One late autumn afternoon, my husband and I were seated before a welcome open fire in our New Hampshire home, when Mrs. Patrick Campbell walked in on us unannounced. Without introducing herself, she said she was visiting a neighbor and in wandering about had stumbled onto our place. She wished to thank the owners for the privilege of sitting alone in the two outdoor theatres we possessed.

She was impressive and still beautiful as she sipped tea and talked delightfully about the stage. Somehow, the conversation got around to the sonnets of Shakespeare. "He wrote them when he was in love, and that's why the mood is different," she declared emphatically, and rather startled us by adding, "The same thing was true of Shaw. No one would have thought his love letters to me were genuine if they had not been in his handwriting."

This was her exit line.

To return to Miss Thomas, with all she had on her mind at this time of year, she still found time to send for me to come to the Deanery again. We were alone, and after a few general remarks she pulled her chair closer to mine. Looking at me intently, she asked abruptly, "Will you be back in the fall?"

I shook my head and replied, "You won't understand my not wanting a degree, but I'm not a student like my sister Bertha and other Putnams." Her steady gaze without speaking made me feel self-conscious. "Your own tremendous battle for a Ph.D. must make my attitude incomprehensible to you," I managed to get out after an awkward pause.

"I had to have it," she said with a firm line to her mouth. Then, with a charming smile she said, to my amazement, that a degree was not the whole story in education.

As I rose to go, she seemed rather absent-minded, as if her thoughts were elsewhere. But they weren't, as her parting remark showed:

"You are so intensely alive that your brain can't remain dormant, and in spite of yourself, Bryn Mawr has taught you how to use it."

Thus ended my academic career with a touch of the dramatic.

7

LEARNING TO LIVE

MY FATHER was on his annual spring business trip to London in 1895, and Bertha and Ethel were also in England. My mother and I were about to go to Lake George, our summer home, when she was stricken with a fever that soon was diagnosed as typhoid, from which she died in a matter of days.

After that my mind was a blank until one morning, when the sun was pouring into my room, a maid stood behind the bed with a tray in her hand. Aunt Minnie's voice was kind, but firm, when she said, "Sit up and eat all the food on it." I did, and from that moment I was able to concentrate.

It was not until Aunt Minnie's next visit that she mentioned my two weeks of mental collapse. No one could have spared me my grief at my mother's death, she said. But had she been notified of the illness, she would have come at once and prepared me for the inevitable, which would have prevented the shock from being deliberately kept from me.

Then she spoke of my father's desperate loneliness, and said the blow had been harder since the office had failed to cable him of my mother's illness until she was unconscious, and he had landed the day after her death.

After this her thoughts switched to my relations with Papa. Although he had been bitterly disappointed at my failure to finish college, he felt for me a very special sense of comradeship. This she described as a rare attitude in a father towards a daughter, and that it was up to me not to lose it, for my own sake as well as his.

Her words aroused my determination, and I arranged to be with my father whenever he had any spare time. He told me about the Civil War by campaigns. He got out maps and explained the factors that led to defeat or victory in battle, and their effect on Lincoln, as painstakingly as though I was in a class in history.

We played tennis a good deal together, at the West Side Tennis Club. By now my game was good enough to get me invited to make a fourth with ranking players in exhibition doubles. But I preferred the less strenuous ones that included my father. Our tennis matches served to further strengthen the ever closer bond between us.

From choice I had been very little with young people, but during a visit in Washington with a Bryn Mawr classmate I went with three boys about my age to see the Washington Monument. The freshness of early spring made me feel lively again, and I dared my escorts to race me to the top by the steep inside flight of steps. Two accepted, and I beat them both by a wide margin.

A reporter happened to see the finish and found out who I was. A news item in the papers publicized the stunt. It also stressed the fact that the time kept by interested guards below and at the summit showed I had made a record.

On my arrival home, I told Papa frankly that I was not in the mood to read the complete set of Edmund Burke's treatises he had left in my room. I wanted excitement. This led to my developing a sudden taste for horse racing, undoubtedly dormant since my wild riding as a child. Bareback and mounted on spirited western horses, my Pumpelly cousins and I tore over country roads.

For speed in horse flesh, however, I preferred races on the New York Race Track. Somehow I managed to get there often, taken by frivolous relatives of some of my father's conservative friends. How the horses did run! And how sorry I used to feel for people who saw only the sedate, fashionable horse shows of that period.

With Lake George summers a thing of the past, and my father abroad in 1896, I had not stayed much with my sisters but drifted into decidedly sophisticated house parties, usually arranged for me by Frank Crowninshield. But in the fall I threw my full energies into the political campaign. Father classed himself as an independent, but he was an ardent free trader, and on the tariff issue voted for a democratic president. When William Jennings Bryan was nominated, however, Father supported William McKinley on the free silver issue and with less reluctance, because Teddy Roosevelt was running for vice-president on the Republican ticket.

I spent long hours daily at New York local Republican headquarters, ran errands, distributed pamphlets, and did many odd jobs, including personal interviews with independents from whom I got promises of support. Occasionally I spoke at small meetings representing the views of girls too young to vote, an idea which Teddy himself had pushed.

After the Republican victory, my father wanted to give a dinner in Teddy's honor at the Century Club, but Teddy said, "Have fewer and in your home, Haven." Papa agreed. This would be the first large dinner without my mother, and as I was doing the housekeeping, the planning and work devolved on me. I had been about enough in formal society to know the kind of food that should be served, and the appropriate wines. Father offered no objection even to my rather timid suggestion of champagne.

I was enthusiastic about serving Teddy again, as in the old days, assisted by girl friends. The guests were thirty men, among them intimate friends like Henry Holt, Richard Watson Gilder, and Lawrence Godkin.

Teddy burst into the parlor like a tornado. His tremendous vitality was something that had to be seen to be believed. No occasion could remain formal with him as the star performer, and he was in wonderful form that evening. His responsibilities as governor had not lessened his contagious sense of fun, which affected all his fellow guests, even the most sedate among them.

Teddy in one of his mischievous moods began to tease my father for having had to "stretch his conscience" to vote for a Republican president. This gave Father a chance to retaliate. He gravely informed the assembled company that it was only logical for him to give a personal vote for Teddy Roosevelt, with whom he frequently differed politically, he interpolated, because he had been responsible for his first Republican election.

This was the story: Soon after Teddy's return from the West, he had come to my father and said he would like to invest quite a considerable sum of money in the firm of Putnam's as a silent partner. "Gentlemen," continued Father with mock solemnity, "I wish to draw your attention to the fact that a silent partner was a position our distinguished guest of honor was incapable of filling."

He went on to say that the silent partner did his best to take over the work of each department in the varied processes of producing books and selling them. Soon the entire office was in an uproar and the business of publishing came to a standstill. It was in this dilemma, Father said, that he found it convenient to have some influence in reform politics, and he had suggested to Teddy that he run as a Republican candidate for the Assembly in a district that included the Roosevelt home.

Teddy consented and was elected. When the legislature was in session, he spent five days a week in Albany, and Putnam's resumed the routine of book publishing. On Saturdays, Teddy would return to his desk with a fresh batch of impractical publishing suggestions.

When the laughter had subsided and Teddy could make himself heard, he told a joke on himself. It was about a Boston woman who, in writing congratulations on his becoming governor, reminded him she had been present at both of his weddings. She told him that she kept a diary, and the entry after attending his second marriage read, "It is strange that two such charming women married a man who will never be heard from in connection with anything important."

"Well, I seem to have been heard from," Teddy said, "and I don't intend to be a silent vice-president, as the politicians will soon find out," he added, with a now familiar truculence.

When the long table was cleared and cigars passed with coffee, Teddy invited the waitresses to remain in the room and be seated. The guests settled down to asking him questions. Teddy's clear-cut, frank answers brought out details of some of the scandalous transactions he had blocked by official opposition as governor. His flashing eyes and whole attitude revealed honest indignation and the strength of his determination to resist influence.

After mentioning a particularly outrageous attempt to put over a deal, he abruptly pulled out his watch and said, "It's later than I thought—I must be off." But on second thought, he could not let the evening break up without a final word about "our host and my dear friend," and declared the incident he was about to relate would show Haven Putnam to be dynamite to evil-doers. Then he gave an account of my father, when he was foreman of the grand jury, coming to Albany to inform him, as governor, that Asa P. Gardiner should be indicted as district attorney of New York for cause.

Teddy had replied by saying that no grand jury would dare to act, because of the extent of Gardiner's power. "But Haven went ahead," he declared. "The jury did indict the District Attorney, who was publicly disgraced."

It was like Teddy to be generous about the performance of duty by others than himself, my father commented to his guests.

Crashing parties was unknown in the eighteen nineties. But Frank Crowninshield was popular with hostesses. Thanks to him, and the persuasiveness of a number of older men I met, including foreigners, I received invitations to some of the fabulous entertainments given by the self-constituted clique that dominated New York Society, known as the "Four Hundred."

Papa took exception to my "gadding," as he called it, because I

54

was living beyond my means. He pointed out that the same yearly allowance of one hundred and fifty dollars he gave me sufficed Bertha and Ethel for clothes, hats, shoes, and other accessories. When I told him that my dancing slippers and evening gowns could not stand the fairly constant use I put them to and had to be replaced, he contended that my argument was based on the false premise that frivolity was a must.

But for all his seeming severity he would ask me how much more money I needed. He gave it without question and always seemed pleased when I came to show myself dressed up before going out. He was also reassured by the fact that in these establishments, filled to overflowing with fashionable guests, with champagne flowing freely, I stuck to water.

But when I became a frequenter of New York night clubs, he was aghast. In those days, the clubs had a different and altogether pleasanter atmosphere from today's. A girl did not go alone with a dancing partner, but in a group, boys and girls together. The music was on the quiet side, and smoking was at a minimum—it was to be another twenty years before women smoked in public. No hard liquor was served and nobody became drunk on light wines. There was a courtesy and a genuine cameraderie that sustained a convention which permitted strangers to talk and dance together without a formal introduction.

In one of the most popular night clubs of the time, I was picked up by Diamond Jim Brady. He was an extraordinary personality with amazing eyes. You could not turn away from their gaze. He was stout but distinguished-looking. When he bowed low and invited me to dance, I was surprised but rose at once. I could not get very near his person because of the way he was built. An enormous diamond, in the center of a bulging expanse of shirt front, kept me far from his shoulder-line. He did not really dance but just stood in the middle of the floor with his feet shuffling slowly, in perfect time to the music, and very slowly we moved around the room. All eyes were focused on my partner—particularly those of a flock of blondes, who apparently resented even the temporary claim of an outsider.

Diamond Jim asked me who my father was and seemed amused

55

when I told him. After a long waltz and an encore, he took me back to my party and, seating himself with us, treated the crowd to ginger ale—until the aforementioned flock of blondes took him away. Next day a long box of orchids was delivered at our house with Diamond Jim's card, on which he had scribbled, "This kind of exotic flower would not appeal to your father."

I showed the gift to Father. He decided that a drastic change in surroundings was needed at once, and in an attempt to develop in me what he called "desirable Putnam tendencies," he took me to England with him in the spring of 1897.

8

ENGLAND AND THE HIGH TALENTS

ON REACHING London, we settled in lodgings, where Papa (or Father, as he suggested that I call him, to avoid startling the English with an Americanism) had stayed before. To him, the convenience of being located around the corner from his office in the Strand compensated for the dreariness of rooming in the heart of the city, and he knew I was adaptable.

A telegram awaited him from Strachan-Davidson, the Master of Balliol, inviting him to Oxford for the coming weekend. He was expected to occupy his usual quarters at Balliol, and the message ended with the statement, "Find someone in Oxford to put up the young daughter. I want her at a dinner given in your honor Saturday."

After three days in London, I was deposited in Oxford at the home of Edward Augustus Freeman, the historian, in time for a quick change before being escorted by an undergraduate to the entrance of one of the famous old halls in Oxford. Strachan-Davidson welcomed me at the door with a charm and cordiality that made me feel at home. He nodded towards a rather large group of men, of which my father was the center. "We're glad to have him back," he said, beaming. He fumbled in his pocket until he found a note, which he handed me. It read, "I am looking forward to the novel experience of sitting next to an American girl at Balliol." It was signed C. L. Dodgson. "That's Lewis Carroll, keep it as a souvenir," my host advised.

At first sight, his clean-shaven face and classical features, and the way his hair grew off his forehead, reminded me of Emerson. But there was not the same serenity in the expression of the eyes and lines of the mouth, as he stood looking disapprovingly about him, as though he were considering taking French leave from a dinner he found too large to suit his mood.

Instead, however, he responded to my presence, as I stood quietly waiting for his initiative in beginning a conversation. He did so by saying, with mock solemnity, "I have been deceived, you are too old."

"Too old for what?" I asked.

His quick look of surprised interest showed that my giving him the correct lead was unexpected. "After seventeen a girl no longer believes impossible things," he said with a smile that revealed an inherent kindness. His quaint originality, the product of a complex personality, somehow challenged me to reply, "I still believe everything your White Rabbit said."

As we followed the rest of the guests into the Senior Common Room of Balliol, I saw from his manner that I had broken through his reserve and that Lewis Carroll had accepted me in spite of my being four years beyond the age limit of girls who were his friends. When we sat down, he informed me that his curiosity about my being entirely at ease in such an august gathering would have to be satisfied. I explained that since childhood I had seen my father's authors at home or in his office, and that the majority were scholars. Therefore I was used to them.

This he answered by saying he had been among scholars most of his active life, as a lecturer on mathematics at Christ Church College, which was his home, but he usually felt either shy with them or annoyed and aggressive. And furthermore I could get confirmation from my father's good friends, York Powell and Dean Paget of Christ Church, that he (Dodgson) was a complainer who grumbled about the inefficiency of people and was frequently unreasonable. He laughed, but it was laughter without heartiness, and he seemed somehow older than his actual years (sixty-four).

"But I am sitting next to Lewis Carroll, not Dodgson," I said. He nodded approval of the distinction I had made and said the important matter to be settled was what we were to talk about. He offered as an opening the device of asking your partner whether the bread placed to the right of the plate was his. This, he assured me, by a series of conversational steps, would get us to a discussion of the world economic situation, which would fit in with the generally serious atmosphere of the dinner.

When I objected that I might miss the cue to one of my steps, and that I preferred having no subject, he declared that would be a delightful innovation for Oxford. My attitude, he said, emboldened him to invite me to join a club, of which to date he was the sole member, the purpose being to have public dinners without any speakers. It was not long before he was inquiring at what age in America youngsters were forced by their parents to listen to *Alice in Wonderland* read aloud.

Ignoring the slight emphasis on the word "forced," I replied, "They begin to absorb Lewis Carroll's make-believe at about twelve and keep on loving it." I referred casually to American youngsters' instant responsiveness to Uncle Remus and his friends, and he insisted on my quoting extracts about Brer Fox and Brer Rabbit, and why Brer Wolf did not eat the little rabbit, and about the trickery of Brer Mud Turtle, and being an Englishman, he did not realize how poor my imitation of Joel Chandler Harris's rendering of Southern dialect actually was.

I mentioned my father's imagination in appealing to children with his fantasies. In particular, about a gingerbread man who came to life with quaint mishaps and breath-taking adventures, ending in tragedy. This short story, with illustrations in color, had become an American classic. And hardly less so, the dream of a husband who created an artificial mother to look after their children, so she could devote more of her time to him. The little gingerbread man and the fear of the arrival of the artificial mother were very real throughout my childhood, I said.

Lewis Carroll expressed such genuine interest in both of these fanciful characters that I promised to have the books sent to him. When he invited me to see something of Oxford in his company the next morning, I almost stammered in the eagerness of my acceptance. He asked where he could call for me, and I told him at the home of Mr. Freeman. "What an extraordinarily dull household for a young girl! Why are you there?" he asked, bursting into peals of laughter.

My expression checked his merriment, as I told him my father intended to have me included in most of his weekend visits, and this first one had been difficult on such short notice. After two refusals from intimate friends, on the plea that having an American girl was "too much to undertake," my father had turned to Mr. Freeman in desperation, because he could think of no one else. Freeman's telegram in reply said, "My wife and I don't mind putting up your young daughter provided we are not expected to entertain her." It was very kind of them to take me in.

At my reproving tone, he stared at me incredulously, murmuring, "And American girls are reportedly badly brought up."

The dinner was about to break up, and I was thanking him again for his invitation when I heard him repeat in a conversational but rather low tone, "I hate Oxford."

"If you hate Oxford how can you be a good guide?" At my question he jumped to his feet with a pretense of excitement. "At last I have found a listener," and he proceeded to enlighten my bewilderment by saying that this was a test, to which the unusual answer was something completely irrelevant. "Little did I expect to find in an American girl that rarity in the human species, a listener," and it behooved him to make preparations for our tour accordingly.

That Sunday afternoon late, I was in Strachan-Davidson's study with him and my father, still starry-eyed from seeing Oxford with

Lewis Carroll. I mentioned having been taken into spacious courts with trailing ivy, and to look at large trees and grass that had grown a long time, up and down dark stairways, into great halls and impressive smaller ones. "He was so wonderful," I said with unashamed rapture.

"What did he tell you?" Father asked prosaically.

"That he would permit the sound of the chapel bells to remain real." I continued that "Lewis Carroll's spoken words put everything I saw into a world of make-believe, more real than reality."

"You're talking nonsense," Father broke in.

"Yes, that's what Lewis Carroll called it," I said. "Nonsense to make important things become real."

"Are you feeling all right?" Father asked with a concern that silenced me from further dwelling on my fanciful journey into the wonderland of Oxford through the magic of my recent host.

An amusing analogy to my father's reaction on this occasion was Charles Frohman's to *Peter Pan*. "Barrie has gone mad, quite mad," he is reported to have said.

England at the turn of the century was a cluster of all the talents, from the remembered brilliance of Gladstone and Disraeli, to whose eminence many a youngster aspired; to Lewis Carroll, whom none could imitate; the modern artists, Edwin Abbey, Sir Lawrence Alma Tadema, and Sir Edward Pointer; writers like George Meredith and Thomas Hardy; and figures in ferment like Sir Walter Besant and still another Besant, Annie, not his own.

Sir Walter Besant, who lived at Hampstead on the outskirts of London, had established in his middle age an Authors' Society, and was a fiery opponent of publishers. But apart from what became almost an obsession, he was a loyal friend and was devoted to my father, who always stayed with him for a time during his annual visits to England. In Sir Walter's home, I was to meet Annie Besant, by curious coincidence, since she was not related to him. She had come for a chance to talk American publication of some of her work with my father.

Sir Walter's was a rambling old house and garden, without much form to it, but producing a pleasant effect with gay flowers and some fine old trees, among them some particularly superb oaks. By now he had reached the age when he enjoyed finding a quiet nook where he could sit relaxed.

It seemed to me that my father evaded the other and unrelated Besant, Annie, as far as was compatible with politeness when he chanced to be placed in company with her. But I, on the contrary, never missed an opportunity to be within earshot when she went into action with visitors who dropped in, or with professional people by appointment. She was in her mid-forties at the time of our visit and already had a reputation as a brilliant lecturer on socialism, though by now she had become completely absorbed in theosophy, in which she was the great leader for the remainder of her life.

One evening I heard her expound to a group of satellites the doctrines of theosophy; I did my best to follow, but got lost in the intricacies of the transmigration of souls and the seven heavens. Just before the meeting broke up, one of the older women, who had known Annie Besant at the time of her active work for socialism, prevailed on her to tell about having led a successful strike of grossly underpaid girls who sold matches at a well-known shop. As the story unfolded, her eyes flashed and she was magnificent with a power and an evident strength of purpose that made even me, a young girl, feel I was in the presence of a person who would never fail in anything she undertook.

As I say, talents in this age—at least in England—were everywhere for the asking. Max Beerbohm, later, Sir Max, was getting on with that peculiar and unique genius which was to delight his contemporaries, in caricatures, the essay, criticism, and the novel *(Zuleika Dobson)*. But just beginning was a gentler spirit, Logan Pearsall Smith, whom I was to meet for the first time in Surrey.

We were to stay, my father and I, in one of the most remarkable family circles of the time, that of Robert Pearsall Smith, a retired clergyman from Philadelphia, and his wife, Hannah Whitall Smith. He had settled in England at a place called Friday's Hill, later to become associated with the name of Bertrand Russell. Pearsall Smith's Quaker wife, like Annie Besant, had a cause. Hers was the fight against alcoholism, and she brought to the campaign an indefatigable energy and wholehearted enthusiasm that built up a large following. She was also well known as an evangelist.

Their three children were very unlike their parents in character and interests. Logan, the son, was tall, with delicate features, and although he had smiling eyes, there was a touch of melancholy about him. He had quite a collection of art objects, which he described to me as indicating a range of interest rather than definite tastes. He did not appear over-confident about really getting anywhere with painting, to which he was devoting a good deal of time. Someone once said of Logan that he wouldn't "find a wife or a career to suit him."

I did not seem his type, with his sophisticated conversation, quick mind, and a genius for apt phrasing, but we struck up a friendship that was to last. And it was Logan who asked his mother to invite me to stay on when my father had to leave. Coincidentally, his many publications, which he continued to send me in later years, were to be much sought after, as literature and as examples of a method of expression.

Mary Costelloe, the Smiths' elder daughter, and her two children, both girls, were living at Friday's Hill while she flitted back and forth between her former home and Paris. She talked to me about the marital difficulties that had ended in separation, as though I were a contemporary in experience. Her many kindnesses to me made a deep impression and laid the foundation for a real friendship during the long years when, as Bernard Berenson's wife, her intellect found an outlet in helping him in his work.

At the same moment I was being disillusioned about marriage, I came in contact with romance in the same household. Bertrand Russell had married Alys, the younger Smith daughter, three years before, and obviously they were very much in love. She was unusually tall and very graceful, her wavy brown hair, bright blue eyes, and exquisite complexion made her a striking figure in my eyes.

"Bertie," as Russell was called, was not handsome, because his forehead was too prominent and his chin receded a little, but his was an arresting face, full of character, with clear-cut features and keen eyes. He was so frank in mentioning his dislike of being bored that

I kept out of his way until one afternoon, after tea, he invited me to join him and Logan in a game of croquet, a procedure that continued throughout the remainder of my stay. He attacked the ball on the croquet grounds with the logic and devastating skill he used in demolishing arguments contrary to his unconventional opinions, and as effectively.

Logan was no match for him, and the only time I beat him Bertie attributed to my luck, not skill. When I told him this was not fair, he sized me up in a searching glance, as though considering my words, and remarked, "You are right."

When Father and I were back in our London lodgings, I found plenty to occupy me. Just to be on a bus and watch the kinds of people who got in and out, how they looked, and what they did and said, or to stand at crowded circles such as Piccadilly Circus and near Saint Paul's Cathedral, gave me vivid impressions of the differences between us and our English cousins.

A most striking example took place in Putnam's London retail store, where I had gone to meet my father. A pathetic-looking, elderly American woman had buttonholed an English clerk, from whom she was trying to buy a book. She did not remember the title or the author's name, but went into detail about her reasons for wanting it. My eyes were on an American man, who, very red in the face at the clerk's rudeness to a fellow citizen, was about to intervene when the woman scuttled away.

As I was leaving I saw the same woman re-enter Putnam's by a second door, opening onto the Strand, thinking she was in a different book store. When she addressed herself to the same clerk, with the same questions, not having recognized him, he was really insolent. The American, rushing up to him, said, "You're no gentleman." Instead of the expected blow that would have been the response to this insult, the Britisher replied calmly, "Of course, I'm not a gentleman, what can I do for you, Sir?"

I found much to amuse me at my six-penny lunches at the ABC shops (Aerated Bread Company), and on the evenings when I was thrown back on my own resources in lodgings, I read Macaulay's *History of England*. But I did not mention to my father that what he dismissed as Lewis Carroll's nonsense had inspired me to acquire a first-hand knowledge of England's history and traditions.

Soon English young people were planning interesting jaunts for me. John Atkins, a junior member of the staff of *The Spectator*, was very obliging in taking me to cathedral towns, Winchester, Canterbury, Salisbury, and many others. The reverence expressed in stone, the dignity and fine proportions, simplicity in details, the vast empty spaces—gave me a new sense of religion and the meaning of the words, "Church of England."

Strong contrasts in out-of-town weekends appealed to me. For instance, one week we were an integral part of the family life of a great scholar, where his wife and daughters did the housework, and the next at Knebworth Castle, let to an American because the then Lord Lytton was too impecunious to live there. The American was Henry Phipps, a partner of Andrew Carnegie's, but in spite of his wealth, he, his wife, and their half-grown sons and daughters proved to be the simple, high-minded people who represented the best type of Americans spending money abroad. They were unpretentious but perfectly at ease with an imposing array of servants standing about in impressive rooms. A great private park with hundreds of deer was in keeping with the grandeur of the enormous estate.

The London stage took up many of my free afternoons. Matinees at a number of theatres took place every day of the week, not merely on Wednesdays and Saturdays, as in New York. William Gillette was in London acting in *Secret Service*. He had been on our steamer, the *Saint Paul*, with his company, and I ventured to remind him of our having met at Bryn Mawr with my classmate, and his niece, Margaret Warner.

He and my father got on very well, and on one occasion I overheard Gillette explaining why he had incurred expense in bringing over about twenty men to take very small, non-speaking parts as confederate soldiers. He said English faces would not look right, but admitted his real reason was that in one scene they had to arrest him as a Yankee spy, and he was not going to have Britishers lay a hand on him after the way they had behaved in the Civil War!

Ethel Barrymore was an understudy in Gillette's company. We

had become friends on shipboard and saw something of each other in London, where she was living in the same kind of dreary lodgings I was. It was she who took me to the Henley Regatta, with Richard Harding Davis as our escort. Ethel had an irresistible urge to buy hats, the larger, the better, she thought, and her height made her carry well enormous wide-brimmed affairs trimmed with huge birds. She was the most beautiful girl imaginable, but no flirt, and seemed absolutely unconscious of the effect she had on men of all ages and nationalities.

Daniel Frohman, the brother of the better known Charles in the theatrical world, was Gillette's manager. During his few weeks in London, they frequently were to be seen in boxes, put at Frohman's disposal for matinees of popular English plays, and Gillette gave me a standing invitation to join them.

It was interesting to watch Frohman in action. The first experience I had was at a performance of the *Princess and the Butterfly*, with Julie Opp as leading lady. She had merely walked across the stage at her entrance and had spoken only one sentence, when Frohman said to Gillette, "I want that actress in America." "How about the play?" Gillette asked him after an excellent second act. Frohman replied that he never decided on a play until the final curtain had fallen on the last act.

Incidentally, he did take the *Princess and the Butterfly*, as well as the actress, and Julie Opp, as Mrs. William Faversham, began a long and successful career on the American stage.

Behind the scenes, I was taken for granted, as a very minor member of Gillette's company, or a young relative, and no one paid any attention to me. It was the same when the box door would open between acts and prominent English actors and actresses walked in, most of them looking less well in street clothes than they did on the stage. I will always remember Sir Henry Irving discussing stage production with Frohman, in violent disagreement as to ideas and methods, while lovely Ellen Terry gushed over Gillette. Or it might be a playwright in the news, such as Sir Arthur Wing Pinero or George Alexander, who came in.

When Gillette knew I was in town on a Sunday, he often sent me a message and we did something together. Once I received a hastily scribbled line in pencil saying, "The more I see of humans, the more I crave the company of animals—how about an afternoon at the zoo?"

Almost an hour alone with John Hay in his study was a fitting climax to my first summer in England. President McKinley had appointed him ambassador to the Court of St. James's. My father thought he knew him sufficiently well to ask to bring his daughter to the Embassy for a few words with the co-author of the *Abraham Lincoln*, which she had read with interest.

The Ambassador and Mrs. Hay received us in one of the smaller reception rooms. In appearance and in his speech were agreeable traces of Hay's Scotch ancestry, and like the majority of men at that period, he wore a short beard and mustache. Although unimpressive in size, being conspicuously short, like my father, seldom before or since have I met a man whose personality made such an instant impression of greatness.

After a few words of greeting had been exchanged, he asked me abruptly what had started my interest in Lincoln. I told him that when I was very little, the words, "Lincoln, the man of sorrows," fascinated me. Father added, "She could not have been more than six when, on being left with an elderly bachelor friend of mine, not used to children, she began a conversation by announcing, 'I love Mama and Abraham Lincoln.'"

"An incident likely to be remembered," Hay commented with great gravity, then as he saw guests about to enter the room, he took me into a small study—"the one place where I am not disturbed," he called it.

He seemed surprised that my response to some remark of his showed my familiarity with the Civil War by campaigns. He reminisced about some remarkable prison experiences, and this led me to tell him my father had survived both Danville and Libby prisons. He spoke of the terrible anxiety in Washington when, near the end of the war, the city was threatened by a raid by Jubal Early, with expected reinforcements nowhere in sight. I told him of my mother's having been a nurse at the military hospital in Baltimore at the time,

66

and about her graphic descriptions of the effort to get the sick and badly wounded into uniforms and on picket duty. The Confederate scouts' report on the large number of pickets convinced Early that the reinforcements had arrived. He turned back and Washington was saved from destruction.

Hay also seemed surprised when our conversation brought out how much I knew about his own career. I said that was what had made me understand why he had been able to make Lincoln's character come alive in the writing he had done about the President. His seeming pleasure at my explanation caused me to enlarge on the theme by saying that things like the printing of the many drafts of Seward's and Staunton's notes, with Lincoln's longhand modifications of them, made reading the ten volumes like actually knowing him personally.

This really got Hay started, and he referred to the rare opportunities he and John G. Nicolay had had in watching Lincoln's mind at work, because one of them was present at all his official interviews. He responded to my spellbound attention by recounting several dramatic interviews resulting in momentous decisions which only Lincoln could have shaped.

"I find myself conversing as though you were an old greybeard like myself," Hay said, laughing.

And then Mrs. Hay came and took him away.

9

OLD STATESMEN AND NEW

My father and I landed together in England for the second time in May, 1898, and we occupied the same lodgings which had been ours on the first trip. London was in gloom because of the death of William E. Gladstone, the former prime minister. I entered Trafalgar Square alone, to find literally thousands of people standing about sobbing, the clear evidence of an overwhelming mass grief. As the crowds slowly drifted towards the Embankment, I drifted with them in the direction of Westminster Abbey, where Gladstone was lying in state.

Friendly English bobbies made way for me through the kindly throngs of people, to the entrance, and into the Abbey. Everywhere men and women were kneeling or slowly advancing down the main aisle. No one pushed, no one hurried. Inside that vast and historic interior, the silence was even more moving than the sobbing, as I reached the bier.

I had seen the early morning sunlight on Nelson's tall monument in Trafalgar Square, but now the glow of the setting sun was over buildings and on the Thames as I emerged from the Abbey, completely unmindful that I was to have lunched with my father and John Morley, Gladstone's biographer.

Morley was so impressed by the length of time I was a part of that great mass of men and women, as well as the fact that I had actually got into the Abbey, that he again asked father and me to lunch, and this time I did not forget to go.

Morley was understandably eloquent in talking about Gladstone. It was a terrific blow to him (Gladstone) to have his Home Rule Bill thrown out in 1893, he said, and then the next year the First Lord of the Admiralty proposed an addition to the navy. This was imperialism which Gladstone had consistently opposed, and he threatened to resign on the issue. Colleagues in his cabinet did not back him up, and Gladstone's political career was ended. "He was never more magnificent than in his acceptance of defeat," Morley said.

On one of Father's leisure afternoons, we got on a bus which deposited us at St. John's Woods, an old-fashioned residential district of London, rather run down but with an atmosphere of gentility. We poked about among streets cut through since the days when my father's parents had lived there for a number of years, and the identification of the site of the house in which he had been born put him into a delightfully reminiscent mood. Among his family

68

anecdotes was one connected with an ill-featured, sallow-cheeked young Frenchman, named Louis Napoleon, at the time living in exile in London. He became a fairly frequent visitor, often accompanied by a number of his compatriots. Unquestionably, he had abused the Putnam hospitality by using the house as a convenient meeting place for himself and his fellow conspirators, for planning the details of the plot that would drive Louis Philippe in flight from Paris and result in his (Napoleon's) being elected president of the French Republic in 1848. By the *coup d'état* of 1852, he began his long reign as Napoleon III. It was characteristic of grandfather that, during his many trips to Paris, he never got in touch with the man he had found to be the "self-seeking schemer of France."

I was never tempted by any invitation that would prevent me from sleeping in our lodgings when Father was to be in town. The shabby sitting room, with an old settee that needed recovering, and faded chintz on armchairs, rather dark and chilly on some mornings, was to me a palace of delight, particularly during our cozy breakfasts, which were served punctually at 7:30.

A letter from Father to Aunt Minnie which she had mailed back to me made me walk on air. It started by saying that my responsiveness to what England meant to him, and my careful attention to conversations between him and his friends, made me a real comrade. Then he wrote, "Corakins' audacious spirit and joy for life is making me less sedate, which is a good thing, and she has developed a sense of discretion that has relieved my anxieties for her future." He added in a hasty pencil scribble that he had quite a time in persuading me to join in the festivities of the undergraduates at Cambridge, rather than be with him when he was visiting his old friend James Bryce.

After many of Father's entries in his engagement book for luncheons and receptions, and even a few dinners, he would add, as a memo to himself, "Try to get Corakins included."

Through his inherited friendships, as well as his own increasing number of friends, and the fact that the majority of his efforts to have me included were successful, I met a great many people. We were in London more than we were on the first trip, and some of the well-known hostesses were very kind about entertaining a stray American girl.

Lady Charnwood, whose husband wrote a life of Lincoln, asked me on a special afternoon made memorable by meeting Viscount Grey of Fallodon. I knew he was an ardent fisherman, so I told him of my experience in landing my first salmon trout in Canadian waters. We had a quite long conversation, mostly about fishing and camping out. Next day Father received a note from Lord Grey mentioning our meeting, how unfortunate he had been the season before in missing him (Father), and wouldn't he bring his daughter to Fallodon for overnight!

To Father's amazed "How did you manage that?" I replied casually, "I caught him with a fly."

I went to a garden party given on a large estate not far from London. Handsome tall Englishwomen in gala array, with escorts in the fashionable London afternoon attire of Prince Albert coat and top hat, strolled leisurely about among magnificent garden surroundings. There were flower beds with specimen blooms stretching as far as the eye could see, with wide green paths between them, and stately old trees in the background. A scene of sunshine, gaiety, and laughter.

An entirely different note was introduced when a middle-aged man was brought up to me whose name I did not catch. He had the sort of solemn face my father described as that of a nonconformist clergyman. Ideas and ideals in government burst from him with the violence of a volcano in eruption. I was tremendously impressed by the intensity of his earnestness and sincerity.

When he paused for breath, I found myself telling him about my reaction as a child to my father's being a Mugwump, explaining what the word meant, and how I had been made to realize that it was everyone's responsibility, and especially of the young, to make good government a reality.

"Exactly, exactly," he repeated and lapsed into silence.

The name of the serious man was Herbert Asquith, who at that time was considered politically promising. (He had been Home Secretary, 1892–95.)

The London family whose latchkey was always out to me, and where I could come and go without notice, were the Hardcastles. She was the granddaughter of Sir William Herschel, the great astronomer. The eldest Hardcastle daughter, Frances, was a friend of my sister Bertha's, and there were other girls older and younger than I. Henry, the father, remained rather a shadowy figure—the only definite recollection of him that has remained was once when he announced to me from the depths of an armchair, in which he was busy with the London *Times*, that on his marriage he had insured himself with Lloyd's of London against twins.

They lived in a stately mansion on Eaton Square, set well back from the pavement, and fronting a small private park, accessible only to the householders on the square. To avoid the extra tip expected by a cabbie from an American put down at such an establishment, I descended at a little distance and walked in.

Under Mrs. Hardcastle's auspices, I was at moments on the fringes of brilliant social events, but I did not bother to record the names of notables, if acquaintance was limited to a mere "How-do-you-do?" or having them pointed out to me.

She had been lady-in-waiting to Queen Victoria, a fact which caused me to ply her with questions. It intrigued me to learn what the Queen wore, what she did in the privacy of her room, and what the duties were for ladies-in-waiting and of the bed chamber. The realization that Victoria was never alone, and that important documents were taken to her to sign at any time, day or night, made me appreciative that a queen leads a very interrupted life.

I was fascinated in all I learned about court etiquette and protocol. Once Mrs. Hardcastle said to me abruptly, "It's a pity, with all your father's distinction, he cannot be given an audience with English royalty." "Why not?" I asked, only to receive the, to me, astonishing reply, "Because he is in trade."

I remember a rebuke Mrs. Hardcastle administered to me. I had mentioned someone high up in the Conservative government, which was then in power under Lord Salisbury as prime minister, as a "politician." "We call them all statesmen," she said severely, and added, "We never invite Liberals into our home—they are politicians." Those who remember English history will recall that Gladstone had suffered from the same stigma, in Victoria's eyes, and Benjamin Disraeli had enjoyed a corresponding advantage.

She expressed great satisfaction that father and I had tea on the Terrace of Parliament with Lord Salisbury. What I remember most about that momentous occasion was the sight of my father standing beside the Prime Minister as he was stressing policies with which father was politely disagreeing. Salisbury was so tall that he had to lean far down to look into father's eyes as he murmured,

"You have no idea of the pressure brought to bear on a prime minister."

Mrs. Hardcastle took me on a Sunday afternoon to see Sir William Herschel's great telescope at Slough. As we drove to Windsor and beyond, through beautiful country, she told me he had been born in Hanover, Germany, and brought up as a musician, and the study of harmony had led to mathematics and astronomy. He had discovered the planet Uranus in 1781 when he was forty-three, and after several moves he had settled at Slough, where the house and gardens were still known as the "Herschels."

As we left Slough, Mrs. Hardcastle was saying that, before her grandfather's death in 1822, he had put on the market huge telescopes that "counted the stars visible in the same telescopic field in different directions." She commented that he was rather upset as a scientist because he had made a fortune through the sale of large-size telescopes, but the family had found the money convenient.

On the Fourth of July, father and I were with Sir George Darwin, the well-known mathematician and physicist, and the son of Charles Darwin. I came down to breakfast with American Independence violently displayed on my person in the form of a gilt spread-eagle and an American flag.

My father was engaging Sir George in an animated conversation, but he jumped up politely and held out a chair for me. "Do you know what day this is?" I asked Sir George.

"It's July 4, 1898," he replied. Then taking in my ornaments, he continued quietly, "And a great day for England, on which we got rid of you bumptious Americans."

I was at Cambridge in a whirl of festivities at the end of the term. The ball at Trinity College, with its tradition and dignity and the way it was conducted by undergraduates in charge, I had to admit was on a more impressive scale than class day at our home colleges.

My conscience was troubling me for acknowledging that anything in England was better done than in America, when several letters reached me from New York members of Troop A. I was severely reproved for a lack of patriotism in being away in foreign lands during the war with Spain while they were fighting for their and *my* country.

I was still feeling rather miserable next day at the bumping boat races, a sport unique to England. Instead of ending at a finish line with the first boat across the winner, the aim was to bump with the bow of your boat the stern of the one immediately in front, which, on being bumped, was out of the race. Spectators in a mad rush followed along the shore, encouraging their favorite colleges.

The small college of Peterhouse (pronounced Pot-house), starting as the head boat of the second division, had accomplished the rare feat of getting two bumps in the same race, and I was invited to celebrate the victory the next afternoon at a party given by Peterhouse undergraduates.

On my way there, to my indignation and dismay, I saw floating triumphantly above the weathervane of the main building of the college a Spanish flag. This public insult to America by favoring our enemy, I took to be my personal affair, but exactly how I was to deal with it must wait on circumstances. Restraining my wrath, I went to the party, where I managed to have presented to me the undergraduate who had raised the flag.

He turned out to be a mild-eyed youth holding an Angora cat in his arms. He kept insisting he had reached for any flag, and had not deliberately chosen the Spanish. He had managed to get it to stick to the weathervane by a lucky fluke involving a stone and a thin rope. When he explained the only way to get the flag down was by shooting at it, my desperation knew no bounds. But I finally persuaded the perpetrator to put an American flag still higher.

I tore through the stores of Cambridge to buy an American flag.

73

No one knew what it looked like. Salesmen offered me one of the flags of South America. I then wired to Putnam's to get off immediately a good-sized flag of the United States of America. They did so. I took it to the undergraduate, to whom my final word was *"Excelsior!"*

A few days later he sent me a Kodak picture showing the top of the main building of Peterhouse College with the American flag, larger than the Spanish and above it. Indeed it was *excelsior*. He wrote that the authorities were perturbed and did not know who had raised the flags or how to remove them.

In a letter to Frank Crowninshield, I remarked that Dewey was being acclaimed for raising the American flag at Manila Bay, but I was responsible for our flag being raised in the heart of an English university town, above the Spanish. Frank thought the episode too good to keep, and in due course it ended up in the *New York Times.* This was not my wish, but the lark, as any old Oxonian or Cantabridgian can attest, was then and might now be fully in keeping with the spirit of undergraduate fun at England's two oldest universities.

IO

VISITS TO MEREDITH, HARDY, AND BURNE-JONES

FATHER HAD TOLD ME that George Meredith and Thomas Hardy were the prime movers in giving him a testimonial for his part in the passage of the International Copyright Law. This consisted of a parchment signed by all the great authors of England. It meant far more to him than decorations which had been bestowed on him by France and Italy.

By 1898, Meredith was living in retirement. Physical infirmities had reduced him to a state of invalidism, the harder to bear because

74

his mental faculties remained unimpaired. He suffered the further handicap of being deaf. All this Father pointed out when I urged him to take me to see Meredith in his home in Surrey.

At our luncheon with John Morley, he had casually mentioned that he was one of the few old friends who continued to visit Meredith during his enforced inactivity, his writing career at an end. His response to my suggestion of a personal interview was that "it would do Meredith good to see an old friend and a young new admirer."

While he was arranging for us to have lunch with Meredith in his home and return to London by a late afternoon train, he talked to me about the author. He referred to Meredith's long years of struggle against poverty, the son of a tailor who was without sympathy for the literary aspirations of his son. Added to this, for twenty-five years Meredith wrote without recognition as a novelist. Morley said it was generally conceded that Meredith had created some of the greatest women characters in modern fiction. But his plots were condemned by the critics as fatiguing, with tedious analyses of human behavior, and the style labored.

Morley considered that what Meredith had gone through had driven him back upon resources within himself, and had developed in him a feeling for the beauty of nature, which he later expressed in lyric verse.

Then reverting to the novels, he said that the instant acclaim of *Diana of the Crossways* had led to a uniform edition of Meredith's works in England, in 1894, including many of his novels which had long been neglected.

Father was amused when I told Morley that America some years previously had recognized Meredith's genius as a writer of fiction.

After a short walk from the station, a gravel driveway on the slope of Box Hill, with marvelous box hedges all around, brought us to Flint Cottage, where Meredith lived. He rose with an effort from a lounge chair in the garden outside to receive us. His frailty was obvious and he controlled his legs with difficulty. He greeted us in a voice made high in pitch by his deafness. I was fascinated to watch his sensitive face with grayish eyes, deep set and observant, clear-cut features, and wavy hair. He was wearing a quilted jacket, an informal flannel shirt with the collar open at the neck, and no tie.

We met his wife at a simple lunch. She was a French woman and apparently a congenial companion, after his first unhappy marriage. Meredith's zest for conversation equaled that of my father, who was many years his junior. He recalled having met in his extreme youth at Grandfather Putnam's London home, Mazzini, the Italian patriot, and Louis Napoleon, "the rascal responsible for the downfall of France."

When he offered to take us to the Chalet, his famous workshop, his wife whispered to me that he had not been in it for two years. A young man assisted Meredith, whose movements were pathetically slow. Father and I followed to a terrace above the garden.

As our eyes swept approvingly over a wide expanse above the slope of Box Hill, to ridges encircling neighboring towns beyond, Meredith said proudly, "An unparalleled view, even in Surrey." The interior of the Chalet consisted of two good-sized rooms, splendidly light and airy. Father's comment that here was everything essential for a study and nothing superfluous, delighted him. In this workshop for the past twenty years, he had found a much-needed detachment, Meredith said.

He gave a quickly suppressed sigh at the thought that his writing days were over. Then, in an abrupt change of mood, he mentioned having been a journalist during the American Civil War. Under orders from his superiors, he was compelled to write articles attacking Lincoln, when his sympathies lay with him and the cause of the Union. He reminisced about John Bright's having upbraided him for acting against his convictions, to which he had retorted it was that or starve, as he had no other means of livelihood at the moment.

Before we had to leave for our train, Father considerately drew attention to my presence by mentioning my admiration for Meredith's novels. Whereupon, turning towards me, Meredith said, "So the lovely Diana with her wit and charm appealed to you."

When I said it was *The Egotist* that had remained my choice among his novels, he appeared surprised and insisted on my telling him why. My answer was that I had searched the pages from cover to cover without discovering a single reason for his charming heroine's having fallen in love with such a preposterous man. But in the process, I realized that every character created by him, in every novel, had a purpose.

Soon I was talking excitedly about what his poetry meant to me. Inadvertently, I confessed to repeating aloud to myself his poems on nature. At his request I even recited several. Then I stopped suddenly and began to rub my eyes. He inquired whether I had a cinder. "No," I told him. "I want to make sure I am awake and not dreaming that I had the opportunity and encouragement to repeat some of Meredith's poems to Meredith himself."

A similar memorable occasion was an overnight stay with Thomas Hardy, which took place some days later. Once again Father and I got out at a railroad station for the purpose of meeting a literary giant. This time it was Dorchester, reached by the London and Southwestern. Dorchester Road was cut deep between high wooded banks, and in the middle distance were rich farms, whose thatched-roof cottages added to the indefinable charm of Wessex.

Max Gate, Hardy's home off Wareham Road, was built in a secluded spot among tall trees and was vine-covered, with an impressive turreted entrance. He had been his own architect, and the house, which deserved the designation of mansion, reflected the influence of the years he had been an able assistant to an expert in Gothic architectural construction.

He was totally unlike what I had expected from his gloomy books, which had everything going wrong in the lives of his main characters. He was just below middle height and had an attractive personality. A contagious laugh revealed a sense of humor, curiously in conflict with intensely sad eyes, and a face that was thoughtful in response to conversation. At first sight, gentleness seemed an outstanding quality, but a fierceness in the lines of Hardy's mouth made one believe the tales about the short shrift he gave tourists and unannounced reviewers who ventured to intrude upon his privacy.

The sun streamed into a solarium, and all was friendly and gay as we settled down to a quiet conversation before an early lunch and a tramp over the countryside. Hardy was a young fifty-eight, four years Father's senior, and the cameraderie between them was agreeable to see. He was quite willing to talk, and about himself if pressed, and Father did press him for my benefit.

The three of us were good walkers, and Hardy knew exactly what he wanted to show us of what he termed his "special bit of countryside." He kept us at a good pace but every now and again we sat down on some knoll to enjoy a particularly fine view and catch our breath from a steep up-grade. Gradually, from snatches of his detached talk, I got a picture of his early life. During school days he showed no aptitude for study. He was shy and held himself aloof from boys of his age. This threw him back on the companionship of villagers, which in his case was to prove a mercy in disguise. His father decided arbitrarily that both social contacts and an academic training would be wasted on him. At the age of twenty, he was sent to London to be a draftsman in the office of John Hicks, an architect, in Bayswater. He gave a vivid account of his utter frustration when his urge to write verse was thwarted by his father's insistence that he must stick to architecture.

He did stick for five years and overcame his loneliness by using his leisure hours in visiting art museums and picture galleries. This led to his taking up painting for amusement. He wrote articles on art for the newspapers, and attended evening courses at King's College at the University of London. In this fashion he had overcome the early handicaps which had threatened his career as a writer.

Throughout his life he remained a prolific reader, became thoroughly conversant with English literature of every period, and managed to achieve in the originals a working knowledge of both Latin and Greek. But first and foremost, he had familiarized himself with the Bible, both the Old Testament and the New. "Whenever I was at a loss for the correct remark to be made by one of my characters at a critical moment," he said, "it was safe to turn to the Scriptures for a quotation in Biblical phraseology. I always found it." His statement was made with a lack of emphasis which was overwhelmingly dramatic.

The sun was declining on the western horizon. Time was now a factor in bringing Hardy's amazing career up to the present from his own random recollections, though clearly he was in a mood for reminiscing. Both Father and I had begun to fire questions at him, and he answered the ones that seemed to him most pertinent. Such a question was mine about his poems on love.

He had begun by thinking of love as a tormentor which ended in tragedy, he said. Then he had met Emma Gifford and wrote love ditties to her in a different mood. He had been concentrating on verse, but when he fell in love with her, he turned to writing novels in an attempt to make sufficient money for them to get married. From that time on, beginning in the early 1870's, he had published a novel a year.

But (and this was his final word before we stumbled along in the fading twilight) he had continued to write poetry, and his ambition to become a great poet would never be lost sight of, despite the financial success of his novels.

Time has had the final say, however, and it does not put Hardy in the first rank of English poets, but it has given him a secure and respected place as a novelist.

One day in June, 1898, I went to a function where everyone except myself was rather old and important and nobody took an interest in a young American girl except a Greek named Ionidas. He told me he was an intimate friend of Sir Edward Burne-Jones's and suggested that I go with him to see him in his studio.

I was cold to the proposition because the artists I had met to date were young men with affected manners whom women at studio teas encouraged to talk about their art and themselves, but who did not attract me. A few days later, my father took me to the home of the Rudyard Kiplings, where I saw my first Burne-Jones picture. I realized I was not the type to appeal to an artist who specialized in tall, pale, long-necked, gray-eyed women and girls.

Ionidas continued to be persistent, and when he enclosed a note from Burne-Jones urging me to come, I went with Ionidas rather reluctantly one late afternoon to an old-fashioned house on the out-skirts of London. In my girlish self-consciousness, I felt out of place in a large crowd, mostly women who stared at me in passing without any attempt to be polite. Suddenly I saw Burne-Jones, a slight man, wearing a brown velveteen coat and a necktie of a woven silk sold in Venice by weight. The ends hung loosely through a ring of three large sapphires that matched the blue of his eyes and the tie.

He was unlike any man I had ever imagined as he greeted me with a smile that was unbelievable in its radiance and sincerity. He thanked me for coming and almost at once took Ionidas and me across a vast rambling garden, where gay flowers, casually planted, seemed thoroughly at home with nearby lawns that had grown leisurely for several hundreds of years. At the far end of the garden, near a vine-covered front entrance, we entered a low, very simple studio. It had been adapted from a chicken house, Burne-Jones informed me. On newly whitewashed walls were a number of paintings by him.

He said he had seldom talked to a young American girl, and I with equal frankness replied, "I never go to artists' studios." In spite of my attitude, he doggedly assumed that I would marry an artist and assured me that I would thereby get the best life had to offer. "Remember," he said, "art is an illusive mistress and if neglected or abused will vanish." He warned me against ever urging my artist husband to paint a pot boiler because I wanted a new bonnet.

He showed me a portfolio of black-and-white sketches of women and girls and asked me to pose for such a study the next day. I told him I was going to Paris for about two weeks, which seemed to disappoint him, so I said I would pose on my return.

The shadows of late afternoon lengthened, but each time Ionidas tried to leave, Burne-Jones intervened. I later remembered thinking I had never seen a man as physically frail who looked so intensely alive and interested in what he was doing. I listened to the intimate talk of the artist about plans for the completion of his unfinished work. His mind was never in the past. Ionidas and I were about to go, when Burne-Jones reopened the portfolio containing the portrait sketches: "Choose any one of them you like," he said generously.

Meeting his eyes squarely, I replied, "But what would I do with it?" For a second Burne-Jones looked slightly startled, then catching Ionidas' horrified expression, he chuckled, "I'll expect to see you after Paris."

The following night Burne-Jones died in his sleep.

II

I BECOME A SMITH

I HAD HEARD a good deal about Joseph Lindon Smith for some time, but always had just failed to meet him. I could have met him the summer of 1893, when I was in Dublin, New Hampshire, with my family. This was the only season, however, when Joe, who lived there, was elsewhere. He did visit Dublin for about two weeks, but my Aunt Minnie, in an attempt to improve me, had taken me, much against my will, to the Chicago World's Fair.

The next winter, I happened to be in Philadelphia for a ball given at Horticultural Hall. As we came out by a side door about dawn, someone in a group of young people said to me, "You ought to look at a fresco on the outside of the building, above the main entrance, painted by Joe Smith, a Boston artist." To this I retorted, "Not at this hour!" The next year, Horticultural Hall was torn down.

In 1898, I had stayed on in England after my father's departure, and in early September was about to join friends in Italy when I had a letter from my cousin Elise Pumpelly, saying she was going to be married in Dublin on October 3 and wished me to be with her. On a sudden impulse, I changed my winter plans and took the first steamer home. Joseph Lindon Smith had postponed his own sailing overseas to be at the wedding.

I reached Dublin in the early morning of the day before the wedding and that afternoon I happened to be the one who showed the presents to Joe's mother. She went home and said to him, "That Putnam cousin of Elise's is a girl I believe you'd like." He accordingly went to the family supper that evening, and we met for the first time.

After the wedding I was to stay on with the Pumpellys for a few days. The next afternoon I went by appointment to Loon Point (Joe's home) and saw a rather forbidding looking older man working in the flower garden. I realized he must be Joe's father and said, "Your son asked me to pose for him. Is he in his studio?"

Without stopping his work, Mr. Smith, Sr., glanced up towards a window and called out, "Joe, there's a girl after you."

But Joe was after a sketch of me, and at that sitting and for the next several days, we came to know each other well. In fact, I liked him better than any man I'd known before, and I therefore made arrangements to stay on at Dublin rather than return immediately to New York. In two weeks Joe and I were engaged—at least I thought so.

I returned to New York, and after two weeks of silence Joe telegraphed he would spend the next evening with me before sailing for Italy the following morning. He arrived at our house after dinner, looking white and strained, and kept repeating like an automaton I was to "forget him." From his disconnected utterances, it was obvious that the reason for a decision which, to him, was inevitable was his relationship to his mother.

She felt that his work as an artist was perfectly adapted to having his parents make a home for him, in a studio apartment in Boston, between his painting trips abroad, and it had never entered her head he might fall in love. "She can't face it," he said, simply. She had sent for her sister, "Aunty Pratt," but found no comfort in Aunty's expressed pleasure that Joe wanted to get married, nor could she accept Aunty's blunt opinion that the young should lead their own lives.

Joe's eloquence made me realize all his mother had gone through and her need for him. His father had been a successful wholesale lumber merchant in Rhode Island, until his partner, who was ill, had made commitments Joe's father knew nothing about, ultimately

Henry Francis Smith, Joe's father,
from a sepia sketch made by his son Joseph Lindon Smith.

Sir Edward Burne-Jones had wanted to try a sketch
but it was Joe Smith who succeeded, during our engagement,
with this portrait.

Stage of the Teatro Bambino at our home,
Loon Point, Dublin, New Hampshire,
one of the oldest outdoor theatres in America.

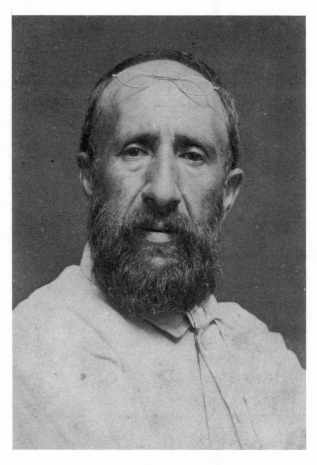

O. Hamdy Bey, Director of the Museum,
Constantinople, 1900.

ruining the firm. After his failure, he became downhearted and refused any further business ventures.

Joe's mother had never lost her courage. She salvaged the remaining resources, pinched and scraped, and finally made it possible for Joe to have two years in a Paris studio to complete his art education after attending the Boston Museum's School of Art.

Joe had come back from Paris to settle in Boston, and thanks to his first art patron, Denman Ross, of the Department of Fine Arts at Harvard, was soon on his feet. He began to make money by painting portraits, landscapes, and frescoes, and by teaching art. This had eased the financial pressure on his mother.

Denman Ross owned the Ludlow, an apartment building, on the top floor of which he gave Joe a large space. Here Joe had made a big, attractive studio, a kitchen, and some small bedrooms. I got the sense of a happy, self-contained family life based on Joe's creative gift in art and his popularity, aided and abetted by his brilliant mother. But he had never lost sight of the fact that, in leaving Rhode Island, his parents had lost a life of their own and were dependent on his friends for companionship.

Joe frequently took his brother Bert with him on painting trips to Italy and Greece and taught him how to carve frames for his paintings. The frames were made from designs suggested by frames on pictures by old masters and ancient sculpture. His father opened a small carpenter shop where he put the stretchers onto Joe's pictures and fitted them into Bert's frames. Thus a Smith industry involving the three men, with Joe's mother looking after them, came into being.

Then Bert, in taking a short-cut across the railroad tracks, had been accidentally killed, and Joe had promised his mother never to leave her.

Thoughts of her natural panic because of me and an understanding of his loyalty rushed faster through my mind than words to express them. As I stood silent, I heard the front door shut and Joe was gone!

My understandable confusion at this moment was occasioned not only by the strange turn of events but the certain knowledge that

Joe Smith was no ordinary young man. This is as good a point as any to say why. Joe had then, and he subsequently developed further, an immense gift in portraiture—a fact which his artist contemporaries and the public well appreciated. He possessed the ability to make people come entirely alive, in lineament, character, and that ultimate glow in portraiture that is the nearest thing to life.

Joe's landscapes were good, although not as good as his portraits, and they are now widely dispersed and hardly traceable. It has become clear in the last sixty years that, if Joseph Lindon Smith had chosen portraiture rather than to dedicate himself to the preservation of many great works of the ancient past, he could probably have been among America's most distinguished portraitists.

His skelate portrait in sepia of his father, which the Century Association of New York thought highly of when it was exhibited there some thirty years after it was done in 1903, represents his talent well, as does his oil portrait of me as a young girl.

The test of his choice of careers probably lies with, and is exemplified by, his color renderings of the sarcophagus of Alexander the Great. The sarcophagus remains, but the colors in the marble are now gone forever, except as they are preserved by Joe's art, executed soon after the sarcophagus was dug out and while the colors were yet fresh.

The holdings of his subsequent work by the Boston Museum of Fine Arts, the Peabody Museum at Harvard, the Egyptian government, and many others complement the written record which was published in the book, *Tombs, Temples, and Ancient Art*, compiled from his journal accounts and published in 1956.

Ignoring the fact he had told me to forget him, Joe wrote during the voyage to Italy. It was fortunate, he said, that my own interests and tastes were not very definite, since to unlearn was difficult, but to learn new ideas easy, given the incentive I had to adapt myself to living with him *and his parents*. An artist's life he described as "never commonplace, nothing essential for happiness lacking, and nothing superfluous in it. An artist knows instinctively what to eliminate." Then he warned me such a life also entailed sacrifices that a wife must accept, but he promised me constant adventure more exciting than poker, horse racing, and night clubs combined!

In a postscript to another letter, mailed from Naples, Joe said that his winter address would be Egypt, instead of the Italian one he had given me, and I had better begin to get used to his change of plans, or the complete absence of any, as that was how the mind of an artist worked. "Possibly you will have to add archaeology to art and in-laws," he scribbled on the outside of the envelope.

After a long gap, a letter came with a pyramid stamp on it, and postmarked Cairo, Egypt. It began, "I found thinking of you and a season of painting in Italy, which was the purpose of my trip, constantly interrupted by thoughts of pyramids rising out of the desert. Now, I have seen three nearby, and many more on the distant horizon, in the glory of sunrise and sunset—and the Sphinx was something to sit in front of in quiet contemplation."

These mixed thoughts were the point of departure, in all probability, for a career which has been fully described in Joe's book.

He told how he had traveled south up the Nile on a small tourist steamer, guidebook in hand, asking innumerable questions of the energetic dragoman on trips ashore. "I saw too many temples and tombs too quickly, wonderful sculptured reliefs jumped at me saying 'paint me.' My bewilderment was like yours when Burne-Jones offered you one of his sketches." He went on to say that when he had sat alone in the great hall of the Temple of Karnak, with the moonlight picking out the details of carved reliefs on tall columns, he knew he had made no mistake in coming to Egypt.

It was more than two months before I heard from him again. He wrote that he had entrusted the letter with money for postage to a native on a passing government steamer and hoped it would reach me eventually. He was with an artist friend far up the Nile, camping out before the rock-hewn temple of Abu Simbel, a commanding edifice with a façade of four colossal seated figures. He had made the exciting discovery that he was able to recreate through his own self-effacement the work of a genius in stone portraiture who had lived centuries before. This was possible by interpreting, through the medium of canvas, both the spirit of the original and his own appreciation of its beauty. He could thus make it understandable to someone else. He could do the same thing in interiors with carved reliefs, painted in reflected sunlight.

For instance, his canvas of the King in his chariot charging fiercely against his enemies, the same size as the original and its exact replica in form and color, was so realistic that he said he stepped back involuntarily from the painted scene to avoid being trampled underfoot.

He summed up what he termed a sensational artistic venture that might determine his future career by emphasizing the encouragement he had received from George A. Reisner, the distinguished Egyptologist, to continue in a highly specialized field of art.

"Each painting is an archaeological record correct in details, but beautiful as a picture," Reisner had said. He estimated surely that collections of such paintings would be of value as a study series in museums.

And, as Joe put it, "less important, although convenient," a fairy godmother had turned up in the person of a Mrs. Phoebe A. Hearst, who was financing an expedition in Egypt for the University of California, of which Reisner was in charge, and she had purchased Joe's entire season's work.

"In the same year, to have met you and acquired a strong link with ancient Egypt through my pictures causes me to believe in the predetermination of all things, which the Moslems here talk about with conviction."

These were Joe's final words to me from Cairo. I was expecting his arrival in New York when a letter came to me from Greece. Another artist friend, Walter Brown, who lived in Venice, had persuaded Joe to make a short trip with him roughing it through Greece. Brown was always short of money but succeeded in being comfortable in out-of-the-way places. He spoke modern Greek fluently, which made it possible for them to get about on native cargo boats along the coast and through the Gulf of Corinth, sleeping on deck.

Joe referred to several painting visits to Greece he had made in his youth with Denman Ross and a classical scholar, and said that his main reason for accepting Brown's invitation was to gratify his curiosity about Greek sculpture. In Greece, his first predilection had been for the archaic rather than for the generally acclaimed statuary of the golden age of Pericles. He wished to see whether his seeing the forerunner of the Greek archaic in Egyptian statues had intensified his preference for the former. And he found it had.

Joe landed in New York the middle of June. Our meeting was well chaperoned by three Putnam aunts with whom I was staying. We had communicated with my father, who was in England, about our engagement, and now the formal announcement to their Dublin friends was to be made during a brief visit to his parents.

In those days, an old-fashioned stagecoach, pulled by a pair of horses, brought passengers getting off the Boston train from a small station into Dublin. On a late afternoon at the end of June, I descended from the stage at the corner of the lake directly opposite Joe's home on Loon Point, and he was waiting for me in a canoe.

In spite of myself, I found Joe's extreme nervousness contagious, as very slowly, in absolute silence, he paddled towards a stone platform at the very end of the point, where, on a wooden bench, two grim figures were seated. Joe helped me out and the four of us stood facing one another. His father, a tall figure with a long mustache, stood rigid. I thought his face stern until I had a chance to compare its expression with that of Joe's mother. She stared at me with uncompromising eyes, and a set determination in every line of a typical New England face, her gray hair parted in the middle and brushed smoothly back from her forehead. Her unusually small stature somehow caused her to look all the more formidable. She was the first to speak.

"Joe's marriage will be hard on me," she said.

And Joe's father added, "We bought white pigskin trunks for our trip to Egypt—I suppose that's off."

Joe flushed and was about to protest at his parents' lack of welcome, but responded to my gesture to keep still as we four entered a frame house, which the men of the family had built. The main feature of the house was a long, very high studio with many things in it I wanted to look at. But we went directly through it into the dining room, made cheerful by walls covered with turkey-red cloth.

Bridget, the maid, a pretty Irish girl, on coming in to serve the customary cold, light New England supper, was introduced to me by Joe. As I rose to shake hands, she set down a dish on the table with a bang, and throwing her apron over her face, burst into tears murmuring, "Poor Mr. Joe," over and over.

Her performance relieved the tension, permitting me to say abruptly to Joe's mother, "If you don't mind having me join the party, we'll all go to Egypt together, including your intimate friend, Lois Anna Greene, who I understand was also invited by Joe, and we'll always live together, why not?"

She looked as though she could not believe her ears, and father broke in, "There, Emma, didn't I tell thee, Joe would not pick out an *unreasonable* girl for his wife!"

Mother became cheerful at once, and she and Joe vied with each other in making plans for keeping the engagement a complete surprise from the community until it could be announced in a play in an open-air theatre on the place.

It was an eye-opener to me to see the Smith family in action as a unit. I could not imagine Joe without his parents, and I told them I wanted it that way. Mother interrupted her flow of ideas long enough to give me a spontaneous hug, then went back to discussing the plot of the play with Joe.

The scene was to open with Joe telling his mother in an exaggerated manner he was in love. She, taking alarm, asked anxiously, "Who is she?" To which he replied he was in love with love and wanted to find a girl. Greatly relieved, she told him she had expected this moment long since and would produce the ideal companion for him.

She left the stage to return arm in arm with a girl who sat down in a chair beside hers. Joe drew near, all excitement, but on taking off a large hat the girl was wearing, to get a better view of her face, discovered it was a dummy who did only what his mother instructed her to do.

The two of them thought up screamingly funny stage business which his father solemnly jotted down for them to remember. In watching Joe, even without properties or make-up, I did not wonder that a Broadway producer, after seeing his performance as the Rabbit in *Alice in Wonderland*, in a large theatre for charity, inquired why he did not give up "dabbling in art" and join "*the* profession." His mother was equally gifted in playing up to him in a character part.

The climax of the play was to be her reaction to the substitution of a live girl for the figure. Joe was giving me my first lesson when mother began to shout, "Lois Anna." And to my surprise, a small Quaker lady with a demure face but a twinkle in her very black eyes appeared from upstairs, calmly stating she thought in-laws were sufficient for my first family meal. "Did anyone think to tell Corinna I *live* with the Smiths?" she wanted to know. Both Joe and his mother were too absorbed in developing their parts, with his father still recording their apt phrases and witticisms, to answer.

But soon Joe began to explain to Lois Anna how to make a dummy exactly like me and what he wanted in the way of duplicate costumes. She and his mother went up into the attic. I heard their voices, and even caught some of their words in a house without plaster or any other means of deadening sound, before they reappeared, Lois Anna with an armful of materials and his mother with a collection of hair from which to match mine. Father, meanwhile, produced a piece of *papier-maché* for Joe to use in molding a face I posed for.

Three days later, the play was given, with all Dublin present in "Teatro Bambino," modeled on a theatre Joe had seen in Siena, Italy, and incidentally among the first outdoor theatres to be built in America. There had been only a partial rehearsal on the stage for the position of the actors' entrances and exits. The dummy, finally come to life, was introduced to the audience by Joe as his fiancée, Corinna Putnam. Then we stepped together quickly to stage left, to leave stage center to his mother.

In a terrific scene, she ordered her terrified husband to change the live girl back into a dummy.

Whereupon he turned helplessly to Joe, "Better obey Mother, Son, and show me how to use the mechanism you invented, in reverse."

But Joe, in open rebellion, with his arm around my waist, defied his mother, saying, "This is what you yourself gave me as an 'ideal companion'."

Her changes in expression were amazing and her gestures even more so as she accepted defeat at the hands of her son. In eloquent silence, she drove her thoroughly cowed husband away, then she turned to the audience and said, "Joe has pulled a fast one on me, but perhaps a live daughter-in-law will have some advantages over a dummy."

The loud applause was not for the New York girl who was to marry Joe, but for his mother, who had managed to capture the honors. And I realized it must always be that way for the happiness of all concerned.

Joe felt he could not delay sailing beyond early October. Miss Emily James Smith had resigned as dean of Barnard College to marry my father in April, 1899, and they were to be abroad until September, which was far too early in the season for a New York wedding. In this dilemma, Uncle Bishop and Aunt Fannie offered their home in Rye for Joe's and my wedding, which took place on September 18. We were to have two weeks alone in Dublin before meeting Joe's parents and Lois Anna Greene in New York to sail for Italy on October 4.

After the wedding, as we came near Loon Point in a carriage, our approach was barred across the road at an avenue to the right. There was an arrow pointing upward through an arbor entrance with bright flowers interspersed among green boughs, with a sign bearing the words, "Greetings to the Bride and Groom." This led through a long, steep incline to the house occupied by George de Forest Brush, the artist, and his family. The children had worked on the arbor for days but had overlooked the fact that Joe and I needed more height than they did. Therefore we had to crawl on our hands and knees to reach the house, with much damage to our traveling clothes.

But the welcome to Dublin by the Brush family was something I shall never forget.

It seemed strange to have only Bridget, the maid, on Loon Point, and the community left us completely alone, until just before our departure from Dublin, Abbott H. Thayer, the artist, whose life was pretty much that of a recluse, came to call. He informed us that the next afternoon at 4:00 o'clock we were to get into our wedding garments for a "surprise" party.

Abbott Thayer had arranged everything, and he and George Brush arrived arm in arm, in formal attire, which neither of them had ever worn in Dublin. Both said their frock coats and waistcoats dated back to their own weddings, as did Thayer's top hat, but Brush had hired one which was far too big for his head and gave a comical effect to his expressive face.

My sister Ethel was there in the charming pale green gown she had worn as my wedding attendant, Elise and Handasyd Cabot were present in their wedding garments, and Thayer had persuaded Denman Ross to come from Boston for this very special occasion.

Thayer was in the gayest of moods as master of ceremonies and the food was delicious. It was a perfect farewell with old and young neighbors assembled. He asked all present to wish Godspeed to the bridal couple, who were about to start off for a year of travel through countries of the Near East, with the groom's father, mother, and her most intimate friend. "Let us drink to an unusual honeymoon!" he said.

12

EGYPT AND THE HOLY LAND

By november we had arrived in Egypt. A party of five, with Joe's bank account rather unimpressive, meant that the strictest economy would have to be practiced. Hotels frequented by tourists were quite out of the question. Joe went at once to Assouan to inspect a *dahabieh* recommended by Dowe, his Nubian camp servant on a bachelor trip the previous winter, for the proposed voyage to the temple of Abu Simbel on the upper Nile.

The rest of us stayed at the Hotel du Nil in Cairo, an old-fashioned hostelry on the famous Muski, which was the main thoroughfare of the native district. Father Smith devoted his daylight hours to watching any kind of business construction going on within walking distance of the hotel. And Mother, freed in a strange land of the repressions imposed by the strictness of the Quaker regime of her girlhood, began acquiring exotic scents and colored fabrics for dresses.

I wandered about the Muski picking up Arabic phrases. In the evenings, a Roumanian scholar on Islam gave me lessons in grammar. I was eager to talk to Moslems in their language about their religion, because, when they prayed in the streets, they looked as though they felt they were actually in communion with Allah.

It was ten days before Joe sent for the family. We discovered that the *dahabieh* he had hired was the *Amir-el-Wuz*, on which Lady Duff Gordon had taken trips on the Nile during the many years she had lived in Luxor.

On seeing the *dahabieh*, resplendent with fresh paint inside and out, it was hard to believe Joe's statement that he had found her on the shore, all but a derelict, with the seams in her hull opened from the scorching sun to which she had been exposed for a long time. He told us that after repairs she had been scuttled and left on the bottom of the river for a few days to rid her of rats, snakes, scorpions, and insect life.

Joe had bought gay rugs from the bazaars, and also had been lucky in finding some old pictures from the Greek islands, painted on wood with a gold background, and two large Chinese plates, with which to decorate white enameled walls. Dowe looked very attractive in a long garment of striped silk and neat turban as he stood with his eyes shining at the family's obvious pleasure at arrangements over which he had worked hard. He spoke a fluent English of a rather strange kind.

Reis Owit's flat features and thick lips were of a more pronounced Nubian type than Dowe's. He was a stern, unbending man, wearing black garments. He entered the cabin, solemnly shook hands all around and retired. The crew, formally presented, consisted of a good-natured, fat second *reis* and six sailors. Dowe was to cook for us, with a boy to help him in the serving.

It was by moonlight, after a leisurely voyage upstream, through country with small agricultural villages, that we moored in front of the Temple of Abu Simbel, and the pale beams on the colossal seated figures of Rameses II brought them forward from the mass of rock, in which they had been carved by the King during his long reign beginning in B.C. 1901. Joe and I left open the shutters of our cabin at the stern of the boat, and at about 2 A.M. we got the full benefit of the wailing of the jackals, whose chorus increased until it became a tremendous volume of sound, with wolves and hyenas joining the chorus in baying at the moon. And later, in a complete stillness, we watched these desert animals come to the shore just behind our cabin. There was the noise of heavy breathing and swift lapping of water, then the dark forms disappeared into the night.

For the six weeks of our stay Joe and I were up at daybreak. We saw the first rays of the rising sun reach the seated colossi, and then brilliant sunlight flooded the interior of the temple, even reaching the holy of holies. The double line of statues and painted decorations on roofs and doorways were gorgeous. Rameses in his chariot charged fiercely over long walls against his enemies. All too soon, the back of the temple would again be engulfed in blackness and we would be seated in the shadows.

It was during the brief period before this happened that Joe worked on details of reliefs on the long walls, and also on those carved on columns in warm reflected sunlight. It was a picture that took in the architecture through the great entrance door, and beyond, a stretch of the river and hills on the other side of the Nile. It was a wonderful view in the freshness of early morning. Later in the day, he painted the heads and figures on the façade.

I sat with him during his long hours of painting, read Dante's *Inferno* in the original, studied the history of ancient Egypt, and learned the names of the kings and their titles in hieroglyphics. One day I was repeating some of the titles Rameses had taken for himself, such as "Son of the Sun." Dowe, who was within earshot, said contemptuously, "That King is big noise in stone."

All too soon our days at Abu Simbel were numbered, and the return voyage came to an end when we touched the Island of Philæ at Assouan and moored just below the Temple of Isis. For more than two thousand years, in the inner shrines of the temple, the rushing bats had shared the privacy with the Greek Ptolemies and their protecting gods. But now the first sound heard in the morning was a shrill whistle summoning the men of Shellal to come to work above Assouan in drilling through the solid granite, to build a dam for an irrigation system that would submerge the temple for the greater part of the year. And when that same whistle blew again at sunset, it was a reminder to these same workmen that, by their day's toil, their own homes and their date-bearing palm trees were one day nearer destruction.

In late March, after ten days of painting at Philæ, we reached Cairo by train. The Hotel du Nil proved itself delightfully casual again in its construction. Water trickled pleasantly in a large tiled Arab fountain in the center of a spacious square court. Vivid bougain-villaea vines trailed over surrounding walls, the heavy fragrance of acacia filled the air. The bedrooms led off rambling terraces, with orange and lemon trees in great tubs, and above everything the tops of palm trees rustled in the breeze. On all sides one caught intimate glimpses of native family life on lower housetops open to the heavens. At the first signs of dawn, Joe and I climbed up to a tall tower on the hotel roof and watched the rising sun illuminate hundreds of golden domes and slender minarets of mosques. The sunset usually found us in the same spot.

Joe painted in the Cairo Museum studies of ancient sculpture, and in his leisure hours we wandered in the Muski. I can still recall the thrill when, with the creaking of hinges, the heavy wooden gates of the hotel grounds closed behind us and we were outside in the bewildering confusion of races and unfamiliar animals. Carried along in a surging crowd, we walked briskly, as though towards a definite destination.

We were often in the bazaars, or in other native districts, where winding streets and unpaved lanes revealed buildings irregular in outline, because of projecting cornices and overhanging windows of closely cut, delicate lattice work. On ramshackle homes were fragments of ancient façades and portals. Behind tumbled-down walls were courts with old trees and a scented mass of flowering vines. It was a proper setting for a honeymoon, even with in-laws included!

After Egypt, Joe and I were to have a unique experience. This was to travel on horseback from the coast, after landing at Jaffa by steamer from Alexandria. We were to cross the land of the Philistines and reach Jerusalem on the heights through the wilderness of Judea.

Our purpose was to be in Jerusalem with pilgrims of every nation converging there to commemorate the Greek Easter. On the riding trip, we were to be guests of the Reverend James Nies, a Hebrew scholar and an authority on the Old Testament; we would sleep in the open, and upon our arrival in Jerusalem be under the auspices of the Greek and Armenian patriarchs.

We landed at the port of Jaffa, where Father, Mother, and Lois Anna took the train for Jerusalem. Reverend Mr. Nies had ready for Joe and me a primitive camp outfit and sturdy Arab saddle horses.

The first night we made camp early, and before dawn we were in the saddle again and on the great plain of Sharon, associated with warfare involving, successively, Israelites, Philistines, Assyrians, Babylonians, Persians, Crusaders, and Saracens.

After the Romans, the Moslems, the Crusades, and the Turks (though the latter remained), Palestine was what it had always been between invasions and varying administrations, a land of gentle, simple, religious people living in a warm, mellow climate, tending flocks and producing small crops of grains, fruits, dates, and nuts.

We were seeing it as none of the present generation can see it, and if our travels revealed a signal fact it was that here, perhaps of all places in the world, the greatest of religions could have found its homeland in that early period when early man was finding God.

Palestine in the last two centuries has had, if anything, a stronger, more persuasive hold upon Western Christian thought than at any time since that great revival of religious devotion which produced the Crusades. For many people of the United States, England, France, and Germany, it evoked, in the fifty years before the first great war, the same desire for a pilgrimage that Mecca has always done for Moslems. That this is no longer so may give special point to that relatively undisturbed world of Christ and the Apostles we were to know and to treasure at first hand.

Several times during our journey, we dismounted, promptly to be joined by Arabs or Bedouins, camel drivers, lean and hollow-eyed. With the courtesy of primitive peoples, they took for granted an exchange of greetings. A few words of Arabic from me would bring a flash of white teeth and a volley of language, understood and answered in kind by our versatile leader.

It was nearing dusk when we reached the summit of a very rocky highland, where we lost all trace of vegetation. The landscape was forbidding and it was rough going for our mounts. Finally the path descended abruptly, and we pitched camp on a level stretch beneath a cliff. The sky was overcast and the wind howled dismally.

I needed no words to make me realize that we were in the wilderness of Judea. It was a relief to leave my bedroll after a restless night. We were soon plunging down between walls of rock in a winding trail on an exit pass.

Through an opening in the deep-cut trench of the Jordan Valley, some eight hundred feet below sea level, we caught sight of Jericho. This oasis in the midst of desolation seemed a desert mirage.

On reaching a fragment of the walls of Jericho, we led our horses to drink from a spring of cool water. I learned that this spring, in its relation to the wall, identified the site (not excavated at the time) of the ancient Jericho. I found it an interesting footnote to be told that the springs and mountains of the Holy Land have been the landmarks by which archaeologists have verified the accuracy of Scriptural accounts.

As we paused to drink, a black-draped young woman, after filling her water jar, started to move away in the direction of a small adobe village surrounded by banana groves. She walked with the erect carriage of races accustomed to bare feet and balancing burdens on their heads. She turned to stare at me, then, with a shy smile, came back and handed me a single bright red anemone. We could have been living in another age—the age of the New Testament, in fact.

We pushed on to the Jordan and made camp near an oleander tree. After a hasty meal, in the light of a full moon, we returned to Jericho. Gone was every trace of the palaces, the aqueducts, the hippodrome of the Roman city of Herod, with its decadence and pomp.

We were up again before dawn for another long day in the saddle. The sun had risen before we reached the Jungle of the Jordan, and flickering sunlight silvered its waters. A lark was singing, with other birds joining in the chorus, and fields of waving grain gleamed. But shortly, as our horses, in single file, picked their way carefully along the rough river bed, the green vanished, to be replaced by land parched and scarred.

Soon we were standing on the shores of the Dead Sea at the point where the river Jordan ended. The view of far-distant, snow-capped Mt. Hermon on the Lebanese border, seen in intimate contact with the deep blue of the Dead Sea, was a combination that only needed life and sound to make it perfect. But there was neither!

My eyes searched in vain for a single bird or a fish leaping in the unruffled surface of the sea. Along the shores there were no weeds, nor water plants of any kind. There was the sickening smell of great masses of sulphur and other chemicals, and above all, salt spread over the edges of the land to a great depth. In the immediate foreground were enormous pillars of salt and grotesque shapes in accumulations of life-destroying deposits.

The Dead Sea was a place to hurry away from at a gallop, on the way to ancient Bethany, built on the shoulder of the Mount of Olives, where we were to spend the night. Almost instantly our horses were plodding doggedly along on a steady upgrade in a rise from thirteen hundred feet below sea level to an elevation of over two thousand feet.

It was a gloomy ride, shut in as we were on both sides by rock formations that made a natural hide-out for bandits. The bad reputation of the area had persisted, apparently, since the days of the parable of the good Samaritan on this same trip, since additional guards were deemed necessary for our safety. We were urged to be at our destination before sunset.

The next afternoon we rode into Jerusalem. Pilgrims swarmed the streets, the rich lost in the vast multitudes of the poor, and Christians from the Western World inconspicuous among those of the Orient. Russians, Poles, Abyssinians, Greeks, Armenians, a number of other races from minority groups of the Turkish Empire, Syrians, and Copts from Egypt dominated the scene.

We were lodged in the home of an Armenian who lived on the immediate outskirts of the old city. From the rooftop in between water cisterns, I caught glimpses of silent pilgrims in the winding streets. The Garden of Gethsemane and the Mount of Olives, where Joe and I had eaten lunch, was in the far view.

Through the courtesy of the Greek patriarch, we were invited to witness the fire miracle on the Saturday evening before Easter. A Turkish guard made a passage for us in the midst of a milling crowd outside and inside the Church of the Holy Sepulchre. Our seats were in the gallery under the great dome.

The ceremony, held jointly by the Greek and the Armenian patriarchs, began with a slow chant in Arabic about the holy fire. It was taken up by hundreds of voices, and banners appeared above the heads of the dense mass of people. I caught sight of the tall black hats of the patriarchs and their long dark robes in the vicinity of the sepulchre, and there was a frenzy of hysterical excitement as tongues of fire, starting from the sepulchre, spread through the church, but no one had burned clothing. Bells rang out and wooden gongs beaten by metal strikers added a note of barbarism to the strangest spectacle I had ever witnessed.

People in the galleries leaned far over to haul up lighted candles attached to long ropes, until candles were in evidence by the thousands. A charming last memory of the holy fire, as we walked towards the old city of Jerusalem, consisted of thousands of tiny lights which illuminated the road like fireflies on a summer's night. They were candles being brought into their homes by the celebrants.

As on all our Palestine trips, we started before dawn for the six hours in the saddle required for a visit to Hebron. We were to be housed at the Russian hospice in the vicinity, dine there with the Greek and Armenian patriarchs, go to the home of a Jewish rabbi, and receive hospitality from Arab tribesmen.

Before entering Hebron, we inspected the ruins of a Christian church built in the time of Constantine. Just beyond was the site of a building with a vague Jewish tradition connected with it.

Hebron in Moslem tradition is known as el-Khalil (the friend) of Allah, because this is the name in the Koran for Abraham, as the first to resign himself to the will of Allah, after Muhammad, the messenger of Allah, had shown him the way. Moslem tribesmen from across the Jordan continue to make an annual pilgrimage to Hebron to visit what they believe is Abraham's tomb.

Nothing remained of the ancient Hebron, beyond a few fragments of old walls on an olive-colored hill slope. But in the modern town, we walked through the district of the glass-blowers, cotton workers, and makers of skin water sacks.

After we had been served coffee by a rabbi in his home, we were about to leave the Jewish Quarter when, suddenly, we were surrounded by Moslem youngsters. They threw mud in our faces and called us "Franks," a term for Christians which had been used, apparently, since the days of the Crusades.

The last day of our stay in Jerusalem we "broke bread" with Arab tribesmen far afield in the desert. Their leader, who was a friend of our American host, had come for us with finely caparisoned, gaited camels, as easy to ride as our own thoroughbred horses. We sat in a circle around a communal bowl of soup and mutton, into which we dipped pieces of bread, while small cups of thick coffee were passed from hand to hand.

By the laws of desert hospitality, as guests of their chief, we were accepted by this group of fierce-eyed, bearded men, who looked as though they made their own decisions about justice. The white of a headdress worn well down over the shoulder lightened shadows cast by a mass of brown cloaks, in the dark interior of a large tent of woven camel's hair.

And in the open desert we witnessed a second miracle, performed this time by Arabs in a sword dance. The dancers soon were jumping about in mad gyrations and drawing swords through their cheeks and lower bodies, apparently with no physical injury. The watching tribesmen swayed back and forth to an accompanying rhythmic refrain, which grew ever wilder and louder. Some of them became almost as uncontrolled as the performers in their religious exaltation, and at moments uttered shrieks of ecstacy piercing to our eardrums. It was a moment when it was better to have these desert Arabs as friends rather than as enemies!

13

TURKEY UNDER SULTAN
ABDUL HAMID II

You could not have lived in the Eastern Mediterranean world at the turn of the twentieth century without feeling intensely many of the things that have since become a part of my most deeply held interests: among them, the fate of the average intelligent Turk lost without the moorings of his Moslem religion, the victim of international intrigue for control of his land, unskilled in anything except a military tradition, groping towards the organized political, cultural and economic life which would remove the stigma of the "sick man of Europe."

After the sojourn in the Holy Land, the Smith party started for Constantinople in the spring of 1901, so that Joe could paint for the Boston Museum of Fine Arts the sarcophagus of Alexander the Great, recently found at Sidon.

A Turkish peasant, who made the discovery while plowing a field near the entrance to a tomb, told the news to two American missionaries. They in turn reported the find to the Turkish authorities, and the sarcophagus, eight feet in length, with its delicately colored sculptured reliefs, was transported to the government museum in Constantinople.

The train part of our journey was through Damascus, where we stopped to get a brief conception of the oldest city continuously occupied in the Near East, an important center, after its even more ancient past, during the Roman, early Christian, and early Islamic periods, in succession.

From Damascus we went to Beirut, where, before taking a steamer to Constantinople, we were all to spend a few days with President Daniel Bliss and his family. He was the founder of the American College at Beirut, and had had long experience in dealing with Turks.

He told Joe that the Alexander sarcophagus was considered the museum's greatest treasure, and the colored reliefs were protected by dark curtains, only drawn aside for visitors a few moments at a time. Furthermore, President Bliss personally knew of several applications to make paintings of it which had been bluntly refused, including one from the Germans, who were in favor with the Sultan. Therefore, he felt that Joe's official request, made by Secretary of State Hay through our Legation, would be ignored. On the other hand, since Hamdy Bey, the director of the government museum, did pretty much what he pleased, Joe's chances of success lay in getting the strong recommendation he had from the Reverend John P. Peters direct to this Turkish official, since they were close friends, having excavated together at Nippur.

President Bliss expressed admiration for both the Grand Vizier and the Sheikh el-Islam, and intimated there were signs of reform that might develop in the midst of plots and counterplots that were a constant threat to all Turks in high administrative positions.

After an uneventful voyage, our steamer passed through the Dardanelles and into the Bosporus, and soon was approaching a dock in the heart of the native city of Stamboul. The Galata wooden bridge, which spanned the Golden Horn, connected Stamboul with the European quarter of Pera, situated on the heights. The Angleterre, where we were to stay, was an old-fashioned hotel, and the pleasant rooms assigned our party looked down into the gardens of Sir Nicholas O'Conor, the British ambassador.

Next morning, Joe and I crossed the Galata Bridge to go to the museum, which was in the vicinity of the Sancta Sofia Mosque and the buildings of the Sublime Porte.

Hamdy Bey opened the door of his office and, by way of greeting, said, "Jojo, you are here!"

Joe looked as bewildered as I felt at the use of a nickname given him in his studio days in Paris, and known only to intimates. He was quick, however, in reviving a non-existent memory of their having been fellow students at the Académie Julien in Paris, a fact, Hamdy Bey was saying, meant much to him, and he added that he had followed Joe's artistic career with interest. Without further ado, he produced an imposing authorization for Joe to paint sculpture anywhere in Turkey for an indefinite period. He explained that the Reverend Peters had already written him.

While Joe and he talked, I had a chance to study this important Turk. He was beyond middle age, thin, with bowed shoulders and an untidy beard. A sallow complexion, pronounced nose, and a growing baldness accentuated the length of a face in which sadness and character were combined. He had a nervous habit of clasping and unclasping his hands and pushing his spectacles above his eyebrows, then back onto his nose.

It seemed rather odd to us, as Americans, to have him boast that, as a Turkish representative on the Council of the Ottoman Debt, he was too valuable to the Sultan to be annoyed by having a spy sent to his home on the Bosphorus when he entertained. This was an indignity, he said, to which every other Turk had to submit, with the exception of the Grand Vizier and the all-powerful Sheikh el-Islam.

Joe got to work at once. Inside the museum, terrorism and sudden death seemed unreal to us as the work on the sarcophagus went forward. He found that the reliefs on the magnificent object more than came up to his high expectations of their artistic value. As he worked, I enjoyed long quiet hours seated beside him studying classical Arabic grammar.

Delightful breaks were provided by informal noon luncheons, served in Hamdy Bey's office by a servant from his home. The Grand Vizier, who was a connoisseur of art, frequently joined us, as did other cultured Turks, and occasionally a European scholar. Art and archaeology were the main topics of conversation, and before Joe resumed work, he took time to look at a number of fine new acquisitions, paid for by Hamdy Bey personally.

Joe and I enjoyed the long brisk walk, twice daily, across the Galata Bridge, where we encountered an intermingling of races, peasants for the most part. In the morning their carts were filled with farm products for Pera, and empty on the afternoon return trip.

One day on our way back to Pera, my gaze was distracted from the beauty of the minarets of Sancta Sofia by the expression on the face of an approaching Turk, obviously a high official. I noticed him glancing over his shoulder, as if he feared he was being shadowed, and at precisely the moment he decided he was not, a man stepped to his side and stabbed him. He fell dead at my feet. Death by a hired assassin was such an accustomed sight that the crowd passed on its way unheeding.

It was after this incident that we met Alessandro Gargiulo, an Italian whose responsibility was to be interpreter between the Sultan and representatives of foreign countries, at audiences.

Gargiulo got into the habit of dropping in on us at odd moments, and from him I learned a lot that was going on *sub rosa* in the Ottoman Empire. He mentioned that pressure was being brought to bear by Zinoviev, the Russian ambassador, to maintain the *status quo* in the Balkans and to secure possession by Russia of the Dardanelles.

The Germans were even more pervasive. The Kaiser had come to Constantinople to assure the Sultan of Germany's friendship for Turkey. As a result, the contract was signed for construction of the final link in the Berlin to Baghdad Railroad to the Persian Gulf. In addition, a German general was reforming the Turkish army and equipping it *gratis* with arms and ammunition from Krupps'.

One afternoon, on our return to the Angleterre, we found a tall, slender, good-looking young Philadelphian in our sitting room. He introduced himself as Lloyd Griscom, chargé d'affaires of the

American Legation. He said that Oscar Strauss, the American minister, had left Constantinople hastily, and that he (Griscom) had just found among his papers a personal note from Secretary of State John Hay requesting the legation to look after us.

Soon Joe and I were spending weekends with Griscom, in his bachelor retreat on the island of Prinkipo on the Sea of Marmara. It afforded Joe complete relaxation, the bathing was refreshing, and there was excellent sailing on the sea.

Griscom would take us in a speed launch far up the Bosporus, where life was as varied as street scenes in Stamboul. We met tramp steamers on the way to Odessa, ferries between Europe and Asia, and fishing boats in quantity.

Therapia, a charming settlement in the midst of cypress-covered hill slopes, was situated in a sweeping curve where the Bosporus widened beyond the round towers of Rumeli Hissar and Robert College, established by Americans.

Joe was invigorated at being on the water with superb mountain scenery on both the Asian and European sides. And both he and Griscom were pleasantly diverted by the aimless chatter of diplomats about intrigues, rumors, and gossip.

Griscom told me that Sir Nicholas O'Conor frankly admitted that England's policy was to keep on good terms with the Sultan at any cost. This was essential because possession of the Dardanelles by either Germany or Russia would be a threat to England's supremacy in the Near East. Therefore James Bryce had urged in vain England's intervention to stop, in 1896, a massacre of thousands of male Turks between the ages of sixteen and sixty.

The United States, under President Cleveland, a Democrat, had also taken no action. But his Republican successor, on taking office, changed the policy.

Griscom said that just before our arrival, Secretary of State John Hay had recalled Oscar Strauss, the American minister. This was in protest to the Sultan's refusal to pay a ninety-thousand-dollar indemnity demanded by the United States for the wanton destruction of Armenian life and property by Turks.

When Griscom presented his credentials as chargé d'affaires, he informed the Sultan that he intended to order an American battle-ship, which was at Smyrna, to enter the Bosporus. "The next day, the indemnity was paid," he said.

All my information had been from diplomatic sources, until Hamdy Bey put me in direct touch with the reforms which President Bliss had intimated were developing inside Turkey. This occurred when we visited Hamdy Bey in his home on the Bosporus.

Soon after our arrival, Hamdy Bey, Leyla, his daughter, and the Grand Vizier's daughter, Fatima, were grouped around Joe, who was constructively criticizing Hamdy Bey's landscapes, with suggestions for their improvement in color and technique. Then he examined a portfolio containing Fatima's water-color studies. He complimented her on her artistic ability and, to her delight, offered to give her painting lessons.

This peaceful scene was abruptly terminated by the appearance of the Grand Vizier. His face was black with rage as he burst out that he had just come from being with the Sultan, after he had killed a man.

He ignored Hamdy Bey's warning glance towards Joe and me and said, "Here I am among friends and can talk freely."

The incident which had aroused his anger had occurred while the Sultan was exercising in a carefully guarded inner court of his residence at Yildiz Kiosk. Startled by the approach of a man from behind a fountain whom he had not recognized as a privileged gardener, he had shot him.

The Grand Vizier expressed disgust at the Sultan's callous reaction to the deed, which, in effect, was the loss of the only gardener in his employ able to cultivate a favorite rose.

The Grand Vizier stayed on to a family dinner, and his tongue, once loosened, continued to talk.

His thoughts turned to the Sultan's accession in 1876, when Midhat Pasha (his predecessor in office, the Grand Vizier interpolated) had compelled him to adopt a reform constitution which he had drafted with the approval of the army.

A year later, however, the Sultan dismissed Midhat from office and revoked the constitution. When Midhat, on the promise of an amnesty, later returned to Turkey, the Sultan threw him into prison and had him strangled.

The Grand Vizier ended his indiscreet tirade by saying that, before the Sultan was deposed, a leader must be found who combined the determination to restore the prestige of Islam, lost under the present Sultan-Caliph, with the ability to establish a modern government based on democratic ideals.

"The matter brooks no delay," he said.

One of the subsequent visits to Hamdy Bey's residence was in strong contrast to this day's events. Izzet Bey, head of the secret police, and reportedly the most dreaded official in Turkey, dropped in. He lived with the Sultan, was supposed to be the only man in the latter's complete confidence, and was most influential among three individuals through whom the Sultan carried out his sadistic commands, including the Armenian massacres.

The only light moment in the evening occurred after Izzet Bey's departure, when Hamdy Bey related the dramatic story of how one of the finest heads on the sarcophagus of Alexander the Great was found missing after its installation in the museum. He knew that there were only seven men who could have had the opportunity to steal it. Hamdy Bey invited them to dinner together, and when they were seated told them that the lights would go out for five minutes. When they came on again, he expected to find the mislaid head in his napkin. He did!

The Grand Vizier brought his daughter to the Angleterre to see Joe's Egyptian paintings. Her lessons were progressing well, and Joe had arranged for a group of her water colors to be shown in a small room of the American Legation.

Later Joe and I went to the Grand Vizier's home to see his art collection and to have an informal meal. Joe found each object worthy of being in a museum. He and the Grand Vizier were absorbed in a lengthy discussion, as I was with the Sheikh el-Islam, who had been invited for my benefit.

He was tall, sturdy in build, and an imposing figure in his long robes. He had the eyes of a mystic but a firmness of purpose in his good-looking, rather stern face which indicated that he was a militant protector of the *sharia* (sacred laws), expounded by him and his *ulema*. Fortunately, his French, although slightly labored, was intelligible. He seemed pleased at my desire to read the Koran in the original.

The Sheikh el-Islam repeated several *suras* (chapters), then he asked, "Why do you wish to know the Koran?" To my reply, because Moslems at prayer looked as though they were in actual communion with God, he said, "They are."

A few days later, both the Grand Vizier and the Sheikh el-Islam were at lunch in Hamdy Bey's office, for the purpose of giving me an idea of the reality of Islam among Turks.

Our first visit was to Sancta Sofia Mosque. The dark interior was brilliant from the sun which streamed over the stations of the first four Caliphs, and the green turbaned heads of *Hagg* (Moslems who had made the pilgrimage) and others in the flowing robes of Moslem dignitaries. Enormous golden circles bearing the name of Allah or of Muhammad all but covered the Christian mosaics in the dome one hundred feet overhead. The slow sonorous chanting reverberated through every crevice of endless arched windows, in the base of the mosque, and through the aisles and galleries, which were supported by arcades with superb columns.

Upon our departure, peasants crowded about the Sheikh el-Islam in the outside court. Their immediate recognition of his presence showed that his revered figure was a familiar one. He exchanged Moslem salutations with each in turn. "They are fine, loyal, cheerful, hard-working people, with religion to comfort them in poverty and neglect," he said.

We made leisurely visits to a number of the two hundred mosques in Stamboul, and in each one were Moslems, seated in silent contemplation, or engaged in their devotions. Among the mosques was one with beautiful blue tiles conspicuous in the striking architecture. We had removed our shoes, and I was standing outside the threshold a little apart when three *ulema* appeared. They completely ignored a man, obviously a spy, who had placed himself within earshot. But the Sheikh el-Islam laid a firm hand on the spy's shoulder and literally threw him down the steps of the mosque.

A final impression was gained on the homeward trip, when half-way across the bridge, our carriage turned inland. It was a long drive up the Golden Horn before we dismounted at a mosque I knew of by hearsay.

I was allowed to look through widely opened doors to view inside sacred relics of the Prophet. As the Grand Vizier and the Sheikh el-Islam rejoined me, the latter, as though thinking aloud, voiced his anxiety about the Sultan's constant attempts to instill politics into Islam.

I was glad to have had this impression of the reality of Islam before Griscom escorted Joe and me to *"Selamlik,"* the Friday noon prayer, which the Sultan, as Caliph of Islam, was compelled to attend. Foreign visitors sat in a garden by the door of a pavilion where the diplomatic corps assembled. It was a brilliant spectacle, with the sunlight streaming over red banners of the lancers mounted on white horses, preceding the imperial open barouche drawn by two beautiful white horses with flowing manes and long tails. As always in a public appearance, Osman Pasha, who was the idol of the Turks, sat beside the Sultan as a protection against a bomb.

Turkish officials in full regalia, most of them fat and puffing from the exertion, followed the carriage on foot, with their hands crossed in front, required as a safeguard against a concealed weapon. I had an excellent view of the Sultan as he got out of his carriage. His very small feet were encased in high patent-leather boots, and he wore a long black coat, with fitted cloth up to his neck. The fez accentuated the reddish brown of his hair and beard, which were dyed with henna. He had a pale, thin face with a conspicuously long nose.

There was a disagreeably furtive air about him as his eyes darted about him suspiciously. Altogether, Abdul Hamid II was a despicable figure in comparison with the Sheikh el-Islam and his accompanying *ulema*—the only Turks with their hands hanging free.

A number of cultured Turks came to the Angleterre to see Joe's paintings, and consequently we were removed from the category of American tourists in whom official Turkey had no interest. My remark to the Grand Vizier that a spy had been placed in our room, disguised as a hotel servant, had unexpected repercussions. He had gone to the Sultan, demanded that the spy be withdrawn at once, and that Joe receive the decoration of the *Medjidieh*. Furthermore, the Sheikh el-Islam put in a plea for me to be awarded the Woman's Order of the *Chefekat*, for my virtue in being with my husband while he worked, and for studying.

It was Griscom, of course, who accompanied us to the Sultan's state apartments at Dolme Bagshe, where the honors were to be bestowed. He laughingly declared that it seemed unnecessary to have an American present the Joe Smiths to Turks.

I noticed that the walls of long corridors, and also those of the enormous formal state apartment, where the Sultan stood, were lined with mirrors, so he could watch everyone's approach.

The squadrons of cavalry that lined the roads, near both the official apartments and the Sultan's apartments, as well as the bodyguards inside the enclosures, were Albanians. The Sultan trusted their loyalty because he was worth much money to them alive, whereas his death meant their immediate destruction by Turkish soldiers, who despised both him and them.

A royal yacht, although at anchor, had steam up, ready for instant flight, thus completing the picture of the life of a ruler living in fear of his subjects.

Shortly thereafter, Gargiulo happened to remark to me that the commemoration of the martyrdom of Hussain, the grandson of the Prophet, was to take place in Stamboul the following evening.

His brief summary of its origin fired my desire to be present. He told me that the Shi'a was a dissenting sect in Islam, holding the belief that the Caliph must be a direct descendant of the Prophet. They were very powerful throughout Persia and in the Iraq (a term applied in ancient times to the region near Baghdad).

The Shi'a had refused to accept the legitimacy of the election of Muawiyah as Caliph, who moved the seat of Islam from Mecca to Damascus.

They maintained that the sons of Ali and Fatima, each in turn, were the true successors. Hassan renounced his claim and lived in retirement in Mecca, where he was joined by Hussain, his younger brother. Hassan's death made Hussain the head of the Alid party.

He listened to his Shi'a adherents in Persia and in the Iraq, and in open revolt against Muawiyah's grandson, when he succeeded to the Caliphate, went to Kerbala in the Iraq. His Shi'a followers deserted him and he was killed.

In expiation of this crime committed twelve centuries ago, every male of the Shi'ite sect had to make a pilgrimage once in his lifetime to Hussain's tomb at Kerbala.

In addition, the Martyrdom of Hussain had continued to be celebrated annually, on the anniversary of his death, not only in Persia, but in all of Persia's colonies, with every Persian family represented by a male member, indulging in self-inflicted punishment. Gargiulo arranged to have Father, Joe, and me join a small group of diplomats to witness the ceremonial in the largest Persian *khan* (covered market) in the heart of Stamboul.

At the agreed-on hour a *kervass* from our Legation appeared at the hotel. He was a fierce looking creature armed to the teeth, in wide Turkish trousers, short jacket and broad sash, all of rich blue broadcloth, heavily embroidered in gold. He placed us inside an official American carriage and seated himself beside the driver. Soon after we entered Stamboul, a traffic jam was caused by a solid front of these Shi'a fanatics, who refused to budge for our passing. The driver looked greatly relieved when we got out of the carriage.

The *kervass*, by a circuitous route, maneuvered us afoot through narrow alleys, past sullen Turks, while drops of a sudden shower stung our faces. Finally I caught sight of a few Europeans on a raised platform, just inside the main approach to an enormous *khan*. To my surprise, the *kervass* motioned us in the opposite direction, and we stumbled along after him in the darkness towards a flickering light. This proved to be a back entrance to the *khan*.

He led us inside, where tall flares lit up the faces of fierce-eyed women and men, who protested violently at our presence. We were gradually being pushed back into the alley, when a milling throng, entering, carried us forward with them. At this moment a distant murmur became an undercurrent of sound. It was electric in its effect on the crowd hemming us in, who were unquestionably the families and friends of the martyrs-to-be.

The face of the *kervass* was transfigured, which made me realize that he was a Persian Shi'a and had decided to combine his official responsibility for the party under his protection with an opportunity to miss nothing of the martyrdom. All eyes focused on the procession slowly advancing. In the lead were two beautiful white horses with long tails and flowing manes, and a solitary white dove tied onto the back of each. From the doves' slit throats, blood dripped over their breasts and wings, spattering the white backs of the horses.

Behind walked men in white garments, splashed with blood; each right hand held a flat sword, and with it every one of them was pounding at the top of his own head or back. At the side of each of these gory participants was a man who placed a short stick between the sword and the open wound on the head or back when the vigor of the blows caused the bleeding to become a steady stream.

There were also men, bare above the waist, pounding their own backs with heavy flails; the thud of these torture weapons made a horrible sound, and the sight of the raw, lacerated flesh and the livid black of bruises was even more dreadful than the sight of blood. The words, "Hassan, Hussain," penetrated every area of that great *khan* in a low, whispered monotone, more compelling than raised voices. There must have been at least three hundred of these crazed fanatics subjecting themselves to self-inflicted wounds. The procession stopped close to where we stood; after a moment the men staggered away and disappeared from the *khan*. The cries of "Hassan, Hussain" became fainter and fainter until they ceased altogether.

Five times the procession came back. The hacking at heads and backs grew more violent as the sharp edges of the swords came into play, so carelessly aimed that they struck near vital organs. The click of the intervening sticks made a refrain that all but rivalled in intensity the subdued monotone of the never ceasing "Hassan, Hussain," as meanwhile the uncertain light steadily became dimmer.

Within my view, a participant dropped in his tracks and blood from his body splashed on the garments of bystanders. Many leapt forward with shrill exclamations of joy and fought among themselves to dip cloths into the blood of the expiring martyr. A woman knelt beside him and raised his head. There was no sign of suffering on his face, as blood gushed from a mouth set in the calm of death.

I became separated from Joe and Father, and struggled to reach them as a steady pressure against me was carrying me in the opposite direction. Men and some women with bloodshot eyes were tearing at the fawn-colored skirt I wore, now dripping from the blood of an expiring martyr, who, in tottering from the procession, had fallen at my feet. It was a scene such as Hogarth might have drawn, but with an Oriental frenzy unlike anything he witnessed. Fortunately, Gargiulo appeared, almost beside himself with anxiety for us, and we returned to Pera with a small group of diplomats.

The stark drama of self-inflicted wounds causing death before my eyes gave me a new understanding of the psychology of Moslem fanatics, who, well into our century, were stirring up massacres of non-Moslem populations.

But against these practices and the corruption of the Turkish court the winds of change were even then beginning to blow. Scutari was their center. There an underground movement had begun to develop. Its adherents were known as the "Young Turks." Their tenure was always precarious: members whom we met one day might the next be limp bundles thrown into the Bosporus, after a careless word had been reported by spies to the Sultan. The more fortunate operated from cellars, or even from locations as far away as Paris.

Kemal Pasha was one of the Young Turks whose acquaintance we made casually. His liberal political views naturally caused him to be a marked man, but his partisans, some of them in high places, had thus far succeeded in saving his life. On our next trip to Turkey thirty years later, in 1931, Kemal had become Ataturk and was president of the Turkish Republic.

Politically, the stay in Turkey was immensely instructive and interesting to me. Joe's stay, on the other hand, had produced something for the ages. In his superb way, with his great mastery of colors, he had captured for all time the delicate but life-like tints on the original marble figures of the sarcophagus of Alexander the Great. In a relatively short time, as might indeed have been expected, the colors on the marble were to fade and become obscure, whereas Joe's renderings of these great pieces of sculpture were to remain. The paintings are now to be seen in the Museum of Fine Arts, Boston.

14

JOHN SINGER SARGENT

AND HENRY JAMES

ONE WEEK after the Turkish sojourn, Joe and I were dining with John Singer Sargent in London, a far cry from the evening of self-inflicted torture in Stamboul. My first impression of Sargent's personality was of his height and that he stood very erect for so portly a man. Protruding eyes and a slight upward tilt to a small nose gave a curious effect in profile to a round, pudgy face that was abnormally and unbecomingly red. As he greeted me, there was an expression in his eyes that made me understand why strangers found him blunt and severe, especially if they attempted to break through a reserve which was like a shield protecting his inner self from intrusion.

I silently appraised this characteristic in terms of an evening with the three of us alone, at Joe's insistence, for the avowed purpose of permitting Sargent and me to become friends. I intuitively sensed that the distinguished painter, immaculately tailored and accustomed to great functions, would have preferred as an alternative his own suggestion of a large formal dinner in my honor, and that, strangely enough, he was ill at ease.

When I neither gushed over him with girlish enthusiasm nor took for granted acceptance of me at sight because of his affection for Joe, a subtle change in his manner towards me clearly bespoke his relief.

Meanwhile, as I remained detached and silent, he chatted with Joe, his attitude that of a man in a particularly sympathetic presence.

I liked his contagious chuckle and quick wit as the two of them reminisced about art experiences and tastes in common, such as their love for the hill towns of Italy, especially Assisi. Also an early predilection for the Renaissance, with a brief interlude of indulging themselves extravagantly in impressionistic principles, according to the trend of their respective Paris studios.

A reference to Florence reminded Joe of his first chance encounter there with Sargent when he was at work in 1886, the beginning of their friendship. He said he was feeling rather pleased with his own water color of an architectural detail of the entrance to a medieval church, until he saw Sargent's sketch, which had handled the same subject from a different angle. Joe expressed admiration for the subtle variations in the color of the stone in bright sunshine, contrasting with the shadows over a nearby tree, caught by a few strokes.

Sargent countered this spontaneous praise of his work by mentioning a water-color sketch of Joe's, also painted with a few strokes of the brush on a narrow bit of cardboard. Several brilliant spots of light, with thin lines of color below, in a deep blue sky had produced an impression of a tremendous display of fireworks, with sparks flying, in Venice. He had been so impressed, he said, that he had invited the younger painter to show his studies on Greece and Italy in his London studio that summer.

One of the best art critics had acclaimed the fireworks sketch "a masterpiece of its kind."

"Please keep on talking Mr. Sargent," I exclaimed. "You are opening a page in a book about Joe before I knew him, and I don't want to miss anything you remember."

Sargent's face was full of charm and responsiveness, as, looking straight at me, he said, with a sudden friendliness, "I believe you'll be a good wife for an artist."

Joe immediately followed up this unexpected awareness of me as an individual by stating that I was beginning to appreciate old masters by only looking at the best in a museum, and a few at a time. By this method he was teaching me to identify those by the same painter.

My lessons in art training brought the conversation to what both of them had learned, in their formative years, from copying portraits by Frans Hals—Sargent, on the initiative of Carolus Duran, his teacher in Paris, and Joe on that of Denman Ross. Sargent mentioned an occasion in his Tate Street studio when Joe's copies were on view. He remembered having done the same head of a man by Frans Hals, and managed to find it. They were shown side by side. Artist friends present adjudged Joe's to be an exact replica, all the more remarkable from having been painted in a different medium, that of "body" water color instead of oil. They considered him to have the makings of an expert forger!

All were also in agreement that Sargent's rendering was a very free translation, in which his own technique had not altered. He recalled having met this criticism by expressing his gratitude for the discipline acquired from an intensive study of Frans Hals in the nature of structure, form, and color which was to have a permanent influence on his career.

It seems relevant to remark here that, later, Sargent was to become generally accepted as the "most important innovator in portraiture since Frans Hals had liberated that medium from the tyranny of ancient techniques." Nevertheless, Sargent refused to be a sponsor for an exhibition of Cézanne, Matisse, Picasso, Gauguin, and Van Gogh held at the Grafton Galleries. Nor was he classed among the revolutionary painters of his day.

Sargent congratulated Joe on having been completely at ease artistically in the ancient civilization of Egypt. He enlarged on the theme by defining Joe's instinct for close observation and the interpretation of what he saw as a rare gift, evidenced in his Egyptian paintings. He confessed that a cursory glance at the monuments of the Nile Valley had left him dazed and inarticulate with a brush. He hoped to go again for a long stay and an opportunity to become familiar with what could be done by a painter like Joe, he said.

By now it was nearly midnight and departure was clearly indicated, but Joe made a final attempt to bring me forward conversationally. "Tell John of your interesting experience in crossing the Nile alone on a native ferry," he urged.

Obediently I began to relate the incident. Sargent's cold, penetrating eyes, fixed on my face without the movement of an eyelash, soon drove away consecutive thought, and Joe's worried frown brought me to an abrupt stop in the middle of a sentence. Sargent looked embarrassed, and Joe broke an awkward pause by a few words, which, to my horror, I realized gave point to my story.

A few moments later Joe and I were waiting for a bus to come rattling along over the cobbled street. It was raining, and drops dripping from an umbrella he held over us both were ruining a new gown. In between sobs, I poured out to him the disgrace I felt at my failure to come up to his expectations of me as a storyteller.

He patted my cheek gently and said, "Darling, I never knew a story to go so well without a point." He said it in a voice so convincing that I was almost persuaded I had done him credit after all!

The few friends Sargent had told us he had asked to see Joe's recent paintings the next Sunday turned out to be a crowd of the best that London had to offer. Distinguished people from every walk of life, with artists and curators of museums predominating, they were animated and interested. I had been standing a little apart, listening to Joe with a pleasurable thrill as he held his own on Egyptian art in a group which contained many ardent admirers of the Greek classical period. Tea was about to be served and people were moving about talking.

The outer door opened and shut behind a stout man with hair neatly brushed to the sides of a well-formed, over-sized, partly bald head. A large nose and a firm line to the chin and mouth added strength to a unique personality. His hands were delicate, with finely tapered fingers. His dress was conventional and formal, in spite of its sack character. I took a second look. The man was indeed Henry James, by now an English American, with all that that designation may connote. He was like the photograph Joe possessed of him but was very much alive.

Involuntarily, I walked towards him, frankly staring and smiling. Later I marveled at my presumptiousness, which would have been fatal in an approach to Sargent. But James regarded me questioningly but not disapprovingly. "I've read everything you've written," I burst out impulsively.

"Let's sit down," he suggested, as Sargent hurried forward to greet him. "I see you know Joe Smith's wife," Sargent said.

True to form, James replied, "Unforeseen circumstances have already introduced us and to our mutual and continuing satisfaction."

James stayed on after the other guests had gone. It was obvious that his affection for Joe was very genuine, as was also his interest in the paintings.

Apparently from something he said, Joe and I were expected to come with Sargent to visit James in Rye the following Tuesday for two nights. "We are not Sargent's house guests and don't have to be included," I felt compelled to tell him.

"It was a different premise on which my plans for having you and Joe under my roof definitely took their ultimate shape," he said.

On the scheduled afternoon, the three of us got out of the train at the country station of Rye. Sargent remarked that this kind of community, consisting of retired army and government officials, afforded excellent relaxation for James's overworked brain. He added that the possession of Lamb House was the attraction which kept him in residence for most of the year.

Our luggage was cared for, and we walked to James's home, a mansion and an excellent example of the Queen Anne period, with an air about it of eminent stability and respectability. A middle-aged couple received us in the hall. Both were impressively in character with the severe interior and its furniture.

Two anachronisms in the otherwise staid surroundings struck me forcibly. One was the entrance door, which was painted a startling and vivid green, the other was the freedom of a pet dog, who was leaping about recklessly and barking loudly.

James, on his return from a walk, joined us for a late tea, which was served under a mulberry tree several hundred years old. Nearby were surrounding walls covered with vines.

Sargent's unpretentiousness was an excellent foil for James's pompous manner. In his later years, literary success gave James social assurance and he was a voluble talker, whereas Sargent was rather inarticulate. James's slow and studied exaggeration in expressing his thoughts in a lengthy disquisition fascinated me.

Sargent had warned us that James's evening meals were banquets, even when he was alone, so the four of us sat down in gala attire in an enormous dining room. To my surprise, Sargent monopolized the conversation and was extremely amusing.

The climax came when James described Mrs. Jack Gardner of Boston as being an inspiration to all cultured and creative men who knew her.

At this tribute, Sargent, with inimitable power of mimickry, gave a screamingly funny account of an evening in Chase's New York studio when he (Sargent) had promised Mrs. Gardner to have Carmencita dance for her and a few other guests. Carmencita, arriving very late and in a vile temper, had refused to dance. To Sargent's horror, the Spanish artist picked on Mrs. Gardner for particular insult. She pulled down her hair, threw the flower she was wearing directly into Mrs. Gardner's face, and made a rude gesture. Sargent recalled that Joe had come to the rescue by picking up the flower and placing it in his buttonhole. His exaggerated thanks to Carmencita, as though she had intended the flower as a gift for him, changed her mood. Sargent succeeded in getting her out of the studio and further placated her by the promise of a jewel. She put her hair in order, pinned a torn skirt, then, smiling and demure, made a re-entrance to the studio on Sargent's arm and gave a spirited performance.

Sargent's story over, we awaited yet another story of larger canvas. James, in fact, had promised to read aloud his *The Turn of the Screw*. As an introduction, he said, with a friendly smile towards me, that he was fully aware Joe and Sargent read his novels as seldom as was compatible with their affection for the author. But this evening he guaranteed to give them the creeps.

After a leisurely glass of port, James settled himself in a comfortable armchair and opened the book. His voice was effective, and, as in a Japanese geisha's acting, he gave full play to scenes and situations where terror mounted far beyond the range of the ordinary mystery story. He wore no spectacles, and his mournful eyes, raised at moments from the page, reflected the horror being created by his own word pictures.

The pleasant old house and attractive grounds of Bly described in the story were, of course, a disguised Lamb House. Even James's unimaginative housekeeper had her counterpart in a scene of comfort and sanity deliberately selected to make the tragedy that engulfed two innocent, radiant children all the more accentuated. As the tale unfolded, I suffered with the emotional young governess in her struggle to break the hold of an evil man and woman, after death, over a boy and girl, now under her charge, whom they had corrupted when alive.

The account of their apparition as ghosts, visible to the children, and finally to herself, was so vivid that, when a door leading to the outside blew open, I steeled myself against the shock of seeing the debased Flint enter the room. The final triumph of the governess in reclaiming the boy through her love and the repudiation of the ghost were manifested by his flinging himself into her outstretched arms—but his heart had ceased to beat.

As James's voice ceased, Joe and Sargent looked as though they were still seeing ghosts. But my thoughts were concentrated on giving James my interpretation of an illusion which his versatile mind had made a reality through words.

I told him rather decisively that I disagreed with some readers and critics who believed the author was describing a situation that existed only in the mind of the governess. To me, the story was an allegory of evil which had corrupted human beings, and which not even an innocent child could escape, in surroundings made for comfort and happiness. It was evil that must be combatted, as the governess had done, otherwise it would work havoc morally even after death.

James looked at me very earnestly as I rose to say good morning, (dawn was breaking). "A tenable conclusion," he murmured.

Sargent had told me that James permitted no interruption to his writing. He ate lunch in his study, from which he emerged to take a walk before tea. I remained in my room to give Joe and Sargent a chance to be together.

After a bite of food was served me, I was lulled to sleep by the rhythmic sound of James's voice dictating and the click of a typewriter coming through my open windows. An abrupt cessation of sound awakened me just before a knock at the door proved to be a summons to James's study, delivered by the housekeeper in flustered astonishment.

Conspicuous in the furniture of James's simple workshop were two extremely large tables, and at either end of the room was a long cushioned bench with a high back. Books were in every available space. As I entered, a secretary was covering the typewriter, preparatory to departure, and James was glancing through sheets of manuscript. He gestured me to a chair facing him, smiling in a way that made me feel my presence was a favor to him. His opening remark, after a companionable silence, even more winning. "In the midst of a sentence," he said, "it occurred to me that a cozy chat with a young woman familiar with the characters in my novels would not be an interruption, so here we are!"

For the ensuing two hours, from James's casual conversation, I gained a series of indelible impressions. He went back to the time when, as a reticent boy, he felt overshadowed by his elder brother William, who was "engagingly outgoing and bright," and whom he admired inordinately. And his dependence on the understanding sympathy of his mother in adjusting himself to a family existence constantly uprooted because of the restlessness of his father.

A social fling in Newport at the age of eighteen gave him a taste for formal society which he was never to lose. Posing for his portrait by John La Farge had caused him to entertain a vague idea of becoming an artist. Although he had not followed through with this impulse, he had acquired from La Farge, and from meeting other great painters La Farge had introduced him to, a realization of the importance of art and culture which was to become thematic in his novels.

After an experiment with law, he had settled down on Quincy Street, Cambridge, and had started his literary career by writing for the *North American Review*. I gathered from his detached, disjointed talk a terrific inner conflict before he had reached a decision, at the age of thirty-two, to break loose from his family and make his home abroad. He intimated that anything alien to life in Cambridge was wrong, to his brother's way of thinking, but for himself, the serenity he needed for writing, as well as the values he deemed essential for development in his own life, could not find fulfillment in America. He left the subject at that.

The financial ease which James enjoyed because of his father's wealth undoubtedly was a factor in the steadily recurring premise in his novels that money was a condition of freedom. He never questioned its advantages, any more than he did the aristocratic ideal. He delighted in placing his characters, frequently Americans in contact with Europeans, in ancestral homes with great halls, upper galleries, and family portraits.

I thought this might have been a throwback to the impression made on him by tall mirrors, marble fireplaces, crystal chandeliers, and other signs of luxury in big houses in New York, where he had lived when he was very young. His detailed knowledge of history, culture, and politics provided suitable conversations for his fictional characters living in style.

Sargent's expression was comical when, on entering the studio for the afternoon's exercise, he found me with James.

Joe's choice of dress was well adjusted to the Surrey countryside, even though Sargent's smartly correct apparel and gold-headed cane suggested town, Joe alleged jestingly. Sargent was always the typical Londoner, James added in the same vein, and when he painted in the evening, wore a dinner jacket or a tail coat. To this sally Sargent retorted that James's outfit today was that of an actor playing the part of the country squire.

Both had admired Joe's neat tweeds and sporty waistcoat, so, responding to James's sympathetic attitude towards me, I told with absolute self-confidence the story of his newly acquired wardrobe. Lloyd Griscom had made me mindful that Joe's clothes were lacking in distinction. Lloyd went even further and prepared a list of what the well-dressed man should wear on every occasion.

It had needed compulsion on my part, I said, to get Joe to Pool's, the London tailoring establishment patronized by the British aristocracy. He had taken an instant dislike to the staff, faultlessly attired in morning coats, who, on reading the warmth of Lloyd Griscom's recommendation, had welcomed him cordially. Also Joe's excellent selection of materials had aroused respect. But he became restive during a lengthy consultation among a group of fitters about how to deal with one of his shoulders, which was higher than the other.

Meanwhile, I found that everything ordered tallied with the prices given me by Griscom, except for the amount charged for the evening clothes, which was much lower. Annoyed by the belief that Joe was being offered inferior cloth, I asked haughtily to be shown a better quality.

"Madame, Pool carries but one quality," I was told in a shocked chorus.

Sargent's spontaneous burst of laughter at this point exhilarated me. I recounted that while I was trying to pull myself together, Joe had created a stir by asking for the bill covering his order. He was promptly informed that Pool's procedure was to extend practically unlimited credit to clients. When he insisted on the account, the staff went into a huddle. Then one of them disappeared, to return shortly with the account. In exchange for ten pound notes which Joe strewed rather ostentatiously over the counter, he was handed an impressive-looking document, which proved to be a receipt, on which was written in large script: "Discount of 20 per cent."

The staff escorted Joe to the door and urged him to patronize Pool soon again. Evidently, on second thought, spot cash did have certain advantages over the British system of extended credit.

I can still hear Sargent laughing.

It was never again to be Joe's and my good fortune to be in Rye, nor to see Sargent and James together, except in passing glimpses in England. Our future meetings with Sargent were to be frequent in Boston, only occasionally elsewhere, and with James, in Italy, which he loved as much as Joe did. Possibly in no place away from Rye was James more at home than in Rome.

His devotion to his brother William's family from their early childhood was, I believe, the reason for his acceptance of the children of intimate friends. This was one of his most lovable, human characteristics, perhaps the more astonishing to those who only knew him formally. He used to say children were "individuals" and "companionable," and seen to advantage when away from a mother or nurse. Both either "repressed" them or permitted them to "show off objectionably."

On one of our several later visits to Rome at the same time, James invited our children, Rebecca and Frances, aged four and three, respectively, to have supper with him in a villa he had rented. Joe deposited them and brought them back two hours later. Upon their return Frances announced excitedly that the nice man who could not talk English "straight" had invited her to feed pigeons with him in Venice.

He did feed pigeons with the children in Venice in the summer of that year (1906). It was there also that there occurred another unforgettable episode. A New York woman had persuaded James to dine with her, she told us, on condition of being "alone with the Smiths." He was in a happy mood, and it was a particularly pleasant evening. After we had left the dinner table, I noticed the hostess looking at the door expectantly. It suddenly opened to admit a woman followed by her husband. She bustled in, saying, "It was 9:30 you asked us for?" Voices coming nearer on the stairs indicated these were not to be the only guests. The hostess had kept technically to her promise of having no one else at dinner, but had been unable to resist showing off her lion at an informal reception.

James acted at once. Seizing me by the arm, he all but pushed me on to a balcony overlooking the Grand Canal and into a seat. He stood beside me. As he heard someone approaching, he leaned toward me, saying, "You are wonderful." The steps retreated. But the persistent hostess came out on to the balcony a few moments later with an impressive looking woman and her escort, introducing them to both James and me. He rose, smiled agreeably, said a few courteous words, then, turning to me, remarked, "You are wonderful this evening, simply wonderful."

After this, the interruptions ceased, and James and I spent the better part of an hour in quiet enjoyment of the stars and the gondolas on the canal below. He said good-night to his hostess, who was seated alone with Joe. The other guests (unexpected by him) had departed.

Valambrosa in Italy was an enchanting place. Joe and I were there more than once, in a charming villa, with Edward Boit of Boston as our host. Once James was among our fellow guests. I was presiding at the tea table, and everyone was in a hurry to be off on an excursion to see the sunset from a particular hill.

After I had poured tea for the women of the party, I turned to James and asked whether he would take sugar and milk, or lemon. He replied, "Sugar," then began a long dissertation on the difficulty of reaching a decision between lemon and milk. I caught Boit's despairing eye, and breaking in on James's peroration, I told him I would give him both.

"No, lemon," he interrupted himself to say, and we reached the hill on time for the sunset.

In the early spring of 1909 on our return from Egypt, we were staying at Garlant's Hotel in London. A dinner was being given in Joe's honor at the Atheneum Club, and James, who was at the Reform Club at the time, had agreed to come. The day of the dinner, however, he sent Joe a note saying his thoughts were not companionable and he had begged off. He added as a postscript, "I feel in the mood for an evening with Corinna."

James looked depressed and ill when he arrived. He had known Whistler, and the atmosphere of Garlant's, where Whistler had often been, was agreeable. His spirits did not soon revive but he began talking. As always when he was with me, he was really more thinking aloud than conversing. First his mind was on the failure of his plays, which had been a bad blow. He did not consider Shaw's verdict correct that the conversations were too literary to get across the footlights. He referred to himself as old and as useless as a pricked balloon.

Unwittingly I intensified his gloom by a chance reference to my father's having fought in the Civil War. "Don't mention it," he said despairingly, and then explained he had never risen above the ignominy of being refused as a soldier because of a leg injury.

I at last got him laughing by telling him that the copy of *The Golden Bowl* he sent me had arrived on a Christmas and I had shamefully neglected the children's tree to devote myself to the book, which I had finished late at night.

We discussed the plot, that of an emotionally immature girl and her development as she fights for, and saves, her marriage. She finally decides marriage is more important than her absorption in her father and the sharing of his enjoyment in the possession of great wealth and a large mansion filled with precious works of art.

I also mentioned *The Wings of the Dove*, where wealth was again a factor, and a losing one. The heroine is a rich, lovely girl, doomed to die in her early twenties. A scheming poor girl persuades a penniless young man to become engaged to her, both realizing that marriage cannot last long, and thus he will soon be free and rich. The rich girl dies before the marriage takes place, but she leaves her entire fortune to her fiancé. He has fallen so deeply in love with her memory that he repudiates the schemer.

There are so many ways money can be dealt with in a novel, James was saying when Joe came in. It was late when he left in the best of spirits. We never saw him again.

Sargent's American success in portraiture was instantaneous. Despite a spectacular career and the ability to earn large sums of money, he was not happy in that phase of art. His favorite definition of a portrait was a "painting with something wrong about the mouth." He told Joe he envied him his courage in deliberately choosing Rameses the Great as a sitter, whose relatives, like himself, were in stone and could not criticize.

By 1910, Sargent had abruptly abandoned doing commissions of important oil portraits, with rare exceptions, but he continued to do charcoal sketches of people. Twice he made sketches of me, but both times destroyed them before Joe and I saw them. "Not satisfactory," was his verdict. In the immediate pre-World War I years he threw himself enthusiastically into the painting of ambitious murals for the Boston Public Library, where there were decorations by Puvis de Chauvannes, Edwin Abbey, and Joe Smith. During the war years, he established himself in a Boston studio to complete them.

Joe and I were among the few friends who were free to drop in on him at work. Once, as we mounted the steps, Sargent was laughing loudly. We opened the studio door to find him alone, seated before an easel where there was a finished portrait of a prominent Bostonian whom Joe knew Sargent disliked. Black lines added to the face and head had turned the man into Mephistopheles. As Sargent engaged Joe in conversation, he removed the lines. "I have had my quiet fun with that portrait," he remarked, still laughing.

Sargent enjoyed dining informally at the homes of intimates, but when he was bored he was at no pains to conceal the fact. I recall vividly one such event, a luncheon he had felt obligated to attend. The hostess had appealed to me to come and sit next to him.

He looked rebellious when the hostess waited a long time for late-comers. Lunch was not over when I explained to him I had to leave for a professional ball game. As I rose from the table, he did the same, and after a hasty apology to the hostess, joined me in the hall. "I'm going with you," he said, "for a first experience in watching American baseball." I knew it was useless to combat the determined look in his eye. My young man escort, whom we met at the entrance to the ball park, good-naturedly relinquished his seat, and Sargent and I were in a strategic position to see the entire field.

Instantly the scene fascinated him as an artist. He borrowed score cards from neighbors and steadily used a pencil in rapid strokes to catch the outline of players sliding bases. Poetry in motion, he termed it, only equaled by the sparkle of sunlight and varied shadows. He jumped about to sketch the teams in play, and his comments, in a voice that carried far in his excitement, soon had people in his vicinity looking at him instead of the game. His insistence that he must come again with water colors was overheard by a man who had recognized him. The man left the game and returned with a sketch pad and paints. Whereupon Sargent was busier than ever.

In May, 1918, Sargent went to France to paint for the British government enormous pictures commemorating the war, with the British and American troops involved treated as a unit.

During the summer of 1919, he was in Boston again and, as in previous seasons, visited us in Dublin, New Hampshire. With his passionate love of nature, the desolation of the French countryside left in the wake of fighting saddened him as much as the suffering and death of human beings. He found me a sympathetic listener, for my reaction had been similar. From my word pictures of individual trees, he actually sketched hideous, distorted skeletons that were the exact replicas of those I had seen.

Sargent came to Dublin on his final visit in the summer of 1924. He had been ill and wanted a quiet week, he said, to sit about in our Japanese and Italian gardens. His comment on a large Chinese wave Joe had made of cement in the Chinese garden was, "How delightful, Joe, a Rodin gone wrong."

All our friends considerately kept away so he could be undisturbed. The climax to his visit was to be a command performance, given in our Teatro Bambino, and at his request, with no other audience. I was behind the scenes, assisting Joe getting the children into costumes of fairies, gnomes, and fauns, when we heard Sargent's voice.

He was addressing imaginary sitters for portraits in the empty boxes on both sides of him. "I hated perpetuating the nose in your family for three generations," he said. Then abruptly turning to another, "Your mouth was just as disagreeable to me, rather more so." He went on to say how glad he was they were not present at this performance given for him alone. He gave a royal gesture and said, "Joe, the play may now go on."

15

EARLY BOSTON

IN THE FALL OF 1900 began a stretch of many years when Boston was my legal residence and home for those seasons of the year we were not abroad or in Dublin. Joe's parents continued to occupy the bedrooms off the large studio in the Ludlow, where they had lived with him as a bachelor.

It was a leisurely era when worthwhile things were accomplished and the arts and intellectual pursuits supported, as a matter of course, by unpretentious men and women with sizable fortunes. The atmosphere was delightfully cosmopolitan, but lacking in the display frequently found among wealthy New Yorkers. The principal places of social intercourse were spacious homes. Some of them included a music room, where musicians of the highest professional rank played for the pleasure of guests. One often sat down to a dinner party of twenty or more people, and luncheons included prominent business executives, professors, scientists, writers, and specialists, who somehow found the necessary time.

The Ludlow was situated in the center of Back Bay, facing Trinity Church. Horse-drawn vehicles were in general use. The broad Commonwealth Avenue, consisting of two lanes for traffic, was the main thoroughfare for reaching social occasions by walking. How delightful it was in the evening to be on the dividing dirt path reserved for foot passengers, its length edged with a wide expanse of grass between a double row of trees! During daylight hours, the charm of the avenue was enhanced by the sight of children rushing about over the green, and baby carriages pushed by nurses in trim uniforms and bonnets. One paused from time to time to converse at benches with friends or acquaintances taking a constitutional.

Many distinguished but less fashion-conscious families lived on Beacon Hill. The houses dated to a much earlier period than those of Back Bay, and when restored were more interesting architecturally, but not as large nor so impressive. The guests who came on foot arrived at the festivity rather breathless from the steep ascent of hillside streets, after passing diagonally through the Public Gardens. In the months of snow, high, fleece-lined arctics protected evening slippers. If the weather was unpropitious for walking, a Charles Street livery stable provided closed carriages. A number of Bostonians had their own sleighs, and the ladies, when a fur coat had been laid aside, removed several layers of woolen material before disclosing evening attire. (Unquestionably, among many other changes during the last sixty years, the winters have become progressively milder.)

An excellent suburban railroad service was available, and many weekends found Joe and me in the nearby country, on large estates in Milton, Ponkapog, and Dedham. We visited in old-fashioned mansions set in the midst of superb trees, and the stables contained beautifully groomed horses and equipages worthy of them. Inside, we particularly enjoyed art objects from the Orient, brought to Boston by the clipper-ship trade, with the histories of the voyages an integral part of the tradition of New England families. Portraits of their forebears were on the walls of homes owned by these descendants. Drives in the vicinity of the Blue Hill reservation were a feature of such outings. We took tramps through the woods, to see fruit trees and dogwood in blossom in the early spring. The bright foliage of autumn and the gay blooms in extensive gardens, to be continued in conservatories after frost, made the environs of Boston unforgettable.

Sundays spent in town afforded unique hospitality to friends of the Quincy A. Shaws in a standing invitation to an open house after church. This included an informal luncheon in their stately, old-time mansion of brownish wood, reached by a horse car to Jamaica Pond, followed by a walk uphill.

An enormous lump of solid copper from the Calumet Mine deserved its conspicuous position on the lawn, as the symbol of what had made possible in the rooms of the house one of the most notable collections of Millets, Corots, and Rousseaus of that day. Shaw had been among the few Bostonians to buy these and other pictures by impressionists before they were popular in France.

He also owned excellent specimens of Japanese kakemono and lacquer, and among his Chinese possessions was a much-admired peach-blow vase, and another white piece with a magnificent incised dragon on it.

The Charles Sargent estate gave enjoyment to visitors because of the perfection of plantings, second only to those in Sargent's own arboretum. The special feature of the estate consisted in the variety in specimen shrubs. The property covered a larger area than any other in Brookline and adjoined the Quincy A. Shaw place. Both took in a stretch of the shore-line of Jamaica Pond. Mrs. Sargent had on one occasion persuaded her husband to open the grounds as a benefit for fallen women, a charity of which she was the head. More than two thousand people were on the place in the all-day affair, yet there was no sense of overcrowding. They strolled along wide intersecting paths to booths selling all kinds of attractive novelties, contributed for the purpose.

Joe was in charge of an afternoon fete. He made use of endless stretches of empty lawn and long, enticing vistas for a series of short theatrical acts, witnessed by audiences of several hundreds at a time and constantly repeated. A particular favorite was an episode of mermaids in a large pool, overcoming by their wiles the evil intentions of pirates against a lone sea captain. For this act there was always an extended waiting line for tickets.

That evening, at dinner at the Sargents, where we were staying, Joe was tired but pleased at the success of the afternoon. Mrs. Sargent was equally satisfied because of the amount of money taken in. She was explaining to us that her organization helped to give a second chance to girls who had fallen *once* (emphasis on the once). At this moment, Mr. Sargent walked into the room, very late for the meal, and his voice broke as he observed that, for his shrubs, there was no second chance, one fall meant complete ruin. "Replacing my fallen shrubs will cost far more than what you made for your fallen women, my dear."

Mrs. John H. Gardner was the only one among Joe's many women friends I had known previously. Her presence at our small family wedding was in character with her unconventional manner of doing things. She had telegraphed, "Hope I'm expected." Her toast at the wedding breakfast, "To the bride, my ready-made friend because of Joe," produced quite a sensation among my staid relatives.

No one was kinder than Isabella Gardner in dropping in on Mother, or for a visit with Father. As for myself, it was always a gala occasion when I was invited to lunch with her alone. I had never been with a more stimulating companion, and she aroused my ambition to try to have her think me worthy to be Joe's wife.

I remember an occasion when our conversation had been intimate and mostly about Joe. I had referred to her influence on his formative years, and his having remarked to me that Isabella Gardner had encouraged him to talk to her about his art ambitions and had made him feel he could achieve them. Her response was that, curiously enough, he had had the same effect on her.

The first Bostonian to become my real friend was Barrett Wendell. His brilliant sarcasm and caustic wit caused him to be dreaded, not only in the classroom by his students in English at Harvard, but even among his peers. I had seen an entirely different phase of his character, one of extreme sensitiveness and consideration, and ours was a friendship at sight. He admired Joe's mother, approved of my attitude towards my in-laws, and took the pains to make a special call on me to tell me so. When he dropped in on the Smith family at odd moments, his talk was always stimulating and entertaining. After our first meeting, he sent me a copy of a much-discussed life of Cotton Mather he had written, scribbling on his card, "Read every word of this account of dreary days that he [Mather] did nothing to make less so." He acknowledged to me later that his purpose was to prevent my being discouraged at Boston society's attitude towards me as a young stranger.

I needed encouragement, since, generally speaking, I was considered a maverick, and even my New England inheritance on both sides of the family was insufficient to overcome the fact of my New York birth and upbringing. Again, Boston had an arbitrary pattern of fitting people into an age group. I was firm in insisting that, as a stranger, I had no age and should not be limited in my companionships simply because I was younger than Joe. Fortunately for my premise, I was asked to become a member of a sewing circle of women, comprised of Joe's friends, who had come out more than twelve years previous to my debut. This strategy proved bafflingly successful as a camouflage for my actual age.

No less rigid was the tendency to classify people according to tastes (if any), cultural or intellectual. Learning to appreciate art was considered too vague, but it was the best I could do. Then by a lucky chance good fortune came my way. Harold Bauer was to give a piano recital for invited guests in the home of a well-known patroness of music. He requested her to include me. "But she is not musical," the patroness of music stated, with an air of finality. His reply that he knew from experience that I disliked bad music was beyond a Bostonian's calculation as to where to place me musically. I went to the recital, and during supper Bauer talked to me about Beethoven, Wagner, Schubert, Brahms, Lizst, and other great composers whose music he referred to our having listened to together in London and Paris before my marriage. Furthermore, Paderewski, when he was in Boston, always made a point of being nice to me at parties, as did Franz Kneisel and the other members of the Kneisel quartet, who were good friends of Joe's.

Another event that assisted materially in my being taken seriously by women of an older generation was having Mrs. George Tyson include me among the few invited to her home Saturday morning, and to an informal lunch served afterwards. Invitations to these regular readings by Mrs. Pratt, the companion of the famous Mrs. Bell, who was a legend in Boston, were eagerly sought.

Joe had met Charles Eliot Norton a number of times at the residence of Norton's older cousin, President Eliot, of Harvard, where Joe was invited frequently to tea as a special favorite of Mrs. Eliot's. Norton, one of the giants among Boston's intellectuals, I was eager to meet, not least of all because he had been a shadow picture in my youth from knowing both my grandfather and father. I heard him much discussed in Boston for having created a new approach to beauty in relation to social progress, culture, and literature, and for his high ideals, brought out in his art classes at Harvard. He had known Ruskin, Carlyle, Browning, and other great figures abroad, had written a life of Dante, and had done an innumerable lot of learned things, yet was an avowed admirer of the city of Chicago, a combination that intrigued me.

By 1900 his failing health restricted his attendance at formal occasions, and it was difficult, except for privileged friends and very distinguished people, to meet him at small dinners. I was overjoyed, therefore, when Joe and I were invited to dine with him at the William C. Endicotts. When my hostess approached me, accompanied by Charles Eliot Norton, she was explaining to him that Edith Wharton, whom he had been told was to be his dinner partner, was unavoidably detained in Philadelphia. His eyes became cold and his expressive face set in grim lines when she said, "I know you will enjoy this opportunity to get acquainted with Joe Smith's young wife."

At table Norton did not deliberately ignore me, he was just entirely unconscious of my presence. I made repeated maneuvers to gain his attention, and for one brief moment managed to do so. Before I could mention my father, and Egypt where he had traveled, he had turned again to his neighbor on the other side, who was a noted classical scholar.

With fighting Putnam blood in my veins, I refused, after this dinner, to be ignored by any among the intellectuals of Boston who, although a great deal older than Joe, had long since accepted him in their inner circle. Barrett Wendell, in whom I confided, seemed greatly amused at my plans for a counterattack on Norton. I made up my mind to learn something he did not know and somehow compel him to listen to me.

My choice was a serious study of classical Arabic under scholarly auspices. I appealed to Denman Ross, who approved of Arabic as a curb to the frivolous tendencies in me, which he admitted had perturbed him because of their possible effect on Joe's career. He introduced me to Professor Toy, the head of the Semitic Department of Harvard. The Professor, with a twinkle in his eye, wanted to know if my purpose was to impress Bostonians. I assured him I wished to read the Koran in the original so that I might get near the thoughts of simple Moslems. I had already made progress in classical Arabic grammar, thanks to a voluntary teacher in Constantinople, and had kept on alone since then. My reference to having been given by James Nies, a scholar whom Toy knew, his copy of the standard and valuable dictionary for classical Arabic counted in my favor.

Toy seemed to think hard before he looked me straight in the eye and said solemnly that, if I were in earnest, he would send me to John Orne, a scholar who translated difficult manuscripts in ancient Arabic for the Harvard Library. Orne was old but great both as a teacher and in deciphering all but impossible scripts. "He will give you of his best, but if you disappoint him, I will never forgive myself for recommending you," Professor Toy said, not without misgiving.

A week later, I stood on a small porch at 104 Ellery Street, Cambridgeport, reached by a temperamental horsecar on Charles Street that ran on no schedule. I rang the bell several times before a face peered out at me through a glass in a storm door which was already in place in the early fall. The door was finally opened by an aged man wearing a skullcap and a black suit. He had no glasses on the keenest imaginable eyes, which were sizing me up. "Is this the Mrs. Smith I have been corresponding with Professor Toy about for Arabic lessons?" he asked without preamble. I nodded. "Well, if you intend to master classical Arabic, youth is a good asset. Come in."

In retrospect it seems incredible that the determining factor in my acceptance of John Orne in my life, on Professor Toy's terms, was a desire to show off to Charles Eliot Norton, who had all unwittingly humiliated me at the house of a mutual friend.

Before Joe and I left for Japan, early in January 1901, I had taken Arabic lessons three mornings a week and studied hard in between them. During my protracted absence, John Orne kept me supplied with grammar exercises, done in Arabic script. That same fall, we were settled again in Boston, in a house on Marlborough Street loaned us for the winter months by a friend. By now I was primed for an intellectual encounter with Charles Eliot Norton.

I got Joe's close friend, Edward Robinson of the Boston Museum, first as curator of the Classical Department, later as director, to invite Charles Eliot Norton, whom he knew well, to come to dinner without informing him I was to be on one side of him. Barrett Wendell was to be on my other side. When we were seated, Wendell repeated to Norton a little-known bit of folklore of Grecian origin across me, as my cue to perform. Norton was interested, and then I opened fire on him by remarking that a legend I had just read, but which had not been translated, seemed pertinent and proceeded to tell it.

"It certainly is," Norton declared with enthusiasm, then inquired what the language was. "Classical Arabic," I informed him casually, and offered to give him a small paper-covered book which contained a number of similar legends about the Arabian desert in Arabic script. Whereupon he acknowledged that he did not read Arabic.

"Why don't you take it up?" I asked patronizingly. He actually chuckled. Barrett put in that I was a daughter of George Haven Putnam's, to which Norton replied that that explained my knowing Arabic. To my great satisfaction, this was to him an adequate reason for his not only taking pains to talk to me when we happened to meet in the future, but inviting me to his home with a few scholars. I dutifully absorbed culture at entertainment given by Denman Ross, Sturgis Bigelow, and others associated with the museum, where I attended endless lectures on art. I felt more at home than otherwise would have been the case, however, from my youthful experiences in my father's company among intellectual groups, many of them Harvard professors, met through Barrett Wendell, and also writers of distinction.

What I greatly looked forward to were the few formal balls given each season. In Boston, as in Rome and other foreign capitals, a debutante daughter made her bow, not only to her contemporaries, but to society. These coming-out parties were brilliant affairs; the sedate came in gala attire and, relatively speaking, a gay mood. They indulged themselves in a stately waltz, and even ventured on a lively polka. One was asked for supper in advance by mail.

My having some partners who danced in the real meaning of the word came about through Henry G. Vaughan, the popular master of hounds at the Norfolk Hunt Club. He was kind in remembering me from the summer I spent at the age of fourteen with my family at North East Harbor, where he lived.

Among Joe's intimate friends, next to Isabella Gardner, I enjoyed Mrs. Henry Whitman, who allowed me in her studio to watch her making stained glass. In her special technique, she was almost a throwback to the great glass makers of medieval times. She was a witty conversationalist whom we frequently met at dinners, and a genius as a caller. She would appear unannounced, never seem hurried, comment pertinently on current topics, inquire sympathetically of each person in the room what he or she was doing, and within ten minutes be gone.

One of Joe's friends of whom we saw a good deal was Russell Sullivan, the author. In Joe's youth, he had traveled with him in Italy, and Sullivan had his own room in the Dublin home. Once he invited me to a Boston theatre to see Henry Irving in *The Bells*, and to a supper afterwards in honor of the English actor, promising he would arrange for me to have a short talk with him.

The supper was quite an affair at the home of one of the leading hostesses. When Sullivan brought up Sir Henry, I reminded him we had met a number of times in London before my marriage, with Daniel Frohman and William Gillette. This struck a reminiscent chord, and Sir Henry settled back comfortably in an armchair, devoting his full attention to me.

Sullivan, with a surprised glance, walked away, and after saying a word to the hostess, she too left us undisturbed. Our ensuing conversation gradually attracted noticeable attention from the other guests.

The play had opened with Sir Henry murdering for gain a male companion during a sleigh ride. His alibi had held but the plot had the murderer being haunted by the deed. He would hear sleigh bells so vividly at odd moments that, whatever he was doing, he believed the bells must give away his guilt to others. He finally confessed.

I was thinking aloud when I inquired why he had not simulated the sound by his acting rather than have bells rung loudly backstage. At my question, Sir Henry turned a brick red in fury, jumped to his feet, and stalked away from me dramatically. Instantly an anxious-eyed hostess was beside him, and so was Sullivan, talking earnestly in reply to the actor's flow of words. Sir Henry returned, shook my hand, then joined a group of men, of whom Henry Higginson was the center.

Later Sullivan gratified my curiosity by saying he had pacified Sir Henry by stating that my attitude was not critical but merely expressed a desire to learn his reason for this interpretation of the part. He had given none, according to Sullivan, who added archly, "But the elder Salvini would have needed no bells rung to have the audience hear them."

Bostonians consistently turned out in force to attend the Lowell Institute lectures and those at the Art Museum and at Harvard. But what occurred at a lecture on "Happiness," shortly after my encounter with Sir Henry Irving, caused the slight social stir I had unwittingly produced to be soon forgotten. The daughter of a famous English painter, whom I consider it tactful to let remain anonymous, was to be in America on a first lecture tour. An English friend of Cecilia Beaux's, to whom that artist was indebted for arranging exhibitions of her portraits in London and securing commissions for her, had asked her assistance towards the success of the lady. It was an ultimatum more than a request. The instructions were very definite for engagements in big cities, New York, Philadelphia, Chicago, and Boston, and in the houses of leading hostesses. To make the matter more difficult, men were to be included in the audience in any afternoon affair.

No one in Boston except Mrs. J. Montgomery Sears could have met such requirements, done cheerfully because of affection for Cecilia, who was willing at all times and in all ways to put herself out for her friends when appealed to. The women of Mrs. Sears' circle responded gallantly. But the rumor got started that Monty (as Mr. Sears was called) had started a rebellion. Then he yielded, and other husbands succumbed to pressure put upon them by their wives. It was finally a representative array of Boston society at its best that poured into the Sears' drawing room, two hundred strong. The many men in formal black afternoon coats gave the audience a rather lugubrious appearance.

The lecturer's manuscript, placed ahead of time on a music stand, was formidable in thickness, but Judge Robert Grant, who sat next to me, hopefully suggested that it included a series of lectures, not simply the one on "Happiness" we had been summoned to hear. But once started the lecturer's voice droned on and on, with every one too dazed to move. The men's thoughts were easy to read. "Theirs not to reason why." The women remained politely composed, prepared to endure to the end. Isabella Gardner was even animated. But the lecture became utterly meaningless to me, absorbed as I was in watching the expressions on the men's faces. Major Henry Higginson struggled valiantly against a persistent yawn. Edward Robinson, always courteous, looked gallant but discouraged. Monty was glum but conquered. Howard Walker, one of the leading architects, on the contrary was resentful. Arlo Bates, a writer, had given up even a pretense of listening. Russell Sullivan's forced look of interest had become frozen. Gentle, artistic Templeman Coolidge, was resigned. Nina Gray, never wanting to hurt anyone's feelings, was keeping a watchful eye on her husband John, the head of the Harvard Law School, who showed indications of impending flight through a nearby door.

Mrs. Sears' gracious invitation to refreshments took some time to penetrate. The lecturer's beaming face at her success in holding the audience was the last straw to Grant, and with the assurance of a judge announcing the verdict of a jury, he said, "A tabby cat has been made a lion."

During some months in Boston between travels, personalities of the old-time Boston tradition became realities for me, thanks to my being a Putnam. Foremost among them was Julia Ward Howe. In later years, Joe and I were to see the daughter, Maud, and her husband, John Elliott, in Newport, where she planned several exhibitions of Joe's paintings. But it was in 1906 that I met Mrs. Howe in the Beacon Street house for the first and only time.

I had answered a telephone ring to hear a crisp voice tell me that Mrs. Howe was to recite the "Battle Hymn of the Republic" the next afternoon at three o'clock to a few friends. She wished me to be present as the niece of her colleague, Mary Putnam Jacobi, in the hard struggle for women's suffrage. I was speechless from excitement as the voice went on, "Did you get the message?" I was told to be prompt and not to stay long, as Mrs. Howe tired easily, though with her indomitable spirit, she refused to recognize her physical limitations.

A group of about twenty, all women, gathered in a library. Every face wore an expression of deep emotion and expectation. Mrs. Howe, seated at one end of the room, greeted each guest with a smile and special welcome. Her hands were transparent and she looked decidedly fragile. A soft piece of white lace over her head became a collar and frill under her chin, and her dark silk dress had very wide sleeves. Her broad brow was wrinkled, but her eyes were clear and the rest of her face noticeably without lines. Her cheeks were plump, her nose straight, and a determined mouth bespoke her ceaseless struggle for the causes she believed in and a strong sense of joy in her work that made her incredible achievements possible.

She rose, apparently without undue effort, to walk to a chair placed under a strong light. She looked shriveled and bent but ageless. Someone placed an opened book in her lap. She pushed it aside, closing it with a gesture that said her memory needed no prodding, and she turned down the light.

No one stirred as her voice, with a slight quaver in it, began:

Mine eyes have seen the glory of the coming
  of the Lord . . .

It gained in strength as the noble words rolled on in an increasing volume of sound until the inspired climax:

As he died to make men holy, let us die to make men free
  While God is marching on.

The silence could be felt as her voice stopped, then the guests, after a few minutes, began to slip away with a quick good-by to her. To my surprise, she motioned me to stay. I sat facing her, a lump in my throat, then burst out, "Words as eternal as Lincoln's 'Gettysburg Address'." Luckily I remembered that her husband, Dr. Samuel Howe, had been the driving force behind the establishment of the Perkins Institute for the Blind and referred to the fact. She was pleased at my mention of him and his work and we talked a little about Aunt Minnie.

As I rose to go, she said, "Kiss me again, dear child." But I had not kissed her once.

16

AMERICAN PIONEERS
AS COLLECTORS OF ART

DURING THE eighteen eighties and continuing well beyond the turn of the century, the United States enjoyed a period of great economic expansion. Capital and incomes piled up rapidly, for we had no income tax. Wives persuaded their husbands to spend quickly acquired fortunes on the construction of mansions. Dealers supplied fountains and statuary as centers of interest in elaborate courts and passage ways, but the main emphasis was on paintings of every description for the wall space in the enormous rooms. Most of these possessions were to come under the auctioneer's hammer after the death of their owners, and this kind of impersonal buying needs no serious consideration. But in Boston and elsewhere in Massachusetts, collectors of the caliber of Denman W. Ross and W. Sturgis Bigelow bought with the Boston Museum of Fine Arts in mind. In this way, the Asiatic Department acquired some of its unique and priceless treasures from China and Japan.

Edward W. Forbes was the first American in the market for Italian primitives before their value was realized. His purchases were for the Fogg Museum of Harvard, of which he was the creator and director.

But American men and women in their travels abroad before the discovery of modern art were thrilled by examples of the great schools of painting to be seen in museums. Rapidly they developed the desire to acquire old masters and have daily enjoyment of them in their homes. They had the means to do so and acted under the guidance of experts. This led prospective purchasers to the estates of certain impoverished Europeans who had inherited valuable paintings from their ancestors, or to the premises of important dealers who handled rare examples of art.

These enthusiastic and often well informed collectors could rarely resist any available picture, whatever the price, that fitted in with what they already possessed. When wall space was inadequate for new acquisitions, special rooms were added to their homes, and the more ambitious built art galleries on to existing structures. To such owners, art treasures were a part of their daily lives and they shared their pleasure in them with their friends.

A natural anxiety on the part of owners about what would happen to their collections after death, combined with a civic consciousness that works of art should be accessible to students and the public, determined their ultimate destination. Many of the important private collections, varying according to the tastes of the individuals assembling them, remained intact and ultimately came to form nuclei of famous periods of art in the museums of today.

Some of the notable collectors of this kind Joe and I knew well and had the privilege of seeing their collections in their homes. There was a rapport between interesting personalities and their art treasures that was lacking when later the collections were on public view in museums.

Charles Lang Freer of Detroit and Isabella Stewart Gardner of Boston were the two who, to me, seemed to derive the greatest satisfaction from constant contact with their art possessions. Both expressed to me the same thought in different words, that, when perplexed by an annoying problem, just to sit quietly before a beautiful object in one's possession was refreshing, and the problem tended to solve itself in the process.

We met Freer by chance at a lecture on Japan which Joe gave in Detroit. At its close, I noticed others fall back as a meticulously dressed man with tired eyes, visible behind old-fashioned pince-nez, and a neatly trimmed beard conversed with my husband. Joe nodded in my direction after a few moments, as though in response to a question, and as the two of them approached, I heard the man say, "I like your attitude towards Japan, Mr. Smith."

"This is Mr. Freer," Joe said to me. "He has invited us to stay with him for five days and he wishes to arrange a date now." Joe's pleasure was obvious.

Some weeks later, towards dusk, we were arriving at an imposing residence in Detroit built of dark stone and shingles, with a conspicuous gabled roof. Inside there seemed an almost over-perfection in housekeeping details. The contrast was great between a veritable banquet served for the three of us, dressed in formal attire, and the charming naïveté of our host's conversation, which Joe skillfully kept flowing.

Freer mentioned his poverty as a boy and his determination to find an escape from a limited existence, as he defined it. He could not agree, he said, with people who looked upon money as the root of all evil. Wealth, to him and others, had made possible an appreciation and understanding of the necessity for beauty, by contact with the best specimens of art. Eloquently but rather shyly, he enlarged upon the theme of his purchase of some Whistler etchings, which had changed his outlook on life.

After the first dinner and on the successive evenings of our stay, we devoted ourselves to a detailed study of Whistler's etchings. They were produced a few at a time by Stephen, a talkative, burly cockney, who had moved up from the position of coachman.

"I expect to own the most comprehensive collection of Whistler's etchings in existence," Freer said, after the final showing, speaking with a sense of awed wonder rather than pride of possession.

The next morning we paid homage to the Abbott Thayer paintings, which were imposing because of their number and the fact the collection comprised many of the most notable of the artist's work. We learned that Freer's admiration for Thayer's art led to their close friendship, and not vice versa. He remarked with quiet satisfaction that Thayer always seemed at ease on visits to his (Freer's) home. As he pointed to details of these Thayer pictures he liked, it seemed delightfully obvious that this exhibition would remain intact long after the artist's rather tragic life had ended.

When Joe admired a Japanese pottery jar, Freer told him it was a most important piece because of its history. Before he had started to collect Japanese objects, he had drifted into a curio shop and this jar had held his spellbound attention. Finally he ventured to handle it and rub a finger over its surface. Completely fascinated, he bought it at an absurdly low price. With a boyish look of diffidence, he turned to Joe, saying that, trained as he was from boyhood to appreciate art, he would not realize what his (Freer's) sensations were on discovering later that he had secured a Japanese masterpiece from instinct—or good luck, he added modestly.

Most of our time was spent examining Freer's superb Japanese pieces, many of which were bought from Ernest Fenollosa.

Freer enthusiastically acknowledged his gratitude to Fenollosa for having awakened his permanent interest in Japanese civilization, as expressed in art, and for guiding him into a highly specialized field as a collector.

Freer's ambition was aroused, he said, to study until he reached a point where experts would confirm his own judgment.

He explained to us the method he had followed in educating himself to weed out mistakes. It was to buy not only fine originals but their imitations and originals that had been restored, and by constant observation he was thus gradually learning what made the original different. He took us into what he termed his study room and showed us a bewildering number of such selected objects. I was pleased at his commenting to me that he could tell from the expression in Joe's eyes his approval or indifference to an object, and that Joe's judgment always tallied with the opinion of experts.

Freer was an inimitable raconteur, with a keen sense of humor. One of his priceless anecdotes was an experience he had had in Japan. Frequently, the head of Yamanaka in Osaka accompanied him, and objects available for purchase were thus made ready for his inspection at various centers he wished to visit. On one trip, however, he had sent word that he wished to be taken by Yamanaka only to great private collections, avoiding anything that was for sale. Freer declared he had spent a wonderful month, for Yamanaka had kept strictly to the agreement. After settling his expense account and saying good-by to Yamanaka, he received word of a three-day delay in the departure of his ship.

Becoming very bored, he had summoned Yamanaka to take him

sight-seeing, without making any conditions. They had gone to a tumble-down temple on the outskirts of Tokyo, where a pathetic priest, threadbare and looking hungry, showed him about. Freer was entranced, he said, by a painting in an alcove. "Could the priest be persuaded to sell it?" he had asked Yamanaka, who promptly inquired whether he was released from the former conditions. He was, Freer had replied.

Freer bought the painting, then other rooms were opened, and in each were magnificent objects.

"Haven't I seen that man at a dealer's in Osaka?" he asked, and pointing to others, "in shops at Nikko, Kyoto, and Nara?"

"Yes," admitted Yamanaka.

"He had heard of the delayed sailing," Freer said, "and the best in the market had been hastily gathered, on the chance I might ask to see antiquities. I purchased them all," Freer ended with a chuckle.

Freer spoke at length and excitedly about the recent acceptance of his offer to give the entire collection at his death to the Smithsonian Institution in Washington. He was to erect the building, which was to be named for him but maintained by the federal government. He informed us that this innovation in the nature of Smithsonian collections had taken Theodore Roosevelt's personal intervention as president before it was agreed to by the authorities concerned.

His decision for Washington was based, he said, on the fact that endless numbers of people came to the capital from all over our country and from abroad. He realized it was a drifting population, there for a political purpose or as tourists. Even so, his premise was that a gallery containing a comprehensive collection of Asian art might attract a different kind of visitor, interested in culture. His determination had been strengthened, he declared, by Herbert Putnam (my uncle), as librarian of Congress, who had successfully instituted an informal luncheon club in the Library which distinguished visitors took time to attend. Also members of Congress were proud to bring their important constituents to listen to discussions on scholarly matters.

In the hours we were with Freer among his cherished art treasures he was serene and apparently a man at peace within himself. We had only one real outing with him, just before boarding our train. He had spoken of a park near the center of Detroit which was open to the public on Sunday for picnics, and he wanted to show us how it looked the following morning.

On this occasion we saw an entirely different side of his character. He flew into a fit of temper at his chauffeur for being a few minutes late, and when we were caught in traffic jams, he became dangerously purple in the face, from loss of self-control, and was arrogant and unreasonable. But he was in a delightful mood when we got out of the motor at a number of places where he led us over lawns and past benches on patios. There was no refuse in sight nor any scattered newspapers. "That's the way the picnickers leave the Park Sunday evenings," he said with civic pride, adding, "It was I who insisted on this privilege for the people against the strong opposition of the city fathers."

Years passed without our again seeing Freer. Then we lunched with him after his move to a New York hotel when he had become a confirmed invalid. He talked intermittently to Joe, with an occasional flash of gaiety about a trip to the interior of China. When Charles Platt came in with some blueprints for the Washington gallery, Freer brightened and pointed out on the plans the proposed installations for his collection, the fulfillment of which, however, he was not to live to see.

The Freer Gallery (opened in 1923) was created for the avowed purpose of placing his oriental treasures on exhibition or making them available for study in storage. On permanent view were his Whistler paintings, etchings, and the bizarre Peacock Room that had aroused a furor of interest at the time of its purchase. There were also pictures of three other American artists: Dwight Tryon's landscapes, Thomas Dewing's interiors, and Thayer's large canvases of figures. The entire collection was an expression of Freer himself.

On the other hand, Andrew Mellon's later gift to the government had a fundamentally different aim. He wished to establish in Washington a National Gallery of Art where his own masterpieces of a rare order would cover but a small amount of exhibition space in a building that extended a number of blocks. Mellon's premise was that his own pictures would attract similar gifts to a government-owned gallery that bore no man's name.

The addition of the superb pictures presented by Joseph Widener maintained the high quality established by the Mellon Collection, enhanced by his Hermitage pictures from Russia. Personally, I would have preferred to see both the Mellon and Widener treasures in less ornate surroundings, but with all the other paintings on exhibition as carefully selected. To me, a setting unrivaled for splendor in any government museum, with enormous marble columns in a great court, having brilliant green as the predominant color, distracted attention from the paintings.

Joe's and my slight acquaintance with Andrew Mellon commenced in Pittsburgh soon after the turn of the century, when Joe was to give two lectures on Egypt in the museum. We were visiting the wife of a steel magnate, who told us with manifest satisfaction that we were to dine with Mellon but he had begged off from attending one of Joe's lectures.

Mellon was rather short and slight with clearly defined features, grey hair and mustache, and he positively bristled with intellect and character. There was something about his fragility and avoidance of publicity that reminded me, as a casual impression, of Freer. Mellon's home was large but not pretentious, and his taste in pictures centered on Dutch landscapes and portraits by English painters, none of them of noticeable significance.

He was an agreeable host but rather taciturn. The seriousness of his demeanor visibly lessened when, during the meal, Joe was telling his neighbor one of his Egyptian tomb adventures, which attracted general attention, including Mellon's. I was seated on his left and Mellon remarked to me with obvious surprise, "I did not realize an Egyptian tomb could be amusing." Incidentally, when he appeared at Joe's second lecture his presence created quite a stir.

It was during the latter part of Mellon's term as secretary of the Treasury that he began the purchase of pictures destined for the National Gallery. Several times, when Joe and I were being shown these masterpieces hanging on the walls of a number of rooms in a

Washington apartment, Mellon came in to greet us. He appeared to have a detached attitude towards his art treasures and to derive no personal pleasure in being surrounded by them.

This doubtless was an over-hasty conclusion by one who, like myself, was accustomed to having art possessions talked about on visits to their enthusiastic owners. Henry Clay Frick, in his huge North Shore establishment in Massachusetts, apparently thoroughly enjoyed himself while escorting his guests through his many galleries while he related pertinent anecdotes connected with his purchases. It was the same with John G. Johnson of Philadelphia. Once inside his hospitable front door, he talked of little but his art collection.

But the name to conjure with among art collectors was that of J. Pierpont Morgan. In his art transactions, as in cornering the market, he brooked no rivals. His tastes were those of a man from a refined cultural background and were extremely varied. For months before his expected arrival at a given place, dealers would sell to no one else, knowing his indifference to what he paid for something he wanted. Even after his departure, prices skyrocketed, on the chance that he would send back for an object he had seen but had not purchased. Joe and I saw this happen in many places.

We were fortunate that, on the few occasions we saw Morgan, it was with friends of his. The first time was after the Philip Schuylers and the Weir Mitchells had been with us in Japan and we were visiting all together in the Schuylers' delightful old family home at Ardsley-on-Hudson. John Cadwalader, a brother of Mrs. Mitchell's, brought Morgan to Sunday lunch, and John Shaw Billings, at the time head of the New York Public Library, was also present.

At sight, I found Morgan rather overwhelming. A high silk hat and long black coat made him look even taller than his actual height of six feet. In build he was noticeably heavy. The darkness of his thick eyebrows and mustache accentuated hair which was already white and gave signs of approaching baldness. I did not dare meet the direct gaze of his black, penetrating eyes for fear of seeming to stare at his conspicuously deformed nose.

At the table, Morgan was genially talking about books to Billings, who looked the librarian, with a strong face and serious eyes. But of the three men, it was Cadwalader who was the impressive figure. Aristocratic features made up for a lack of stature, and a courtesy of manner that has long since ceased to exist seemed incompatible with his reputation as the ablest and the shrewdest New York lawyer of his day.

I noticed that Morgan listened attentively to what Cadwalader had to say about recent law decisions. Morgan among friends seemed neither formidable nor autocratic.

It was Cadwalader who took us for a long afternoon in Morgan's library. He received us in the perfect setting of the West Room, where ancient red brocade on the walls was a wonderful background for Renaissance and other period paintings. He extracted from a vault a number of extraordinary manuscripts, and it was a rare treat to watch him seated at his desk handling them reverently and with absorbed interest as he gave us comprehensive descriptions of each. In the happy environment of his library one could get a genuine impression of the human side of Morgan—the greatest and most patriotic of American financiers.

What was to develop into a real friendship with John G. Johnson began when Joe and I were staying with the Mitchells. Mrs. Mitchell and I dined elsewhere one evening, when the doctor was having a large stag dinner for Joe. Unfortunately, the guest of honor committed a *faux pas* from ignorance. Joe simply failed to comply with what used to be an established ceremonial at the end of a formal dinner. The table was completely cleared and lights turned low. As port was solemnly brought in, the only conversation was expected to be about its vintage and flavor. But Joe continued a story he was telling Johnson.

"The port has arrived Joe," his host observed.

"Has it?" replied Joe carelessly, who went right on talking.

"We will wait until you are ready for the port to be served," Mitchell had to say before Joe's voice ceased. Johnson was greatly amused by the incident, which he thought indicated in Joe an originality. As a strong individualist it appealed to him.

In the pre-World War I years, twice when Joe had professional engagements in Philadelphia he managed to take time off to spend several nights with Johnson in his South Broad Street rambling house, and I was with him.

Johnson was a heavy man, ungainly in build, with a noticeably large head, prominent features, and rather an untidy mustache. He was bursting with good spirits, and although he was over seventy when we knew him, he was singularly youthful in his outlook on life.

In a long legal career, he had been considered in a class by himself both as a corporation lawyer and a member of the Supreme Court.

He was unique as an art collector in refusing to patronize the dealers who sold to the very rich. He preferred to rely on his own judgment, based on infinite study and backed up by friends among scholars who were experts on special schools of art. He was blunt in speech, and his comments about the fabulous prices paid for great pictures were inimitable. As he put it to us, Morgan and others looked upon the buying of art very much as they looked upon competition in big business ventures, or as society women might develop rivalry in obtaining rare jewels. He himself bought to prove the worth of less spectacular art.

His wife had died and he ran the house probably more informally than when she was there to restrain his unconventionality. I never had seen, or would see again, in anyone's home such a bewildering array of pictures. Escape from them was impossible. They were not only hanging on every inch of wall throughout the premises but were stacked in corridors and closets. In the guest room allotted to us, a large wardrobe for clothes was filled to overflowing with canvases. Some of the choicest pictures were in Johnson's bedroom, and it was there that Joe paid special obeisance to the first and rarest painting by that rare Flemish master, Jan van Eyck, ever to come to America.

Johnson's memory was astounding, for he frequently demonstrated his ability to locate at will any pictures mentioned in a conversation. Joe, during his early education in the art of the past on trips abroad with Denman Ross, had been thoroughly indoctrinated in masterpieces of the great schools. This caused Johnson to appreci-

149

ate Joe's knowledge and enthusiasm. The first evening, with a rapid step unusual for so heavy a man, he took Joe all over the house. I tagged behind them as our host dragged invaluable canvases from unexpected places, handling them with the skill of an expert.

Johnson was known as a tremendous reader. After saying good-night to us, he disappeared into his library, and it was almost three in the morning when I heard him coming upstairs.

Next evening, the hours passed pleasantly for me in a lighter vein. Poker was another of Johnson's keen interests. On learning accidentally at dinner that I was also a poker addict, he abruptly left the table and shortly I heard his voice on a hall telephone: "I've arranged a poker game," he said. It was decidedly late, or rather early morning, when the game broke up. I was relieved at having managed to do slightly better than hold my own in a contest against him and other experienced opponents in a game where the stakes were decidedly high for me.

Seeing the art collection of Benjamin Altman in his house came about by chance, and, like the experience of the Morgan Library, through Cadwalader, who was devoted to his sister Maria (Mrs. Weir Mitchell), and because of her affection for both Joe and me, accepted us on an intimate basis. In the early years of our married life, Joe's theatrical performances and lecture engagements took him often to New York. We were always welcome guests of Cadwalader's on short notice. He was to introduce us to many collectors and their treasures.

He was a confirmed bachelor whose home surroundings and way of life belonged to the late Victorian era among the gentry. There was no display, but taste and comfort combined in spacious well-proportioned rooms containing many choice objects that repaid careful study.

An eminently respectable English couple, grown elderly in Cadwalader's service, belonged to the setting. Horn, the butler, who also valeted his master, had an ability in typing that made him invaluable in matters of a privileged legal character. The wife was housekeeper, and in spite of acute suffering from rheumatism, kept a strict control over demure young maid servants in becoming caps and aprons. Before Joe's Newport days, this was the only house where he was assigned a valet, much to his embarrassment and far beyond the qualifications of his modest wardrobe.

On our first stay, we arrived after Joe had produced an evening charity benefit. Horn opened the door and graciously offered the apologies of our host for having retired for the night. He was an impressive figure as he served us delicious food and a refreshing vintage wine in the library. Mrs. Horn answered my bell the following morning, and I sleepily ordered breakfast. She looked surprised but left the room without comment, soon to return, saying that Mr. Cadwalader expected me to breakfast with him at nine o'clock. "This is fifteen minutes longer than he has ever waited for a guest," she added, as a probably successful incentive to getting me out of bed.

The housekeeper informed me that she personally looked after special guests like myself. It was a period when tight-fitting gowns were fastened by hooks and eyes the length of the back. Her exit line was a plea for an extra fifteen minutes, as her fingers were stiff.

I entered a morning room flooded with sunlight. Joe continued to read a paper but Cadwalader laid his aside to greet me. Events happened as in the opening scene of a period play. Horn had placed the food on the table and withdrawn, but soon the door was reopened by him to announce that the bootmaker had arrived. Cadwalader explained that breakfast was his only available time to attend to purely personal matters. The bootmaker was a solemn-faced Englishman, who proceeded to measure Cadwalader's foot for handmade boots while he selected the leather for several pair. Our host's clothes were noticeably well chosen, and when a tailor, also English, appeared I saw why. Cadwalader paid meticulous attention to a wide range of samples, and then we were again alone with him.

The table was cleared and we had lingered on, but Horn came back in visible agitation, followed by a young woman strikingly beautiful and much upset. "The butler tried to keep me out," she acknowledged frankly, "but I had to see you to persuade you to handle my divorce." She forestalled Cadwalader's refusal by saying she realized he did not take such cases, but hers was different.

Our host left the room with her but in about fifteen minutes he was with us again. He said rather deprecatingly that in accepting her case he had made it clear he could not appear personally in the proceedings. "She was so helpless and attractive," he said, by way of excuse for yielding to impulsiveness.

He then proceeded to glance hastily through a bulky mail, sorting it for the attention of a trim young woman secretary whom he had summoned. One opened envelope he continued to hold in his hand remarking to Joe that he wondered what B. Altman, the head of the department store bearing his name, had to say to him. The letter was a suggestion that Cadwalader spare the time to come to his house to look at pictures he owned. From this he inferred that Altman might be considering a gift to the Metropolitan Museum. "Has he any famous paintings, Joe?" he asked, admitting to a lack of familiarity with masterpieces.

"He's in the market for Rembrandts," Joe replied.

At this answer, Cadwalader spoke to Altman personally on the telephone and made an appointment for the three of us to go to his house that afternoon.

At the time, Altman was unknown socially in New York. He told us that it was as a relaxation from business that he had bought Rembrandts and other extremely valuable masterpieces, as well as rare oriental pieces for his own pleasure. Long since they have been made available to the public at the Metropolitan Museum in New York, in a gallery known as the Altman Collection.

17

FENWAY COURT

IT WAS MY PRIVILEGE to have seen the curtain-raiser, as it were, to Fenway Court. This was in the early fall of 1898, when, after our first meeting in Dublin, Joe came to Boston with me to put me on the midnight train for New York.

He took me to dine with the John L. Gardners on their Brookline estate. Mrs. Gardner greeted us in the front hall, then led us into a room where she wanted to show Joe some recently acquired Venetian objects that were effective.

As she talked to Joe, I watched from a distance, interested in this woman about whom I had already heard a great deal. She was of medium height, graceful in her movements, her splendid figure shown to advantage by a simply draped, sleeveless black evening gown, which revealed arms that were extraordinarily lovely. At her throat was a magnificent ruby, her only ornament.

Her face, with wide-set eyes and full lips, was distinguished by an apparent strength of character rather than beauty. One of her greatest assets was a low toned, richly modulated voice.

My first impression was that Mrs. Gardner knew instinctively the importance of being herself. And in years to come I was to see many times at first hand the electrifying quality of her presence among people of all kinds.

In the drawing room, Jack Gardner rose from an armchair to welcome Joe affectionately. He was a portly, kind looking man, with penetrating eyes and a long mustache. Isabella Gardner took this chance to draw me aside to say, "Joe has never asked to bring a girl to dine before—are you engaged?"

But there was more to this than a startling frankness. It was an

153

immediate understanding between us and a sense of ease in each other's presence that was to me as pleasant as it was unexpected. "I don't know," I replied with an equal frankness.

Mrs. Gardner was about to say something further when Jack came up to me with Joe. It was a merry dinner. He cared for good food and wine without pushing it too far. She was indifferent to both.

For my benefit, both of them reminisced about incidents occurring on one of Joe's trips with them after his Paris studio days. Soon, however, the conversation was obviously a continuation of numerous previous ones on the all-engrossing subject of housing Mrs. Gardner's increasingly valuable art treasures. I gathered, from what I heard as an interested listener, that Jack did not consider the middle of a residential block on Beacon Street a suitable place to combine living quarters and an art collection rapidly becoming important. Isabella, however, was still favorably inclined to the proposition.

She interrupted him as he referred to the advantage of a site with open space around it, permitting light from windows on four sides of the building. She told him not to be "practical," or he might tempt her to invent a new system of lighting. To him, apparently, this was a warning signal. The subject was dropped and other matters were discussed.

Unquestionably, they were on the best of terms. Obviously, she relied on his judgment and laughingly told me Jack called her "busy Ella." Then she remarked seriously to Joe that no one knew better than he how Jack had encouraged an Isabella Stewart Gardner collection.

Her husband showed inordinate pride in her ability and achievements and, as I was to learn, was pleased at the admiration she aroused in all men of distinction.

I have remembered as a final scene on that unforgettable evening his eloquent appeal to her imagination in urging her to create a Venetian palace out of barren waste land. I remember, too, a subsequent development. Shortly after his sudden death two months later from a heart attack, she bought the Fenway lot they had inspected together just before I dined with them.

To understand Mrs. Gardner's spectacular career, one must know something about her past. She was the daughter of David Stewart, an enterprising Scotsman. He came to America and made a fortune as an importer of Irish and Scottish merchandise, and later engaged in mining. She came to Boston as a bride, just before the outbreak of the Civil War. Her health was delicate, and she was rather indifferent to formal society.

Dowagers resented her for capturing Boston's most eligible bachelor, so considered both for his wealth and for his impregnable social position. To add to their consternation, it soon became apparent no male could resist her charm, wit, gaiety, and an indefinable fascination that was far above mere beauty. Again, she made no claim to knowledge, but an alert, intelligent mind was immediately recognized by intellectuals as a satisfactory response to scholarship.

Henry Adams, the historian, when he was director of seminar research at Harvard, signalled her out for special devotion; Oliver Wendell Holmes never missed a chance to see her; Charles Eliot Norton instantly made her a member of his select Dante Society. All foreigners of distinction, in any worthwhile field, on Boston visits, spent their spare time in her company.

Neither vain nor conceited, she made no effort to attract male attention. It just came, to the mortification of light-minded women, envious of her when they attempted competition without success. Her wardrobe, for instance, was their despair. Her perfect fitting gowns, with extreme simplicity of line, made them feel over-dressed in her presence. Again, one out of a series of priceless gems, worn alone, caused them to feel over-bejewelled.

A characteristic contrast occurred at a luncheon when one of many of the female guests, wearing a complicated early fall headgear, exclaimed, "Mrs. Gardner, there's nothing on your hat—yet it's just right."

To this Isabella Gardner made the classic retort that it took thought to keep trimming off a hat!

Women were even more frustrated that, at her entrance into a room, people instantly talked of something interesting. She was impatient with the commonplace and at times ruthless in dealing with it. Among women friends with whom she was on intimate terms, she expected and got brains and a range of common interests. But, all her assets considered, it was probably her infinite capacity to listen that provided a large measure of her attractiveness and the real strength she possessed as an antagonist. A man found her rapt attention to what he was saying entrancing at a dinner table, where most of the women were talking too much.

What astounded men and women alike was having her every desire apparently satisfied by the birth of a male child. She was a passionately devoted mother, and with an adoring husband, she was completely happy in retiring to a purely domestic life. The baby's death, a few years later, completely crushed her, especially since according to the medical verdict, she could not bear another child.

Possibly, had the boy lived, there would have been no Fenway Court. As it was, recovery for normal activities was slow. Finally, Charles Eliot Norton persuaded her to resume collecting rare volumes about Dante, for the most part. But this renewed interest proved to be only a transitory one.

In intensive travels abroad with her husband, planned by him to keep her from living with her sorrow, she began to lose herself in the companionship of cultural leaders, who stirred her imagination. In addition, she discovered in herself an unexpected ability for evaluating great schools of art, represented in the museums of Europe. This she found an absorbing pastime in the development of both taste and definite art convictions of her own.

Jack encouraged a craving on her part to own important specimens of art. It was in this mood that in 1886 she met Whistler in London. She posed for a pastel portrait, and he presented her with his first slight sketches for the famous Peacock Room. It was Henry James who took her to Sargent's studio in Paris in 1888. During the process of Sargent's painting her portrait, they began a friendship that was to mean much to both of them.

It was knowing Sargent that made her seriously consider becoming a patron of artists, an idea that was to crystalize on her acquaintance with Anders Zorn and Paul Bourget, both of whom became her friends.

When Mancini was down and out, Sargent sent him to the Gardners. He painted Jack's portrait and left Boston on his feet because of a generous present of gilt-edged securities.

Altogether Isabella had become thoroughly alive again!

It seems appropriate to comment here on the portraits of Isabella Gardner painted by Sargent and Zorn—at about the same time. Sargent's has been much publicized and is installed in the place of honor in the magnificent Gothic Room of Fenway Court.

She is painted standing in a black, tightly fitted evening gown, with a string of large, priceless pearls reaching below the waist. To me it is a portrait of a dashing society woman—nothing more.

But Zorn had caught an intangible something in her spirit that set her apart from other women. She is again standing, a loose white gown of sheer material giving the illusion that she is stepping forward, with outstretched arms waving white draperies before she pauses in the room for a passing moment.

The same idea of aloofness was to be expressed years later by Okakura the Japanese Sage in one of many poems he dedicated to her when he was on the staff of the Boston Museum. He described her as "Alone! White! A cloud."

Curiously enough, Sargent was to express the same feeling of her detachment in a sketch he did of her long after, about a year before her death in 1924. She was seated, helpless physically, her shriveled body as well as her head wrapped in white draperies. Nothing showed except her face, which had a marvelous expression of elation.

On her return home in 1886, her keen interest was aroused in young Bernard Berenson, ambitious and a genius but without funds to study art abroad upon his graduation from Harvard in 1887. She sent him to his destiny. Shortly he became an acknowledged expert in the attributions of old masters.

Berenson soon evidenced an instinct for being on the inside track of unique masterpieces for sale. Mrs. Gardner followed his every move with eager interest, and on her father's death, a large inheritance from his estate provided funds for her acquisitions of great importance—bought for her by Berenson. She was still with no intention beyond owning paintings for her own enjoyment.

During the year 1896 she became the proud owner of a Tintoretto, the world acclaimed "Rape of Europa," by Titian, and a Boticelli, to be followed by a Raphael, a Rubens, a Holbein, a Rembrandt, a head of Christ by Georgione and a Velasquez, all obtained through Berenson. It was these paintings that forced her inevitably to think in terms of a Museum, which I had heard her discuss with Jack.

Soon after Jack's death, a latent dynamic energy resulted in a driving urge to create something Venetian in character, by her own efforts, a gigantic task from which she did not falter. Joe believed that the determining factor that kept her going against every obstacle was the recognition of her capability to carry to completion a great purpose evidenced in the wording of Jack's will.

He had not wished her to be handicapped by a lack of funds in case of need. Therefore she was authorized to demand at any time any part of the principal of his very large estate, left in trust for members of his family after her life interest in it.

This permission was much talked about at the time, on the assumption that, like most collectors, Isabella Gardner would become recklessly extravagant. But those like Joe who knew her intimately were confident she never would spend her late husband's principal, no matter what the temptation—and she never did.

As an artist who had traveled extensively abroad with Isabella Gardner, Joe recognized that she alone, among individuals, possessed the essential qualifications to achieve a Fenway Court. Among them were a sense of proportion, rare artistic taste, and an instinct for construction. He also realized she had the patience and gaiety of spirit to get fun out of a job of selection which she refused to delegate. Her determination caused her to spend endless time picking up in Italy the fragments from old palaces needed in construction.

These pieces comprised columns, capitals, pilasters, arches, staircases, balustrades, and iron grille work. Each must be perfect of its kind, of the same period, and they must harmonize with the others. Later these pieces were to be supplemented by furniture, brocades, and other furnishings meeting the same qualifications, and found by the same painstaking process of search.

Above all Isabella Gardner had the extraordinary gift of having the image of the building so clearly in mind that she knew exactly where each purchase was to be placed. Only in this way could a detail become an integral part of the structure her genius was to make a reality.

In this exacting work she offset the loneliness caused by the loss of her congenial companion of many years, from whom she had seldom been separated.

The architect William T. Sears revised the blueprints, prepared according to her plans for the Beacon Street site, her original choice, from which I had heard Jack dissuade her. The lot, being on the corner of the Fenway and Worthington Street, allowed windows on all sides, as Jack had advocated. Also space for a music room, and later, the buying of the adjacent lot made possible a lovely "Monk's garden."

Her ideas called for having the new living quarters a reproduction of the rooms she and Jack had occupied in Beacon Street. For this purpose, she had everything removable torn out of the former residence, such as woodwork carved especially for her, and fireplaces. Architectural details which would have served to perpetuate her personality, but which could not be removed, she had destroyed before disposing of the property. Eben D. Jordan, who bought it, agreed to renumber the house 150 since she wished 152 Beacon Street to remain associated with hers and Jack's name.

During Isabella's absence, building operations ceased. She was on the grounds all day until the completion of every detail. The construction, as well as the architectural blueprints, was a complete expression of herself. She gave the actual orders to the artisans, wielded a paint brush or an axe with equal dexterity and ingenuity, in demonstrating to each expert exactly how she wanted him to do a specific job, and kept an eagle eye on him to be sure he did it.

She brought her lunch, like the workmen, and ate and drank barley water with them, keeping their hours. They obeyed her implicitly, more from respect than fear, and considered her one of themselves.

I will always feel grateful that she gave me the privilege more than once, during the crucial stage of construction in 1902, of seeing her in action when we were settled in Boston again. It was during this time that our first child was born, a girl named Rebecca for my mother.

At unexpected moments, when garbed for a social event, I scuffed good shoes and ripped new gowns in attempting to keep Isabella's pace, while my stunned amazement grew at the vastness and variety of her self-assigned tasks, each one of which she never failed to conquer. For instance, I was breathless when, taking me into the Gothic room, she pointed to beautiful, hand-hewn beams of enormous size supporting the ceiling. She casually remarked that it had been necessary for her to mount a very high ladder, axe in hand, to show the expert at work exactly how she wanted the surfaces to look, which was at complete variance with what he was doing. As usual, her effect was the correct one.

Among the workmen was an Italian known as Bolgi, who displayed such skill and interest in handling fragments from his native land, and such tact with fellow workmen, that she appointed him foreman. In this capacity, he proved such an efficient ally in carrying out her wishes that he remained on as superintendent of Fenway Court during her lifetime and long afterwards.

He was at her side, and silently on her side, as she gave many bad moments to the contractor and architect by countermanding their orders, necessitating much tearing down and other fundamental changes. She disliked steel construction and city inspectors alike, and Bolgi was useful to her at the times she was compelled to compromise with the dictates of inspectors.

Isabella Gardner's tension disappeared when Bolgi, on his own initiative, pressed Joe into willing service as his handy man and personal assistant in the unpacking of the cases containing the precious fragments from Italy, with priority being given to the endless columns as features of the main floor. Also, in the delicate process of placing the fragments and getting sculptures in position, Joe acted under Bolgi's directions.

By Christmas, plants growing in the large and impressive glass-roofed court gave an air of festivity to a Fenway Court now approaching order. Isabella, who was an Anglo-Catholic, had planned to take Communion on Christmas Eve in the chapel, and to have dinner served in her private apartments to a few friends. Despite all the work entailed, she took time off to invite herself to Christmas breakfast with us, a resumption of a former custom.

To the Smith family, this Christmas breakfast was a solemn commemoration of a magnificent purpose achieved. That afternoon, she sent for Joe and me. For an hour the three of us wandered about Fenway Court.

She drew attention to the fact that her bedroom was an exact replica of her former one, even to Joe's water-color copy of Sancta Caterina in a frame made by his brother Bert, placed on a gondola seat at the foot of her bed, with a bunch of violets beside it.

Joe and I were in Rome on that evening in February, 1903, so long awaited by Bostonians for the first formal showing of Fenway Court. Repercussions of extravagant praise reached us. The philosopher William James found in Fenway Court a "moral influence, elevating the character of all who entered." But Joe had stressed the physical cost to Isabella. He wrote her, "An avalanche of masterpieces in a perfect setting, created for them at the price of your superhuman struggle and self-sacrifice."

To me, even more exciting than being Joe's companion in Rome, visiting well-known dealers and art galleries, was the frequently rewarding search for treasures for Fenway Court, among inconspicuous antique shops or tumbled-down, half-deserted villas. In this activity he said, I think over-generously, that I was an "untrained understudy" for Isabella Gardner.

Soon after our arrival, he found during our prowling about a terra cotta Madonna and Child, Italian fifteenth century. He explained to Isabella that in modern times flesh-colored paint applied to the face and body of Christ had obscured the identity. By his personal supervision of the removal of the paint, the terra cotta was restored to its pristine beauty.

That May in London, where our second girl Frances was born, Joe bought an Italian primitive for Mrs. Gardner, discovered in the shop of an elderly Italian. He described it as being as large as a grand piano—Madonna and Child with saints around her—full of strong individual character—absolutely untouched canvas—marks of a cruel past treatment that can be removed by a little loving care. It is signed and dated.

+ Anno — DNI — Millo — Settimo — Julianus — Pictor — Dearimino — fecit — Octopus — Tempori — Dni — Clementis — pp QUINTI +

It has been said that this is the only known work by this master with a signature and date.

A picture adventure of a very different nature occurred this same visit. On a Sunday morning Joe and I presented an introduction to Forbes-Robertson, the actor. We were admitted to a corner house on an important square, where we were received by a man who introduced himself as a brother of the actor, who was away for the day. We had accepted hospitality for lunch, and in the dining room Joe could not keep his eyes off an enormous painting of a Descent from the Cross. He finally remarked to the host that it was unexpected to find such a magnificent Rembrandt in private ownership. To this he replied that he had been tempted far beyond his means and had decided to sell the painting. Whereupon Joe immediately asked for a refusal for Mrs. Gardner, on a cable answer. Forbes-Robertson agreed, provided Wilhelm Bode, of the Berlin Museum, did not exercise his option, already given. Mrs. Gardner had cabled back to buy the Rembrandt, and Bode had been communicated with for his immediate decision.

There the matter stood, when Joe, delighted with his primitive, went back to the old Italian to see what else he had. There was available, he was told, a superb Rembrandt, a Descent from the Cross, but it would take a few days to produce it from where it was. To Joe's expressed amazement that there was a second one on the market, the Italian enquired whether he had been shown the masterpiece at the palace of the Duke of Devonshire, who owned it, or at Forbes-Robertson's. He also informed Joe that the commission would be very moderate, if purchased through him, whereas Forbes-Robertson's, because of his style of living, would be big.

But Bode exercised his option and the Rembrandt was lost to America.

During the winter season of 1904, the Smith family was back at the Ludlow with the two small children.

Gone was the era loved by the gossips and reflected in the press, relating to Mrs. Gardner's escapades, the direct consequences of freedom from inhibition, a sense of fun, and a lawless spirit.

Hers was a defiant demonstration that she intended to live among Bostonians on her terms, not theirs. Fenway Court was immediately accepted on these terms, and Boston was generous in admitting that the achievement was that of a creative genius, a daring spirit whom the city could never have produced.

The unique feature of Fenway Court was a collection of masterpieces, ranking with those of the foremost museums, but here seen in the kind of surroundings with which one associated them before they had reached a museum. In these rooms, medieval in feeling, gathered artists, musicians, philosophers, scientists, on every occasion dominated and enlivened by the personality of a woman.

Mrs. Potter Palmer of Chicago and Mrs. Gardner were often mentioned as belonging to the same category of prominent American women. But as far as I could judge they had no common characteristics. For instance, Mrs. Palmer was an ideal chairman of civic committees, with adoring females as her subordinates. Mrs. Gardner, on the other hand, firmly refused all such responsibilities, but as a lone sponsor she could put anything across.

Mrs. Palmer had demonstrated an unusual ability in organization and administration as chairman of the Lady Board of Managers of the Chicago Exposition. Her ambition for social recognition was realized and became international when President McKinley appointed her the only Lady Commissioner to the Paris Exhibition in 1900.

Soon she was having private audiences with queens, and even played a round of golf with King Edward VII. Mrs. Gardner cared for creative genius, rather than royalty, equally available to her on trips abroad. Mrs. Palmer sought publicity, but publicity sought Mrs. Gardner's every act. Mrs. Palmer's name was constantly in the society columns, but Mrs. Gardner's was also in the "news," or in feature articles, although she refused to be interviewed.

But to return to art, the thrill of Joe's purchasing career was securing for Fenway Court the Hercules by Piero della Francesca. Volpi, a dealer in Florence, had taken him to see this single heroic figure in the form of a fresco at Borgo San Sepulcro. Successful removal from the wall was guaranteed.

This was during the 1903 winter we spent in Rome. Only after three years of tribulations was the Hercules actually in Mrs. Gardner's possession in Paris, eventually to reach Boston under appalling circumstances—a story in itself.

Even though it had been sold before the Italian government passed a law listing masterpieces that could not leave the country, officials refused to let the Hercules go, since by mistake it was included on the list. It was not until the winter of 1906 that Joe wrote her the Hercules had been delivered to Robert, her Paris agent. "Would that Boston was as free as Paris to welcome it," he added. This was a reference to the recent decision of Leslie M. Shaw, secretary of the Treasury, that duties must be paid on works of art imported by Fenway Court. Before it had been incorporated as a museum, duties were paid without question. This unfair decision was a severe blow which forced Mrs. Gardner to store her most expensive acquisitions in Paris.

At this time, she was particularly handicapped for funds. She had arranged to pay for the Piero della Francesca by installments, and four tapestries from the Foulke Collection had been a drain on her purse. With other unsettled indebtedness, she was in a mood of feeling very poor when she accepted the suggestion of a young woman compatriot whom she casually met in London, where her compatriot had rented an enormous house on a long lease.

This was for Mrs. Gardner to relieve herself of the heavy financial burden of storage and insurance on some of her most valuable possessions. These would be gladly assumed by her new-found friend, in return for temporary possession of priceless works of art. Soon the Hercules, tapestries, and other treasures were installed in England.

Three years passed. Joe was spending a few leisure summer days with Mrs. Gardner in Brookline when one afternoon their privacy was interrupted by an uncouth individual with an aggressive manner, appearing unannounced. He displayed a badge of the U. S. Customs. "You own a Piero della Francesca!" he burst out rudely, murdering the pronunciation, "Four tapestries and . . ." he proceeded to read from a sheet of paper a list of what Mrs. Gardner had on loan in London.

Mrs. Gardner gave a gesture of dismissal to the unpleasant intruder, but volunteered a curt, "Yes, in London, but I can't see . . ."

He broke in insolently, "You can't get away with that talk—they are in the Customs shed in Chicago, as you know full well."

I got the other end of this extraordinary story from the elder half-brother of the London American, a wealthy Chicagoan. This was it! He received a cable from his sister, saying she was coming home for good. He had met her steamer in New York, in the intense heat of midsummer. She was surrounded by an endless array of enormous packing cases on the dock, the contents of which she referred to vaguely as "household goods, mostly pots and pans." He had everything sent through in bond to the Chicago Customs, where he did a lot of business.

On notice of arrival, he went to the receiving shed of Customs, and the head examiner promptly signed a release to the invoice, on his declaration that there was nothing dutiable in it. This formality over, they were walking together towards the nearest exit, when the examiner's eye, by chance, caught sight of the original case, in which the ill-fated Hercules had started his travels from Florence, with all the foreign labels still on it! The sister declared her ignorance of the customs regulations of her own country and had wanted to give Mrs. Gardner a "pleasant surprise."

Before Mrs. Gardner's property could be released, she had to pay the federal government, cash down, $150,000. She refused a refund from the offender's brother, or to accept the generous offer from her husband's Gardner beneficiaries to take the amount from his estate. Joe remembered her mentioning this financial catastrophe to him only once. She had said it took a "stiff upper lip" to resist assistance but she was sustained by the knowledge it was the right decision.

But in the years immediately preceding this disaster, she had continued to buy, mostly through Berenson, old masters such as "Pope Leo X" by Velasquez, and two Gentile Bellinis, one of them a priceless drawing of a Moslem prince. Her Whistlers had accumulated, and even after the Hercules affair, Berenson tempted her with Manet's portrait of his mother, a superb Degas, several Corots, but no Millet, who was an artist she disliked. She acquired them all. With Henry Adams' assistance, she secured a stained-glass window, probably the best in the United States.

I had a rare opportunity to become familiar with the contents of Fenway Court, because as one of Mrs. Gardner's younger friends, I served as a guardian-usher on the occasions it was opened to the public. The hours were strenuous, being from ten in the morning until three in the afternoon, and at these openings Mrs. Gardner was a bundle of nerves.

From my experience, I considered her lament entirely justified that the American public "saw with the fingers." Unlike the usual run of museums, the aspect which gave its unique charm to Fenway Court was the informality in the arrangement of rare objects and hangings which made them within reach. She seemed to find me quick in detecting an intent to commit an act of vandalism, and my job was a roving commission to stop the "patting" of an object. And to eject from the building, with as little commotion as possible, anyone I thwarted in an attempt to obtain a surreptitious souvenir by means of scissors or penknife. At one opening there had been a trying series of outrageous behavior, and in passing, I noticed Mrs. Gardner was near the breaking point.

I entered the Titian Room, where a young woman, timid looking, almost pathetic, was gazing at the "Rape of Europa," her face actually transfigured. On observing she was about to jot down something in a minute notebook, I was about to inform her kindly this was against the regulations, when Mrs. Gardner pounced down upon her like a fury, shouting, "Don't you know you are breaking a rule?"

The poor creature cringed in terror and soon fled from the room. I later returned breathless from a fruitless search for her, to hear Mrs. David Kimball, a friend of Mrs. Gardner's, voicing a protest.

"She intended no harm," she asserted. Then she went on to say that this was an intelligent school teacher in a Worcester high school, eager to improve herself, whom she befriended as an unknown benefactor by making it possible to get to museums. She was always present to enjoy her protegée's pleasure. "The beauty of Fenway Court overwhelmed her, and you drove her away," she ended reproachfully.

"What's her name and the number of the high school?" Mrs. Gardner inquired.

Mrs. Kimball was so flustered about what had happened that, at this unexpected manifestation of interest, she could remember neither. But Mrs. Gardner, with infinite patience, located both by telephone calls. She wrote to invite the little school teacher to spend a day entirely alone at Fenway Court, with lunch served. She could take all the notes she wished. She greeted her guest on her arrival from Worcester by an early morning train, and was back to take her to the station again in the late afternoon.

This is but one example of Mrs. Gardner's consideration, which lessened the drab existence of many insignificant people. In few enterprises did she take more satisfaction than active sponsorship of tenement garden contests, with prizes awarded at Fenway Court.

The Music Room was continuing to play a prominent role in the cultural life of Boston. Here the Boston Symphony had played more than once. Pianists, singers, violinists of international reputation were heard. Arts and letters had not been overlooked in the programs of lectures. Also Lady Gregory's informal talk about what her Irish Players were attempting to do on the stage assured success for the plays in Boston and elsewhere. The same was true in introducing "Everyman."

When Mrs. Gardner bought the entire sets of the Foulke-Barberini tapestry groups, eleven in all, this meant the eventual demolition of the Music Room, to be replaced by a Tapestry Hall. She had intended to have the transformation done after her death but in buying abroad furnishings and furniture for a Tapestry Hall of the future, she decided it would be fun to make the changes herself.

Possibly the thought of having the available space on the ground level, providing agreeable surroundings for the reception of intimate friends in her declining years, influenced her decision. But I believe the determining factor was an urge again to create. This was in line with her saying, in connection with the many museums revisited on this trip, that she had longed "to reinstall their collections."

I believe, in the final analysis, her underlying purpose was a greater honor to Sargent than having his portrait of her prominently placed. The chance came when Jefferson Coolidge presented her with the masterpiece of Sargent's art career. This was "La Jaleo," a Spanish dancer with a seated group of musicians playing on guitars for her spirited performance. Her plan called for a display of the enormous canvas with a dramatic realism.

She had constructed a Spanish cloister to fill the central place now available, and within was an alcove marked off by a Moorish arch for the installation of the painting. This gave the appearance of a stage with a row of electric lights along the floor, making the effect that of a dancer in action.

Her personal supervision of renewed building activity reminded me of 1902. Once again twelve years later, I saw her at work. Dodge MacKnight had bought for her in Mexico two thousand blue tiles of different designs. These kept her busily engaged in sorting and arranging according to the plan she wished used on the walls of the cloister.

Her final contribution to Fenway Court, this time in the installation of a painting, equalled her former effectiveness in the use of a new creative technique.

18

ROME, THE ETERNAL CITY

EARLY IN NOVEMBER, 1902, the family, Father, Mother, Joe, baby
Rebecca, and I reached Rome from Naples by the southern route
through the Mediterranean. We went to the Piazza di Spagna,
which presented a pageant of simple Italian peasant life. Here all
was gaiety and charm. Smiling girls and young women had dark
eyes, jet black hair, and mobile expressive faces. They wore red and
blue striped skirts, black blouses adorned by multi-colored beads,
and brilliant handkerchiefs wound around their heads. The men's
garments were equally attractive, with bright colored sashes and
shirts, and, generally, they wore long gilt hoops in their ears.

Painters' models, both male and female, were in evidence, with
young artists, distinguishable by long hair and affectation in dress,
watching them. The pleasing aroma of roasting chestnuts was in the
air. The only hard work being done was by wrinkled old women
bent over from bundles of faggots on their backs.

Joe had chosen this route to reach the Hotel Eden, high above
the piazza. Idle men soon were carrying our varied assortment of
baggage on their heads up the long flight of steep stairs known then,
as now, as the Spanish Steps. At the hotel our bedrooms, including
a large private, pleasantly furnished salon, all had the dome of
St. Peter's in their view.

Within an hour, Joe and I were entering the Roman Forum
down a steep decline. After a cursory glance at the very tall triumphal arches at the four corners of the Forum, we passed solitary
marble columns and bits of walls with sculptured figures on them,
and stopped before a group of Italian workmen. Joe inquired of
them for Signor Giacomo Boni.

169

"He's down that hole," volunteered one; and another added, "And not to be disturbed."

Joe produced his visiting card and scribbled something on it. "He wants to see me," he said confidently. "Find him at once."

"*Sicuro*," said a keen-eyed, intelligent workman who, taking the card, descended into the pit, which had only a precarious means of entrance and was marked by wide crevices in unevenly projecting rocks. I heard a voice from below repeating:

"Jo-jo, Jo-jo, are you really here?"

"Come up and see for yourself!" Joe shouted back, "And meet my wife."

Blinking in the strong sunlight, a short man with a beard and solemn, very blue eyes emerged, covered with dust and slime. He beamed at Joe, kissing him affectionately on both cheeks.

Joe remarked promptly, "And this is Corinna, my wife."

Ignoring my presence, Boni, with his eyes on Joe and a flush of excitement, went on to say, "Does she like Greek coins? I have some here in my hand found in an amazing stone construction far underground."

Determining to attract Boni's attention, I said firmly, "Of course I like Greek coins and everything else of the ancient world, or I wouldn't be Joe's wife."

Boni grunted approval and showed me a fine collection of Greek coins, their soft glow undiminished by the long centuries. Then he looked me straight in the face and said, "Follow me."

Down the pit the three of us scrambled, Boni with the rapid and certain tread of a mountain goat. My training in entering pits and underground tombs, gained recently in Egypt, stood me in good stead. He led us through winding passages, where I found the obstructions hanging from above the hard way in the semidarkness, by getting bad bumps. We finally were in a kind of mud chamber with a few blocks of marble scattered through it. In rapid Italian, Boni explained the details which made these blocks unique. I understood what he said, and my genuine enthusiasm for his recent discovery appealed to this obviously shy Italian, a genius in archaeology.

"Jo-jo dislikes dates," he stated abruptly. "He does not need them because his instinct guides his interests to the best periods of past ages." He continued emphatically, addressing me, "But you will read what I give you of my reports and then we will talk about them while Joe paints."

It was noon when we came to the surface again with our traveling clothes as disheveled as Boni's working ones were. He took us to his small villa, perched at a height on the edge of the Forum, at the back of which was a garden made attractive by his personal efforts. A large peasant woman with a saucepan in hand rushed out from the back door of the villa and embraced Joe. I took it for granted they had met before. We sat down at a well arranged table and were served plates piled high with steaming hot spaghetti.

After lunch, we went back to the Hotel to clean up and report to the family. Then we returned to the Forum. Boni had insisted on giving me an immediate conception of Imperial Rome, and Joe wanted to select his first subject. The tour started at the far end of the Colosseum. As we walked its length, Boni, in a few eloquent sentences, made me realize the final agony of Christian martyrs, triumphant in death, as they perished for the amusement of the Roman crowds.

Then we were in the Forum again. He told me that the first archaeological interest in the Forum dated back to Renaissance times, when the earliest excavations were made. Unfortunately, before and since that period, and until well into the present era, the Forum had provided a tempting source of marble and other building materials, and had come to be regarded merely as a quarry. He expressed great gratification that King Victor Emmanuel III was extremely interested in archaeology and under his reign there would be no further spoliation.

He produced a small working map of his own and pointed out on it the different levels of civilizations reflected in the inevitable demolitions and erections of new buildings through the ages. Boni was an artist as well as a historian and was facile in the use of charcoal for quick sketches. He created a general idea of the appearance of the Forum, in the period of Emperor Augustus.

Thanks to his sketches, the past captured my imagination, and I could actually visualize basilicas, temples, and other public buildings visible from a great central pavement upon which we stood. To add to the illusion, he identified for me one of the various *rostra* used for funeral orations for the imperial deceased and for festival speeches, and declaimed in Latin one of Cicero's best-known funeral orations!

We ascended a steep incline, originally the Sacred Way, which, after attaining a ridge, finally ended at the forecourt of Nero's great golden house. During our long absence, Joe had had time to draw in a life-size study of the famous Farnese Bull, sculptured in high relief on a great marble slab.

Through the ensuing weeks, I sat beside Joe while he worked, reading Boni's reports, with a dictionary close at hand for the technical terms that my Italian vocabulary did not include. Often Boni joined us, and on such occasions I encouraged his and Joe's reminiscences about their early days together in Italy. Their first meeting took place when Joe was painting a corner of the Doges' Palace in Venice. A young Italian introduced himself as Giacomo Boni and said he had been in charge of recent repairs done to the palace, inside and out, and the Campanile as well. Joe was amazed at restorations which had been carried out so entirely in the spirit of the original construction that he found it hard to distinguish between the new and old workmanship.

Boni attributed his success to the knack of inspiring artisans in his employ with his own enthusiasm for the perfection of what might be considered insignificant detail. His training had been undertaken by John Ruskin, whose genius and energy in large part were responsible for the awakening of Italians to a realization of the need to preserve irreplaceable art treasures of a bygone age. Boni modestly claimed that his selection as curator of art restoration for the Italian government at the age of thirty was due to his having studied harder than Ruskin's other pupils.

Boni told me that he had found Joe an ideal companion on his official inspection tours of monuments, that several times Joe had repaired a delicate design without injuring the surface which he (Boni) had given up attempting. He was so impressed by Joe's skill that he had taken him to see Ruskin, and, with the great man's approval, offered Joe a job as his assistant.

Joe's comment on his refusal was that, much as he loved Italy, he could not bind himself to being there for definite periods of time at regular intervals.

Later that winter we were to see something of Rodolfo Amades Lanciani, from whom Boni had taken over explorations in the Forum after 1900. Lanciani had a gift in popularizing archaeology, he was an excellent talker and writer, and the Lanciani home was a center for those engaged in worthwhile activities.

Boni, on the contrary, lived the life of a recluse, except for entertaining in his villa an occasional scholar and encouraging archaeological students to visit him there. He was self-conscious in speaking English and as his reports on excavations were seldom translated, his discoveries were not as well known as they deserved to be from their importance.

Under Boni's tutoring, I became familiar with the glories of ancient Rome. I particularly reveled in remains of Corinthian columns dating to the Augustan age. I was also greatly intrigued by the later "borrowings" from a previous period. For instance, an altar which a Roman consul had dedicated to Juno was made into a shrine to the Immaculate Virgin. Again, a statue of Mercury had wings applied to its shoulders and became St. Michael the Archangel. This metamorphosis from pagan to Christian use I was later to become familiar with in reverse, in the Near East, where adaptations were made by the Moslems.

I was to find papal Rome of even more vital interest because of the opportunities it afforded for intimate contacts with its majesty and religious traditions. This was brought about quite unexpectedly. When Joe had mentioned to President Theodore Roosevelt that we were going to spend the winter in Rome, the President said that George von Lengerke Meyer, our ambassador, was one of his closest friends, and he volunteered to write personally, asking him to see to it that the Joe Smiths were included in everything interesting.

He described the Ambassador as extraordinarily versatile. He owned the first motor in Rome, a huge Mercedes in which he tore over the *campagna*. He was a great sport and had started a polo club that was being patronized by the younger, less conservative among the princes of the old Italian families. At the same time, he was the only American ambassador ever to be received in papal circles and had learned to speak Italian.

Pope Leo XIII was very frail and his appearances at St. Peter's among the faithful were somewhat curtailed. At one of these services, Ambassador Meyer arranged for Mother and me to be in seats where we could see without being trampled under foot. The Pope, seated in his paladin, was carried by special bearers down a lane through vast crowds and guarded on both sides by papal guards and soldiers. His advent was announced by a row of boys in a balcony over the great entrance door blowing silver trumpets.

We were also fortunate in having an introduction to Cardinal Merry del Val, and in his company, to get a lasting impression of the Vatican. He took us into some of the state and informal apartments. All were of striking dignity, with perfect furniture and matching draperies. He showed us collections of paintings and sculpture exhibited in the seemingly endless galleries. During an hour when the Sistine Chapel was closed to the public while in use by the Vatican, he escorted us inside. A mass was being celebrated for one of the church festivals. No setting could have been more breathtaking, an interior, Greek in the details of its construction, and overhead on the ceiling frescoes by Michelangelo, and from where I sat I faced his "Last Judgment."

Soon after our arrival Sargent wrote Joe, asking him to persuade our American ambassador to give an order for his portrait to Mancini, an Italian artist who was a great genius in portraiture but unfortunately subject to intervals of mental disturbance when he was apt to do erratic things. At the time, he was in Rome greatly in need of commissions. George Meyer consented, provided I was present.

All went well. Mancini was delighted to find that we both spoke Italian; he was gay and interesting in his conversations about art. He was not a rapid painter and the sittings were prolonged, but finally the artist declared the portrait was finished. George Meyer was completely satisfied and wished to take it home with him that

day. He yielded, however, to Mancini's urging to let it remain overnight for the fresh paint to dry.

The next afternoon he and I went together to the studio. We
stared dumbfounded at the portrait. The features were concealed
by a tennis net painted over them and down on to the coat. Mancini
appeared fascinated by his final touches and asked me to pose. He
said he visualized me with a carrot hanging from my nose!

Joe and I were to get an impression of society in Rome during the
final gasp of the late Victorian era. There was a sharp distinction
between the "Whites" (papal circles) and the "Blacks" (government), who were scarcely on speaking terms with one another. At
receptions and dinners given by the latter, we were to meet members
of the diplomatic corps and ranking officials of the Italian government, the least conservative among the Italians with great names,
and English women and Americans with Italian husbands, the latter
predominating; also many wealthy Americans who had established
themselves in Rome or were visitors with the right kinds of introductions.

The Whites, on the other hand, limited their entertainments to
the hierarchy of the Church and *papalini,* as the Catholic families
of Italians with a long church tradition were called—the Borghese,
Colonna, Farnese, and Doria, to name but a few. This Roman society, with its roots in the past, entertained itself with simple evening
gatherings, with light refreshments served and the daughters of the
house charmingly effective as they moved casually among guests, at
least one of whom would be a cardinal. The acceptance of the Meyers
in such strictly limited circles was a privilege they shared with Joe
and me.

At one of these evenings, I was talking to Prince Colonna, when
the doors swung open to admit Cardinal Mariano Rampolla, the
papal secretary of state. Nothing could have been more dramatic
than his entrance. His scarlet robes swept the floor, making him look
even taller than his actual height of nearly seven feet. Under the
cardinal's cap was a stern featured face that seemed to personify
Church and State in all the majesty of uncompromising power.

On several other occasions I was a part of these intimate *papalini* gatherings when Cardinal Rampolla was present, and at the final one for us he spoke to me, saying he had noticed me before. "You are an American who speaks Italian, are you a Catholic?" he inquired.

I replied that I was not but my husband and I were guests of our American ambassador. This fact seemed to vouch for our presence. The Cardinal asked to have Joe presented, said a few gracious words to us, and passed on.

Receptions given by the Blacks were amusing because of the variety of personalities represented in the diplomatic corps and government, met in the confusing din of many languages. But as Joe put it, there was too much standing about, and he got tired of the sound of popping champagne corks and the necessity of refusing caviar. In looking back, I recognized in the noise and confusion of these receptions the ancestors of the all-pervasive American cocktail parties which, in the coming generations, were to invade every capital city of Europe, with a stultifying effect on worthwhile conversation.

The first formal dinner at which the Meyers arranged to have us included was given by a Roman prince, San Faustino, who was married to a wealthy American wife who liked entertaining. The dinner was a late affair and Joe found it incompatible with his painting regimen of long hours. I also was perturbed on discovering that it involved a strange protocol procedure, long since forgotten in Rome. This was explained in a scribbled note from George Meyer received the following morning. It stated that, according to accepted custom, I, as a stranger, must leave my card within forty-eight hours on every woman at the San Faustino dinner, even those to whom I had not been introduced. The right hand corner of the card must be turned down as evidence I had gone myself but on no account was I to ask to see the person. It was up to her to decide whether she wished to pursue the acquaintance by an invitation.

A list was enclosed prepared by an Embassy secretary consisting of thirty-six names and addresses, with a chart showing their proximity to one another for my convenience. In addition, there were names of four men, all Italians, and above them was written: Attention, Mr. Lindon Smith.

Early that same afternoon I started forth, dutifully hiring a carriage by the hour and taking my baby and her Italian nurse with me. She was late for her evening meal and yelled loudly after I had reached the eighteenth name, with eighteen to go. I had to give up.

Such a protocol observance, which seems incredible in retrospect, caused Joe and me to go on strike. He declared he had no time to leave cards on young Italians so they could call on me. And I had a better use for my late afternoons than scattering cards. The Meyers good naturedly spread the word that artists never paid any attention to social etiquette. I received no more lists with names and addresses but we continued to make delightful friends of our own choosing, many of them Italians.

Mrs. James T. Field of Boston had given us a letter to Mrs. George Berdan, an American and the mother-in-law of Marion Crawford, a much admired writer of fiction. She was one of the most charming hostesses in Rome, and I never failed to meet interesting people when present at one of her salons. The most unexpected among them occurred when she presented to me an Italian, who, from his appearance, was apparently from the Vatican staff, but I had no idea of his exalted position. I happened to mention my great religious emotion at attending the celebration of Christmas High Mass in St. Peter's and how much it had meant to Mother to have seen the Pope on another occasion. To my surprise, about a week later I received a formal notification from the Vatican that she and I were to have a private audience for a few minutes with the Pope. An accompanying note of instruction was signed with this Italian's name, who was one of the Pope's chamberlains.

We entered the Vatican by a side entrance from a carriage belonging to our Embassy. Swiss guards in striped yellow uniforms were in evidence through long passages and anterooms through which we were escorted by a tall footman in red damask. In the vicinity of a great hall, through the opened folding doors, I noticed hundreds of Albanians, Montenegrins, Bulgarians, and Armenians. Obviously, these Christians among the Sultan of Turkey's subjects were about to have an audience with the Pope. The chamberlain, whom I met at Mrs. Berdan's, awaited us in a small enclosure beyond the hall.

With him we entered a high studded and dignified room, with a few red and gold armchairs, where private audiences were held. It was empty until the arrival of Pope Leo XIII. He was dressed in white. His long, transparent hands rested on the arms of the paladin in which his attendants carried him. He looked very small and frail as he stood without assistance. I was conscious of the clear, penetrating gaze of his marvelously clear eyes, which lit up a face absolutely without color, even in the lips, as at a signal from the chamberlain, Mother and I knelt. The Pope blessed us each in turn. He spoke a few words in Italian about the importance of religion and the audience was over.

By a strange juxtaposition, the next day Joe and I were presented at court. I was escorted into a large anteroom by one of the Queen Elena's ladies in waiting, to join there a group of fifteen other Americans. Joe had been taken elsewhere to await the King's pleasure. It seemed an interminable length of time that we stood stiffly, with few words spoken, before being summoned.

After going through a number of rooms, we reached a large hall where Queen Elena received us. She was noticeably tall, with a jeweled crown on top of very dark hair, worn in a high pompadour. At a nod from our Ambassador I stepped forward. He said, "I have the honor to present Mrs. Joseph Lindon Smith." I made three curtsies, and that was all there was to it. Joe had practically the same experience with King Victor Emmanuel III, but bows were substituted for curtsies.

I persuaded Joe to attend one great function. This was a brilliant dinner followed by dancing given by the Waldo Storys. Mr. Story, like his father, W. W. Story, was a sculptor, and I had posed for the head of an angel he was doing for a Belmont memorial in Newport. The evening ended in a cotillion at which I was to dance with Richard Norton, the son of Charles Eliot Norton. Joe was preparing to leave when George Meyer approached with a vivacious and lovely looking young Italian matron. "Your partner for the cotillion, Joe," he said, introducing her. She gave him such a whirl, teaching him fancy dance steps, that when the party broke up he was wide awake.

We had turned into the Piazza di Spagna, attracted by singing.

To our surprise an Italian woman, seated quite alone on the Spanish Steps, was going through a series of grand opera roles in a gorgeous, rich mezzo-soprano voice. We listened at a distance so as not to interrupt her mood. Suddenly, she disappeared just as dawn broke and the early marketers were arriving with their produce. We mounted the steps and went onto the Pincio to watch the rising sun cast its rosy glow over the dome of St. Peter's, visible from behind a fountain, with two overhanging trees as a frame.

Joe and I often had a hasty meal alone with Boni, but avoided his formal entertaining of visiting scholars, including a lunch he was giving in honor of a great authority on the painter Raphael. Several hours before it was to take place, Boni turned up in the Forum greatly agitated, reporting that Bernard Shaw had telephoned that he wished to be shown the Forum. Whereupon Boni had told him anytime at his convenience, except at lunch that day. To this Shaw had replied, "I'll be there," and had rung off. Whether Shaw had caught only the words lunch today or was provoked at not being immediately included was beside the point. Boni had heard that Shaw could be difficult and feared the worst. Joe and I thought this alarm justified but did not say so.

Under pressure we yielded to Boni's insistence that we help him out by coming. This meant thirteen at table, which would not do. I solved the problem of finding a suitable guest on such short notice by telephoning George Meyer, who broke an engagement to be present.

Poor Boni was in despair about placating his cook, who was in an uproar at having to stretch her meal and reset the table. I succeeded in calming her, and with her capable assistant, who was to serve, the three of us lengthened the table and found additional china and crystal that did not match too badly. Joe and I rushed back to the hotel to change our clothes and therefore were late. Upon our arrival, a cursory glance disclosed that the lunch was off to a poor start. Boni's face was strained, the Raphael expert looked furious, and the other guests dazed. Bernard Shaw was saying decisively, "It's an exploded theory that there is any merit in Raphael's paintings." The experienced diplomat George Meyer intervened with appropriate questions addressed to the expert, only to have Shaw answer them.

The lunch was a complete failure and broke up early. Next morning, Boni, still upset, appeared at the Forum with a note addressed to him by G. B. Shaw. The contents were to the effect that, at the lunch the day before, so many of the guests were trying to talk in praise of Raphael's pictures that his curiosity was aroused about a painter whose work he had never bothered to look at. He had gone to a gallery where several were on exhibition, and to his surprise had found decided merit in Raphael's work!

I did some riding, both with George Meyer and with Don Gelasio Caetani, one of the Italian leaders in the field of sport, who had been an enthusiastic promoter of the polo club started by George Meyer and Herbert Haseltine. I was in my element at the hunt breakfasts, on the *campagna*, and could hold my own conversationally with the Italian sportsmen, who were excellent riders and had the means to provide themselves with first-class mounts.

Caetani was the first Italian to follow Meyer's example in purchasing a motor car, though his was far less pretentious than the enormous red Mercedes driven by the Ambassador. When others in the younger group among the Italian aristocrats followed suit, society ladies took alarm. Was the privacy of fashionable drives in the afternoons ending on the Pincio and the Villa Medici to be invaded by motors? They could not but disturb the even gait of well-trained horses between the shafts of stylish carriages. To set such fears at rest, Mrs. Meyer rather reluctantly joined the afternoon parade in a high-backed, specially made Victoria, while the American Ambassador confined his red Mercedes, driven by a taciturn German of enormous bulk, to the *campagna* and environs of Rome not patronized by fashion.

With his usual tact in accomplishing what he set out to do, George Meyer invited some of the most conservative Italian matrons, such as Princess Rospigliosi, Marchesa Rudini, and Contessa Palavicini for a spin over the *campagna*. The strategy worked! They were soon spreading the news in good Irish fashion that there was a distinct place for motors in Rome, entirely apart from the advantages of horse-drawn vehicles.

Boni had frequently lamented a lack of transportation for reaching archaeological sites in the *campagna* and beyond. At my suggestion, George Meyer invited Boni to accompany us on the frequent tours we made within a radius of one hundred miles of Rome.

Boni, who had never been in a motor, called our first trip a *viaggio* (voyage), and prepared for the adventure by wearing an odd-looking ulster and a cap with a wide visor pulled down over his ears. On fast turns, he gripped firmly the outside edge of the open Mercedes. Gradually, however, he learned to relax and keep on talking when the chauffeur, on being told to reach a given destination, headed straight for it, preferably taking a road, but if none existed, with his skill and the tremendous power of the engine, he chose to get there without one.

The *campagna* was a plain in name only, being traversed in many places by ridges or shallow ravines. There were reminders of extinct volcanoes in the smell of sulphur, and deadly swamps, often difficult to detect, were a menace to be avoided.

Boni's descriptions gave reality to ancient centers of civilization as we admired distant landscapes visible in the clear air and blessed by the kind of blue sky known only in Italy. On the horizon, we never lost either the Alban group of hills or the Umbrian and the Sabine Apennines.

One of my favorite trips was that which took us along the banks of the Tiber, with its quaint old quais, whose counterparts had long since vanished from the vicinity of the San Angelo bridge inside Rome. At the end was Ostia, with its great tombs and fragments.

Another favorite was Frascati and the ruins of ancient Tusculum. By a steep ascent, we reached the top of the Alban Mount, from which I looked down to the sea and lake while Boni pointed out the site of the great Temple of Jupiter. But the most rewarding excursion of all was a walk through the confines of Hadrian's Villa. For a distance of three miles, Boni led us on foot past a mass of ruins of amphitheatres, porticos, halls, and other architectural features which a Roman emperor considered necessary as a setting for his own greatness. We got the perspective of his residential possessions from the rocky heights of nearby Tivoli.

19

DUBLIN, OUR SUMMER HOME

Loon Point, consisting of nearly five acres, jutting far into the lake from the main road at Dublin, New Hampshire, offered creative possibilities to Joe as relaxation after strenuous working winters, mostly in the Near East among the ancient art treasures of Egypt. Dublin was the only town among those encircling Monadnock that lay actually on its lower slopes. Also it was the highest town in New England, and an altitude of fifteen hundred feet had given it a peculiarly health-giving summer climate.

The first known inhabitant was an Irishman from Dublin, Ireland, hence the name. A few Scotch-Irish families were there when permanent settlers from Massachusetts incorporated themselves into a town in 1771. Dublin had historic significance, even as only one of many similar scattered farming settlements in New England. For it was early composed of solid citizens with strong convictions who became leaders in the Revolution. The able-bodied to a man fought in the American armies.

A high ethical and cultural level was maintained during the first part of the nineteenth century. Theodore Parker, a disciple of Thoreau's who spent summer vacations there during that period, declared in print that, with the exception of the already famous Concord and Lincoln, Dublin held the palm over the rest of the New England towns. It had one of the very first libraries in the country to be supported by contributions.

But as early as 1830, migratory tendencies developed. The lure of the West took the restless from the tedium of the farm, and others with initiative, both men and women, drifted away into fast-growing Massachusetts factory centers, while local businessmen of ability became city executives. The decreases in population and wealth continued when no manufacturing opportunities offered themselves, and response to the call of the Civil War was a further drain on ever-diminishing resources.

A town attempt to take summer boarders was an immediate success. The boarders found in Dublin the privacy and simple living, permitting the enjoyment of rare beauties of nature, all the more welcome after the responsibilities of city winters. A small group of Bostonians built cottages and became summer residents.

Among the first were Mrs. Copley Greene, Mrs. Munro, whose daughter was to marry George Gray Barnard, the well-known New York sculptor, and the Daniel Dwights.

Also Henry B. Hill, professor of chemistry at Harvard, who married my mother's youngest sister. And a little later Raphael Pumpelly, citizen of the world, whose wife was another of my mother's sisters.

Ten years after Joe's advent in 1890, fifty cottages had been constructed on hillsides in the vicinity of the lake, with a majority occupied by artists, writers, and professors.

Colonel Leighton and his family from Saint Louis had already taken over an extensive abandoned farm and put it under cultivation, and his son George ran it after his father's death.

Franklin MacVeagh of Chicago, who was to be secretary of the Treasury in President Taft's administration, did the same on a less ambitious scale.

Early, the important Saint Louis colony included Ethan Allen Hitchcock, secretary of the Interior under President McKinley, and his wife. Their daughter Anne married Admiral William S. Sims, U.S.N. And there were the Daniel Catlins.

Local business thrived as never before. Labor was employed all the year round. There was a profitable market for forest wood and ice cut from the lake in the slack winter months and for summer farm produce. Summer residents were willing to be taxed for good roads for phaetons, landaus, and other luxury vehicles. Through the years, the Dublin community was to remain distinctive by not becoming a summer resort in the sense of high fashion, thus avoiding a display of style and a rivalry in entertaining. Participation in town affairs by members of the same families has continued through the years, with Mrs. Robert D. Sterling a prime mover.

The activities of the summer community centered about a simple Dublin Lake Club, started in 1901, of which Joe remained the president. Its management was ably seconded by two Saint Louis men, Lawrence Mauran, who married Isabel Chapman, whose parents were among the first settlers, and George D. Markham, with Mary McKittrick, his wife, in the same category.

At a later period, Frederick F. Brewster of New Haven, Connecticut, who purchased the Leighton estate when it came onto the market, developed the golf course. And his wife created the most notable garden in New England.

In these days, Mrs. Franklin MacVeagh and Miss Rebecca A. Caldwell of New York, in turn, were responsible for the social activities of the club.

Dan Catlin the younger, who became its president after Joe's death, his sister Irene Allen and her family, and the younger generations of the Charles MacVeagh family of New York have been among those who today are carrying on the Dublin tradition of their parents.

The Smith family, increased by the birth of a second child in the summer of 1903 and the acquisition of an English nurse, all crowded into the Dublin home. I urged the necessity for more space on deaf ears. Father insisted we were all comfortable, and Joe was cold to my suggestion of building again. Then in a chance encounter, Sturgis Bigelow remarked to me he had forgotten to give us a wedding present. It was, he said, a unique Della Robbia mantel, supported by two caryatids that Joe and he had purchased together in Florence. The stipulation was that Joe must locate it personally in one of the endless rooms, in endless warehouses, containing Bigelow's oriental and Italian possessions, "mostly unlabeled," he warned.

The very next evening, Joe returned from a trip to Boston on a truck, bringing back far more in the way of antiquities than the mantel. He was to be his own architect, and on his way home dropped in on a local contractor, who agreed to start building on receipt of the blueprints. Father and he got busy moving the house to a nearby lakeshore site, and the rest of us departed for Cape Cod to stay with my sisters in a rambling, elastic establishment.

The succeeding Thanksgiving holidays we spent in Dublin as a reunited family, camping out in an Italian Villa, with the mantel built into the middle of the back wall of a long, paneled, narrow living room, over an open fireplace. Nothing could have enhanced its magnificence better than a Della Robbia plaque of the kneeling figure of a woman, holding a lily, ending in a sweeping curve. This piece, which fitted exactly above the wide glazed mantel shelf, Joe had found in an old Sienese palace which was being torn down.

The room was built plumb with the existing Italian garden, which was entered from it through a wide columned porch with a wing at each end extending to the first flower beds. The further one consisted of a dining room, Japanese in character, and the other, to the right of the front door, was a library. Fortunately, Joe's and my tastes coincided: he liked antiquities without books around, and I greatly preferred books, without antiquities. Shelves reaching nearly to the ceilings, with broad windows between, left space for nothing else in the library except a fine old desk.

Highboys and other fine early American pieces, once owned by Smith ancestors, looked thoroughly at home in a strictly Italian setting, as did English Sheraton chairs. Father told Joe to have an adequate furnace installed. In early May, however, when the family again showed up, bag and baggage, there was no sign of a furnace. But beyond the dining room, an ingeniously contrived Chinese porch, forty feet square, was breath-taking in its effect. It overlooked the lake on two sides, and whenever the structure permitted, revealed Chinese sculptured wood, either in the round or in carved relief.

In early August, after Joe's return from a short trip to Spain with Denman Ross, he dedicated the Chinese porch to Isabella Gardner. Joe appeared, to the guests assembled in it, as an old Chinese sage strolling in a Chinese garden below. Then he slowly ascended a few steps and entered the porch through a wide square opening, painted dark blue. At the Sage's repetition of a magic formula, the opening, now a Chinese vermilion, further changed into a large round moon gate, used in China as a feature leading from a building into a garden.

The simple ceremony closed with Isabella Gardner stepping inside the moon gate, which she formally accepted as her own by right of gift, and promising to come back to it every summer. It was a promise she faithfully kept.

The water of the lake nearby was then and is now pure and very clear, with no visible inlets except tiny rivulets from the surrounding hills which fed it. It was here that Professor Alexander Agassiz, on one of his visits to Abbott Thayer, identified a small, juicy trout as a species previously known in one lake in Switzerland.

Mother gradually developed a fish ritual which she came to perform daily at noon from a sand spit in a little cove under the lea of the house. At the sight of a bright tin dish in her hand, and a peculiar sound produced by a rapid movement of her tongue against her lips, her tame fish (as she called them), as though in response to an expected signal, came shimmering forward in great shoals, close to the surface of the water, until she was surrounded by them. She scattered food and, stooping, carelessly picked up at will individual fish, including the shy trout, then threw them back into the water.

She firmly refused to exhibit to the curious, but Thayer turned up quite frequently and once brought Agassiz. The great scientist stared in complete silence, broken finally by his saying, "For the first time in my life, I cannot believe the testimony of my own eyes."

As a family, we seldom did anything the customary way, and so it was with the recording of visitors. Signatures of the Smith house guests were carved on the front and sides of a tall, old-fashioned American settee which stood on the porch leading into the garden. They afforded us pleasant reminders of striking personalities and varied episodes. This novel guest book attracted the instant attention of anyone who happened to be on Loon Point for the first time. For instance, Isabella Gardner, with the use of her given name only (like royalty), somehow achieved in a conspicuous flowing script, with a long S, and prominently placed signature, the attention which she intended. "Tell me anything you know about that remarkable woman," was the request frequently made, and the Smiths knew a lot. An awed staring, without a word, at St. Gaudens' signature told its story even more eloquently.

Next to Mrs. Gardner's, those of Mark Twain and Ethel Barrymore tied for interest. Often comments on names served as stimulus to conversation. James Bryce's and Cecil Spring-Rice's signatures producing an amusing, "Oh, I say!" in a British accent. Brooks Adams' appealed to a very few, over that of his better known brother Henry Adams, also there. Later, John J. Pershing and George C. Marshall, whose names were carved close together caused some casual callers to be very late to subsequent appointments, as did the signature of Amelia Earhart, still later, after her solo flight across the Atlantic. Amelia had married one of my kinsmen, George Palmer Putnam.

Baron Kaneko represented Japan at the Peace Treaty ending the Russo-Japanese War. Directly after it was signed at Portsmouth, New Hampshire, in September, 1905, he came to us in Dublin for recuperation and meditation. Four years earlier, at an informal dinner at the White House just before Joe and I sailed for Japan in January, 1901, President Theodore Roosevelt had spoken of Baron Kaneko as a good friend. He generously gave us an introduction to Japan's leading statesman at the time, and during our stay in Japan we came to know him well, and through him achieved an understanding of Japanese culture which was rare then.

Kaneko was delighted that everything in our guest suite was Japanese. The creation of a Japanese garden across the driveway close to the lake had been precipitated the summer before by Father's protest at having barn space, which was needed for hay, occupied by a heavy stone Buddha, Kwannon, and pagoda dumped on Loon Point from a Japanese freighter. These were presents from Kaneko, who praised Joe highly for his strict adherence to symbolism in the use of an existing boulder, some odd-shaped rocks, gnarled stumps, and other vagaries of nature, all carefully considered in their relation to the stone objects. Kaneko sent for two dwarf Japanese maples, which he planted himself with grave ceremony. He dismissed the insistence of a local horticulturist that delicate Japanese maples would not live in New Hampshire, saying with a tone of authority, "These maples are in the only genuine Japanese garden in New Hampshire." Apparently this did make a difference, because they are still thriving, after more than half a century.

On his own initiative, he gave an informal talk to the Dublin community from the stage of our Teatro Bambino. In the absence of the press (at his request), he plunged into his subject with entire frankness. The President of the United States had consistently urged on him (Kaneko), he said, the necessity of making his government realize that the great powers would not allow Japan to reap the fruits of her victory over the Czar's forces, when the outcome of hostilities was but a matter of weeks away. This had been done by personal communications over the telephone in Japan, in private interviews after his arrival in America, and by telephone again at Portsmouth.

It had been no easy relinquishment, the speaker pointed out, but finally Japan had accepted extremely adverse terms from a thoroughly defeated Russia. After an amazingly dispassionate presentation of the Japanese case he stated categorically that the rule of an emperor was in no way in conflict with the development of Japan as a modern industrial nation along democratic lines. He cited as two essentials for success the obtaining of raw materials from overseas and the control of a strongly entrenched Japanese military leadership by wiser civilian heads.

Before Kaneko left, I heard from George von Lengerke Meyer, who had become our ambassador to Russia in 1905, writing from St. Petersburg. The fact that none of the court advisers had dared inform the Czar of Russia's overwhelming defeat on land and at sea had complicated the settlement at Portsmouth. He was insisting on only an armistice. It had taken the threat of his official withdrawal from Russia, Meyer wrote, to obtain an audience. In an interesting two hours with the Czar alone, the latter had finally agreed to peace, but stuck to the position that Russia would pay no indemnity—and got away with it!

Mark Twain was a welcome addition to the community when he rented a house for the summer of 1905. His was soon a familiar figure on Loon Point, in white flannels always spotless, and with his distinctive features set off by a shock of white hair pushed back from his forehead, a rather heavy mustache, and the inevitable cigar.

I think the reason for his finding the Smiths congenial as a family was that none of us tried to guide his mood by questions. He would straddle a rock in a locality where Father and Joe were busy, chatting idly, with witticisms interspersed, varied with long lapses into silence. Joe might be watering and Father dragging a heavy stump from an adjacent lawn. "I'm all beat out from watching them work," he would say to anyone about. He waited patiently for callers to depart, to visit Mother in her kitchen, to return, munching a handful of doughnuts, remarking cheerfully he could resist anything except temptation.

Once I found him alone in the garden examining the perfectly matched flat stones in the surrounding wall, fitted evenly together without plaster, built by Joe and Father. He abruptly inquired how much time Grandma needed to prepare hot cakes of Rhode Island white meal that Abbott Thayer had mentioned. My answer, "Half an hour," brought the prompt announcement, "Notice given now."

He expressed pleasure on finding all his publications in our library. Picking up *The Jumping Frog*, a literary landmark, as it has been called, about a frog which was filled with lead by a stranger so that his own competing frog could win in a race, Mark Twain said chuckling, "Let's see how it reads aloud."

This was the beginning of many pleasant evenings, including those when Mark Twain read to us portions of *Eve's Diary*, which he was writing that summer. In the printed copy he later gave me, he wrote, "'Tis noble to be good, 'tis nobler still to show others how to be good—and less trouble." It was an autograph eventually to prove prophetic, since in many phases of my extremely diverse career, I was to do just what it suggested.

He volunteered to give one of the afternoon lectures at the club sponsored by Mrs. Franklin MacVeagh, who was chairman of entertainment. He informed an enormous gathering that under the title of "Caprice of Memory" he intended to mention anything that came into his head. For two hours without a pause, he played on the emotions of a fascinated audience, evoking rapid changes from solemnity to peals of laughter. A number of his fans, many coming from a distance, concurred in never having heard him give as absorbing or more self-revealing a talk. When his voice ceased, he was cheered to the echo and carried through the audience on the men's shoulders.

Next summer he was back, but in an isolated house, and depressed from the recent death of his wife. At the beginning of the season he shunned companionship, then, becoming lonely, sent for Joe to arrange for him to give another afternoon at the club.

His scheme was based on the premise that the most popular after-dinner speakers rarely touched on their advertised subjects and merely told excellent stories apropos of nothing. He was to be announced as about to give lessons, in the form of a debate, to two pupils, George Brush and Joe.

They were each to have three absolutely irrelevant stories, always introduced by the formula "How fortuitous what the previous speaker has just said is exemplified by the . . ." then tell a story. This was essential, he emphasized. Incidentally, the subject was to be whether the world would have been a better place if Adam had never been born, if Eve had not, or if neither had lived.

Mark Twain was in top form on the afternoon of the lesson. He made monkeys of Brush and Joe, in their pretended confusion as to which side they were on in the debate, as they constantly interrupted themselves and each other, by leaning forward, and in confidential asides to the audience, after the formula, telling such screamingly funny anecdotes that they even distracted attention from Mark Twain's brilliant nonsense. The audience began to roar with expectant laughter on hearing the words, "How fortuitous."

The lecturer summed up by saying that his friend Professor Pumpellys' learned dissertation (which he misquoted), on the superiority of man's skull over the skulls of brute beasts, had failed to prove man's value. A few instances would suffice, such as planting tobacco for his own gratification in smoking, and much more in a similar vein. Eve's claim as necessary for the propagation of mankind, he dismissed as a mere detail. He concluded with a plea for a world of nature and wild creatures, with no humans to mess it up.

Ethel Barrymore was staying with us on one occasion when we

had planned an evening surprise party for Mark Twain. She expressed enthusiasm for a fantasy Joe was to produce in the Italian garden entitled *Jack Frost Comes in Midsummer*, and impulsively asked to play the role of the Spirit of Summer. Except for the part of Jack Frost, to be taken by Joe, the cast were youngsters.

At the one rehearsal, he read aloud the simple plot and then distributed the parts. "Yours, Ethel," he said, "like all of them, briefly outlines the points to be covered, cues, action, entrances, and exits."

Under his direction, the children took their places in the garden, representing flowers, their costumes the counterparts of brilliant August blooms, with the stalks, supplemented by property leaves, concealing their figures from the audience.

Each flower in turn rose from her light foliage, until the garden was a blaze of color, gaiety, and movement. A lovely little moth, with a lightness of step suggestive of Pavlova, literally floated about in her delicate rendering of leading a flower ballet. Chilly blasts (represented by Father) caused havoc, accented by the terrific noise of music. Jack Frost made a dramatic descent from a treetop (more of Father's mechanism). At his icy touch, an illusion of actual desolation and wilted flowers was created by imaginative children who needed but little coaching. Jack Frost, still threatening the little moth, who had become a realistic heap at his feet, now provided the signal for the entrance of the Spirit of Summer from inside a large fountain.

"Ethel, your cue," I prompted. When nothing happened beyond a faint murmur, I beckoned Joe.

"I can't emerge gracefully, as the instructions read, or improvise appropriate words," Ethel gasped at him.

After one glance at her, Joe called to the cast, expectantly waiting to be revived by the great actress, "Of course, Miss Barrymore needs no rehearsing." Joe went through Summer's part for the benefit of the cast. After he had dismissed them, Ethel asked him to take up his position as Jack Frost terrorizing the little moth, "That's my cue," she said. Immediately she was Summer personified, hurling contemptuous epithets at the arrogant intruder, until Jack Frost, completely cowed, vanished as though into thin air.

Her performance was exactly according to the conception Joe had just given us, in facial expressions, positions taken, the significant gestures, even the letter-perfect character of the words spoken. She told him that the part was so entirely out of her line that she had to see it performed.

I was with her after the play when Mark Twain, joining us, said, "The audience thought you wonderful in it, because you are Ethel Barrymore, but frankly you tried too hard to be spontaneous."

"How understanding you are, Mr. Clemens," she replied feelingly, "Instinctive spontaneity in acting can only be imitated, alas."

Then Dublin paid homage to them both, as they stood side by side.

It made a great stir in the community when James Bryce, known as the great commoner, established the British Embassy in Dublin for the 1909 summer season. I did not know he had arrived when a smallish stranger, standing on the threshold of the Chinese porch while we were still at breakfast, announced himself as James Bryce. Then stepping toward me with a quick, sure tread, as we all rose, he added that someone in Washington had given him a memorandum to look up the daughter of his good friend, George Haven Putnam, "And here I am." He pointed to his high spiked boots and knickerbockers, as he told us he was just down from climbing Monadnock and was hungry. "Are there any kippered herrings about?" he enquired.

At my information that there were, because they were a favorite dish of my husband's, he turned to Joe, remarking with a radiant smile which lighted up his sharp-featured face, that he knew instinctively when he admired his Egyptian paintings at a Washington exhibition that they had a further bond in kippered herrings.

Joe explained that the trail Lord Bryce had traveled down Monadnock was named Pumpelly, because he personally had laid the cairns that marked this longest and hardest route, up each rocky, steep peak to the highest pinnacle of Monadnock. Obviously Bryce's mind was on the man himself rather than his trail.

"It's exciting to have Pumpelly as my nearest neighbor," he said. His agile mind next darted to his pleasure in having a chance to know

Thayer. Then in mock solemnity he said that the presence of Mrs. MacVeagh with her husband, now secretary of the Treasury in President Taft's administration, precluded all hope that his overworked tail coat could have a respite in camphor. Any such ceremony was to be tabu at the British Embassy, he declared, with a stubborn set to his jaw that was an indication of his reputed obstinacy. He would not let Father drive him back to the Embassy, since he felt that he must settle his kippers by walking. He expected to bring Mrs. Bryce around soon, he said. "She'll be as intrigued as I was, in a cursory view, to find that none of the antiques, inside nor out of doors, appear uprooted from their natural habitat."

Heresay about Bryce's informal method of making acquaintances had been more than confirmed by his approach to the Smiths.

Joe once introduced Bryce to a club audience. "Your President," said the Ambassador, "egged on by his Putnam wife, I suspect, selected for my topic *The American Commonwealth.*" Then he modestly attributed its wide acceptance to one fact, which he defined as a study, through personal contacts, of the people governed, after a thorough perusal of every pertinent document available in American archives. This he acknowledged to be a startling innovation in the methodology of scholars who had analyzed various forms of government.

He, as a stranger with an inquisitive mind (which had caused him to be called behind his back a "human interrogation point"), had undertaken to make himself thoroughly familiar with American habits of thought before he engaged on a stupendous, self-imposed task. The happiest and most instructive experiences of his entire life were wanderings throughout the United States, without a railroad timetable or a schedule, covering many sections of a vast expanse of country, as varied as its population: from districts of small farms to the great wheat fields of Iowa, from Maine to the state of Washington. After visiting great industrial centers like Pittsburgh he had gone to isolated regions of the "Deep South."

"Everywhere, I ran across people with ideas, ready to share them, and friendly beyond belief," he said. He classified his travels as invaluable towards an understanding of why the American form of government continued to work among a large and varied population, with strong, and usually conflicting, sectional interests, as well as a mixture of nationalities. Briefly but eloquently, he analyzed salient points of government, frankly critical of a few. "The book wrote itself," he said in conclusion.

Among many questions, a woman aggressively British in her manner asked rather sarcastically, "Can you imagine, Lord Bryce, the British parliamentary process in operation here in a crisis, with the majority party in control of the government at the time calling for a vote of confidence?"

"Why should Americans want anything so entirely at variance with their own procedure, now so satisfactory to them?" Bryce came back at her quick as a flash, and the Britisher subsided.

Even more gratifying to me than diplomacy at work in Dublin was an occasional emphasis on literary personalities. Among them, the name of Albert J. Beveridge is written indelibly in Dublin annals. It was here that he began his final compilation of data for his erudite life of Chief Justice John Marshall. One night when we were dining at the Beveridges', he exclaimed suddenly to Joe, "I wonder if I can make the life readable!" He agreed at once to Joe's suggestion of trying it out on a club audience.

No one who heard what Beveridge called a first tryout in presenting his material will ever forget that event. His closing words were spoken with great earnestness. "There is so much new material that will eventually turn up," he said. "There must be," he reiterated. "When it does, I only hope it won't prove wrong my every conclusion from the data now available."

A very real literary adventure, continuing for a number of summers, came about when I joined two other women who went to Amy Lowell's house for scheduled readings of plays of the Elizabethan Period, selected by her, and occasionally a French drama. We insisted that she take the leading roles of both sexes, which she did with astounding versatility. An even rarer gift than her remarkable intonation and diction was her tending to actually become the character she was portraying in words. Part of each evening, as an interlude, was devoted to literary criticism, including French drama, early or current. I often wished a concealed stenographer could have taken down her very definite opinions, expounded with originality and complete assurance.

Her choice of words from a rich vocabulary was peculiarly arresting at a time when her thought of writing poetry was still in embryo. To me, this ability reached its climax just after the end of World War I, during an evening on her Brookline estate when she was late, even for her, in joining her guests. In fact, dinner coffee had been served when she appeared.

"Listen," she said. And standing with her back to the fire and facing us, she repeated in epic form an account of the sinking of the German fleet at Scapa Flow. Through the mere use of words, each mighty battleship in turn went down before our eyes. "Well! How about it, Joe?" she asked.

"I really don't know, Amy," he replied. "I'd have to read it in print, without you punctuating the word pictures by acting, which gives an impression far more vivid than any geisha's performance I ever witnessed."

Before the war, a high-powered, enormous Mercedes, owned by George Leighton, whose father had been the earliest gentleman farmer in Dublin, was the only motor to invade our sylvan privacy. The loudest voice raised in protest was that of Amy Lowell. She was a noted whip, and a drive with her, as she handled a lively, fast-trotting pair, was a hair-raising experience I often shared with others who possessed strong nerves. On a long excursion to some distant forest or to a laurel grove, a picnic was combined with several hours for the horses to be freed from harness and shafts, then back at a whirlwind speed, against the oncoming blackness of night, over the uneven surfaces of roads without lights.

Her defiance of the Mercedes was magnificent, and in a head-on encounter, it was the Mercedes that yielded ground, often to the extent of being forced down a bank, later to be ignominiously hauled up by co-operation between man and work horses.

An immediate and fundamental change occurred after the war, when it became apparent that the motor was here to stay. Amy Lowell was one of the first to succumb. She turned her horses out to pasture and bought a motor, American made, which competed in size and elegance with the hated Mercedes. She complained she was so used to the rapid pace of her horses that she found it difficult to pass through Concord, Massachusetts, where speed laws were strictly enforced. The only way to avoid arrest, she said, was by walking behind her motor, with a conservative chauffeur at the wheel!

Dirt roads vanished! Riders took to the woods! I missed our mounted visitors, who left their horses at our unique hitching post, a six-foot Stone Henge-like boulder! The village began to deliver supplies on wheels, and Sir Cecil Spring-Rice brought a flock of motors to be used by his British Embassy. Dublin had accepted a new and less pleasant era.

Austrian Ambassador Constantin Dumba, before the exposure of the intrigue with Mexico disclosed by the Zimmerman letters, appeared to the community, when he was a guest of Sir Cecil's, to be a harmless, rather light-weight diplomat. I was frequently his doubles partner in tennis. But Count von Bernstorff's presence in Dublin, visiting a neighbor, produced an uproar. He was informed curtly to keep off the main roads and was socially ignored.

President Wilson had made Cornish, New Hampshire, about sixty miles from Dublin, his summer residence since 1912, and was still there when war was declared. It was not until much later that it developed von Bernstorff's purpose in coming to Dublin was to have a secret meeting with Wilson, at the President's request, in some out-of-the-way locality accessible to both Dublin and Cornish.

20

ITALIAN INTERLUDES

Two years later, in the spring of 1905, we were again back in Rome, on a detour from Naples as we returned to America from Egypt, in connection with a purchase by Joe for Mrs. Gardner.

Associations with papal Rome caused my mind to revert to the conclave which followed Pope Leo XIII's death in July, 1903, resulting in the election of a Venetian cardinal as Pope Pius X. I recalled having learned at the time that, when Cardinal Rampollo apparently was gaining a majority of the votes, as had been generally expected, the Archbishop of Cracow pronounced a veto against his consideration. This he did in the name of Emperor Franz Joseph of Austria. Incidentally, this was the last time such a veto could be exercised, since Pope Pius X subsequently abolished Austria's privilege.

Joe was greatly interested in the election to the papacy of the Venetian whom he had known as Giuseppi Cardinal Sarto, Patriarch of Venice. The Cardinal had enjoyed watching Joe at work, particularly, as in former years, when he had painted the interior of San Marco. Frequently in the late afternoons they sat together at a small table in the Piazza chatting casually. On going to see the Patriarch in his official residence, Joe brought as an offering a sketch of San Marco's high altar. The Patriarch had been quite overcome by the gift. Joe had remembered his beautiful round face with its fine mouth and earnest eyes. "A simple soul with qualities of a saint," was his prophetic description.

Nothing could have amazed him more, however, than to receive a summons to the Vatican delivered personally by Cardinal Merry del Val, the Pope's secretary of state. The Cardinal explained it was not to be an audience but in the private apartment of His Holiness. The Pope received Joe alone and, like an old friend, talked reminiscently about their days together in Venice. Not even to me did Joe repeat the words that had passed between them, but he mentioned the Pope's saying to him that he had kept as a memento his return ticket from Rome to Venice, bought at the time of the conclave. Joe was greatly moved by the interview and considered that Pope Pius X had not yet found in the beauty of the Alban Hills a substitute for the Grand Canal and Piazza San Marco.

An encounter with one of the striking personalities of the day occurred at Anacapri. I had gone there to leave the two children with my sister Ethel before joining Joe and Boni on an inspection of Paestum and recent excavations in Herculaneum.

American tourists and artists flocked to Capri, a popular island reached by boat from Naples. But we preferred the little-advertised Anacapri on the heights above, where we stayed in a small inn fittingly named Il Paradiso. The whole Bay of Naples lay at our feet, with a superb view of the Sorrento Plain and Vesuvius. Further away was the long range of the snow-capped Apennine Mountains. Higher up than Il Paradiso stood a little round chapel riveted to a steep rock. Accompanied by the children, I decided to attempt to reach it. We mounted by a winding narrow trail. I did not realize we had reached private property until I noticed extensive gardens and a voice said, "Someone must have given you an introduction to me. I am Axel Munthe."

No one had, but even so, he invited us to come with him, and I was only too delighted. Thus informally I made the acquaintance of a man whom I, like everyone else, had heard much of. He pointed toward Roman columns and arches dominating the top of the hill, with a building beyond, also Roman in character. "San Michele, my home," he told me, "restored from the ruins of a villa on the site, a favorite retreat of the Emperor Tiberius from affairs of state." And he added his own villa was an exact replica, with much of the ancient material employed in its construction.

At first sight I would have described Munthe's appearance as ordinary, with small regular features, hair brushed back carelessly, and a short beard and mustache. Then on meeting his direct gaze, I changed my mind. In deep-set eyes was a quality of clairvoyance that made his face arresting and rather terrifying. Before proceeding to the villa, we entered the round chapel, which had finely carved medieval stalls and cloisters in keeping. Nearby was a library built of polished Roman marble slabs. Down the center on a long refectory table were endless piles of ancient manuscripts and terra cotta fragments.

On leaving the library, we went through an avenue of cypress trees that were from the Villa D'Este in Rome, he informed us. Just beyond, balanced on the corner of a Roman bath, was a mutilated bust of Emperor Augustus, dating to his period. We were on the edge of a cliff with a sheer drop of two thousand feet to the sea below. Before passing through a columned hall reminiscent of ancient Rome, we entered a small antechamber. Here we sat down to a supper of minestrone and macaroni, facing a Roman copy of the Winged Victory, placed on an enormous cinquecento Florentine mantel.

The longer I listened to our host's conversation, the more I understood the peculiar power over women for which he was known. He was one of the first Paris physicians to use hypnotism in the practice of medicine. His patients were ladies of fashion and high rank, even including royalty, who traveled from all over Europe for his diagnosis and treatment.

Henry James was a bond between us, and during my short stay at Anacapri I saw much of Munthe. Fortunately I was there in an interval between visits of patients whose position was so high that he found it impossible to refuse them an invasion of his privacy at San Michele. From what I heard, they came in a steady stream, more for a few days of his cherished companionship than for medical advice, I gathered.

I will long remember Axel Munthe's brilliant and original mind and his vast fund of intellectual information. But above all, I found it striking that in his island retreat he had succeeded in creating the illusion of being actually back in the times of the Emperor Tiberius.

Another striking personality with an extraordinary effect on women was D'Annunzio, the Italian writer. It had been the talk of Rome when an Italian princess appeared with him at a hunt on the *campagna*, and at his insistence, with her reddish-gold hair, inherited from an English ancestor, falling free to her waist, and holding a lily as she joined the riders. D'Annunzio's publicizing of his relationship with Eleanora Duse in one of his novels, in which he used the text of her love letters to him, was the culminating factor in the contempt with which men regarded him.

On one of Joe's and my visits to Florence with the children, I decided impulsively to go to Pisa to see the Leaning Tower. This entailed a rather tedious railroad journey, possible in a day by an early start. I went alone and felt fully repaid for the effort we made. On a very crowded train back to Florence, there was no vacant seat. I was standing in the corridor when I saw I was opposite a compartment containing only two men—Italians. I entered before noticing a "Reserved" staring me in the face, and was about to beat a hasty retreat when one of the passengers motioned me to be seated.

In traveling, I always read one of D'Annunzio's books. His Italian was unexcelled for poetical expression, choice of vocabulary, and formation of sentences. I was soon completely absorbed in what to me was an Italian lesson of a high order. Suddenly I became conscious of one of the Italians, who was glancing over my shoulder.

"Why do you, a stranger, read D'Annunzio?" he asked.

"For the perfection of the Italian language," I replied.

One look at the speaker sufficed for identification. It was D'Annunzio himself. He responded to my commendation by directing his conversation to me. I answered his inquiries as to who I was and why I was in that train. Then shutting the pages of his book, I listened in spellbound admiration to his flow of language, which covered a wide range of subjects. In the fascination of his discourse, I forgot his reputation and, to me, unpleasant personality.

My reaction to the train's being greatly delayed was that it gave me more of an opportunity to hear D'Annunzio's spoken Italian, which was equally as perfect as his written expression. On our arrival at Florence, he helped me out of the compartment and without releasing my arm he took me down the platform, talking and laughing gaily. Joe, waiting at the gate, almost cut me dead on observing my obvious enjoyment of being in D'Annunzio's company.

Memories of Florence will always be associated in my mind with a number of brief visits to the Bernard Berensons, through a period of over thirty years.

Berenson, or B.B. as his friends called him, had developed fast after Isabella Gardner gave him an opportunity for art training abroad.

His extraordinary gifts and a highly retentive memory took flight under the influence of Walter Pater, who introduced him to Renaissance art. He was to become, in comparison with others in the same field, almost infallible in his attributions.

In spite of the difference in our ages, a real friendship continued between me and his wife, the former Mary Costelloe, begun during my girlhood in England, when I had visited with the Robert Pearsall Smiths, her parents.

As for Berenson, he had an exhilarating effect mentally upon everyone with whom he came in contact. Joe had known him in his bachelor days through Isabella Gardner, and I had met him at Fenway Court after my marriage.

Mary, being a Catholic, was not free to marry again until the death of her former husband Costelloe, which occurred in 1889, after many years of separation. Berenson had joined the Catholic church, and in December, 1900, they were married by a priest.

For some years previously Mary had been closely associated with Berenson in his writing and was later to become his able assistant.

I Tatti, which they had rented after their marriage, was situated on one of the hillsides of Settignano, near Florence, with a superb view. Joe and I had made a brief stay with the Berensons during our many months in Rome in 1903. Their place was then a large, rambling farmhouse, with surprisingly fine old furniture and fifty surrounding acres, uncultivated for the most part. By 1907, Berenson had achieved his dream of buying I Tatti. This was made possible by his having entered the service of Joseph Duveen, an association that put an end to his financial worries.

I think it cannot be too often repeated that Berenson never gave an attribution of which, at the time, he was not convinced. And it was on this issue that his severing connections with Duveen was brought about in 1936, when Berenson refused to give an attribution which he believed to be erroneous.

On a visit in 1907, we found Berenson and Geoffrey Scott, his secretary, busily engaged in rebuilding I Tatti on a grandiose scale. Within three years the farmhouse was transformed into an enormous villa of unparalleled beauty and grandeur. The plan called for the eventual housing of a tremendous library on art, literature, history, economics, poetry, biography, and memoirs. And for a collection of Renaissance paintings of a quality and size hitherto known only in great museums. But they were shown not in galleries but in great apartments and corridors and were hung on a level with the eye.

A comprehensive photographic record of paintings, their whereabouts and facts concerning them, was a gigantic task in itself and formed another invaluable collection at the villa.

The villa opened into a formal green garden, planted with a profusion of cypress, junipers, and box, and was reached by a descent of broad steps on several different levels. There soon developed long avenues of trees, endless paths, and fine individual gardens.

In 1916 Berenson looked me up in Paris and we had an evening alone. He spoke of the war and how it had brought about incredible dislocations of worth-while pursuits in the countries engaged. Then, in an emotional mood that led to self-analysis, he said the trouble with his life had been that early he had begun to look upon luxuries as necessities.

I saw Mary and Berenson often at the time of the Armistice, when they were in residence at Paris. Both were despondent, and Mary frankly hoped that after the war Bernard would be satisfied with a simpler life.

The burden of running an establishment with an army of retainers and secretaries was becoming an increasing burden, and she had lost much of the gaiety and joy of entertaining that had made her a charming hostess. Shortly thereafter she had a nervous breakdown in Paris, from the effects of which she was never entirely to recover.

During the 1930's we were at I Tatti several times. In 1923

Geoffrey Scott had left Berenson, to marry Lady Sybil, the widow of Bayard Cutting, a great friend of ours. We had stayed with them in Milan when he was American consul. Their child Iris, at the age of eight, knew Greek and parts of Shakespeare's plays by heart.

On Scott's departure, his place as secretary was taken by Nicky Mariano, to whom Mary was devoted. And to her relief, in addition to being Berenson's secretary, Nicky took over the burden of house-keeping.

Berenson's great compilation of data on Italian paintings, the most complete ever made and published by the Clarendon Press, Oxford, in 1932, enhanced his fame. When we were at I Tatti, en route to Egypt about this time, in a mood of reaction to the general acclaim given him as an authority, he seemed a trifle bored with his life of pomp and circumstance, in a setting of natural beauty, and was restless for new experiences.

Mary made an effort to come downstairs, after a series of illnesses, but asked me to preside at the tea table. One afternoon, with other guests present, Berenson said to Joe that he wished he could join us in Egypt, "but I'm tied to an invalid, as you see." It was a cruel remark that revealed an inner resentment.

Both of them had remained in Italy after Mussolini entered World War II on the side of Germany. At the intervention of Mussolini's son-in-law, neither the Berensons nor the property were molested, and they were befriended by many Italians who protected his hidden art treasures.

It was in 1946 that I last saw Berenson at I Tatti. Mary had died the previous year. He was rather bowed, hollow-eyed, emaciated, and very bald. But he was the same Berenson, and still talkative. He expressed decided views and high interest in changing world events.

But most of all his thoughts were on the prospect of I Tatti's being preserved, under the safekeeping of Harvard. Actual possession did not take place until some months after Berenson's death in 1959. It was accepted as a gift with an endowment.

I had first known Italy in the days of the monarchy, established in the middle of nineteenth century, after a successful challenge to the temporal power of the Pope. Later I was to become familiar with the Italy of Benito Mussolini, at the height of his power. Foreigners were impressed by fact that trains now ran on time, that beggars had vanished from the streets, and that construction of imposing buildings and creation of parks were going rapidly forward. But Italian friends spoke of city slums that were worse than ever, and of the neglect of schools.

It was in Italy that Joe and I had our first intimation of approaching governmental chaos in Germany. In 1931 we were spending a few days in Genoa with the daughter of old-time English friends, married to a Dutchman who was consul general for Holland.

He had recently been in Berlin and talked of his horror at the effect on street crowds made by the harangues of Adolph Hitler, a young fanatic. "Is that a name I should remember?" Joe had asked.

My final impression of Italy was in 1946, particularly of Rome, with the prevalent riots and disorders. These were the political repercussions after Mussolini's forced resignation and his subsequent ignominious death at the hands of the partisans.

21

THREE GENERATIONS
ON THE MOVE

BETWEEN OUR Italian sojourns, during the winter of 1904, Joe received many commissions for Egyptian paintings. Therefore, when Dr. F. M. Sandwith, the leading English physician in Cairo, assured me by letter that their climate and river life were suitable for very young children, we made our plans accordingly.

Dowe was instructed to have a *dahabieh* ready for the entire family to take possession of at Assouan by December 15, 1904. Dr.

Sandwith had volunteered to have a nurse on hand who knew the country and spoke Arabic.

After a long and uneventful voyage, we met Dowe at the Cairo railroad station. With him was Jeannette Yakovitz, a smiling young Levantine who looked capable. The children took to her at sight.

A few days later, we were off for Upper Egypt by train and at Assouan boarded the *Abu Simbel*, moored to the island of Elephantine. The gigantic Assouan dam was now a *fait accompli*, with endless sluices, canals leading to an enormous storage reservoir for surplus water, and navigation locks. The country people of Egypt believed the famine, coincident with the years of building the dam, was caused by the anger of *afreet* (evil spirits) living in great boulders, which had been blasted from place by dynamite.

Sir Colin Moncrieff was the engineer whose imagination conceived and carried to completion the project which was expected to revolutionize the economic life of Upper Egypt. The dam was a mile and a half long. When he came to our *dahabieh*, our servants all but refused to serve dinner to that bad man, as they called him.

The Nile was still rising, and the approach to the court of the Temple of Isis, on the Island of Philæ, had to be made by boat. The whole former lovely island was desolate with tottering masonry, and the bas-reliefs had wide disfiguring cracks. Much of the beautiful vegetation was already destroyed by floodwaters, as was the attractive town of Shellal.

Joe, seated on a plank placed on a staging against the temple wall above the water line, managed to paint a few of the figures which remained intact and still had color on them. Philæ henceforth was to be visible only during the low-water season in summer time. We were glad to depart from this once lovely site, to drift downstream to Luxor, the prevailing north wind against us, but a strong current aided the crew, rowing with long sweeps.

On Christmas eve a full moon made it possible to continue the voyage through the night, and at dawn we moored against the western sand bank of Thebes, opposite the modern town of Luxor. Behind ancient monuments, within our view on the vast plain, rocky cliffs extended the length of the horizon.

Our native servants took over the entertainment of the children in the sand. Their toys of European manufacture failed to compete with the improvised ones, of ingenious mechanism, made by the crew, who instantly assumed the children's entertainment on the beach.

Even Rebecca's doll, Polly Flinders, to whom Joe had added the name Petrie in honor of the great Egyptologist, was discarded in favor of an odd contrivance of rags and wood. Black wool represented hair, colored beads features, shells were ears, and dangling silver ornaments gave an added charm to Polly's successful rival.

A favorite pastime indulged in by Rebecca and the crew was drawing pictographs on the hard sand with a stick. What interested Joe, as artist, was that the rather complex designs produced by a native adult and an American child were similar in artistic expression. Also, the fact that, while each knew what the other's drawings represented, to Joe both alike were meaningless. With the adaptability and imitation of a child, Rebecca was soon making herself understood in Arabic, and she knew what the crew was saying to her.

I had insisted on a personal inspection of the cow that furnished milk for the children. Dowe and I dismounted from donkeys on the outskirts of a village and he led me through a court and up narrow stairs onto a flat roof, where a woman was cooking over an open oven. Close by, a large, healthy-looking cow was chewing *dhoura* (corn) stalks. "Milk good," the woman remarked.

"How does the cow get down to the pasture?" I inquired, only to receive the astounding information that the cow, as a calf, had been carried onto the roof and had never come down. The question of how the cow became fresh, I leave to the conjectures of experts.

This was one of many examples of living conditions I was to see at first hand because Joe's work in tombs and temples took him to the vicinity of simple communities, seldom visited by Europeans, and under Dowe's auspices, I gained authentic information about native life and hospitality.

Since the days of the Ancient Empire, Egypt had remained an agricultural country, with the political organization in the Nile Valley practically unchanged in Lord Cromer's era. The Pharoahs filled their granaries by the forced labor of the tillers of the soil. Today the struggle was with "absentee landlords," enriching themselves by taking most of the crops from this same black earth.

A casual visit to a village disclosed a deplorable lack of amenities. Even in the better homes, usually situated in groves of date-bearing palms on the outskirts, sanitation was nonexistent, and water for household purposes had to be carried from the Nile, or, nearer, by canals.

From break of day until dusk, the patient tillers of the soil, together with their animals, were in the adjacent fields. In the evening they returned home, where, in a court, a hollow depression served as a stove. The little available food was cooked over a few available sticks in the one utensil owned by such a household. At dark, since there was no spare fuel for lighting, the *fellah*, his wife and children wrapped themselves in any coverings they had and slept on the mud floor of a single windowless room. The restricted space was shared with domestic animals. This was the way many millions of Egypt's agricultural families lived.

There were even greater hardships to face when the people passed weeks on end, among their growing crops, sleeping inside roofless enclosures made of *dhoura* stalks, placed close together, in a vain effort to break the chill of an Egyptian night. Yet the *fellah* was always cheerful. In a fairly large village, the inhabitants formed two or three major clans, arranged in family groups, and members of a different clan had but little to do with one another. This lack of unity among villagers played into the hands of the wealthy and often unscrupulous landowners.

One's entrance to a village was greeted by children shrieking, the cackle of women's voices, and chickens and pigeons underfoot. As strangers, we were received in the formal room of an important home, or by the *omda* (mayor) in his office. My ability to speak colloquial Arabic enabled me to interject remarks that led to interesting information. Among pleasant village acquaintances was the agricultural expert, usually old, who held his position by self-appointment. He had a profound wisdom in everything connected with the growing of crops. When drawn out, he showed an incredible amount of technical information but advocated the same procedures used successfully in ancient times. His reputed knowledge was verified by an English agricultural expert, who told me he had "come to Egypt to instruct, and had stayed on to be taught."

One typical evening in a village near Keneh, Joe and I were the guests of the chief of police. Among the dignitaries present were the *omda*, *kadi*, and the station master. The latter, who was young and alert, gave a description of a lecture by an English *hakeem* (doctor) in Cairo, who advised Egyptians not to drink from irrigation ditches in their villages.

Bursts of laughter greeted this, to them, absurd statement. But the Coptic doctor burst into a tirade against polluted water in stagnant ditches, reminding the notables present of their having opposed his plan of digging a well for drinking water. He glared at each solemn face in turn and said truculently, "You all prefer to drink water with germs in it."

When someone asked what germs were, the angered Copt floundered and finally announced that germs were "worms living in men's stomachs and made them ill."

The fat *kadi* stared unbelievingly at the medical man. "Worms live in the soil," he stated firmly. These words spoken by the local judge were accepted as a legal pronouncement. The sheikh of the mosque promptly took up the cudgels against any change in the local water supply. "Water comes to the ditches from the river Nile, where Allah put it for our use," he declared.

"Allah is generous," echoed all.

It was obvious the course of village hygiene would make but slow progress in this district.

The main emphasis of our life was of course on archaeology and Joe's painting in connection with it, but in between being with him in tombs and temples, I managed to see a good deal of the villagers. Unexpectedly, this was to lead to my having some intimate talks with Lord Cromer about Egypt of the provinces.

We had decided to continue *dahabieh* life on reaching Cairo, and had moored near the Palace Hotel, on the Island of Ghezireh, close to a park where the children spent their days.

Dr. Sandwith held a unique position, in being *persona grata* with Lord Cromer, was popular with English residents, but also had a wide acquaintance among distinguished Moslem families, many of whom he had first known professionally. At the Mehemet Ali Club, comprised of a mixed membership of English and Egyptians, he was depended upon, when conflicting ideas arose, to modify the views of the English and persuade the Egyptians to become more reasonable.

Dr. Sandwith's reply to a comment I made about the absence of Egyptians at functions in English homes was interesting. It resulted, he said, from "social isolation," and according to him was bitterly resented by the Egyptians. He defined some of the racial characteristics that served as a barrier between the two peoples. Conversationally, there was no common meeting ground. The English talked about sport, in their exclusive Turf Club, and about other things connected with the English way of life. Whereas the Egyptians discussed political intrigues and personal grievances. A further bar was that, to a Moslem, Islam gave him a consciousness of his religious superiority over non-Moslems. This caused him to seem arrogant. In all other respects, his mind functioned so entirely at odds with that of an Anglo-Saxon as to arouse mutual suspicion. For instance, in an Egyptian's dealings with an Englishman, he was inclined to tell him what he thought he wanted to know, rather than the truth, or else something to his own advantage. It never occurred to an Egyptian that this might destroy confidence in his integrity.

None of Dr. Sandwith's friends interested me more than his Egyptian colleagues at the School of Medicine. My own accounts of village superstitions in conflict with modern medicine were more than matched in Cairo. For instance, I learned that wearing a bone taken from a dead Jew or a mummy and worn on the person gave immunity to all fevers. This was practiced by both Moslems and Copts. The cure for a sty in the eye was to eat bread obtained from seven women, all named Fatima, after the daughter of the Prophet. These were examples of many preventive measures and remedies, ancient in origin, with which the doctors still had to contend, even in the poorer districts of Cairo.

No one could be in the presence of Egypt's great administrator,

Lord Cromer, without a realization of a nobility of character and steadfastness of purpose that towered above other men's as noticeably as did his physical stature. Every line of his strong face and the direct gaze of his eyes spoke of integrity and sincerity. Dr. Sandwith had told him of my familiarity with village life, and even in a casual conversation at the opera I caught his feeling of personal responsibility for the protection of the patient *fellaheen* against the greed of landlords and others in and out of high office.

I had seen sufficient of the crosscurrents in Cairo to recognize that the actual governance of Egypt, nominally ruled by Khedive Tewfik (selected by the English) under the suzerainty of the Sultan of Turkey, had required the dominating will and ingenuity of Lord Cromer to keep relations between the educated Egyptians in Cairo, proud and sensitive to slights, and the occupying British from the breaking point during the past twenty-three years.

Foreign intervention was universally accepted as inevitable in 1882 for the protection of the Suez Canal, when the misrule of Ismail Pasha had brought the country to bankruptcy and a rebellion led by a native fanatic had brought political chaos.

With the consent of the powers, the British fleet bombarded Alexandria and order was restored. At this point Evelyn Baring, later to become Lord Cromer, took over, his immediate interest being in the bewildered *fellaheen*, on whose ceaseless labor depended the prosperity of the entire population.

By legal status, Cromer was only one of many accredited representatives of foreign powers, but in fact, and again with the consent of the powers, he shared with the Khedive the administration of Egypt. The Khedive governed through a council of ministers but Cromer appointed a British adviser to each minister. Neither the Khedive nor his council was permitted to forget that behind Cromer's suggestions was a British army stationed in the heart of Cairo.

I had seen for myself the system at work. To the *fellaheen* in the Valley of the Nile, England meant young inspectors living among them, speaking their language and preventing their exploitation by ruthless pasha. I was favorably impressed by several English inspectors I met. They seemed to have an understanding of the mental process of the *fellaheen* and a sympathy for their needs. I learned from them that the *mudir* (a native governor of a province) knew to his cost that injustice to *fellaheen*, unless remedied promptly when reported by the British adviser to the minister concerned, would be followed up personally by Lord Cromer's taking it up directly with the Khedive. Not unnaturally, this was a situation Egyptian officials found increasingly irksome.

By the next time I saw Lord Cromer, in the home of a mutual English friend, he had heard of my study of the Koran and he talked to me at length of the importance of Islam in the life of a Moslem.

He referred to the *fellaheen* as deeply religious, neither interested in, nor fitted for, taking part in representative government, as a daily routine concerned with the hard realities of village life. He also questioned the advisability of Moslem youths of wealthy families being constantly in the company of younger members of the diplomatic corps. He feared it might lead to their adopting social practices of Christians, prohibited in the Koran.

Following this line of thought, I repeated a pertinent experience of mine, about being informally in the home of a conservative, rather wealthy Egyptian woman, married to an *alim* of the el-Azhar. In the intimacy of the communal bowl, she confided to me their anxiety about a half-grown son who was frequently with Christians who were a part of the social life of Cairo. She and her husband had taken alarm at his references to "freedom."

When the son joined us, the mother whispered to me to inquire about his interpretation of freedom. He replied casually that it was something Christians had which made it unnecessary to pay attention to Allah except on Sunday, and even then it was not obligatory. "It wouldn't work for us," he added, "because Allah calls Moslems to account for every act, every day of the week."

I responded to Lord Cromer's spontaneous expression of interest by telling anecdotes revealing an equally wide gulf between the ideas of villagers and those of Europeans or Americans.

One afternoon about a week later, as I rested on the upper deck of our *dahabieh*, leisurely reading, Dowe rushed up to me so excited that he could hardly make himself understood, announcing that the

Great Englishman himself was approaching the *dahabieh*. "Bring him up here and serve tea," I managed to get out.

Lord Cromer told me he had dropped in on the chance of finding me, to continue our talk about village life. This was the first of a number of informal, and to me, illuminating conversations.

El-Azhar dignitaries whom I met were constantly expressing gratification at Lord Cromer's knowledge of the Koran and his interpretation of some of the passages in terms of modern life. This seemed advisable in view of what had occurred at the building of the first railroad. Ignorant *fellaheen* either tore up the rails or went to sleep on the tracks.

To prevent the recurrence of these performances, Lord Cromer, in a speech which was widely quoted, prepared the *fellaheen's* minds for a further innovation in transportation. He referred to a verse in the Koran about ships on the sea, and camels and donkeys, on which men got about in the days of the Prophet.

He explained the concluding words, "Allah will create other advantages," as meaning cars, motor trucks, and aeroplanes, which before many years would be in general use. His statement unquestionably influenced a vast number of conservative Moslems to use transportation of a kind unknown to their Prophet. This was but one of many examples of Lord Cromer's tact and wisdom, and his qualities of human understanding.

Our final evening on the *Abu Simbel* has lingered on in my memory. The family had gathered on the upper deck to watch a superb sunset reflected in the absolutely still waters of the Nile, and the black hulls of *feluka*, rosy clouds, and the Mokattam Hills in the distance. And then the full moon rose. My trend of thoughts, tinged with sadness at our approaching departure, was interrupted by Dowe's announcing guests. It was Dr. Sandwith, come to say goodby. He had with him two Englishmen, one of them with a name made familiar by his close association with Lord Cromer.

The three men were on their way to dine at the Turf Club. They joined us on deck and stayed on long past our usual dining hour. One of them remarked suddenly, "Many of us living in Cairo never have a chance to feel the spell of Egypt as we are doing now."

Impulsively, I invited them to dine with us, instead of going to the Turf Club, and rather to my surprise they instantly accepted. What with the moonlight and a general sense of well-being after a good meal, our guests became communicative and discussed many current issues between the English and Egyptian officials. The man who had been delighted at seeing Cairo from the deck of a *dahabieh* was obviously a member of the Liberal party, from his criticism of what he termed treating Egypt as a "Crown colony."

There was favorable comment about Lord Cromer's action in changing the Department of Education into a Ministry as a step in the right direction, and about his introduction of the policy of sending Egyptian girls to England to be trained as teachers. Even more evocative was his action in making an Egyptian minister officially responsible for curbing Egyptian students, whose passion for politics was causing them to be trouble-makers.

Dr. Sandwith spoke of his sympathy for the unknown Egyptian, Zaghlul Pasha, a member of the Court of Appeal, whom Cromer had insisted upon the Khedive's appointing to this almost impossible job. The unruly students were fully aware that they had both the Arabic press and Egyptian politicians behind them. Little did anyone present or elsewhere in government circles realize that this same Zaghlul, before many years had passed, would be the Nationalist leader of the people of Egypt, demanding a break with England.

Dr. Sandwith also voiced sympathy for Cromer in his increasingly difficult position. "I should think he would be glad," he said, "to pass on to younger shoulders the burden of carrying out reforms in the economy, finances, and judicial system of the country which his genius had initiated. Above all, his ceaseless struggle to protect the *fellaheen* from the ruthlessness of the upper classes."

The Englishman closely associated with his chief's policies stated that Cromer was always absolutely confident that his decisions were the right ones, and also had general approval. He added in a surprising burst of frankness that, in his opinion (with which I silently disagreed), Cromer was totally unaware of the fundamental changes that would come perforce immediately after his departure. Suddenly conscious he was being indiscreet, he refused to be drawn further.

I was to remember as prophetic the other English guest, who remarked with some heat that when the Liberals came into control in England they would not ignore the loud clamor demanding that a date be set for the evacuation of British troops from Cairo, their presence having been referred to as "temporary" in 1882.

And on that note the Englishmen left!

22

MEMORABLE EXPERIENCES
IN WASHINGTON

I COULD NEVER FORGET that the first time I was in the United States Senate, I had watched Theodore Roosevelt preside as vice-president. Afterwards, at lunch, he sadly equated a very long-winded speech by a senator to the number of young trees required for the wood pulp used in having the speech printed in full in *The Congressional Record*!

Later, during a period of years, I was to have official contact with Congress in matters of legislation concerned with Indians, for the most part. And in reading *The Congressional Record* regularly, I was always reminded to count words spoken as so many trees.

A delightful custom during the Roosevelt administration was a New Year's reception held in the Blue Room of the White House. One hundred representative women from the country as a whole were invited to receive with the President's wife. Members of the Cabinet were there with their wives.

It was an honor eagerly sought and I was pleased to be included when, on President McKinley's assassination, Theodore Roosevelt became president. But truth to tell, my first experience of it was rather a dull affair, in spite of Mrs. Roosevelt's being very gracious. Everyone was standing about not knowing exactly what to do or say. My eye was on Elihu Root, the secretary of War, who was trying hard to suppress a yawn, when suddenly all was changed.

The President's daughter Alice burst into the room like a whirlwind, and picking out the staid Secretary of War for attention, slapped him genially on the back. He cheered up and so did everyone else! She had her father's physical vitality and dynamic force.

Another eventful occasion occurred in connection with Prince Henry's visit to America. It seems strange, in view of what was later to occur, that the Kaiser's brother was one of the most popular of foreign visitors. Boston entertained him generously, as did all the large cities. George Meyer was secretary of the Navy at the time, and Joe and I were both asked to go on the President's yacht, the *Mayflower*, with Prince Henry for a day's trip to Mt. Vernon.

In going about the many points of interest at Mt. Vernon, Prince Henry expressed constant enthusiasm for what George Washington stood for as a great statesman. In addition, I found it amusing to observe from the sidelines that his volley of questions about significant details in Washington's political career kept the brains of Cabinet members in attendance constantly on the move, as they tried to answer off the cuff. Each looked willing to have one of the others take up the intellectual challenge offered by the German.

In the few moments I had alone with the Prince on the *Mayflower*, mention was somehow made of the Pacific. He spoke of the roughness of the ocean on an official trip he had made. He told me, shuddering even in retrospect, that for days he had "swallowed up" everything.

I had never heard a better description of seasickness.

Joe had particularly enjoyed Alice Roosevelt, who had asked him to give her a comprehensive idea of Egyptology and excavating, subjects about which she knew nothing, she said. He found her an apt pupil, with "rare ability in grasping and digesting all the essentials."

We were in Washington fairly frequently in the Theodore Roosevelt era, usually staying with Miss Emily Tuckerman, who was almost an adjunct to the White House staff. One visit was for the opening of an exhibition of Joe's Egyptian paintings, and she arranged for him to give the President as well as Mrs. Roosevelt a special preview, with no one else present.

A subsequent visit to Emily Tuckerman occurred during the Ballinger–Pinchot controversy. This *cause célèbre*, which was rocking President Taft's new administration to its foundations, grew out of charges made by Louis R. Glavis, chief of the Field Division of Department of the Interior, that his superior, Secretary Richard A. Ballinger, was reversing the Roosevelt conservation policy.

As President, Theodore Roosevelt, in one of his appealing campaigns had aroused the American people to the need for conserving our forests and other natural resources. Now his devoted disciples, headed by Gifford Pinchot, and aided and abetted by Roosevelt, pursued the charges. Consequently there was widespread prejudgment against Ballinger, both popularly and by a clamorous Washington.

Social Washington was out in force at a hearing Joe and I went to, our special interest being that the Pinchots were good friends. We became separated in the crowd, but Joe's account later was that, to his amusement, he was pushed far to the front and seated between Mrs. Pinchot and Mrs. Ballinger. Apparently neither had seen the other as they sat down, and both considered it would attract attention to move—so there they were!

Joe said that he had happened to be watching the faces of both Mrs. Pinchot and Mrs. Ballinger during the testimony of a witness who, for the most part, had insisted on quoting endless statistics. Suddenly Joe couldn't resist saying, "Ladies, there must be something wrong in relying on statistics, since you are both looking triumphant at the same moment."

With President Taft's support of Ballinger and his dismissal of Pinchot, Republican party unity was to be destroyed. Even with the close ties Elihu Root had with Roosevelt, he considered his loyalty, as secretary of State, was to President Taft, but his intimate friend, former President Roosevelt, whose secretary of State he had been, backed Pinchot, as did Henry L. Stimson, the secretary of War.

The political breach had not been healed when Joe and I attended the Republican Convention held in Chicago in June, 1912, where Root was chairman.

216

Taft's nomination by the convention left Roosevelt no alternative but to withdraw from the Republican party. The Roosevelt delegates met and declared their intention of nominating him as the candidate of the new Progressive party. This was done at a convention also held at Chicago in early August.

Whatever has been said and written to the contrary, my own conclusion about a very complex situation is that Roosevelt was absolutely sincere in his belief that his nomination, forced on the conservatives, would accomplish the ends that he and his followers visualized as necessary to the salvation of the Republican party.

When Taft was nominated by the Conservatives and Roosevelt by the Progressives, the result was inevitable—Woodrow Wilson was elected by the Democrats and became the war president.

Another time when, without Joe, I was with Emily Tuckerman for a special occasion, Justice Oliver Wendell Holmes came to lunch. She intended to defy protocol by putting me on one side of him, she said, because his nephew, Edward J. Holmes, of the Boston Museum of Fine Arts, was one of Joe's and my best friends.

All through the meal, distinguished lawyers present attempted to get the Justice's opinion on matters of legal importance over which public opinion was widely divided, but not, of course, under consideration by the Supreme Court. The Justice, however, remained completely absorbed in talking to me about how much Ned and his wife Mary meant to him. I caught a twinkle in his eye that would have dispelled any doubt, had I held such, about the sense of humor which characterized this great justice of the Supreme Court.

He made his excuses as soon as lunch was over and disappeared without law having been discussed, but not before arranging for Emily Tuckerman to bring me to call on his wife.

Nothing meant more to me than seeing John Hay again, after a long lapse. It was in the early fall of 1903, before we were to sail for a winter in Rome, that I chanced to encounter him in the street in downtown Washington as he was about to step into his conveyance. I had seen him occasionally at functions since my girlhood meeting with him in London; he recognized me and suggested that I go home with him for a chat. As he got into the car beside me, he

217

said with a delightful smile, "Still interested in Lincoln?" I assured him I was, and when I mentioned the Pacific, he added jokingly, "We have found another bond."

He led me into his study and ordered tea, then excused himself to give some instructions to a waiting secretary. During his absence my thoughts reverted to 1897, when I had seen him as our ambassador to Great Britain at a period he was generally recognized as a literary figure and a writer of poetry, a volume of which he had sent me.

But now I was about to talk to him, or rather listen to him, as our secretary of State. I remembered his pronounced views about America's role in the Pacific.

In the summer of 1898, he was being consulted about what our terms of peace with Spain should be. By the fall he had aligned himself with those favoring the cession of the entire group of the Philippine Islands to the United States. And with his views well known, President McKinley had appointed him his secretary of State.

Hay's face looked drawn as he sat down and drank in rapid succession two cups of tea I poured for him. But in spite of signs of ill health, he was eager to talk about the Open Door in China.

In his summary of the sequence of events, Hay continued to stress his satisfaction that, as secretary of State, he had been able in August, 1899, to prevent the dissolution of China and a scramble for her vast territory by the European powers.

He further stated that he had insisted on America's keeping the Boxer Rebellion localized by dealing with the Peking government, even though it lacked courage and made no effort on its own behalf.

As we parted, he made a remark I will always treasure. It was that he was glad my marriage had not interfered with my being my father's daughter.

While James Bryce was British ambassador, I could always stay at the Embassy in Washington on notification by telegram. Many of Bryce's statements have remained in my mind, such as that he was brought up on the Bible and the *Arabian Nights*. Being often under the same roof, I could fully realize his extraordinary energy. He always seemed in a hurry to get on to the next obligation.

But first and foremost in the nature of prophecy, I recall Bryce's saying that he never refused an invitation to speak to the student body of a college or university. He wished, he said, to do his utmost towards guiding the thinking of young Americans who were potential leaders. There was the influence of the powerful Hearst papers to combat, and he always found, he said, an eager response to his pleas for sound principles in government. Bryce expressed himself as being appalled at the lack of guidance of students by their professors. He considered that teachers tended to restrict instruction to specific subjects, losing sight of their responsibility to train students for useful lives as citizens.

The last time I saw Bryce was in the summer of 1920, at his home at Hindleap, Surrey. I motored to have breakfast with him before sailing home that afternoon.

He appeared with a bundle containing the first proofs of his book, *Modern Democracies*. He apologized for keeping me waiting until he got them ready for mailing to his publisher. "I must get the book in print while there is still a democracy left," he said.

23

ONE EXCITEMENT AFTER ANOTHER

EARLY IN NOVEMBER, 1905, the entire family was back in Egypt. Joe hired the *Stella* through a Greek merchant in Cairo for the voyage to Luxor, where he was to paint, and the return trip in the spring. While the *dahabieh* was being prepared for travel, the children with Jeanette and the grandparents stayed at Helouan, a health resort near Cairo. Joe and I were in a small hotel near the Cairo Museum, except for a few days in Saqqarah, for me, with the Edward J. Quibells, where Quibell was excavating.

At noon on November 23 we boarded the *Stella*. Reis Inowe inspired confidence, his tall body looked agile, and I liked his friendly smile. Dowe, our principal servant during our Egyptian years, lingered, after a brief visit of ceremony in the main cabin, to inform us the Reis was not pleased. Ousman, the second reis, and Ali, his cousin, and one of the crew had only just arrived. Now with a strong, favoring north wind, we were waiting for the bread for the crew, baked by Ousman's harem.

Ousman did not meet Joe's and Father's eyes, on shaking hands. A nervous twitching of his face was a sign of emotional instability, and a stubborn set to an undershot jaw indicated he might prove dangerous in a crisis. Ali's appearance was even less reassuring; in a yellow turban, slightly awry, his single eye fierce, he waved his arms about, shouting to the crew, obviously paying strict attention to his wild utterances.

By the time the bread came, the wind had dropped. At the Reis's reprimand for the delay in delivery, Ousman retorted defiantly that the harem had not expected a start on Friday, the Day of the Mosque. At this strained moment, Ali, trembling violently, screamed "Allah! Allah!" The crew was unnerved, and the subject of the bread was hastily dropped.

After dusk, however, the crew, squatting around a minute charcoal fire, laughed and chatted over their food. Ali broke into a love song about a girl with beautiful teeth and eyes like a gazelle's, in a singing voice with an agreeable rhythm. Reis Inowe, having finished his sunset prayers, joined the circle. Under these auspicious conditions, I persuaded Joe to take the night train for Luxor, as planned, so that he might have additional painting time.

After he had left and I was inside with the children, I heard a scuffle and the sobs of a youngster. Dowe explained, when I arrived on deck, that the boy he had by the scruff of his neck was a stowaway. He was about to throw him ashore. But the urchin grinned, on observing from the dragoman's displeased manner that the *sitt* (woman) was inclined to be friendly. He told me his name was Mohamed Abdul Rasoul and that he was twelve.

"You will work hard, Mohamed, if we take you?" I asked.

"No," he replied, "I am no good, lazy, and I steal, but I intend to go to Luxor on this boat." His large eyes in a tear-stained face met mine appealingly.

"There is nothing useful you do?" I asked again.

"Nothing," he admitted with the same candor, as, squirming free from Dowe's renewed grip, he stated forlornly, "I read the Koran."

I produced my copy and heard the sacred words roll off the urchin's lips, intoned in the traditional style used by imam and sheikh. Here was a teacher from whom to learn to pronounce words which John Orne's earlier patience had trained me to understand but which I could not repeat in correctly spoken Arabic. Thus we entered into a bargain which gave me a strong start toward competence in Arabic, and which on one occasion saved my life.

The following morning we started in a light westerly wind, which dropped at noon, soon changing into a strong blow from the south. We remained for the next three days moored against an unattractive mud bank, there to remain until, on Thanksgiving Day, ironically, the wind developed into the dreaded *khamseen*. The atmosphere became an ominous yellow, flapping of canvas never ceased, the boat rocked. It was impossible to be rid of, or forget, the pursuing powdered dust at every move. The children whimpered, all of us choked ceaselessly!

That evening Dowe told of a *fellah* who had killed his wife and children during a *khamseen*, but was freed by the judge, since during a *khamseen* a man "was not responsible for his action." This story did not help nerves already on edge.

Ali, without warning, fell to the deck screaming. At this the crew cried, "*Sheikh betarhu*," in awe of the notice by Allah, who had "possessed Ali with a spirit." A wild scene ensued, with dust whirling in sand devils, breaking window panes, Ali wailing steadily like a banshee as he lay in a heap covered by a canvas. The crew was restless, talked excitedly, or were too silent and refused cigarettes with unsmiling eyes. The Reis had worried lines in his face.

In a sudden let-up, a day opened with no sun, but the storm was over. The men sullenly took the long towrope and made a couple of miles, pulling the heavy *dahabieh* along the shore against a strong current. A sharp shower brought the men on board drenched. When hailstones hit us, Ali, who had been sitting quietly on the deck, leapt to his feet and jumped into the Nile. He was rescued by the prompt action of Reis Inowe, who jumped after him, followed by Dowe.

Khamseen, the ominous yellow sandstorm, rain, and hail were intermittent as we progressed toward Luxor. Each time the hail occurred, Ali became possessed. And just when we thought our luck had turned after successive days of bad weather, disaster came during our attempt to get beyond a point of land in a light breeze.

Owing to a strong current, the *Stella*, out of control, collided with a *feluka* heavily loaded with *gulleh*. The outrigging went right through our kitchen and pots and pans and bits of broken jars flew in every direction.

All my life I will remember the faces of the crew, unreal in the wavering light, lips tight, narrowed eyes visible under head shawls. Ali was a creature apart, with the yellow turban unwound and his twitching body electric with excitement as he crouched in the midst of splintered wood and forbade imaginary enemies to approach.

We made an emergency landing against a high bank on a level with the windows. Next morning, soon after dawn, we crawled out of our bunks, the children bleary-eyed and crying. Dowe announced tersely, "Ali tell crew *afreet* (evil spirit) on board, they gone."

The canvas had to be lowered and shutters closed on the shore side, as villagers joined the mutinied crew on the bank, their bundles beside them. An occasional stone and mud were hurled against the shutters. The gangplank was put out and the Reis and Dowe descended, to be plastered with mud by the crew, Ousman with them.

The Reis could not leave the besieged boat, Dowe's command for donkeys was ignored, and the *ghaffir* stood sullenly aloof. Father and I accompanied Dowe on foot, to put our case before the *kadi* of the nearest village, three miles away. We had to walk over rough ground with a fierce sandstorm blowing. Ali leapt about, speaking in a tone of unnatural exaltation. Among the crew, led by Ousman, were many of the local inhabitants making disparaging remarks, but there was no open attack upon us.

We were rather dismayed by the characterless features and weak mouth of the waiting *kadi*. Through Dowe, as interpreter, Father read the contract, whereupon the *kadi* decreed the crew must take us to Luxor before any money was paid. Our triumph was short lived! Seeing the effect on the villagers of Ali's wild gesticulations, the *kadi* agreed to his plea that Ousman be heard.

"The contract was read exactly as written," Ousman said, "but even so, must we remain on a boat with an *afreet*? Is that the will of Allah?" All knew the habits of *khamseen*, he continued, "and that it never lasted more than three days." With the adroitness of an agitator, Ousman made a dramatic appeal to the court audience, which had crowded into this hot little room where the flies were thick and the atmosphere foul with stale smoke.

"Has the *kadi* or anyone else in this room ever heard of ten days of *khamseen* in succession on one trip?" he asked rhetorically, pausing tellingly as a particularly strong gust of south wind shook the walls.

"That man has talked enough!" Dowe said to the *kadi*.

"Let him go on," came the roar from all sides. The *kadi* again yielded to the clamor.

The Second Reis's voice had gained in confidence, and he defied Dowe in a scornful glance. No oriental court could have withstood the strength of the case against us, when Ali, clinging to the *kadi*'s garments, shrieked about the wickedness of attempting to start a voyage on the Day of the Mosque, and told of rain, more rain, and hail, both as unheard of in the villages of the Upper Nile as ten days of *khamseen*. And that was not all! A good north wind springing up to aid the *Stella* had enraged the *afreet*, and it had seized the wheel from Ousman to bring on a collision.

Ali sank groaning to the floor, and Ousman, standing over him, implored Allah to save all in the room from the anger of so powerful an *afreet*. The shuddering natives panicked. It was inevitable that the *kadi* should reverse his decision. And Reis Inowe was compelled, in the presence of the *kadi* on the river bank near the marooned *Stella*, to produce his canvas bag and pay off the crew, who departed with the villagers.

At sunrise, a brisk northerly breeze was blowing and apparently the favoring wind was evidence that the *afreet* had relented and all would be well! At least this was the expressed opinion of a thoroughly chastened crew, who, shivering and hungry, asked to be taken back. They complained that the bad villagers had stolen all their money from them. But Reis Inowe was adamant in his refusal to come to terms with a crew that had mutinied.

The huge sail was unfurled, and the *Stella* headed for Assiut, one hundred and fifty miles away, where we expected to find a new crew, supplied by the Cairo owner. It was extraordinary how smoothly the voyage continued without a crew. Father was as good as several sailors, Abdul Rahman and Abdalla were also helpful, and Mohamed and I did the less important jobs, under the Reis's orders, in managing a large boat under full sail.

The crew awaited our arrival at Assiut, and when no word was received from Joe, we took for granted he had changed his mind about joining us and sailed at once. About a mile above Assiut, when Reis Inowe was at the wheel, Rebecca's bright eyes spied Joe on a donkey, frantically signaling from a sandspit as he was being passed at full speed. She rushed up to the Reis shouting, "That's my father and I want him."

On the forty-first day since leaving Cairo, on a trip that should have taken less than twenty, we moored by the light of a full moon once again on the sand bank of Thebes. Here we settled down to a family regimen attuned to Joe's painting schedule on ancient monuments.

Father told Joe that even the *khamseen* had given up the struggle against my voice, which continued steadily intoning the Koran "hour after hour," when the storm had been at its height. The lessons continued, but I noticed that Mohamed was becoming very restive under my steady demands for instruction. It took more and more bribes in the way of sweets and other delicacies to persuade him to continue the lessons.

One day a crisis in our relations was reached. From our deck, little Mohamed jumped on to a passing *feluka*, bound for Assouan, that had come close to us for cigarettes. He called back that he was tired of the Koran and being with the *sitt*, and vanished from my life.

I soon found myself compelled to accept the Moslem belief that in the "predetermination of all things by Allah," I, a Christian, and a woman at that, was destined to learn the Koran. How could I think otherwise when, only a few days after little Mohamed's desertion, he was replaced. Sheikh Mutr, of a local mosque, appeared at the *dahabieh* as my self-appointed teacher, without notification. His was a grim personality, tall and forbidding, with high cheek bones, a large hooked nose, and eagle eyes.

Without preamble, the Sheikh announced that, since I insisted on reciting the Koran, he intended to train my "bad" tongue as a Christian. He promptly produced a copy of the sacred book and we started right away. He came daily and seemed satisfied with my progress, which was fairly rapid, thanks to Mohamed's previous efforts.

On the third successive Friday of lessons, he turned up early, with an air of suppressed excitement. He told me he was taking me to the home of Mohamed Muhassib, whom I knew as an honest dealer in antiquities, dealing mainly with museums.

It was not until he was leading me towards a small room in the dealer's home, dedicated to reciting the Koran, that he enlightened me about the reason of my being there.

The Imam from the el-Azhar, seated with the local sheikh inside, had not believed him, Sheikh Mutr said, when he had told of knowing an English-speaking woman who had the Koran "on her lips," although "not in her heart," and could answer questions about the tenets of the Islam.

"You will need your wits," he warned me, as he pushed open the door.

I saw, at a quick glance, an imposing figure, alone at one end of the room, and squatted, with their heels behind them on cushioned benches on either side, were sheikhs. No one moved as the Imam gestured me to an empty place facing him.

It was he alone who did the interrogating, which lasted over an hour. I repeated chapters of the Koran, demanded by name in a staccato voice, or verses from them, as indicated. I also answered questions fired at me in rapid succession.

I was relieved to discover from Sheikh Mutr's expression that he considered I was holding my own. Finally the Imam rose. Everyone else, including me, did the same. "Sheikh Mutr has spoken words of truth," the Imam said, "and you will attend noon service in the mosque in our company."

"But I am a Christian," I said.

"I know. You will remain in your ignorance but, even so, you are to come," he said.

Shortly thereafter I was again seated on my heels, on a bit of red carpet at the rear of a mosque, with the Imam and sheikhs nearby. No one had taken the slightest notice of my presence, such is the concentration of a Moslem in his devotions.

I had never seen anything of a religious character to equal the sight of six hundred Moslems, standing, bowing, seating themselves, kneeling, in absolute unison, with perfect timing, and in rhythmical movements and sounds. The sequence was repeated over and over again.

I was still under the spell of reverent faces seemingly in communion with Allah, when there was a slight commotion. *Darwishes* among them had risen and with joined hands were moving in a wild circle. Their leader, catching sight of me, gave a protesting growl and broke into the refrain of "dog of a Christian" in this *zikr* or circular dance.

At once the Imam leaned over me to say peremptorily, "Go at once, they don't like your presence."

"A Christian does not run away," I replied, with all the fortitude I could muster.

At once the Imam and the sheikh perceptibly edged away, showing I was no longer under their protection. Action on my part was imperative as the chorus of "dog of a Christian" echoed and re-echoed. The circle was in wild motion, and several *darwishes* had fallen to the floor in religious ecstacy.

I rose, with my heart beating loudly against my ribs, but I managed to walk steadily towards the leader, realizing my one chance lay in impressing him. I pursued him in his gyrations and held his eyes, which were by now aflame. "I am a Christian but we have the

226

same God," I shouted in a voice that carried above the tumult, and by sheer force of will gained control over him.

My gaze never wavered from his face. There was a moment of hesitation, then he motioned the circle to move in the opposite direction and started a new refrain, "Praise to the Christian."

In the momentary lull, I stole quietly out of the mosque, to find myself with the only sheikh at the interrogation who had opposed my coming to the noon prayer. He was the sheikh of the intrusive mosque within the confines of the Luxor Temple, dedicated to a Moslem saint since 800 A.D., known for the fanaticism of its adherents.

The sheikh motioned me to follow him uphill to the entrance of the mosque. He took me inside and for a long time repeated the Koran.

When he at last paused, I requested permission to depart, but in doing so I asked a question. Why had he invited me, a Christian, to enter his mosque? His answer was revealing.

"I admire a fierceness in religion, even though it is the wrong religion," he said.

About ten days later word came from the Imam that I was to learn to repeat the Ninety-nine Attributes of Allah. After that I would be admitted to noon prayer on Friday, in any mosque of Egypt even as a Christian.

The Attributes did not rhyme and had to be repeated in a prescribed order. I went to a class of Moslem boys to learn them. The teacher was nearsighted and hard of hearing, so he missed seeing small cakes of mud thrown at me surreptitiously when it was my turn to recite. For the time being nothing seemed to exist for me except those elusive words.

One day Sheikh Tiyib, who was very much respected in the district for his piety, came to the class. I was the only one who repeated the Attributes correctly. As a reward, he presented me with his own beautiful prayer beads of special sandalwood, which had made the pilgrimage to Mecca on his person six times.

On the return trip to Cairo, we decided to make a stopover at El Amarna, the city Akhenaten had built and lived in after changing the religion of Egypt to a single godhead, Aton, instead of the long-entrenched Amon-Ra of Thebes. We had walked across the fields to see the pavement in bird and animal designs of Akhenaten's famous palace. It was a region never visited by strangers on foot, and on the way back to the *dahabieh* our crew got into a row with villagers. The difficulty had been straightened out by the *mudir* (governor) of the province, who chanced to be passing, and we had invited him on board.

He was magnificently garbed in silken robes, but for all his grand clothes completely unsophisticated. In an apparently first encounter with strangers of our kind, he looked around the interior of our *dahabieh* with the frank curiosity of a child. He stayed on and on, Mother and Father disappeared, and Joe became restless at awkward silences.

I had made the usual inquiries about the height of the Nile and the local crops. One never mentioned wives to a Moslem, but a reference to his "household" was expected to produce a conversation concerned with children, with emphasis on sons and what they did. Unfortunately, the *mudir* had only one child, a girl, so that topic did not last long.

Finally Joe burst out, "Tell him you read the Koran!"

As I bluntly stated the fact, the *mudir*'s eyes turned on my face with a comical expression of incredulity. "You, a woman and a Christian—impossible!" he said.

I nodded to Dowe, who brought my copy. Soon I was seated beside the *mudir*, the opened Koran between us. I read from chapters, as requested, or we repeated verses together. His eyes were aglow, and he seemed concentrating on an idea taking shape. Suddenly he closed the Koran and exclaimed, "Life with you would be worth living!" He proceeded to tell me how fabulously rich he was, promised to divorce his two wives, if I preferred, and went into rhapsodies at the joy of our repeating the Koran far into the night.

Joe's amazed voice broke in abruptly wanting to know what the *mudir* was talking to me about so volubly. "The Koran," I replied evasively. Dowe's increasing uneasiness recalled me to the fact that the district had a reputation for lawlessness. By now I really began to fear the *mudir* was planning to kidnap me.

Meanwhile he was boasting of the splendor of his home and taking for granted my interest in visiting it. All smiles, he rose, "I hasten to prepare for the reception of your party," he declared and departed.

I was watching with relief his galloping Arab pony disappearing in the desert when Joe commented that the *Stella* was in motion. He was voicing disappointment to Dowe, as he wanted to visit the many ruins, when Abdalla began to fly around with a broom, sweeping everywhere the *mudir* had stepped.

Dowe answered Joe's surprised look by explaining that after sunset a Moslem did not sweep a friend's footprints from a room, for fear he might not return. "But," he continued, "we must make certain the *mudir* does not come back for the *sitt*."

Whereupon I informed Joe of the result of the Koran reading.

During a visit to the Quibells at Saqqarah with Joe, before sailing, the *omda* of Bedrechein devoted much time to indoctrinating me in phases of the Koran. He seemed greatly impressed by my attendance at Friday noon prayer in a Luxor mosque, and the mastery of the Ninety-nine Attributes of Allah.

Several times he lamented the sad fate decreed for me, a Christian, on the day of resurrection in Jerusalem. He reminded me that, starting in the Mosque of Omar, a bridge, narrow as a hair and sharp as a sword, would be stretched across the pit of hell. Jews, Sabians, and Christians, as well as Moslems must pass over it.

The prophet Muhammad would be there as each, in turn, stepped on to the bridge, which would be enveloped in the blackness of night. Esa, son of Mary (Christ) was at the other end, to light up the body of a Moslem at the first stumble, for Allah to notice and summon into Paradise. All others, unseen by Allah in the darkness, must fall into the pit of hell.

One day the *omda* turned up to report he had put my "special case," as he called it, to a group of *ulema* friends, at the el Azhar. After careful consideration, the conclusion reached was that, perhaps because of my knowledge of the Koran, my body might be lighted, just a little, and I would be saved.

24

KHUTMEH, 1906

ON A VISIT to the Quibells at Saqqarah before leaving Egypt that spring, while the darkness outside was yielding to a grayish light, I crept silently downstairs, mounted my donkey, and was on the road at the precise moment when a black thread can be distinguished from a white, as the Koran describes dawn. My journey was in response to a message from Abdul Wahed to come to Bedrechein that my soul might be benefitted. Consumed with curiosity, I was galloping along the embankment of the canal when, clear and arresting above the first faint sounds of animals and humans in a nearby village, I heard a *muezzin*'s summons to the faithful. The sky brightened and the mist lying low over wide stretches of desert sand and cultivation slowly lifted, the Step Pyramid of Saqqarah, the pyramids of Abukir, and those of distant Dashur and Giza were gorgeous. In a world of so much beauty, how could I dread the eternal fire of hell that my Moslem friends told me was predetermined for Christians!

At the outskirts of the village Abdul Wahed awaited my coming. I was instantly relieved by his demeanor. He looked cheerful but cold, with his head enveloped in shawls. His eyes were shining. "You are in time," he said in a voice bursting with excitement. He trudged beside me through narrow, turning streets, empty at this early hour. An Arab town asleep has very black corners and is so silent that every sound is intensified—the protesting snarl from a watchdog, the sliding back of a heavy shutter, or noises of domestic activity inside a tightly closed house. I shivered, more from the expectant thrill of what the *omda* had planned in my behalf than from chill that penetrated even my warm garments.

He helped me to dismount and gave careful orders to a boy to water and feed the donkey well during the day. I noticed an open door opposite, leading into a dim interior, and was listening to a murmur of voices from inside and pondering what might be an all-day affair, when Abdul Wahed cut into my thoughts. "If God so wills," he said with impressive emphasis, "You are about to listen to a *khutmeh*."

In the wildest flights of imagination I had never expected this experience. I was completely overwhelmed and stared stupidly. "A *khutmeh*?" my voice trembled with awe.

A pleased smile showed the *omda*'s pleasure at an emotion that all but choked me. "Even so," he replied, and having once started, his words came with a rush. He told me that Sheikh Abd' Allah of the Delta would repeat the Koran from cover to cover, that he was very old and seldom left his village, his eyes were sightless, and things of the world no longer interested him. "He lives mostly with God," he said simply, "but my father was at the el-Azhar with him, so he was willing to do this good talking for the *sitt*."

My stunned amazement grew. I had heard of the Saint of the Delta and felt perturbed at this effort made expressly for me. "He knows that I am a Christian?"

Abdul Wahed nodded. "Perhaps never again will the *sitt* hear the entire Koran recited by one man—it will be an occasion that must reach the heart of even a Christian—that was what I said to the old Sheikh, and he is here." The *omda* was exultant at what he had accomplished. His words seemed to travel a long distance to reach me: "Generally three or four *fikees* (chanters) relieve one another, as the voice and memory become tired, but Sheikh Abd' Allah is never tired when saying the words of God."

A greeting from within interrupted further conversation. I stepped over the threshold and sank down on a strip of red carpet placed in the shadow of the entrance door to which I was motioned. The small room had high windows with gratings over them; the walls were stained by a bluish wash; there were no furnishings of any kind; a group of men in a half-circle were seated motionless in front of me; the moving white of their turbans and the glint of moving prayer beads in their hands were the only suggestions of animation. All this I took in at a glance as my eyes became accustomed to the semi-darkness focused on the old Sheikh, who sat alone in the center of a raised platform facing the entrance door, on a small prayer rug. He wore a black robe of ceremony with long, wide sleeves, and his loosened white shawl fell like a cloud over his head and shoulders.

Other details of his apparel were lost to me as his extraordinary face held my attention from the moment I gazed into it. His scanty gray beard was trimmed Moslem fashion, the prominent forehead overhung sunken eyes, with no impression of blindness but rather of visions not permitted to ordinary mortals, and a radiant smile lighted a face which invited one to share the visions. His bowed frame gave an impression of extreme physical frailty but there was nothing of the feebleness of age in the sound of his low, well-pitched voice, beautiful in tone and of surprising strength. In the slightly raised face, as he began to recite, was a beatitude of expression and the authority of an inspired prophet.

Laugher from children playing in the streets, sounds of women's chatter, the loud buzzing of a fly—all seemed unreal. The actualities of life were inside these walls, where a single voice had lifted religion beyond the realm of dogma and its contradictions back to a fundamental principle—the love of one true God.

I had a strange, satisfying feeling of a common interest with my fellow beings gathered together in this bare little room where I sat cross-legged, without anything to lean against or a cushion to sit upon. As the hours passed, the Sheikh's voice grew stronger rather than weaker and the musical ring and the never-failing rhythm intensified. Never once did he hesitate for a word. At the close of the entire *sura* of "The Cow," which comprises one-seventh of the entire Koran and is a recitation by itself, he merely paused for a second, changed his position, cleared him throat, and then began again. The steady refrain swept on with an eternal quality, and occasionally a special admonition would ring in my ears as though it were a message to me.

"Verily those who oppose God and his
Apostle shall be brought low, as those
who preceded them were brought low."

As this verse was repeated for the moment, I lost that pleasant
sense of oneness with the silent figures all around me and stared
down at the stone floor, disturbed and helpless, in my Christian loneliness. But my contact was restored when I looked again at Sheikh
Abd' Allah. His sightless eyes saw no distinction of race or creed.

"The Family of Imran," "Women," "The Table," "Cattle," "Al
Araf," "The Spoils." He said all these long chapters with a complete
freedom from physical limitations that I found incredible. When
coffee was served, all stood except myself. A murmur of satisfaction
from the others expressed their approval as I motioned away a chair.
I heard a voice say, "The English woman is not restless, she listens
attentively, she sits like us."

After a brief pause, Abdul Wahed and the others were listening
intently and untroubled to the verses of *Sura IX*, entitled "Repentance," the last of the long ones, delivered with the same beauty of
diction in that tireless voice. But it was then that something struck
me as not only unfamiliar but distinctly wrong. It came to me in a
flash! The Sheikh had omitted the *bismillah* (in the name of God).
I was personally hurt that Sheikh Abd' Allah, after all, was not infallible in giving the exact words of God as sent down to his servant
Muhammad.

Every *sura* in the Koran begins with *bismillah*. How I had had
this fact drilled into me by the many sheikhs up and down the Nile
who had given me lessons, I was thinking, when the Sheikh's voice
abruptly stopped. He took from an inner garment a string of prayer
beads. "*Subhanna Allah*" (Praise God), he was saying over and over
quietly. No one moved until a *muezzin's* call to the noon prayer
penetrated the farthest recesses of the room. All rose, including
Sheikh Abd' Allah. I watched him step over the threshold alone and
walk out into the sunlight with a certainty of tread that was unbelievable for a blind man.

As I stood, going over in my mind the names of the many *suras* which had been recited, recalling also the remaining ones to be repeated, I was so intent in my memory test that I started when I saw Abdul Wahed at my elbow, and close at his heels most of the group who had been present throughout the morning. He nodded to me and left the room with the men. I heard a confused sound of voices, all speaking at once, before he re-entered. He seemed in a very good humor. "Those men are pleased about the true religion being in your heart. 'It is confusing when the *sitt* is a *Nasara*' (Christian.) Such were their words."

I followed him through the court and up a narrow stairway. "You will prefer your food in the harem!" It was a statement of fact.

"I will be honored," I said.

"It is the family that is honored," he responded. He raised a curtain over a door and mumbled a few words. A high cackle of female voices answered, and he left me.

I found myself in a room about the same size as the one I'd been in downstairs and as empty of furniture, but what a contrast from the Koran to a harem, where the ladies were without the restraining presence of the master! Quick adaptation is a requisite in the Orient for getting the most out of an occasion, but I was confident I could overcome the stiffness with which Orientals receive a stranger.

Abdul Wahed's mother's firm chin had not been passed down to her son, the *omda*, but there was much of his inflexible will in her slight body and tight lips, and it was obvious at a glance that she ruled with no light hand her daughters and daughters-in-law with a firmness that is advisable for discipline in the harem quarters, where the younger females are inclined to be volatile in character, readily amused, and curious to find out many things unknown to them because of the prescribed restrictions of their daily routine. The mother and I exchanged greetings, and with a flashing eye, and in no uncertain tones, she ordered back the girls of the family who were crowding too close to me for courtesy. They stood gaping at me, giggling and whispering comments to one another. Whenever I caught an eye I smiled encouragingly. A slim, pretty, half-grown girl, a granddaughter no doubt, brought in the silver *ibrik* (pitcher) and ewer, and I enjoyed the refreshing coolness of the water poured over my hands. The same performance was repeated for the *omda*'s mother and wife. We were about to eat!

A large round brass tray was put on a low stool near three cushions placed on the floor in close proximity.

"*Tafadal*" (Do me the honor to accept my food), invited the mother with a regal graciousness. I seated myself on one of the cushions, she and the *omda*'s wife took the others. *Aish beledi* (small cakes of bread) were the only things on the tray. I took one and broke it in half, preparatory to serving myself from the communal dishes as they appeared, holding the bread between my thumb and forefinger of the right hand. The entire family was at ease on finding that the guest was familiar with their ways. A small copper bowl containing a stew of some kind was brought in and left on the center of the tray. A strong flavor of garlic was immediately noticeable, and liquid grease, the native *semn*, had unappetizing condiments afloat in it. I dipped in my bread gingerly, knowing there was no chance to slip anything into my purse, with so many eyes upon me. I swallowed hard. The food was dreadful to the European palate. The empty bowl was removed, to be replaced by another kind of meat, mixed with horrible sweets, and so they came, dish after dish. I took them all! And even worse were the sickeningly sweet sherbets served in covered glass cups.

The climax in hospitality made all that preceded it, in the culinary art of a Moslem kitchen, almost appetizing in comparison. In the acme of despair, I watched the mother's expert fingers extract from a dish the eye of a sheep, which she smilingly handed to me as a special honor. Somehow I got it down. All I can say is that the sight of that glassy eye was worse than its taste. Meanwhile, the mother and I conversed, if a series of interrogations on her part and my answers can be thus termed.

"Do you have children?"

"Yes, three girls."

"Your husband has not divorced you?"

I shook my head, laughing.

"He is satisfied with the sons borne him by other women?"

"There has never been another woman," I said.

"A kind, patient man," she exclaimed, and in her amazement at hearing of a husband who could be so reasonable with a wife, she relaxed her vigilance. Subtly, each one present was aware of that fact and prepared to take advantage of her absent-mindedness. She mentioned America, "Far, far away, how brave to venture such a distance!"

"It was not difficult," I assured her.

Had I ever flown in the air—like a bird?

At this question from the *omda*'s wife, her mother-in-law glared at her for having dared to speak in her presence without permission, but the thrill of listening to an account from someone who had actually been in a horseless carriage broke down completely the mother-in-law's customary control, and in their eagerness to miss nothing, all the women and the young girls grouped about me, squatted so near that I could feel their hot breath down my back. They chatted freely, quite unafraid of the old woman, whose own eyes were aglow. Between mouthfuls of a reviving watermelon, I talked to a spellbound audience. Children drifted in, girls and boys up to the age permitted to roam at will in the harem. One small tot pulled at her mother's breast, standing on her plump legs for the meal. "*Ahlan wa sahlan!*" I heard frequently. I was being treated as "family."

What did the ladies of America wear in big cities like Bedrechein? I suppressed a smile and did the best I could in my description, but as questions came from all directions at once, it was hard to keep up with them. Was it true that women had very high heels to their shoes, making it difficult to walk?

"Yes," I replied.

A chorus of enraptured "How wonderful's!" "Of what were these shoes made?" and so forth. They asked about jewels. I tactfully admired the ornaments they had on, good silver work and turquoise, and some gold, especially the mother-in-law's. I commented on the attractiveness of their flowered silk house garments, which were all in excellent taste. The mother accepted my praise but, she, too, preferred to hear of exciting events so different from what any of them would ever experience. Several times she apologized, but half-heartedly, at an indiscreet question from one of the young girls to which she wanted an answer as much as they.

"They hear things," she explained, "from a friend who had a friend in a harem in Cairo who once knew a Christian woman." I nodded sympathetically. Was it true that sometimes in a very big room men made love to women and everyone looked on?

This query came from a girl with a restless eye and discontented expression. I was completely at a loss, and then suddenly I realized she meant the theatre, the rumors of which had reached her, many times removed from the actual experiences of the eye witness. My language rather failed me in trying to explain that it was "not real," but "make-believe," "just pretending." I fumbled for the correct words in Arabic.

"Do the women understand that the men are not serious?"

"Yes!" I said, and let it go at that.

Several times the *omda*'s wife seemed on the point of a question, and finally it came hesitatingly. She prefaced her remark with, "I know it is not true, but I have been told more than once—" she looked in sudden terror at her mother-in-law.

"Continue," the latter said.

"Of course everyone understands about a *ghawazee* [dancing girl] who would not be allowed in a respectable harem—" again she stopped.

"Go on," ordered the mother-in-law, in intense excitement.

The *omda*'s wife said that she knew that *ghawazees* were in other countries than Egypt and men would go to see them. What she wanted to know was something quite different, about Christian women with good homes and a husband, possibly one or two sons, themselves not very young, and yet still far from too old. Then she burst out, "Do women such as these dance with men not their husbands, touching hands, their bodies close, and quite openly, with music?"

"That is so, but without evil intent."

All were thinking over my reply, trying rather unsuccessfully to believe my words literally, when one of the younger girls with large luscious eyes and a charming dimple cried:

"How pleasant to be a wicked Christian woman!"

The *omda*'s mother rebuked her sharply for her discourtesy to the religion of a guest, but I laughed heartily. I could think of nothing further to say in explanation which they would understand. The merry mood was contagious.

An approaching step was heard on the stairs, and the *omda*'s voice came to the room, "Come, now, wife of the painter."

"Have I your permission to depart?" I asked his mother ceremoniously.

"Permission is granted," she replied.

We embraced affectionately! All crowded about me and gave impulsive little hugs, even the children kissed me. Suppressed giggles, a waving of brown hands, then the curtain over the harem door fell behind me. What a different place from the sensational harems conjured up by uninformed writers.

Back again to the room of the Koran. Many more men had crowded in. "The *ulema* who discussed your situation about being saved from hell fire have come," Abdul Wahed informed me. This time everyone present exchanged greetings with me, including the *ulema*. Sheikh Abd' Allah was again seated alone, in an aloofness that was more than physical. He appeared unconscious of his surroundings, fingering his prayer beads rapidly, his lips moved in a low murmur that was inaudible. Then without warning the recitation began from where it had left off. Gradually my head swam and I was dizzy, it was difficult to keep my balance. The lack of ventilation and the strain of my complete absorption was telling on me. With a distinct effort I pulled myself together. The verse being repeated was:

> "Yet do they amuse themselves with
> doubt. But observe them on the day
> wherein the heaven shall produce a
> visible smoke which shall cover man-
> kind, this will be a tormenting plague."

I was thinking idly that I had last heard this *sura* of "the smoke" chanted in the funeral procession of an important *darweesh*; my memory brought back vividly the sunlight on the unfurled banners of the order to which he belonged, the faces of the group of *fikees* on that occasion were clear, and many other details of those carrying the coffin. Suddenly my sight was blurred. I toppled slightly. A touch on my arm steadied me. I looked into the face of Abdul Wahed, whose kindly eyes expressed concern.

"Drink this coffee," he insisted.

I obeyed. The room stopped swaying and Abd' Allah's figure was again clear-cut and the deep sunken eyes held mine. The *sura* of "The Smoke" had ended and the old Sheikh was sipping coffee, as was every one else in the room.

Abdul Wahed led me into the fresh air outside. I took long breaths and felt revived. He still had an anxious eye on me when on hearing the word *bismillah*, I hastily started towards the door.

"Your soul is happy but the body needs relaxation. When the men stand and talk of village affairs for a few moments it is well for you to forget religion also."

I followed this advice during two other such interludes. A few candles protected by large glass shades were placed on the platform beside the old Sheikh, and the shadows cast by their feeble light played over his face, accentuating its gauntness. He looked ill but indomitable. The sunset had come and gone. The flames of a small fire, over which an evening meal was being prepared, could be seen in an open court across the street. A pleasant aroma of baking bread reached me. The same animals I had seen going forth in the morning were now being brought back, their day's work over. Night sounds were audible; the village was about to go to bed.

The last verse of the final short *sura* had been uttered. All, with one accord, and with a triumphant shout, repeated the *fat'ah* in unison, in which I joined. The old head of Sheikh Abd' Allah sank on his shoulders. He sat alone and fingered his beads. One of the candles gutted and went out.

"Come," said Abdul Wahed to me. "Now his bed will be spread and he will sleep."

The room silently emptied, with no disturbing shuffling of feet. A pale moon was in the sky, turbans, a profile, an eye with a rapt expression of religious exaltation, the click of moving prayer beads, a general "May Allah preserve him"—all this made a composite picture as I mounted my donkey and rode off into the night back to Saqqarah. I went directly to my room and picked up the Koran, which was always beside my bed. I opened it at the page beginning *Sura IX*, "Repentance." There was no *bismillah* preceding it. I almost shouted in my joy!

The old Sheikh had not made an error in repeating the words of God.

25

ENGLISH CHARACTER

JOE HAD COMMUNICATED with Dowe, before we left Egypt in the spring of 1907, asking for a *dahabieh* for the 1906–1907 season, and received the following discouraging reply: "Must respectfully announce sad news. Nile changed like Philæ. Now smoke from steamers instead of sails on *dahabieh*. Everything too quick. Villagers sad like Nile."

Under the circumstances, we decided to leave the children with Joe's parents in Boston, and Joe and I accepted an invitation from Arthur Weigall and his wife for our sojourn in Egypt.

Weigall had replaced Edward J. Quibell as inspector of Antiquities for Upper Egypt when Quibell took over the Egyptian government excavations at Saqqarah. He had moved the inspector's quarters across the Nile to the town of Luxor, and therefore we lost the Theban Plain as well as river life.

In Luxor we constantly saw a varied assortment of officials high up in administrative positions, both English and French. And their main topic of conversation was Lord Cromer's coming departure in the spring. The view I heard generally expressed was that Lord Cromer had looked upon Egypt as his personal responsibility. Sympathy was expressed for his successor, who would be without a suitable policy because of Cromer's long regime, by now quite out of touch with the demands of a changing, restless Egypt.

The Smiths were greatly honored to be invited to one of the final dinners given by Lord and Lady Cromer. Except for our American minister, we were the only Americans present at a large gathering, mostly English in complexion.

I felt fully repaid for the overnight railroad trip from Luxor when I had a few words with Cromer in his study. His carriage was noticeably less erect, and he seemed to me weary in spirit as well as let down physically.

In saying good-by, I remarked that village life in my mind would always be associated with one sight. That of *fellaheen* who, in taking the customary oath with a hand on the Koran to bind an agreement, added "*Kalam inglesi*" (word of an Englishman). I had the distinct impression from Lord Cromer's expression that he considered that I was referring to something belonging to a fast-disappearing era.

In Joe's and my subsequent trips to Egypt alone, instead of returning home by way of Italy and the southern route, we preferred a stopover in England. There is something admirable about the solidity of an English friendship; it always makes possible intimate glimpses of English home surroundings on short notice.

This occurred with Sir Hamilton and Lady Lang, of whom we had seen much in Constantinople many years before. She was closely related to Constable, and they lived in his former home, with nothing changed since his death.

The surrounding landscape, still known as "Constable's country," composed itself into the scenes of beauty and peace the artist had loved to paint. Somehow, in my leisurely strolling about, I felt completely relaxed, perhaps other-worldly. It seemed likely that the future even, and the thinking of country people we met, would remain as pleasantly static as the past.

Sir Hamilton's nephew, Reverend Cosmo Gordon Lang, soon to be Archbishop of York, made a point of being a few days with his relatives during our stay. His presence livened up our thinking. I have remembered his sermon at the country church. It was powerful, stated with strong conviction, and imbued with such certainty that one felt he must be right. Above all, he was a great church-man, beyond the reach of compromise. Everything in his character, brought out in casual conversation as I tramped with him through the countryside, indicated what his decision, made thirty years later, as Archbishop of Canterbury, would be in the abdication crisis of King Edward VIII.

After our stay with the Langs, we changed into a completely different atmosphere with Lord Carnarvon at Highclere, his large country estate. In England his name was associated with horse racing and his stable produced frequent Derby winners. In these years, before the discovery of the tomb of Tutankhamen made him world famous, he had spent his winters in Egypt as an exile for ill health. There he engaged enthusiastically in small archaeological enterprises as a diversion.

Our fellow guests were interested only in horses, and I found far more in common with them than Joe did. They, in turn, were frankly bored when, the first night at dinner, Carnarvon talked archaeology across them to Joe and continued to do so throughout the evening.

I scored a hit with Carnarvon on a long visit to the stables, by calling attention to a filly overlooked by the horsy guests. Carnarvon, on a re-examination after my recommendation, decided that the colt did deserve watching and special training. Eventually, when she became a Derby winner, he sent me a valuable Egyptian antique.

The next spring we were back in London. This time in lodgings at Garlant's Hotel on Suffolk Street, Pall Mall, where meals were served in one's private apartments. Garlant's had remained famous since the days Whistler patronized it, and his relics were all over the place. These were quarters much sought after, but seldom successfully by Americans. It was Carnarvon who got us in. It was he also who showed us Baron Rothschild's wonderful collection of pictures, tapestries, and ceramics. And his introduction to Sir Ernest Cassel resulted in our seeing some of King Edward VII's superb pictures. Sir Ernest also included us in one of his enormous dinners, where Joe and I felt utterly lost and, I fear, showed it.

Again we spent a weekend at Highclere. This visit, unlike the previous one, was marked by an absence of friends addicted to horse racing. Carnarvon, throughout a memorable stay, displayed to Joe a side of his character with which he was thoroughly in tune. Fellow guests included a member of the Doria family we had seen something of in Rome, the head of the National Gallery, and several keepers of private collections.

A rare treat for me was our visit with Edward G. Brown, familiarly known as "Persian" Brown, in his Cambridge home. He knew not only the thoughts of ancient Persians but from reading modern Persian literature, what the emerging women of contemporary Persia were thinking and doing. He was personally familiar with Persian home life of the time and told anecdotes concerned with it which were unrivaled for variety and humor.

A dinner given for us by our host provided Joe his first contact with professors from an English university. He later described them to me as having "no stop signals for their brains."

After Brown's and my first meeting in Egypt, we had kept up a desultory correspondence, based on what he kindly termed my Arabic potentialities. An English colleague in Cairo with el-Azhar affiliations recently had written him about my experiences in the Luxor mosques and with the Sheikh of the Delta.

On the strength of these experiences, one of Brown's guests, who was a librarian at the Ashmolean Museum at Oxford, brought with him, at Brown's request, some copies of the Koran for my inspection. After dinner, the three of us sat down together to look at them.

One special treasure was a Koran of a very early date, beautifully illuminated, written on parchment that had become very fragile, temporarily bound in stiff paper. As I handled it with great care, I noticed at once that page after page was put together incorrectly.

On my calling the librarian's attention to the fact, he apologized profusely and, to my amazement, instantly accepted Brown's suggestion that I rectify here and now the error made at the Ashmolean Library.

The librarian tore off the binding and separated the pages, which I rearranged and handed back to him in correct order. It was perforce a slow process and the other guests had departed before it was completed.

Brown was delighted at my achievement and much amused at the utter confusion of the rather opinionated scholar.

What always struck me afresh was that Englishmen in important positions always found the leisure to devote to stray visitors like ourselves. Another characteristic was that, instead of the Americans' universal use of the typewriter, they still wrote personal letters in a flowing script learned at Eton or Harrow.

At the British Museum and elsewhere, we were often with Egyptologists, who were familiar figures to us for their work in tombs and temples where we too had worked. Also it was interesting to listen again to the significance of ancient events, explained with nice regard for ancient language by such great philologists as Alan H. Gardiner and Francis L. Griffith.

Another agreeable pastime was reminiscing with Sir Grafton Elliot Smith, at one time the mummy anatomist for the Egyptian Antiquity Service, about mummies we had met together.

Roger Fry, the art expert, and distinguished artists whom we knew through Sargent were generous of their time in showing us private art collections not open to the public. In between engagements, we would drop in at the National Gallery, which attracted us more than modern exhibitions.

Nothing to me was more worthwhile than renewing contacts made through my father. I was glad to have Joe meet Lord and Lady Charnwood at a quiet dinner in their home. He represented the best the English of title had to offer, both in character and in scholarship. His volume on Lincoln was an extraordinarily sympathetic evaluation to have been written by an Englishman.

I had the temerity to communicate with John Morley, then secretary of State for India, saying I thought he would like Joe, and he invited us to have tea with him on the terrace of the House of Commons. With the amazing capacity of an Englishman to remember trifles in the midst of great responsibilities, he referred to my having seen Gladstone lying in state in Westminster Abbey and visiting Meredith. Then he encouraged Joe to talk about Egypt. In doing so, Joe tactfully avoided any reference to Gladstone's having abandoned Gordon to his fate in the Sudan, which Morley as his biographer had found difficult to explain.

Morley took us for a brief moment to meet Sir Henry Campbell-Bannerman, the Prime Minister, whose failing health was causing anxiety about party unity. His final words were that, for the moment, his own difficulties with India had lessened.

Another red-letter event was having H. A. L. Fisher, whom I had met at Oxford as a girl, come to London for the express purpose of seeing Joe and me. He was a notable figure, subsequently to become warden of New College, Oxford, and what I particularly liked was his rare gift, as a great scholar, in being able to converse about people of distinction in a way that made one see them through his eyes. Tall, spare, with regular features, he somehow seemed not striking in personal appearance, but in conversation there could be no doubt about the striking quality of his mind.

When much later he sent me his life of Bryce in two volumes, I remembered his having mentioned on the London visit that he would find it impossible to get all he had to say about the great commoner into one volume, which his publisher preferred.

We saw Fisher again in Boston in 1920, when he represented England at the commemoration of the landing of the Pilgrim fathers at Plymouth. Joe had constructed an artistic pavilion on the Boston Commons for the afternoon ceremonies. Fisher was the principal speaker then and afterwards at a banquet. He amused me by emphasizing, when all the other speakers were indulging in flights of fulsome praise of the Pilgrim fathers, that the Puritans could not have been pleasant people to live among. He was greatly impressed by Fenway Court, where there was an evening reception, and we were overjoyed when he spared time for a quick visit to our place in Dublin.

The climax of our London interlude was connected with American Ambassador Whitelaw Reid. George von Lengerke Meyer, an intimate friend of the Reids, insisted they should have the "privilege" of seeing something of the Smiths. With this end in view, he wrote two longhand letters to the Ambassador about our charm and

245

importance. A prompt response came in the form of a cable from Paris, signed Whitelaw Reid, stating that he was anticipating seeing us immediately on his return to London within a few days.

Meanwhile Ridgeley Carter, the first secretary at the Embassy, whom we had met in various previous diplomatic posts, came to see us. He said the Ambassador had sent him to find out what we wished the Embassy to do for us, and his manner indicated that nothing would be too much. He looked distinctly pleased, I thought, when the Smiths had no requests.

An invitation to lunch came promptly from the Reids. On our arrival at a palace only smaller than Buckingham, we were shown into a small reception room, where a number of guests had already assembled. The Reids were cordial, and Prince Colonna recalled knowing us in Rome with the Meyers. There was an unduly prolonged wait for lunch to be announced, but finally, after the Reids had had a whispered word together, Mrs. Reid said, "I'm sure they would not want us to delay any longer."

Part way down the table on either side was a vacant seat. I was placed at the Ambassador's right, and Joe at his wife's. She as hostess at once plunged into the subject of juvenile delinquency and how important it was to curb it by a correct handling of the problem. I noticed Joe looked perplexed when she said, "Tell me about the workings of your court."

Before a glimmering of the situation had penetrated my dazed consciousness, Mrs. Reid's thoughts had turned to the missing guests. She rang a bell and, when a secretary appeared, said, "Bring Mrs. Lindon Smith's letter."

Joe and I exchanged horrified glances and looked at Ridgeley Carter, who, for once at a loss over diplomatic procedure, remained silent.

Mrs. Reid read the note and called to her husband at the end of the table, "It isn't our fault about George Meyer's friends. They accepted."

There was nothing for it but for Joe to deal as lightly as possible with an awkward *contretemps*. It turned out that the guests of honor, Judge Ben B. Lindsey of the Juvenile Court of Denver and his wife, had failed to appear and the butler, in attempting to do the best with the humble name of Smith, had swallowed it and over-emphasized the Lindon, which the Reids had mistaken for Lindsey.

The Reids were both very apologetic about not having identified us, and to make amends gave us their opera box twice and had us to a grand but extremely dull dinner.

Joe declared this incident must be a lesson, never again to present a letter to one of our ambassadors for merely social purposes.

26

I BECOME A PROFESSIONAL

BEGINNING WITH THE FALL OF 1909, the pattern of my life changed materially. Joe's parents were perceptibly aging, and our children required a mother's attention. In addition, I had returned that spring from a trip to Egypt, made alone with Joe, with my sight tempo-rarily damaged from a violent attack of trachoma, which, for three months overseas, threatened me with complete blindness. There was to continue for me a period of semi-invalidism.

Consequently, Joe "commuted" to countries of the Near and Far East, to paint, while the rest of the family reconstructed life on a home basis. The Ludlow in Boston had been torn down, and we found a subletted furnished apartment unsatisfactory. Therefore, we were delighted when chance offered the taking over of an un-expired lease from a friend moving from Boston to the country. The lease was for a delightful house on Chestnut Street, below Charles, instead of in the area patronized by fashion. But as artists we could live where we pleased without impugning our social status.

Two anxious years ensued, because of our daughter Frances' hav-ing an illness that affected her heart seriously. For some months she had to lie flat on her back, day and night, on a strict regimen watched over by nurses. It would have been a difficult time without Father to share my responsibilities in the crises of the illness, when Mother also needed a good deal of attention. Moreover, because my optic nerve was slow in recovering, I was dependent on his reading aloud to me.

In our close companionship, Father became articulate as never before, and one evening unburdened himself by reviewing a damage suit, decided against him in court, which he had never before mentioned. It had occurred years before, when Joe and I were overseas, else we would not have permitted it to reach the court stage.

The case arose when Father brought with him to the Ludlow a frame-maker to collect one of Joe's Egyptian paintings. He became annoyed when the elevator did not respond to signals, because the boy on it was chatting with a waitress between floors instead of answering the call bell. When finally the door was opened, the waitress got out with her tray, whereat Father sharply reprimanded the boy. He dismissed the matter, although the boy did not report for duty again.

A few days later a lawyer visited Father and told him he represented the boy. He asserted that the sharp blow dealt by Father to the boy's abdomen had necessitated an emergency operation. He offered a settlement for eight hundred dollars.

Father had a witness in the frame-maker, who said the statement was false, and he accordingly refused a settlement out of court. When the case came to trial, the lawyer produced a surprise witness, who testified he had been in the elevator unnoticed. This was contested but was confirmed by the waitress.

The frame-maker got confused, and father's lawyer, a friend and not very quick-witted, lost his head. The boy's lawyer made a strong class plea to the jury against a rich Back Bay merchant, angry with a poor elevator boy for stopping to assist a waitress with a heavy tray before answering his call. The verdict was against Father to the amount of four thousand dollars.

The judge told me later that Father should have come to him for advice. He had talked with the foreman of the jury after the trial was over, and described him as a decent chap who recognized the case was doubtful, but who had been forced into a compromise when most of the jurymen wanted to stand out for the full amount demanded—ten thousand dollars.

The case had greatly shaken Father, who was now determined to spend his share of a two-thousand-dollar purse, presented to him and Mother by the Dublin community in the recent celebration of their golden wedding anniversary, to repay part of the legal costs.

Mother wanted him to buy a fur coat and other personal things, he told me, but he felt impelled to restore something to the family account for the settlement, which had never ceased to rankle.

At his words, the thought suddenly struck me that I had a possible means of my own for earning money. I felt, I told him, that I must in any case struggle against mental stagnation while being without the full use of my eyes. Wasn't it true that I could still talk? And what did he think of my registering at a first-rate Boston bureau that supplied lecturers, as a "substitute speaker," ready to respond on very short notice to calls within a radius of one hundred miles? The conditions would be that I must be free to select my own subject, after learning what to expect in the way of an audience, and that I was to receive the fee of the lecturer whom I was replacing. Finally, would Father take a part of my fees?

It was his response that decided me in my action. He promised to buy the fur coat and other things Mother had suggested that very day, and in turn he would use money I should earn to repay his debt.

Finances had been a subject of discussion between Father and me at the very start of my married life. "Did Joe think to tell you he has no bank account?" he had asked abruptly. His relief was pathetically obvious at my cheerful acceptance of what many young brides would have found an unendurable situation. He explained that Joe handed over his earnings to him and he paid the family bills, investing the surplus.

When we traveled abroad, Father arranged for the funds needed and settled all indebtedness incurred by the party. It seemed to me little short of a miracle that, without a word of any foreign language, he left his financial opponents, including over-eager guides, cowed in their attempts to best him. Equally amazing to me was his mastery of the intricacies of exchange in different countries and the instant detection of counterfeit coins, of which there were many. And I found myself fascinated at the speed of his handing over the correct amount of unfamiliar currency in important financial transactions.

Father was happy and content in a life devoted to looking after an increasing family. In the proceedings, I found but one obstacle. This was that my own father had a strong conviction that a girl, when married, should be entirely supported by her husband. Therefore, having no money, I had to go to Joe's father for cash, and with his New England thrift, he compelled me to state exactly what it would be spent on before he gave me even a few dollars.

I was not extravagant and my clothes presented no problem. A delightful old dressmaker from Bohemia, who had sewn for me and my sisters in New York since we were adults, came to Dublin every summer. In between mending Joe's valuable old textiles, she achieved artistic triumphs in a wardrobe for me, making up dresses from wonderful oriental silks and other materials which were purchased by Joe on our journeys. And there was always antique jewelry to set them off.

Father never objected to bills for anything Joe wanted to get me. And he liked nothing better than shopping with me for the children. I had to restrain him from buying too many toys and other non-essentials. But if I wanted something for Mother, he always refused the money, saying she had more things than she could use already, and that we all spoilt her.

I was equally frustrated in appeals for funds for presents for Joe. He insisted that antiquities were all that were wanted by Joe, who somehow always managed to outmaneuver him in his attempts to circumvent the purchase of any coveted object, no matter what the price.

Father's steady refusal of money for me to get him things he badly needed was what troubled me most. Now I was exultant that he had actually asked for my first thousands earned by lecturing. Full of enthusiasm, I made my proposition to the lecture bureau

I had in mind and, to my delight, got a good hearing for it. In fact, I became a lecturer.

I attribute my immediate success as a "substitute" lecturer to my principle of putting as much enthusiasm into the preparation for, and delivery of, a lecture for a fifteen- or twenty-five-dollar fee from a small women's club as for one carrying a very large fee. It is undeniable also that I had a ready-made claque resulting from the large number of talks I gave for nothing in Boston and the vicinity, to church groups, about my horseback trip in the Holy Land soon after we were married.

I well remember my first large-fee lecture. Severe bronchitis had prevented a noted explorer from talking about his experiences as a big-game hunter in Africa. The audience was to be mostly men, at the meeting of an organization representing sporting interests. The chairman became more and more desperate when no suitable substitute could be found. Finally, with many expressed misgivings, he accepted by services, but not before trying to get me to come for less than had been promised the original lecturer. This last I refused to do. His expression was very grim as he met my train at Salem, Massachusetts, where the lecture was to take place.

Later, as I stepped onto the platform, I realized from the look of stunned disappointment in the faces of the large audience that there had been no announcement about the change of speakers. The chairman spoke at some length about the explorer's career and extraordinary achievements in Africa, quoting several examples of his lion and elephant hunts. "No one looked forward more than me to listening to him," he declared bluntly. "Unfortunately for us all, he's ill——." After an awkward silence, he glanced towards me as I sat nearby and said, "It's very kind of Mrs. Joseph Lindon Smith to come on such short notice to fill the gap. Her subject is——." He hesitated, fumbling frantically in his pocket for a mislaid paper. "I'll let her tell us," he finished lamely, with a forced smile.

I did the only possible thing under the circumstances—I rose and burst out laughing. "From big game hunting to adventure in Egyptian tombs is a terrific disappointment, but give me a break," I urged. The audience did! Just before I left the hall, two men, who had introduced themselves separately, invited me to lecture before an association, without naming its purpose. But both, with an amused twinkle, acknowledged that big-game hunting was one of their main interests. Nevertheless, I was to name my subject and date and not be a "substitute." From a sense of fun, and expecting a hedge on my proposal, I laughingly chose, "Henry James and Thomas Hardy," for one and, "The Place of Islam among World Religions," for the other. But the joke was on me! The first man was president of a literary society, and the second a leader in a group which studied comparative religions.

My most memorable experience as a lecturer resulted when Dr. Weir Mitchell telephoned me from Philadelphia. He and Owen Wister, who was with him, were disturbed, he said, because society was not flocking to a recently opened wing at the Philadelphia Museum. They had thought of a plan to remedy the situation and it involved me. As a preamble, Dr. Mitchell stated that Joe's professional popularity in the city would arouse interest in finding out what his wife could do. The plan was for me to give a lecture and be present at a reception and tea afterwards in the new wing. "My Friend the Prophet Muhammad," was to be the title of the lecture. "Curiosity will bring the kind of audience we want," the famous doctor predicted happily.

"The title makes me cool to the proposition," I told him firmly. But both he and Owen Wister were adamant about it. Decidedly ashamed of myself, I yielded, against my better judgment, to the persistence of the two very persuasive tongues coming to me over a telephone wire. Nothing was right about the occasion, from my point of view, beginning even with the large amount of the check awaiting my arrival in Philadelphia. I felt like a prize pig seated on the platform between my two sponsors, plastered with orchids, facing an audience of fashionably dressed, bejeweled women and immaculately tailored men. I was even more depressed on rising to speak after an introduction of fulsome praise, combined with subtle wit, by Dr. Mitchell. In response to the atmosphere in which I found myself, I started in a light vein and told an amusing anecdote.

Then I caught sight of a dark man with a face that held my gaze, seated quite far back in the hall. On noticing he was about to leave, I changed my mood abruptly and spoke to him alone and with great earnestness. I noticed that he was listening. As I progressed, his concentration on what I was saying stimulated me; nothing seemed important except that I make him understand that I sincerely believed I had a contribution to make towards an understanding of Islam.

My talk ended. Owen Wister gave a laudatory few words. People were pressing forward towards him and Dr. Mitchell, expecting to be introduced to the speaker. I brushed past them and reached the side of the swarthy man still seated. "You didn't always agree with me, but you listened," I burst out abruptly. "Who are you?"

"My name is Jastro," he replied.

Anyone who had studied Arabic knew of Morris Jastro, one of the greatest Semitic scholars of his time, then teaching in the University of Pennsylvania. Here I was, actually face to face with him. Meanwhile he was speaking, "The orchids and the surroundings put me off," he said. He had been at the point of leaving when suddenly he realized, he said, that I had scholarship and, in addition, something students of Islam like himself often lacked. This was a knowledge gained from contacts with simple Moslems in villages, as well as from *imams*, *mullehs*, and *muftis* who spoke to me about Islam, as their knowledge had come down by word of mouth.

"I can't afford to miss you," he said simply, adding that as he had been told my husband was fairly often in Philadelphia, why couldn't I come with him, taking a train several hours in advance, so he could meet me to discuss Muhammad's influence upon our times.

From that occasion, I spent memorable, never-to-be-forgotten hours with the great Jastro. It was a cherished friendship to me, lasting until his death, and I had the satisfaction of knowing, in all humility, that it also meant something to him.

In my engagements, I determined to stick to the "substitute" qualification, and not become a real lecturer. It proved to be a means of acquiring money, during Joe's absences, with no serious effort on my part. Moreover it was great fun. Within less than two years, Father's indebtedness was wiped out, and I still had a nice cash balance left over. He began to consider it an act of economy when he used my eagerly offered money for unexpected expenses, instead of taking the amount from the family account. Best of all, he no longer refused little extras for himself.

27

MY CAREER
AS ASSISTANT STAGE DIRECTOR

SOCIAL ENTERTAINMENT at the turn of the century in New York, in other large cities, and at fashionable summer resorts was characterized by lavish splendor on a competitive scale. One orchestra at a ball had given place to two; creamed chicken became pheasant; vintage champagne flowed freely. Florists covered the walls of ballrooms with rare flowers. In the quest for display it became increasingly difficult to find new worlds to conquer, and a few, not impressed by mere outlay, began to find parties dull.

Balls and masques and theatricals had been developed for social intercourse in eighteenth-century England, but the higher reaches of American society were ready for these kinds of divertissement as the gay nineties spilled over into the first decade of the new century. Money, after all, was increasingly plentiful in an era of developing industrialization, marked by the growth of cities and accompanied (temporarily) by freedom from war. Most important, there was no income tax!

Joe was appealed to by hostesses with imagination for something different in decoration and novel in the way of entertainment. It soon developed that his parties were talked about with gratifying enthusiasm.

The guests arrived at one of his Boston parties to find a familiar hall transformed into a Japanese theatre, with actors from Japan and himself playing the major roles. He planned a Persian fantasy in St. Louis which involved the construction of an entire pavilion in the spacious garden adjacent to the hostess's house. In Newport, during a ball, he was asked to provide five minutes of acts, given by professionals, every hour on the hour, on the lawn outside, from midnight until dawn. The host told him that if the guests did not appreciate this feature and continue to dance, to abandon the experiment. But each performance found the guests lined up in eager expectation.

Hand in hand with providing original decorations and entertainment for private parties, Joe had developed to a high degree the art of creating symbolic plays, given by wealthy patrons in Newport homes and gardens for an exclusive, sophisticated society.

Joe's success in the field of drama, as in his profession as a painter, was owing to the fact that he had a distinct gift of expression. He appeared often both as producer and as actor. He not only excelled in a part he interpreted himself, but had the power to make each actor in his plays "feel" the character he or she, child or adult, professional or amateur, was portraying.

His first production in Newport, for the dedication of the "Blue Garden" on the estate of Arthur Curtiss James, was acclaimed by artists and *Town Topics* alike.

For his civic pageants, there were local leaders to depend on, and a homogeneous group to work with. But in productions for invited guests, arranged by the wealthy in the years interrupted by World War I, conditions were very different. Joe was hired to produce something that might prove a breath-taking allegory, with professionals in the leading roles.

This meant personality complexes to be kept under control, amateurs to be dealt with, in minor parts, and there were always house guests under foot. On such occasions, he considered my active assistance was essential. He trusted me to save him from unimportant decisions, but to refer immediately to him any real crisis.

Consequently, my lecturing languished when he was at home. He insisted on my receiving a stipend for my services, and once again

I was a professional in another field. Two examples will suffice to explain the tribulations I encountered as an assistant stage director, when I had to be prepared, at a moment's notice, to cope with varied emergencies that threatened catastrophe.

After the "Blue Garden" triumph, I went to Newport with Joe on one of the many occasions I was his assistant there. This time it was also at the Jameses'. Joe had built for Mrs. James an amphitheatre which had the unusual attraction of many beds of rare specimen roses, ingeniously distributed among wide tiers of grass, where folding chairs would accommodate the audience. The amphitheatre, which could hold three hundred, faced a vast expanse of level lawn, with tall trees beyond, thus suggesting a natural stage. The entertainment had been left to Joe, who arranged variety acts that would be spectacular for movement and color.

The publicity value of placing an act, to be seen by Newport Society in advance of a circus appearance, was an opportunity eagerly sought after by heads of agencies. In this instance, Joe felt himself particularly fortunate in the selections he had accepted from the many possibilities offered. First and foremost were twelve Arabs who did amazing tumbling acts in groups, intermingled with extraordinary postures, ending in two pyramids that changed their component parts several times at a run. These primitive, untamed tribesmen, with superb figures and dashing manners, had just landed from the Middle East. He had also decided on eight Hungarian gypsies who sang and danced in a fashion only equaled by similar bands in Hungary itself. There were also four skilled French women fencers.

As a culmination to the expected thrills, and in honor of the host, Neptune, seated on an enormous throne, was to be carried in by ten sailors from Arthur James's yacht *Aloha*. The god's attendants were a bewildering array of personages well known in folklore of the sea. To the accompaniment of a Greek chorus and music, they were to perform incredible stunts, directed by Joe.

We turned up at the James estate three days before the party, to find sixteen friends visiting them. The performance was to be at ten in the evening, with a seated supper and ball afterwards. All signs were propitious! Dressing rooms near the outdoor stage, designed by Joe, were constructed in a way to add a picturesque note to the landscape. Under the superintendent's genius, the amphitheatre, as viewed the evening before, was a dream of beauty, caught up in the radiance of the full moon, enhanced by artfully concealed lights.

But alas, clouds threatened at dawn, and by noon the downpour came, and it did not let up until an hour before the guests were to arrive. Fortunately, Joe had insisted that a huge tent for the audience and stage be erected over the lawn, adjacent to the ballroom. A large corps of experienced men got to work under his instruction, supervised by the superintendent, and transformed a canvas background into a near replica of the outdoor setting.

Joe's calm was contagious. While he set the stage, my job was to see to it that the hearty professionals, unaccustomed to Newport society, were kept under control when not on the stage, in quarters downstairs, including improvised dressing rooms and a temporary kitchen for feeding them, situated near the tent. Since Neptune and his entourage would make their entry by the ballroom and through the audience, they would have to dress in the spacious breakfast room used by the men guests.

The organization completed, I persuaded Joe to have the Arabs and others try out their specialty features, with me in charge, before the formal rehearsal. They filed in, brilliantly costumed, and took seats awaiting their turns. When I called for the Arabs, the leader demanded the "boss." There was a disturbed murmur, indicating insubordination, which was immediately quelled when I burst into voluble Arabic demanding instant obedience. I got it! Even the pyramid climax worked! The gypsies assured me laughingly that they had sufficient imagination to accept an artificial moon and stars, and the fencers were unassuming and tiptop.

Then Joe took over for the rehearsal! A painted vista, for intended entrances, through tall trees created a charming illusion, and a cleverly adjusted, curtailed stage did not seem to lessen the effectiveness of his grouping. Both the Jameses and their early guests were present, and at the close of the Neptune fantasy, everyone had forgotten the rain.

Joe and I had supper downstairs with the cast; then, leaving

257

stalwart ushers to guard the exits, he returned to the stage. I meantime took the Neptune actors into the breakfast room and installed myself in an anteroom next, with the main door out of it locked. No actor became boisterous or attempted to disturb the peace during the long wait until performance time came.

The actors in the variety numbers performed and won long-sustained cheers from the audience, then disappeared downstairs. Neptune and his attendants were letter-perfect and vanished to thunderous applause. After a word with Joe, before he joined the supper guests, I was on my way downstairs to join the cast, when Radford, the butler, told me that Mr. James expected me to sit next to him at supper. I sent back word that I could not appear among the guests until I had got the professionals fed and off to their different train junctions.

Everything had gone like clockwork, and by 1:30 A.M. the last actor had departed and I was in the ballroom, feeling relaxed and thoroughly enjoying dancing with an unusually good partner. But my tribulations had not ended! To my dismay, I caught glimpses of four sailors darting about the ballroom, eluding the ushers who were after them. As the music stopped, Arthur James, seeing my watchful eye on members of the *Aloha* crew, said smiling, "They are having such a wonderful time, don't turn them out."

But knowing what the hostess's reaction would be to the sailors' presence, I did. By 2:30 I thought Joe had done his duty to the party. I persuaded him to go to bed. An hour later the last guest had gone and the Arthur Jameses went upstairs.

I got into working clothes and stole down the great stairway in semidarkness, through empty salons, and into the breakfast room. Here was a blaze of light as Radford went about restoring order from chaos. As I entered, he said approvingly, "I knew, Madame, you'd come."

As dawn broke I staggered upstairs. Mrs. James's male guests would breakfast in the usual place, thanks to Radford and me, who had both earned our pay that night.

A test of my ability to cope with complex circumstances came in February, 1916, in connection with the celebration of Louis C. Tiffany's birthday in New York. It was to be done on a grandiose scale. He wanted Joe, he wrote, to produce a masque that would be "featured in the press as the artistic sensation of the social season." It was to be given in the largest of the Tiffany studios on Madison Avenue, immediately following a luncheon for three hundred guests. It must surpass the success of the Egyptian fantasy Joe had given for him three years before, he scribbled in an almost illegible postscript.

A few days after Joe had accepted the commission, in between war benefits, he and I were visiting Mr. Tiffany to get the arrangements under way. Joe lost no time in telling his host he could provide a sensation by the "dome" lighting system, recently invented in Germany and not yet in use in any American theatre. It would only be possible, however, through the employment of an expert summoned from Germany to install the complicated equipment, which would require additionally eight experienced operators, needed to manipulate, under the expert's direction, the lighting effects the producer's signals would indicate.

"Do you have such a technician in mind?" was Tiffany's only comment when Joe observed that the cost probably was prohibitive for a private entertainment, being fifteen thousand dollars for lighting alone. Within an hour Joe had talked to a firm in Hamburg and made a verbal contract which Mr. Tiffany's secretary promptly executed in typed form and sent off.

With the stimulation of this staggering opportunity for the lighting of a creative production, Joe's ideas crystallized rapidly. He knew that the audience would be representative of American art and letters, as well as society, in the best sense of the word. This was not the first time Mr. Tiffany had assembled such people to witness brilliant fetes within these walls.

In an allegory called "The Quest for Beauty," Joe's aim was to symbolize Mr. Tiffany's career as painter, decorator, and master glass craftsman. The theme was that art was the search for beauty and the effort to express it in many mediums through the ages. The scene opened in semidarkness showing beginnings of civilization, with the hero, the first artist, despised and his life threatened by his warrior tribesmen for refusing to fight against their enemies. In his hand he held a clay bowl of his making, with a rough design on it.

Suddenly distant thunder and lightning flashes! Only the youth was not frightened, as Fire appeared coming up from the ground, for he perceived the present use of flame and its service to coming generations. Fire exhausted her rage in a wild dance and in token of servitude to mankind tore a living flame from her side, a symbol of the inextinguishable divine fire. This she left in the artist's bowl, then disappeared within the earth, and the stars shone over a world in darkness.

Faint suggestions of dawn stole on, the stars grew paler and gave way to the bright colors that heralded the coming day. In the clear freshness of the morning sky, Beauty, personified in the form of the wife of the chief barbarian, was awakened by the first golden rays of the sun. Under the influence of her smile, the sleeping artist also opened his eyes. He saw with amazement the fire burning brightly within his bowl. He pledged the work of his hands and lifelong service to Beauty. She, in turn, to aid him in the realization of his ideals, gave him dominion over all materials: metals! minerals! wood! gems! semiprecious stones! silver! gold! and pigments for a painter's need! Answering Beauty's call, these now appeared in a riot of color and variety and swore fealty to their lord, the artist. Each in turn was drawn by Beauty over the rim of a great circle, like spirits invoked from the air.

As a climax (by way of allusion to the shimmering, iridescent glass bowls and vases that bore the Tiffany name), a globe of blown glass, thirty-six inches in diameter, within which a pearl was represented by a little girl, moved across the circle. Beauty stooped and the pearl inside the crystal shell responded with a smile reflected in the delicate tones of iridescent glass, brilliant in the sunset glow.

In the closing act of the spectacle, the artist renewed his fealty to Beauty as she stood surrounded by her handmaidens, Painting, Sculpture, Music, and Architecture.

I was not back in New York again until the final rehearsals. Joe's procedure in selecting a cast was to get most of the actors from dramatic schools, first carefully testing them for adaptability. For principals he needed actors and actresses with imagination and a willingness to perform a part according to his ideas, not their own. There-fore he was decidedly concerned when Mr. Tiffany admitted rather shamefacedly that he had promised the leading women roles to par-ticular friends of his, Fire to a premier danseuse of the ballet of the Metropolitan Opera, and Beauty to an actress soon to appear as a star on Broadway.

Joe visualized this masque as a symphonic poem, played to soft music accompaniment, with a tremendous variety in the movement of his forty-five characters, and changing color effects in scenery and costumes, from brilliant hues to sombre interludes, to rest the eye and emotions. The musical motif was in harmony with the sky, from the darkness of the latter to pale starlight, with the rosy glow of dawn repeated in the sunset. He felt that success depended on the mood created in the audience by an absence of undue emphasis on any one personality. In this he was anticipating German theatrical experimentation by twenty-five years.

During the first of the week before the performance, one day after a series of minor episodes had been rehearsed, the orchestra waited almost an hour for Fire, who came to the studio with Mr. Tiffany. She was lovely and fully aware of the fact. She listened casually to Joe's instructions about the method of her emergence from the ground, and how later she was to dance in a fury, to awe the artist who refused to be intimidated. Her normal technique was grace personified, characterized by intricate ballet steps and sophisti-cated postures, entirely out of place in an interpretation of the force of uncontrolled fire in an age of prehistoric barbarism.

Mr. Tiffany looked at a loss as the famous dancer was about to depart, when Joe quickly requested her continued presence while he showed a child how to become a living flame from Divine Fire. "I'll be Fire, so you'll see she doesn't interfere with your grand finale," he said reassuringly, responding to her doubtful glance at our little Rebecca, who was to take the part.

Joe's imagination, poetically expressed in co-ordinated move-ments of his whole body, inspired the musicians, and our child's experience in dancing to symphony orchestras made it possible for her to keep pace with her father's extraordinary leaps and quick whirls.

261

Out of the corner of my eye I watched a transformation in the attitude of the stylized dancer. She became vividly alive and, as Joe paused, she rushed towards him, saying excitedly, "I see how Fire should be interpreted, let me do the dance again with that wonderful child, and you coach me."

Mr. Tiffany was entranced. "She did have it in her after all," he said delightedly to Joe.

Beauty, on the other hand, was tall, and her beautifully shaped shoulders, arms, and legs showed to advantage, draped as she was in an enormous tiger skin, with not much else on. The artist was a "natural" in his part, which made Joe's many critical suggestions to Beauty in their scenes together the more obvious. Her acting lacked a sense of rhythm and spontaneity, instinctive qualities in the youth, which was the reason for Joe's having chosen him from a number of applicants for the role of the artist.

I warned Joe that Beauty was increasingly dissatisfied, and asked if he could afford to let her go. "She won't," he replied tersely.

Then the blowup came. Beauty began a mad tirade to me against the "boss" for his treatment of her, stating angrily she had about decided to quit. Joe, at a little distance, realized from my expression a crisis had arisen and approached. "Beauty thinks of walking out on you," I said, trying to keep utter dismay out of my voice.

"If she does, get ready to be her substitute, and call an extra rehearsal at seven this evening," he replied without batting an eyelash. As he passed on, Beauty was left gasping at his indifference.

I told her firmly that the "boss" was a first-class director, a fact which was clearly evident in his insistence that a part be played as he saw it. "You'll be the hit of the show if you do Beauty his way; otherwise you will be only a tall woman conspicuous in a tiger skin," I said as convincingly as I could.

After seemingly weighing my words, she replied smilingly, "You win!"

These incidents were trifles in comparison with the near-chaos when, at the light rehearsal immediately before the dress rehearsal, everything went wrong. Joe called a temporary halt and, nodding towards me, said, "Stop the German from shouting!" referring to the principal technician who had been brought over from Hamburg. I did. Joe looked white but calm when, at his command, eight heads stuck out from boxes high on the wall above the stage. He told the technicians to study their light schedules during a ten-minute recess.

The German technical chief got hold of himself and the situation was soon under control. Joe read through the signals rapidly, and they were repeated by the German to the technician responsible in turn, for a given effect at a given moment. All were letter perfect! Then the rehearsal took place. It was a stupendous triumph, cheered to the echo by lighting experts from New York's leading theatres, there as guests of Mr. Tiffany's following requests from their respective managements. As a sample of the revolutionary change in stage lighting this production represented, theatres of the day were using only six different reds, but the "dome" system Joe employed had thirty-three. There were other advances in proportion.

The real test of my nerves at the rehearsals (and performance later) was having a youngster placed in a glass bowl of extreme fragility, with air sufficient to last only fifteen minutes. Moreover this youngster was our own daughter Frances.

When the guests assembled for Mr. Tiffany's birthday masque, they were justifiably eager, for New York had already had rumors of the dazzling private theatrical venture which was long in the making. Half a century later, the masque and its audience become inextricably intertwined: a tableau of lavish elegance on both sides of the footlights. It left everyone—not least of all Mr. Tiffany—completely satisfied at its conclusion, and it was to be talked about for at least a decade.

Today, scarcely an adult American has failed to see a widely published picture of another of Mr. Tiffany's parties: the dinner for gentlemen only held at Sherry's, with all of the guests in white tie and tails, seated on horseback. Indeed, the Gilded Age was a long time dying. But having died, it was to be quickly replaced by another, equally strange, and another, and now still another. The Tiffany era or the Beatnik? Take your choice.

28

THE HOURGLASS RUNS DOWN

SHORTLY AFTER Lois Lindon, our third daughter, was born on February 21, 1911, the sublease to the Chestnut Street house expired. Fortunately, through a real-estate friend, the Smiths were given first choice of a property on Beacon Hill at 93 Mt. Vernon Street, before it was put on the market.

It was available for purchase by taking over a mortgage, but the option was for three days only, and Joe was away for two weeks. In this dilemma I broached the subject to Father, who, to my surprise, was interested.

The house had four stories and a large extension dining room in the rear, built over a garden. A flat roof above provided an excellent place for the children and their pets.

Father looked approvingly at the interior of a fine, old-time Boston residence, with beautiful mantels and woodwork. Altogether, it was a perfect setting for Joe's primitives, other ancient paintings, and antiques in general.

Father was very serious when he said abruptly that he knew I realized he was not well and that Mother was noticeably failing. A permanent winter home would be a relief, he added, as though thinking aloud.

"That settles it," I declared decisively.

Joe was overjoyed at the purchase, and within a month we had moved in. No one in the family got more satisfaction out of being permanently settled than Father. His tool chest was busy overtime, at needed repairs or improvements.

He had grown increasingly dependent on my companionship. I did not feel easy away from Mother for long at a time, and Joe similarly accepted as many engagements as possible in the vicinity of Boston.

On one occasion in Boston itself, he was making preparations for a ball which entailed intricate construction by skilled carpenters. He had picked men who loved the job. They were engaged in complicated details long after midnight, when an agent of the union to which they belonged appeared. He demanded to see Joe's contract and was starting to make a scene when eight burly carpenters took over. "Boss," they said, "get out, we're busy; tomorrow we'll send a delegation to the office to resign from the union."

For several years Jennie Brown, an attractive young woman from Wales, had been our working housekeeper. Joe had hired her because of her rich contralto voice, which was useful in his shows. Also, she handled costumes efficiently. Her talents included acting, and she had been equally good as Jeanne d'Arc and as an Indian squaw.

More and more frequently I had Jennie substitute for me in small shows. Father sensed that I was marking time so as to be with him and Mother, and it was he who got me into an enterprise which I could do at home in between lecture engagements.

A neighbor had told us about having started a co-operative market, whose subscribing members consisted of families living on Beacon Hill. But he was about to drop it because it steadily lost money. Father interposed by saying that a co-operative was sound in principle and he believed that I could make a financial success of it.

The other advocate of my involvement in a venture entirely out of my field was Brooks Adams. We had been friends ever since my early married life in Boston. Bostonians had classed me as a maverick because I was a New Yorker and Brooks Adams was called the erratic grandson of John Quincy Adams because he had voted for Bryan for president. Brooks's brother Henry had done the same, but no one assailed him for it.

I resented Bostonians' ignoring the fact that Brooks was a clear thinker and statesman, with a vision of the Pacific in terms of trade as a deterrent to war. I had heard this aspect pointed out in 1903 by no less an authority than John Hay, the secretary of State, over the tea table in his Washington home. He told me that Brooks Adams saw eye to eye with him about the need for an effective merchant marine in the Pacific. He had said also that it was Adams's personal influence with President Theodore Roosevelt that had made possible the political acceptance of his own Open-door Policy (put into effect in 1899) to prevent the dissolution of China and a scramble for her vast territory by the European powers.

Furthermore Brooks Adams had predicted far in advance of others, and correctly in timing, Japan's war with Russia (1904–1905), resulting in part from Japan's need of Russia's deposits of iron and coal in Shansi province. Also, in connection with Japan's position as a highly organized industrial nation, dependent on manufacture for survival, he had been brilliantly prophetic. He warned deaf official ears that, with the monopoly of these raw materials in North China, an area which was rapidly deteriorating and threatening to lapse into a state of administrative chaos under quarreling overlords, Japan would inevitably secure her needed industrial materials by fighting.

Brooks Adams's delightful sense of humor made an appeal almost as strong as his insight into the conditions controlling the future trend of world events. Once he remarked that his brother Henry would be happier if he could forget that two members of the Adams family had been presidents of the United States.

Now, in urging me to take on a co-operative market, he said owlishly that Henry would produce in advance the reasons for its probable failure, whereas he, on the other hand, believed it would be a success, just because there was no tangible reason why it should be!

I had to convince myself that I had something to contribute to a situation before I was willing to make a definite commitment. When I was pondering the advisability of assuming responsibility for a venture which had failed, I chanced to read an article in a business digest that propounded the doctrine that a corner store always succeeded provided the manager was highly paid. I found the former in a temporarily vacant store on the corner of Mt. Vernon and Charles streets, and the latter seemed called for by a newspaper ad inserted by an applicant seeking a managership of a market, with satisfaction guaranteed in return for a large salary. When I per-

suaded a wealthy Bostonian with a Swedish inheritance, and therefore a believer in co-operatives, to finance the venture for two years,
I was all set.

I started with a nucleus of still loyal members of the old co-
operative, and soon a large percentage of families living in the neighborhood joined. It was a compact district, easily covered by a delivery
boy with a hand cart in a single daily delivery.

The manager proved to be a wizard in the twin aspects of wholesale meat purchasing and cutting things to a profit. In addition, his
salesmanship was amazing. Without apparent persuasion, he sold
what he was determined to dispose of at any given moment. Yet he
left the member on the receiving end perfectly satisfied both with
his purchase and with the quick abandonment of a carefully planned
menu.

The most rewarding feature to me was the fact that the co-
operative afforded Father a much-needed occupation. He was general handy man at the store, doing up packages and attending to
endless chores. Brooks Adams frequently dropped in to see us and
to pick up the latest news.

The co-operative continued under the same manager until we left
Boston in 1926 for residence in New York. It maintained a high
quality of food and paid dividends. The press gave us good write-
ups as a success story. And our enterprise forced down materially the
prices in nearby retail stores.

The winter of 1912 had been a hard one for both Mother and
Father, but by Christmas, 1913, Mother seemed her old self. Isabella Gardner had breakfast with us, and Mother took part in a
Christmas play Joe gave that afternoon in the Gothic Room of Fenway Court.

It was a great relief to me to have Dr. C. Allen Porter, the head
surgeon of the Massachusetts General Hospital, assume medical responsibility for the family. He was always available in an emergency,
even at night, and he personally brought to the house other doctors
as needed. Every few days he dropped in to see how Mother was,
and his visits always did her good.

Because of Dr. Porter's absolute medical authority with the family, when Father got him to insist on my taking a long vacation, I had to obey. Joe accompanied me on a visit to one of America's famous playgrounds, southern Florida. We went with the Arthur Curtiss Jameses in their private car from New York. They, with two neighbors, James Deering of Chicago, and William Matheson of Long Island, owned enormous adjacent properties. Between them they controlled the entire waterfront of Coconut Grove, situated five miles from the center of Miami. In addition, Matheson had a large key, which he had made into a valuable experimental station for the growth of rare tropical plants and fruits. As of today (1962) the Deering place has long since been a city park, and the other two properties have been cut up into real-estate developments accommodating hundreds of small houses. The same is true of the key.

Joe and I found the climate physically debilitating because of its moist heat and life stultifying because of its absence of intellect. One changed clothes, ate delicacies unknown in the North, and paid motor visits to northerners who lived on equally huge estates at West Palm Beach. For exercise, the ladies rode bicycles, their chauffeurs driving ahead of them to clear the roads as they wavered unsteadily back and forth over the road's width.

One of the advantages of wealth, however, was that it made possible the ownership of houseboats. We had several cruises among the Florida keys on the Jameses' *Lanai*, and were joined by other houseboats, whose owners and guests exchanged visits during the long afternoons and evenings at the bridge table.

Every male guest was expected to get at least one tarpon. Joe obeyed the orders of an expert guide seated beside him in a boat. After a two-hour struggle he landed a tarpon weighing 190 pounds, the largest caught that season.

An amusing aftermath to Joe's tarpon experience occurred with the arrival of a good-sized box, shipped to our Mt. Vernon Street place, containing endless fish scales. Instantly Mother decided to give a series of dinners, so they could be used as place cards. On the beautiful iridescent surface, Joe had space for including a tiny water color sketch, with the guest's name. Mother responded to the presence of company, who paid her special attention, and thoroughly enjoyed herself.

This resumption of social activities, which Mother had long since avoided, aroused her ambition to give a large formal dinner in honor of Grandpa Put, as my father was now called in the family. It was a busy Boston season, and I thought that, by inviting thirty, we would get the distinguished people to the number of about eighteen with whom Grandpa Put had much in common. It was, in fact, a table that seated only eighteen.

After mailing the invitations, I had to be out of town until three days before the dinner. Upon my return, Mother greeted me full of vitality and bubbling over with enthusiasm. She showed me how ingeniously Father had lengthened the dining table. All thirty had accepted, she said, and assured me that everything was under control. Once again she was the efficient hostess who in the past had planned all Smith parties.

The food had been ordered, appropriate wines selected, and Father's formal clothes pressed, I was informed. All I found to do was to buy a very beautiful gown for Mother. Isabella Gardner sent Mother a beautiful corsage and on an accompanying card wrote, "To the head of the Smith family."

The dinner was a memorable event. Father looked handsome, Mother was a charming hostess, and her appearance rivaled that of Isabella, who was perfectly gowned and wore her diamond tiara.

The conversation was brilliant and much of it general, which was unusual at so large a dinner. But it was Mother who held stage center in a series of inimitable anecdotes. Among them was one about one of her frequent meetings with her cousin, the poet John Greenleaf Whittier, coming by train from her Pawtucket home for a day in Boston with him. The occasion was a funeral.

On her arrival in town, she found she had an hour to spare before their appointment. She went to a milliner's shop and bought a bright red hat. By mistake, she shipped home the bonnet she was wearing, which was suitable for a funeral, instead of her new purchase. She remembered afterwards, she said, Cousin John's startled expression when they met, but he made no comment. They went to the funeral, where, because of his prominence, they were placed in conspicuous seats.

When he put her on the train for the return trip to Pawtucket, he said, "Emma next time thee comes to attend a funeral with me, please leave thy gay bonnet at home."

Three weeks after our gay dinner party, Mother had an illness which culminated in a severe heart attack. Dr. Porter, who had seen her through it, told me that he planned to call in a specialist next day who had been out of town.

"Please now," I urged.

He looked surprised but did so. The specialist arrived that early evening after Dr. Porter had to leave. He assured us every sign of the attack had disappeared, but he had lingered on with me to watch Mother's breathing a while. I felt completely at ease about her condition, and the specialist was about to take his departure, when baby Lois, who never asked for her grandparents after being put in bed for the night, kept calling "I must see Grandma." The doctor told me to bring the baby downstairs. Lois threw her arms around her grandmother, who was sitting up, and kissing her, said, "Soon you will be all better Grandma."

The heart man remarked that he had never seen a sweeter, more responsive child of two. Mother acquiesced, then turning to face me, with a wonderful smile, and leaning forward to pat me affectionately, told him no daughter of her own could have meant as much to her as this girl, then she fell back dead!

Isabella Gardner was the only one not of the family who was at the interment in the burial grounds at Friends Meeting House in Providence, where the same small band of friends gathered who had come to Joe's parents' golden wedding anniversary.

Father was so desperately lonely after Mother's death that I seldom left him, and Isabella Gardner's visits always cheered him.

In the early spring of 1914, I had to replace Joe at a series of three lectures on Egypt in Buffalo. Just as I was stepping down from the lecture platform after the final one, I was handed a telegram saying Father had pneumonia. Within an hour I was on a train headed for Boston. Upon my arrival Father was unconscious. For the next forty-eight hours until the end came, I sat beside him, reliving the full life we had shared.

In a drawer labeled on the outside "Attention: Corinna," were a number of neatly arranged bundles of business papers and a scribbled line of encouragement about Father's entire confidence in my ability to manage the family accounts. It was clear that I had earned and kept his confidence.

29

WORLD WAR I—FRANCE

THE COMING OF WAR IN 1914 could not fail to disrupt the far-reaching research which Joe and his associates had been conducting into the archaeological past. All expeditions in Egypt, except George A. Reisner's at Harvard Camp and in the Sudan, had closed.

From the first few weeks of the war, after the German armies overran Belgium and northern France, Joe and I knew we must lend ourselves to the serious business of relief, particularly for children. Our sympathy, like that of many others in the East of English ancestry, was with the Allied cause. In wishing to contribute a total effort, he and I seemed to complement each other, in opposition to those who looked to governments alone for assistance to war victims. Forty years ago the world revolved, as a matter of fact, much more on voluntary effort than it does now. Joe's versatile career included managing outdoor fetes and producing allegories for guests on large summer estates. With his talent, fund raising was no trick at all. He had merely to persuade these same wealthy hostesses to open their homes for relief. Well-known actors and actresses offered their services to him, and prominent society people as patrons guaranteed audiences ready with pen and check book.

The money we thus raised helped materially in the purchase of food, clothing, and other necessities, which began to go across the Atlantic in a steady stream. On reaching Paris these things were distributed by American volunteers, both men and women, from offices established for the purpose.

Early in the war it became clear that even for neutrals the world was completely changed. While Joe made brief trips to Egypt during the winters of 1914 and 1915, he considered his own work an interruption and immediately abandoned it when a proposal was made to us by Mrs. Robert Woods Bliss of Dumbarton Oaks. This was to involve us both completely, because we could not dissociate ourselves from what was happening daily in France.

Mildred Bliss's husband was in the American Embassy in Paris and both of them played important roles in the creation and administration of committees doing actual relief work. On a brief visit to New York in the spring of 1916, Mildred eloquently sketched for us the scope of an undertaking called the "Children of the Frontier" that arranged for the boys and girls who lived in the war zone. They had to be housed, educated, and trained as future citizens while their fathers were fighting, and the mothers, if still alive, were clinging to the ruins of homes destroyed by the enemy.

At the moment, the committee had assumed responsibility for two thousand such children. They were being looked after in chateaux belonging to French friends and other buildings loaned to the committee, with Sisters of Charity in charge. August F. Jacacci, an American citizen of foreign birth living in Paris, art critic and a leader in the world of culture, was the president, Mildred vice-president, and Mrs. William H. Hill of Boston, Jacacci's right hand in the actual work.

The headquarters of the *Comité des Enfants de la Frontière*, as it was known in France, were at 77 Rue d'Amsterdam, Paris. Mildred Bliss forecast the war as a long one, and felt that with America's inevitable entry, our Red Cross would take over relief on a gigantic scale, with no place for the individual child, who would then be temporarily deprived of his parents' care and guidance. She was sure that constant and ever-larger demands on American purses would require careful planning at the outset, so that there might be no interruption of needed funds for meeting this special problem.

Mildred Bliss invited Joe and me to come to France in the fall, as her guests, for a two-month stay, to visit different war fronts on motor trips. A pass from the minister of war would give us an idea of the actual fighting, its effect on the normal life of civilians, and a dramatic story for American audiences.

On October 24, 1916, we landed at Liverpool on the American steamer *St. Louis*. During our brief stay in London I read bitter attacks in the British press about America's neutrality. The situation was one that Joe and I, as Americans, found difficult to take, and we let English friends make the first move to see us.

James Bryce, who had been created a viscount in 1913, urged us to spend a night at his home in Hindleap, Surrey, but warned us it took patience to travel on a goods train. Darkness was upon us when we finally reached our destination.

Bryce had aged considerably since I had last seen him as British ambassador to the United States. He was more bowed and his short figure was thinner. His pasty complexion showed the strain of war years, but his eyes were as keen as ever and his smile was the same old smile.

At dinner we were served the Bryces' weekly allowance of roast beef, while he spoke of his happy years in the United States and of mutual friends. He referred particularly to my father, with whom he was in constant communication in connection with the American Rights League, founded after the sinking of the *Lusitania*, with my father as president.

Once seated with Bryce in his study, we listened to him as he discussed German atrocities committed in northern France and occupied Belgium at the start of hostilities. "All documented," he said with flashing eyes. He also said that perhaps no Englishman understood as well as he did the difficulties over neutrality which confronted President Wilson. He then added, "Wilson would have been a great president," and did not mention him again.

Dawn was about to break when we went to bed. "Breakfast at 9:00," Bryce said, "and then a tramp through my woods to listen to the birds."

"But how about the trip back to London?" Joe asked.

"It's all arranged," Bryce declared, adding that it would be uneventful since he had done everything short of actual theft to assure the petrol needed for a neighbor's motor to deliver us to a junction where trains ran. "You don't have to leave me until after lunch," he said with a charming smile.

At parting he threw his arms around Joe. "The painting will go on again after the war," he said. Then turning to me, he remarked that my father had been like an old war horse, springing to action at the scent of battle. But he was ignoring the limitations of his physical strength, he warned, urging me to assist him in his crusade upon returning home. "America, once aroused, will come quickly, and her soldiers can bring the war to a successful conclusion."

On Friday, October 27, we departed from London by an early afternoon train to Southampton, to make a crossing of the channel to Havre on the *Hantonia*, but owing to German submarine activity, we did not reach Paris until November 4. By the twelfth, Joe and I were on our way with Mildred Bliss in a high-powered open car, driven by Picken, her Scottish chauffeur, to the French war zone.

We entered the headquarters of the French Fifth Army, of which General Henri Giraud was in command, at Châlons-sur-Marne. He was leaning heavily on a cane, a fact which recalled his having helped save the Dardanelles Campaign from utter disaster. The campaign had cost him an arm and had given him wounds in both hips. His face was drawn and the pain he was suffering was evident.

His eyes were searching yet kindly, and as he greeted us, a smile lit up a face which had been sad in repose. He looked every inch the fighting soldier, capable of service in another Gallipoli, if needs be, as he motioned us to be seated and remarked with a twinkle in his eyes that it was a rare pleasure to receive ladies at his headquarters office. Although he gave the appearance of complete leisure, his alert mind stuck to essentials on each subject he brought up throughout a brief interview.

He explained strategic places on the map, which showed the Allied lines more favorable than at this time a year ago, but he added it was no secret that shipping losses from submarines were alarmingly on the increase. In his analysis of the very close recent American presidential election, he disagreed with the currently expressed disappointment that the Republican candidate had not won, as was first stated (and applauded) in the Paris press.

It was General Giraud's firm conviction that America would have to come into the war, and within a few months. If this had occurred through a change in administration, many would consider that party politics had influenced the decision. But when President Wilson, re-elected because he had kept his country out of the conflict, declared that America must fight in her own interest, the American people would enter the war united, from a realization that it was inevitable.

In an abrupt change of subject, he glanced at our passes, which he was still holding. The *carton bleu*, he explained, issued at the direction of the minister of war, permitted travel on military roads over which the machinery of war was passing. Camouflage protection meant danger. "Use discretion in reaching your objectives," he advised as he instructed an aide to mark our route between Châlons and Nancy.

In the vicinity of Toul we were in the midst of the French Second Army, on its way to a new position in the Vosges. Endless lines of armored cars, munition wagons, and huge guns rolled over cobbles with a suggestive roar of power, moving with the regularity of freight trains. As darkness fell, our dimmed headlights shone on artillery resembling knights on tapestries with long spears, shadows, taking shape for a moment, then to be swallowed up in the night.

The morning after our arrival at Nancy, its préfet, Monsieur Mirman, took us into a large hostel for refugees. I retain a vivid recollection of a little, old, bowed-over French woman, with snapping eyes, who, to my surprise, spoke English. In response to my query as to what I could send her, she replied promptly, "A rocking chair, I got in the habit of them in America where I lived for eighteen years with a Vanderbilt family."

Equally vivid was a chance encounter with a *poilu* at Saint Nicolas du Port. In guiding us to the *état major*, he told me of a little song-bird he had caught in a front-line trench. He made a cage for it, and the bird remained with him for several months under constant bombardment. Finally, the *poilu* got permission to go to Paris on leave. All went well with his bird until they entered the city gates and the bird chirped madly from terror. "The noise of a city was too much for the little creature, so I shortened my leave and returned to trench life," he explained.

Madame Mirman was as energetic and remarkable a personality as the Préfet. She was promoting an active lace industry among women living in homes frequently bombed, who had consented to have their children in the refugee village.

M. Mirman was describing to us the harrowing sufferings inflicted on thrifty, industrious peasant families before they reached the shelter of Nancy when, during the evening meal we were having with the Mirmans in their home, such a family came in.

It consisted of an old woman carrying a half-naked baby and three small children with bleeding feet, out of breath from running. They crouched on the floor, and with wide-eyed, agonized faces, shrieked as they looked at the walls and ceiling. "The last time my grandchildren saw a room was in our farmhouse when the enemy was setting fire to it," she said by way of explanation.

I caught the drift of her story, related between sobs to the Préfet. The father of the children was fighting, and the grandmother and children had lived in a dark cellar. She and their mother (her daughter) had supported the family by making lace from thread brought from a long distance by a *poilu* on foot. He also took the finished product away for sale. "My daughter was killed by a stray shell while searching for food and—"

At this point the Préfet interrupted the narrative to remind her that the children needed her attention.

One afternoon, accompanied by Commandant Chapui, we made a long motor trip from Nancy and, after a steep climb on foot, arrived in Sainte Geneviève, which was badly knocked about because of its exposed position. After taking us to what he significantly called the wood of the widows, we reached the completely demolished village of Pont-à-Mousson, on an adjacent hilltop. Here, for the first time, I descended into trenches that twisted and turned through damp, smelly passages, where occasionally I caught sight of the bright pinpoint of a rat's eye before it disappeared. Lanterns picked out figures of *poilus* standing at their posts in stained, faded uniforms.

I stumbled along with the others and blinked when we climbed out of the trenches into a high *observatoire* that afforded an extended view. "Those wooded hills conceal enemy batteries, and the village to the right of us is occupied by the Germans," the commandant said tersely.

A brief visit to the recaptured Alsatian town of Thann was a fitting climax to our trip through northern Lorraine. At headquarters, a large group of school children in neat garments and with their faces scrubbed clean was a moving sight. A young girl gave a labored address of welcome in French, spoken with a strong German accent. This was followed by a very small youngster, who struggled manfully through the *Marseillaise* with an occasional German word interspersed.

We had been warned that the road from Thann to Belfort, where we were to take a night train back to Paris, was a dangerous one, since along its route were many ammunition factories which supplied the French armies of the region, and the Germans were determined to destroy them.

Frederic R. Coudert, an international lawyer of renown and of French ancestry, was in Paris in August, 1914, and got permission to go to the front. In the town of Belfort he lost interest in seeing the fighting, in his horror at finding two hundred French children, scantily clothed and half starved, wandering about in a field as the bombs fell in their midst. He took them back to Paris in freight cars, with the permission of both military and civilian authorities, and sent a cable to his wife which read, "We now have not four but two hundred and four children." He appealed to intimate friends to help him care for his large family. This was the beginning of the Children of the Frontier Committee.

Our next war-zone trip, and again with Mildred accompanying us, was into free Belgium, a small coastal area beginning at the town of Ghyvelde, beyond Dunkirk. Count Charles de Broqueville, the Belgian minister of war, and the king and queen of the Belgians were in residence at La Panne.

This was the center for Belgian relief activities being carried on by the Belgians themselves, under the personal supervision of the queen. The reason for our visit was that our Committee was looking after about two hundred Belgian children, cared for by their own nuns, refugees from the Convent of Ypres at the time of its destruction by the German advance.

From Paris we motored directly to Le Havre, the seat of the Belgian government in exile, where arrangements were made for our stay in La Panne, as guests of De Broqueville, and we were to be received by the king and queen.

We had French papers, but were to be looked after by the British military during the first part of our trip, which was through their lines.

At Montreuil, British headquarters of the expeditionary force in France, we were given an escort to Boulogne, where we were to spend the night as guests of the British military.

As in the case of the mountains of empty shells we had constantly passed, one had to see to believe the reality of the British channel transport service. This same service saw that a man wounded early in the morning in France was generally that same night being cared for in a hospital in England. Only the most severely wounded were kept near the front, because they could not be moved. Floating hospitals, of which we visited several, had to cross the channel in a steady stream, since one day's hold-up would congest the entire system. Such was the efficiency of the British that this had never happened.

Our next stop was at the coastal town of Calais, a tremendous center for channel transport. In all directions one saw nothing except supply warehouses, surpassing even Boulogne's facilities for the care of the wounded.

As we approached Dunkirk, so frequently in the news, antiaircraft guns stationed on boats along the canals were conspicuous. The town had suffered cruelly from bombardment. One aisle of the Cathedral was completely destroyed but the intact altar was dramatic in its simplicity. Tommies in numbers, wearing sheepskin sleeveless coats against the penetrating chill, knelt reverently beside French women and children less warmly clad. As the Mass progressed, a priest, reciting the litany in the wavering light of a candle, gave symbolical voice to man's hopes above the sound of guns booming with resonant distinctness.

At Ghyvelde, the military entrance to free Belgium, a captain presented us with the purple paper required for passing the frontier, but failed to produce a letter of instructions, expected from De Broqueville, and an escort, to take us to tea with the king and queen and then to his house for the night.

Under the circumstances, there was no alternative to an uncomfortable night in a poor hotel. Next morning when Mildred got De Broqueville on the telephone, he apologized for the stupidity of the Belgian intelligence for not having located the only civilian car in Belgium that day.

On our delayed trip to De Broqueville's chateau, we visited Miss Fyfe, who was one of the first English women in the early days of the war to establish herself on the Belgian frontier. In makeshift quarters, she had cared for frantic Belgian families fleeing before the German army. At the present time she was running a maternity barracks and hostel for children from the firing-line districts, until mothers and children could be moved farther back.

Marcia Stack, whom we also saw, was another English woman of an equally undefeatable character. She was in charge of a primitive hospital at Hoogstadt.

It was long after dark when, guided by a sentry from the Ministry of War, after poking along country roads and sand dunes, we came to a chateau surrounded by a moat. At dinner De Broqueville told us that the population in occupied Belgium was rapidly declining, because thousands of able-bodied men were being deported by the Germans, who were also deliberately separating families. He then abruptly changed the subject, pointing to a revived Belgian Army, re-equipped and drilled by the British. It was now increased to 250,000 men, from 70,000 at the beginning of the war.

He referred to the magnificent heroism of civilians, who continued to run the risk of almost certain death in crossing the frontier into free Belgium, to join in fighting their way back again into their occupied country. When he spoke of the Belgian soldiers who were holding over fifteen kilometers of sand-dune trenches, I told him I had some idea at least what this meant in the way of hardship, having seen some of the coastal defense on a dismal beach.

We had walked over a desolate stretch to pay our respects to the memory of Madame de Page (who went down on the *Lusitania*), on a site marked by a simple cross. We had paused for a brief conversation with some French-speaking Belgians standing beside trenches built high with piles of sandbags. Underground construction was out of the question here. Water would have flooded them. The wind, with hurricane strength, was blowing sand into faces blue from cold, but we had heard no complaints from soldiers on as lonely a vigil as the British were in the trawler service.

At breakfast, our host apologized for a disturbed night and seemed amazed that his guests had slept until called by a servant. He explained that the British had responded with a deafening roar of artillery to an attempted gas attack near La Panne. I replied that, to be traveling at the front to report war experiences in subsequent lectures in America, and to sleep through a gas attack, was a mortifying situation.

De Broqueville had arranged, at the queen's request, for Mildred and me to visit a number of the Belgian refugee colonies, while Joe, in the care of the military, entered front-line trenches. At Poperinge, we were to meet Countess Van den Steen, a lady-in-waiting on the queen, who was to take us to the palace.

Delays were caused by a recent shelling on the road to Poperinge, which necessitated, at stated intervals, telephone permission to proceed over it. The travel was very slow, owing to a division of Canadian troops coming down from Ypres. Even after the torture of constant bombardment in that exposed salient, they appeared nothing daunted at the prospect of a return to that death trap after a week's rest.

Darkness had fallen when we followed the chart given us by De Broqueville to use in reaching the palace. Picken took a wrong turn and landed in a blind alley of mud. In attempting to turn the car around, it bogged down and had to be extricated by a combination of chains and horseflesh. It was after eight when we finally reached the palace, to be received by three distressed ladies-in-waiting with the news that the king and queen had retired for the night. An aide-de-camp told us Her Majesty had remarked that she found it difficult to understand how guests could be lost for two successive days in a kingdom now no larger than a pocket-handkerchief!

30

NEUTRAL AMERICA

When we got back to the United States in early January, 1917, filled with impressions of thousands of homeless French and Belgian youngsters under the guns of both sets of combatants in northern France and Belgium, America was still neutral, if not always in thought, then certainly in deed. Eighteen months earlier, the sinking of the *Lusitania*, with the loss of many American lives, produced an immediate and violent reaction against Germany by many thousands in this country, but President Wilson came forward with the plea to Americans to be neutral even in thought, adding the further suggestion that there was such a thing as being too proud to fight.

Joe had written an allegory entitled *Love of Country*, which was produced as a benefit in the ballrooms of private homes in big cities. It ended with the appearance of Jeanne d'Arc, whose heroic appeal was never-failing, followed by talented Ruth Draper in her monologue *"Vive la France."* All I had to do was to explain to audiences how their money would be spent and gather in the checks, frequently with three or four ciphers written on them.

In addition, the backing of an important group of men and women on the Children of the Frontier Committee insured audiences for Joe's frequent war lectures, the tickets to which produced large amounts, not only in the East, but in the Middle West. He had long since developed his own public. This left me free to heed Lord Bryce's words, spoken in England, to the effect that my father needed the strength of my youth to assist him in his own campaign against American neutrality. I decided upon Kansas City for a first attempt on my own in telling audiences why America must join the Allies. My ideas and persuasiveness were fortified by my spending a few days in Washington with Sir Cecil Spring-Rice, the British ambassador, and by a lucky chance, Teddy Roosevelt was in town! All together, it was what might be termed a fortuitous combination for gaining inspiration, based on facts and common sense.

My hostess in Kansas City was engaged in effective work for Allied relief and her welcome and arrangements for me were heartening. The schedule was to include talks at several boys' and girls' schools and a guest speaking engagement at a Rotary lunch. It was to achieve its climax in an evening gathering in my honor at a country club, as part of a fund raising campaign. Best of all, I was to make a brief appearance at the Chamber of Commerce, thanks to the prominence of my host in business.

All augured well until I drew a blank on my inquiry about when I would be interviewed by the press. "Kansas does not like the war," my hostess said. This being the case, before the Rotary lunch I dropped in alone at the offices of the *Kansas City Star*, and sent in my card to the editorial department. After a long delay the editor saw me. My statement that I had recently come from the war zone in France produced no comment. But the fact that I was the daughter of George Haven Putnam did—adverse. "He's trying to drag America into the war," he said bluntly. He knew that Joe was associated with ancient Egypt and art, but this did not lead us anywhere conversationally.

The editor was obviously extremely busy and I was about due at the Rotary; when I arose, reluctantly and defeated, he did the same, promptly. His rather hesitant manner, as though he was sorry to be unco-operative, emboldened me to say, "Can't I find some contact with the war?"

"Where do you live?" he asked irrelevantly.

When I told him Boston, he wanted to know if I happened to know Mrs. Jack Gardner. My answer to this question did the trick; everything changed for the better at once.

Next day, when I was looking up trains for my departure, my hostess said with a flutter of excitement that William Allen White of *The Emporia Gazette* wished to speak to me personally on the telephone.

"Why didn't you communicate with me about publicity?" he asked, adding that dear old Jacacci was about his best friend. I was practically ordered to take the next train to Emporia and stay with Mr. White and his wife.

I found him a human dynamo, bursting with enthusiasm and good humor. I told him that to date the majority of my scheduled meetings had been arranged rather casually by Bryn Mawr friends living in the West. But the fact that a number of people in my Kansas City audiences had invited me to speak, on a return engagement, to organizations composed of men, was encouraging.

He appeared greatly impressed by the auspices for my meetings in Salt Lake City, for which I was bound. The engagements had been brought about when Senator Frelinghuysen of New Jersey took me, during a Washington stay, to see Senator Reed Smoot of Utah, with whom he was intimate. "Mormons are good people to have for you," William Allen White commented.

He was on the telephone a good deal in my behalf and suddenly announced that supper would be early, as he was taking me to give an evening talk from the pulpit of a church. We motored a long distance, over a very bumpy road for the final part of the way. The interior of the church was dark, and as I stood in the pulpit a glare of light in my face prevented my getting more than an impression of many black-bearded men in the audience. I was still under the spell of White's praise of my father, and his own varied experiences in combating America's neutrality.

It was in that mood I started to talk, as though to a sophisticated, emotional gathering in New York. Suddenly White's expression of dismay interrupted my trend of thought. He, realizing that he had attracted my attention, leaned forward in the pew directly below and whispered, "Stop being an understudy for Jeanne d'Arc. These are simple Kansas farmers."

I nodded and with an abrupt change in my tone of voice said,

"How about an enemy that sets fire to crops, slits the throats of live-stock it can't take away, and girdles fruit trees—is that fair fighting?" I could actually sense the wave of interest that swept through that audience, and from then on the attentiveness to my every word was confirmed by White's beaming face. Understanding grunts satisfied me that the minute details I gave about the damage done on farm after farm were convincing these assembled hard-headed farmers that I had actually seen the sights I described. This, of course, was long before the days of TV, which came to record an event at the time it took place.

After two hours, White rescued me and, as I sat down beside him, an old, long-bearded man took my place in the pulpit. His face was grim and determined and he spoke slowly with solemn conviction. "When men put on a soldier's uniform during a war, it's their job to fight and they are paid for it; if they're killed, it's hard on their families. Attacking farms, however, is a different matter." His neighbors had been able to judge for themselves that I spoke truth, since no highly educated woman from Boston could have invented such accurate details about farming. He concluded by advising that a collection be taken up, to be sent to France as a token of the fact that Kansas farmers would not stand for tampering with livestock, grain, and orchards.

White and I left the church, dragging between us a sack heavy with quarters, dimes, and nickels. I got a further knowledge of Kansas farmers because he would not permit me to leave Emporia without accepting invitations to talk to other farmer groups in the vicinity. "I didn't know they could be so stirred up," he said happily.

On the long trip to Salt Lake City, the train was snowed up by a blizzard for twenty-four hours on a mountain pass. The heating system broke down and food had to be rationed. The passengers were good sports and I made some helpful friends among them for the Allied cause during the many hours we were dependent on one another's company.

I finally reached Salt Lake to find the Mormon audiences I addressed surprisingly generous in responding to the needs of our committee's French children. They wanted to know exactly how the colonies of youngsters functioned under the Sisters of Charity, and enjoyed anecdotes about individual children. One orphaned Belgian boy of twelve, I told them, had been rescued after six months of trench life with Tommies. When I asked him how he was getting on in the colony of youngsters, he replied, "It's hard being bossed by women, but in war times one must not complain."

After Salt Lake, White's schedule called for a tour beginning with Cincinnati and continuing through many other German centers. On the trip from Salt Lake to Cincinnati, my thoughts had focused upon a line of approach to audiences in cities with dominating German populations, or with families where the man was American but his wife German. I felt a pang of sympathy in the difficult situation of the wife and mother, living in a state of a divided allegiance, with sons who might soon be drafted into the American army. It came to me in a flash that her salvation lay in being persuaded that the Germany her parents had caused her to love did not exist for the moment. Therefore, she had but one loyalty, and that was to her husband's country, where their children belonged by birth.

With this as a premise, I intended to recall by name German-born leaders in American life, notably Carl Schurz, who, having left Germany in protest against conditions there in 1848, decided to make America his home. Many Germans similarly assimilated to American life had fought on the side of the North to preserve the Union, and their descendants were now important in the continued upbuilding of our country.

I became obsessed with a pertinent idea which needed co-operation to put it into effect. At the next station, I rushed into a telephone booth and by luck managed to catch William Allen White in his office. I shouted to him, over a poor connection, to get for me in each city on my itinerary a list of familiar names among the German population dating back to pre-Civil War days. Before I could answer his question why I wanted the names, I hung up on him, as my train was slowly pulling out. But quick-witted White had thought that one out for himself, and I was shortly paged in my car with a telegram from him giving the names requested for Cincinnati, and saying the others were in the mail.

I began my speech in Cincinnati by stating that just before Christmas I had been in the fighting zone of France with the armies of the Allies. I paused for the implication to sink in, then went on with great earnestness.

I explained that my father had been educated at Göttingen, and that he had life-long friendships with German colleagues who were new American citizens. With this as a preamble, I referred to some of the Germans whose work was familiar in the annals of Cincinnati. I took advantage of this responsive atmosphere to point out that I had been brought up by a German nurse. My German was rusty, I said, but still usable. A few sentences in it were greeted by applause.

I mentioned that the Kaiser was so sure of my father that he sent instructions on exactly what was expected of him as a New York agent for Germany in the war. His reply, that he had sent the document to *The New York Times*, as well as the nature of his refusal, brought forth a further communication from the Kaiser stating that the brain of George Haven Putnam was a howling wilderness.

Now, for a look at the record in France, I said abruptly. As though mentally turning page after page in my war journals, I conjured up one episode after another as examples of the brutal treatment of civilians by German soldiers acting under the orders of the German High Command. I was conscious of the breathless attention of an audience actually reliving in imagination scenes difficult of acceptance in a civilized age. "Your reaction is the same as mine, or any other good American citizen's," I said in conclusion and sat down.

Through January and well into February, I felt like a traveling emissary, as, in response to White's orders, I kept on the move almost constantly, with only an occasional few days at home. I often retraced my steps on long trips, to take part in some special occasion. I never spoke fewer than five times a day, looked in at committee headquarters of many organizations, saw club groups of all kinds, and always took part in an evening meeting. Each audience had to be handled differently. To my amazement, checks in sizable amounts, earmarked for French children, poured in. The signatures on them spoke eloquently: so many of them were German names, or American ones, accompanied by a scribbled line saying that a wife was a

German, and expressing gratitude for what I had done for her.

As the weeks passed, a gradual change was noticeable in the attitude of the people with whom I came in contact, on trains, in the streets, and in hotel lobbies. America's entry into the war was being discussed more and more as a probability rather than as a possibility.

On January 22, President Wilson had advocated "peace without victory," and I, like many other Americans, was disquieted about what the words meant. Furthermore, unrestricted submarine warfare, after having been abandoned during the latter part of 1916, was in effect for the second time as of February 1, 1917. A flying trip to Washington seemed indicated, and I telegraphed to Sir Cecil Spring-Rice my date of arrival, as I always stayed with him and Lady Spring-Rice at the British Embassy.

I was shocked at Spring-Rice's unhealthy color but was struck, as always, by his contradictory and appealing personality. His hair was sparse, his short beard, scraggly. His brow was broad and smooth above a conspicuous nose. The gentleness of his eyes, not dimmed by large-rimmed spectacles, was contested by a supercilious curl to his lips. He was noted for his brilliant phrases, as well as a caustic wit that got him into hot water when his quick temper was out of control.

In representing England as ambassador, he was not only under an almost insurmountable handicap because of a constant conflict in American policies, but both President Wilson and Colonel E. M. House distrusted him personally. To make matters worse, their dislike was fanned into official flame by the fact that Spring-Rice was a close friend of Senator Henry Cabot Lodge's and Theodore Roosevelt's, and he was on a cordial basis with Elihu Root. Oddly enough, at the other pole of strong personalities, Spring-Rice found much in common with William Jennings Bryan, whom he described as an "inspired fanatic and crusader."

Spring-Rice said of himself that he always "talked too much and said little of value." But until America's entry into the war, his diplomatic success lay in his genius for knowing what *not* to say in the moments of terrible strain between England and America.

The first evening at dinner, both Roosevelt and Henry Cabot

Lodge were present. I was horrified to learn from their table conversation that several times America's declaration of war against England had been narrowly averted. The plain truth, as stated by Roosevelt, was that England was in conflict with American material interests and Germany was not. American supplies reached England but the British fleet, in spite of the vehement protests of American exporters, prevented trade with Germany from American ports, at first direct and later through neutrals. According to Roosevelt, to make matters worse, it looked as though both the President and Colonel House recognized no difference in the relative rightness of the case of England and France over Germany.

Cabot Lodge repeated to me a casual remark of President Wilson's, to the effect that, if facts were given him, the logical conclusion came automatically. I replied that my father had never lost confidence in the President's ultimate leadership. He considered, I said, that his egotism was a hopeful sign, because another sinking would soon occur which would blatantly infringe the rights of America as a neutral. Suddenly, the logical conclusion would result in a declaration of war, and the President would wage it conclusively, because it was his war.

February 26 the President broke off diplomatic relations with Germany and Count von Bernstorff was presented his passport. Although he was not to declare war until April 7, he made the official announcement on March 17 that a state of war existed with Germany, after the sinking of the *Algonquin*, which fulfilled the conditions my father had foreseen.

On that historic evening, I was in Milwaukee, attending a mammoth gathering of about seven thousand people in the city auditorium. This citizen support of America's entry into the war had been the culminating effort on the part of Paul O. Husting, the junior senator from Wisconsin. Since the beginning of hostilities, he had made a noble fight towards that end, in committee rooms and on the floor of Congress. Later his campaign was strengthened by the participation of Irvine L. Lenroot, one of the Wisconsin Congressmen. During the week previous to the meeting, *The Milwaukee Journal* contained an advance story, daily, promoting it.

I was in Madison when Senator Husting telephoned me personally. He said his good friend William Allen White had suggested my being invited to join at the meeting a group of Wisconsin women engaged in war relief activities. He planned for me to talk briefly on the fighting zone in France, and my confidence in our German citizens.

He insisted on coming to the station upon my arrival and having me included in a dinner at the Milwaukee Press Club given in honor of the principal speakers. Senator Husting, of whom I had heard much, was a bitter disappointment at first sight. He was short and clumsy in his movements, shy, and with an unattractive face until he smiled, and he spoke with a hesitation in his speech that was painful in the extreme.

Guy D. Goff was an excellent chairman and all the speakers were amazingly well stocked with intelligence. But Husting was the bright star. He completely lost his stammer and rose to a height of eloquence I have seldom seen rivaled and never surpassed. He was cheered to the echo—in Milwaukee, a German city.

I will always think of him as he stood on the station platform waving a cheerful good-by to me at one o'clock in the morning. We were never to meet again. In the early fall, he came to an untimely death by accident, at the peak of his power of usefulness.

The next day found me seated at the desk next to William Allen White's in his office at *The Emporia Gazette*, reading items in the western press. The general trend on that day, and for the three subsequent ones of my stay in Emporia, was that the West had been expecting America's entry into the war for the past eight months.

Two weeks later I was again in Washington, at the summons of Newton Baker, the secretary of War. Since our first meeting through a mutual friend on my return from a trip to the fighting zone, I had made a personal report to him. On this new visit he had arranged for me to have a brief interview with President Wilson.

I was impressed by the calm exaltation in the President's demeanor. He seemed like a man whose soul was at peace after an inner struggle. In a short monologue addressed to his Secretary of War and me, he emphasized the fact that he personally was sending

American troops to France. Consequently, the logical conclusion was that everything pertaining to their well-being and efficiency must have his immediate attention. I knew then and I know now that, of the scores of men I came to know in high position, at home and abroad, his was the most supercharged personal ego I had encountered. He struck me as being a person singularly impervious to new ideas, even the best. This impression obviously has to be reconciled with Wilson's admittedly great capacities as a scholar, as demonstrated during his teaching and research career before he entered politics. He simply did not fit easily into a political context.

31

CHILDREN OF THE FRONTIER

THE DECLARATION OF WAR by the United States brought to an end the intensive campaign which many Americans, Joe and me among them, had waged in favor of America's joining the Allies. After April 7, 1917, that matter was settled. But as I have indicated in earlier passages of this book, the care of temporarily homeless children must still remain, in varying degree, the responsibility of private effort. The time when these functions became almost exclusively the tasks of government was not yet.

After America's entry into the war, the Red Cross did away with the American clearing house in Paris as a center, and many organizations carried on by American initiative in the war zones were absorbed by the Red Cross. In our case, it was necessary to function as an independent effort, because the care of the French and Belgian children, for whom we were responsible, must be under the nominal charge of French and Belgian sisters, and the success of the undertaking entailed having the children brought up according to the standards and methods of their own countries. The American way would possibly have proved disruptive of their lives, making it difficult to fit them again into the social scheme of homelands.

The clothes the children wore were those they were accustomed to. Their education was suited to them. Our committee kept in close touch with French and Belgian committees doing relief work in the pattern they had put before us. This was the second and even more important reason for me to make trips into the fighting zones to study (and assist) the planning required for the care of refugees. The experience was to prove vital later, after the Armistice, when, through private initiative as well as French departmental machinery, the gigantic achievement of reconstruction was to be realized.

Anne Morgan and many other Americans were doing valiant work in the relief of families late in the war, particularly after we had joined the Allies, under French organization and direction. But there was a tendency at the time, unfortunately not corrected in the years since, to credit American voluntary relief workers with a much larger performance than they were capable of or had the machinery for accomplishing. In Free Belgium, relief was carried out very largely by Belgian committees, staffed almost entirely by Belgian nationals, aided to a limited extent by the British. These committees were prepared to function in a well-organized way after the Germans were driven out.

Similarly, seven-eighths of the care of civilians in the invaded departments of northern France was being carried forward by the French themselves.

The presence of the United States in Belgium and France as a full-fledged combatant immediately suggested certain changes of direction—notably in voluntary work of the type many of us had been carrying on. With American organized effort in the prosecution of the war came also the great ancillary services sponsored at home, and now abroad, by such organizations as the Red Cross, the Salvation Army, the Knights of Columbus, the Y.M.C.A., and others. Yet to salvage the organization and the work of the Children of the Frontier Committee seemed of importance to the continuity which, in any effort, is slow building.

I was personally interested in keeping the committee, not selfish-

291

ly, I believe, and largely on the twin grounds of continuity and practicality. After all, we had got the hang of things under the most difficult of circumstances—and we had had great experience in raising money as well. Fortunately, there were men of great influence at home and abroad who shared this feeling with me. Among them were Paul Cravath and Frank Cutcheon, to name but two. Both were high in the councils of the Red Cross. Moreover, both had come to France to advise with General Pershing on military and legal decisions during the American offensive. Fred Coudert, our treasurer from New York, had influence both with the French government and with our own, and C. A. Coffin, the head of General Electric and the central figure in raising relief funds by the millions, insisted on the integrity of the committee. To make things still more solid, Samuel Mather of Cleveland, who was high in the Red Cross, was a loyal supporter of the committee and its work.

I sat in at a number of heated conferences held on the subject of the discontinuance of the committee, between these stalwart protectors of our continued existence and Henry Davidson, the head of the American Red Cross, a situation incidentally which Mildred Bliss, with her usual vision, had foreseen.

The garments made from French patterns by our garment centers at home, principally in New York, Boston, and Chicago, kept up the interest of a large number of volunteers engaged in the clothing of four thousand children who were our responsibility. Also, these garment centers provided an excellent forum for lectures by me and many others.

The showdown came when the Red Cross refused shipment of these American-made French garments to France. Coudert came to the rescue by getting the French government to ship them free. And through my friendship with Hendon Chubb, Chubb and Son paid the insurance required by law.

In this situation, Davidson dropped his insistence that the Committee of the Children of the Frontier be dissolved. At the instigation of Cravath and Coffin, he even agreed to have the Red Cross underwrite a part of our steadily increasing annual budget. This was indeed an expression of appreciation for our taking off his hands the problem of the child made homeless by war. I like to remember that the final $100,000 the Red Cross spent in France for children was through our committee. Davidson informed Jacacci that he considered the committee could put it to better use in individual rehabilitation than could the Red Cross.

The committee did not go out of existence until 1924. It had found a living relative to whom to return each of the four thousand children who had been in its care, with the exception of thirty who had been in government institutions for epileptics and the blind located in the invaded districts.

Our committee had worked with the regular French departmental health machinery, instead of as an independent health unit, in the care of sick children for whom we were responsible. We had co-operated closely with Dr. Jacques Calvé, head of the government sanitarium at Berck-sur-Plage for children suffering from bone tuberculosis. We left him and his staff, as a legacy from the war, a first-class, well-equipped hospital. Thanks to the active participation of Dr. James Miller and Dr. Linsly R. Williams, the New York tuberculosis authorities, the committee had added to Berck a *femme école*, the first of its kind in France. The école not only furnished fresh vegetables, milk, and butter to the patients, but served for a trade training school for the youngsters as market gardeners during long convalescences.

The committee had established the first preventorium in France, at Calvados in Normandy, which the government continued to use after our organization went out of existence. Also it left a hospital for babies with tuberculosis, on the highest point of the Seine and Marne, in a building that was the gift of Robert and Mildred Bliss.

Altogether, the Children of the Frontier Committee had fully justified the need for its continued usefulness during the war and long after hostilities had ceased, both in the care of children temporarily deprived of a home and education, and in a lasting contribution to the departmental health machinery of France.

Voluntary work in a war zone has its perils as well as its privileges. Soon after the United States joined the conflict in 1917, Joe and I were again on our way to the region of heavy fighting in northern France, to help in carrying relief to the youngsters and to gather first-hand information which would be invaluable in working up lectures for delivery to audiences in America on our trips home. Once again, we were accompanied by Mildred Bliss and Picken, her chauffeur. As before, our *"laisser passer"* permitted travel over military highways, and the choice of roads between points mentioned in the permits was left to our discretion.

Our first objectives were the towns and villages in the vicinity of Noyon, first occupied by the Germans in their sweep for Paris in 1914, and only freed by the French and British advance in the spring of 1917. A chart was furnished us, indicating side lanes to isolated farms, far off the beaten track. Coucy le Chateau, on the heights overlooking the valley of the Aisne in an exposed position, and Rheims, under frequent bombardment, were on our passes.

Rheims was an official stop for us, at the request of Archbishop Luçon, who wished a report of children from there who were still with our committee, and arrangements were to be made for our taking still more. But it was sheer adventure, suggested by James Hazen Hyde, to include the ruins of Richard Coeur de Lion's famous fortress castle at Coucy le Chateau, with its enormous buttresses which were continuations of natural rock. All civilians had long since been evacuated. The justification for our going was that it would be good lecture material. Before we were to get there, however, we were to see much devastated countryside.

It was easy to distinguish damage done in retreat rather than in an advance. We went through several small manufacturing towns where the products were necessities for civilian life, with no military advantage. Factories had been gutted and machinery, hacked to pieces, was lying about in the open. From these towns we followed instructions on the chart and came to deserted lanes of uneven surfaces that took us through a series of villages and farm lands. We were surrounded by burned houses and barns. Acid had been poured over demolished stonework in the vicinity to prevent its use in rebuilding. Occasionally the flames had spared a charming archway or a grape vine, where ripening grapes trailed over a broken wall.

We walked on what was left of bypaths, through fields, to see blackened ruins of stacked crops and wagons. Strewn about were scattered bones and bits of carcasses of livestock. In orchard centers, we picked our way between countless lines of fruit-bearing trees that had either been cut down and left in a tangled mass or were left standing with the trunks girdled. On a number thus mutilated a few apples had managed to ripen in a final spasm of productiveness before death.

A characteristic account of the destruction by the retreating Germans of once prosperous farms was given us by a lone farmer whom we overtook as he trudged along one of the side roads. "Yes," he told us, "the *Boches* came to my farm and killed my pigs and other livestock, although they had no time to take them away." He went on to say, in an expressionless voice, "I fled with my wife and daughter. We sat on a hill and watched everything we owned go up in flames." They were not hungry, he said, but from nervousness they ate all the food contained in a haversack they were depending upon for several days. "Now I am ready to begin all over again," he said, his face full of courage.

Back on the main road, it was a relief to catch fragments of cheerful songs and gay laughter coming from a convoy of French soldiers whom we overtook as the sun set over a distant landscape.

We wandered through churned up streets in villages where the only living thing apparently was a butterfly. In one partially wrecked home a sewing machine was suspended in mid-air, in another a child's crib was visible, and nearby a string of bright beads rested in a child's armchair. Toys, saucepans, stoves, beds, bureaus all bore witness to the war's savagery. A little dead bird in the corner of a cage, and a child's school diploma on a wall seemed poignant beyond the power of words to express.

As we sped away Joe quoted Kipling's warning, "Rise up and meet the war, the Hun is at the gate."

As we passed on we encountered permissionaires haying in fields close to groves of tall trees—a beautiful view, symbolic of peace. But the road we were on was protected by camouflage nets containing leaves and dry grasses, for again we were approaching danger.

When we reached the entrance to Coucy, blocked by a chain, a sentry stared incredulously at two women and a man in mufti in a civilian car. His examination of our passes obviously increased his respect, but also eliminated his responsibility, for us. He pointed to a road beyond the barrier that we were to take on foot to the *état major* above, emphasizing, rather to our dismay, that the road was within range of enemy guns and that the motor would be a target.

We started the ascent, which became steep almost at once. Walking was made difficult by deep craters and exploded shells over an already uneven surface. We were all out of breath but increased our pace when the "upheavals" looked recent, as we approached buildings which were mere silhouettes, with blue sky showing through their partial walls. There was no sign of human habitation until we reached the *état-major* sign over a cellar door.

A jovial-faced colonel named Rey was in command. He inspected our credentials before welcoming us cordially. He soon escorted us to the only remaining part of the Richard Coeur de Lion's castle still intact—a tower—but I noticed in passing several demolished buttresses, and even the adjacent rock formation had been blown into separate boulders. By the light of an electric torch, we mounted a short, dark stairway and, to our astonishment, were ushered into a real room of impressive proportions. There were good rugs on the floor, a baby grand piano, comfortable stuffed arm chairs, and on a long table were two large shell cases, used as vases, filled with a mass of gay flowers. However, as a reminder that this was not merely a drawing room, military maps covered a vast amount of wall space. He termed our unexpected visit a very special occasion for the officers whom we would meet at tea, inasmuch as his colleagues had seen no ladies in Coucy for more than two years. He then took us up another stairway, very narrow and winding, with badly broken steps, where the torches cast eerie shadows. I had seen nothing like it except in parts of the interior of the Pyramid of Cheops at Giza. We emerged suddenly to a stupendous view over the valley of the Aisne, seen from the terraced roof of the tower, from which we could look into the enemy lines.

After this, Colonel Rey showed us what had been the main part of the castle. Huge blocks of stone, in formidable piles, looked as though one or more pylons of an Egyptian temple had fallen. He said this old fortress had been so solidly built that even though three thousand sticks of dynamite had been used in blowing it up, the cellars had remained intact and were occupied by a very large French garrison.

Since military service was compulsory in France, one met in the war zone in the officer class a cross section of a society that included artists, musicians, and distinguished men of letters. For example, in this group, consisting of about twelve officers, one played Chopin and another recited one of his own poems as we awaited tea.

As we sat about afterwards, the officers stood less on dignity, and we got an idea of what was in their thoughts during anxious days in a very lonely outpost. Coucy was then the only bulwark against advancing enemy hordes that threatened to sweep through the Aisne Valley and within striking distance of Paris for the second time. We heard it hinted that the French army was dismayed at not being backed up by the government, which, it was said, was playing politics, and that civilians were becoming weary of their sacrifices.

As we were about to leave, Colonel Rey said, "Of course you have gas masks?" And was disconcerted when we replied, "No." He told us that the new colorless, odorless gas now being used was instant in its effect and very deadly. He wrote an order for masks to be furnished us at Soissons. "Take the road to the left," he instructed us. "The other is unsafe. I trust you will get into Rheims but I fear it is doubtful."

Next morning, just beyond Soissons, we found the *état major* at Belleau so successfully camouflaged that we passed it several times. We looked at the masks vaguely as they were handed to us by a lieutenant. They were neatly done up in a case with straps for slinging them across one's shoulder. "If you expect to enter Rheims, I must show you how to adjust them—it's a bad place for gas attacks," the lieutenant said. Joe was used for demonstration purposes, but when our lieutenant came to Mildred and me, he had his eye on our hats. "Now I am helpless to advise, but you must be able to get into a mask promptly," he warned.

As we made our way toward Rheims, anti-aircraft guns in position and many camouflaged camions made the presence of the enemy seem imminent. On the wall of a lovely little church, we read in large letters the words: "*Attention au Gaz, préparez vos masques.*"

A farmer plowing in a field, at which we stopped to eat a simple lunch, got into conversation with us. He criticized the minister of agriculture, who was urging the necessity for larger crops. "How can a farmer take in his crops when his barn is filled with soldiers quartered on him?" he asked. "Not that I have anything against the soldiers, '*au contraire,*' but crops and soldiers cannot be housed in a small barn to the advantage of either—I have fifteen." He concluded his harangue by saying that, in spite of the mistakes of the government, which was not '*très raisonnable,*' "We must continue the war '*jusqu'au bout.*'"

I was still thinking of his words when the scene changed completely. An air fight was going on high above us. There were two *boche* planes and several French ones, flying faster and lower, giving chase. These white birds, with outspread wings catching the sunlight, followed by silver puffs, afforded at once a wonderful and a terrifying sight. I counted eleven exploding shells before the *boche* planes escaped over their own lines.

At the foot of the hill, a group of *poilus* started towards us making frantic signals for us to stop. As the motor came to a standstill, we heard a shell explode, and flames leapt up from the roof of a house. This was at a crossroad, and its importance was borne in upon us as we saw disappear a little bridge on which we would have been at that instant if the *poilus* had not attracted our attention.

We got out and Picken put the motor behind shelter. We were joined by the group of *poilus* whose timely warning had saved our lives. The enemy, they told us, was attempting to interrupt ammunition supplies and had the range of the road. The tremendous whirr of a shell passing through the air was unlike any other sound. Then came flame and explosion simultaneously, followed by clouds of smoke. This was a very ugly corner, the *poilus* said, but the enemy did not often keep up bombardment for more than an hour consecutively.

The commandant told us that the enemy was bombarding heavily in the direction of Rheims. "Use your discretion," he urged.

We started off at a breakneck speed, passing from time to time camouflaged hospitals. From Fismes on, twenty-six kilometers to Rheims—a straight road ahead and at a mad pace we went! Military were in abundance and the camouflage was more pronounced. I read on a milestone, "Rheims four kilometers." I could see the cathedral as we were hauled up by a sentry whom we almost missed because of the dust. *"On bombarde maintenant,"* he said. He looked at the pass again, obviously impressed by "Generals to facilitate passage." Then we passed on.

At the entrance, a sentry on the canal called out, *"Le laisser passer."* He inspected it with grave attention and in silence. As he spoke, I saw the flames and heard a shell exploding a little to the right of us. "There is probably time to enter the town before the direction of the shells changes," he said, unmoved.

Not daunted by the "probably," we entered Rheims. Nothing in our expectation could come up to the reality! We got out of the car and walked to the square in front of the cathedral. I stood motionless, my eyes riveted upon the once marvelous façade and towers, the stones of which were now scorched beyond repair. The only thing untouched in the midst of desolation was the equestrian statue of Jeanne d'Arc. In her hand was a remnant of a French flag.

The whirr of the shells was alarmingly close as we noticed a *boche* plane directing the firing of German artillery against the French positions beyond the town. We managed to find the broken gate of a badly damaged court, where a servant led us across and up a flight of steps into a small, dreary reception room. The glass was gone from the windows and the building shook from the force of the bombardment. My eyes were on a small altar in an alcove, when from a door behind it Archbishop Luçon approached us. I looked with instant admiration at this priest who was serving his fellowman so gallantly.

As we sat with him, he talked as unconcernedly as though deafening shells were not making conversation all but impossible. He told us that only a few of the inhabitants remained, the number daily becoming fewer, because of deaths from odorless gas and artillery

299

shells. "Some families refuse to go while I am here," he said simply.

Mildred Bliss handed the Archbishop some letters written by Jacacci to the mothers of children who were being cared for by us. While we were talking, the two mothers concerned came in and stood silently watching us as they listened to what Mildred recited concerning the welfare of their children and the progress they were making with their studies. Finally a wan smile changed the hitherto expressionless faces.

Arrangements had been made with the Archbishop for two girls and an older boy (who was delicate) to come to one of our children's colonies. We talked with them and their mothers. But suddenly the Archbishop interrupted himself to say firmly that the direction of the bombardment had changed and we must leave at once. He escorted us to the gate in the outer court. As we exchanged good-bys, he said in a ringing voice, "Remember, the spirit of beauty always has been in the world and always will be, and the comfort of religion."

32

PERSHING THE MAN

JOE AND I could not know that, when we sailed for France in late September, 1917, the care of French children uppermost in our minds, we were to acquire another type of responsibility that was entirely new to us. It centered in troop morale, but it had ramifications even in the corps of commanding generals of our army, as will be seen shortly.

General John J. Pershing, who had arrived with his troops only a few months before we entered the American war zone, called this thing "getting behind the soldier's salute." My part in it was purely fortuitous. I just happened to be the first woman whom he encountered after being among our soldiers at the fighting front. I was then, and always have been, a person interested in people and how they were getting on. I literally fell into the role of talking with soldiers. I didn't know what "morale" meant, but I was to find out.

It was perhaps an irony that I, a woman, had already seen at first hand a vast amount of the war which young men from the East, the South, the Middle and Far West had come to France to fight. They had only the vaguest idea of what actual combat was like—after all, there was no immediate reportage by radio or television, and there was no commentary of the kind available today. My knowledge of what lay ahead of them made of me a prime informant for these young men who were later to wade into the thick of things at Cantigny, Belleau Wood, Chateau-Thierry, and in the Argonne.

In the early evening of November 1, 1917, I had my first glimpse of American soldiers on duty in France. It was obviously an historic occasion. Edward Carter, the head of the Y.M.C.A. in France, had wanted to bring us face to face with our own forces before we returned to the United States to lecture for French relief and for our own war effort. This first meeting with American troops was to lead to a significant association with General Pershing, whom we were shortly to see.

We had entered a town in the area just behind the fighting front, only a short distance from Mailly, a center where we were to stay overnight. As we slowed to a stop, our motor lights picked out four strapping lads in khaki, standing around a fountain in the middle of the square, with provost marshal bands on their arms. They were pathetically glad to see us, especially me.

For the next ten days in the fighting zone, which extended as far as Gondrecourt, I was in friendly contact with several thousands of these lonely Americans, many of them rather dazed. As more than one of them put it, "I don't know where I am or how I got here." They were gathered in groups around stoves in "Y" huts, glad to be out of the mud, or in their camps, and even more anxious to talk to a "lady from home," as they all called me, than to listen to her talk. I had found a characteristic informality in their manners and speech, but also a morale in embryo, thanks to General Pershing's constant admonition: "Let us work hard and be inconspicuous, since we are not yet ready to be useful in fighting." But I found morale problems too, but more of them later.

On our return trip to Paris, we stopped at Chaumont, the headquarters of the American Expeditionary Force, where these young men of a sudden ceased to be individuals and had merged into the American Army. The Stars and Stripes floated triumphantly over a gate in the center of a large square with imposing buildings. Officers were coming and going and army trucks passed in a steady stream. We walked down a long corridor, to find the office of Major Robert Bacon, an aide to the commander-in-chief, whose guests we were to be. Over all doors were signs indicating the technical type of work going on inside the rooms. With a sense of pride, I viewed the American headquarters, which was every bit as businesslike as those of the French and the British with which I was familiar.

Major Bacon took us to an imposing villa in a side street near the cathedral. He left us in old-fashioned attractive rooms, after reminding us we would be called for to dine punctually at seven with General Pershing, at the chateau where he lived with his immediate staff. We said good-by to our Y.M.C.A. escort and sat in the salon before an open fire, comfortably relaxed, awaiting the arrival of Mildred Bliss and Ernest Schelling, with whom we were to go to Verdun on our way back to Paris.

At 6:45 there was no Mildred, the car had not come for us, and the villa was without a telephone. In this dilemma we accepted the offer of a young French girl to show us the way to the chateau. It was pouring rain and with neither umbrella nor overshoes, we started off on foot to have our guide promptly get lost in the blackness of the streets. When by chance we were again in the vicinity of the villa she left us. American soldiers to whom we appealed for directions deliberately misled us, and we wandered about aimlessly. As a number of clocks struck eight, we had just returned from a street that ended on a muddy country road. At the moment we were before a gate we had passed many times, now it stood open and at the end of a courtyard there was an American flag over the entrance to a large chateau.

"General Pershing is expecting us for dinner," Joe stated to a sentry who, without presenting arms, merely stared at us, making no attempt to restrain his laughter. Joe flushed angrily. I intervened and with all the dignity I could muster said firmly, "Summon an orderly at once." Greatly to my relief he rang a bell, and an orderly came out of a door from across the court. Joe mentioned our names and he said with a broad grin, "If you are as hungry and as mad as the General, don't waste time talking, go inside." In the hall, General James G. Harbord, the chief of staff, whom I knew by sight, stepped forward and said bluntly, "You are an hour late."

"We certainly are—due to inexcusably poor management at headquarters," I replied with equal bluntness. Without further exchange of words, we followed him into a brilliantly lighted room with heavy red draperies, small gilt chairs with spindly legs, a gilt piano, and other elaborate furnishings. It was a fantastic setting for the soldierly man standing in the midst of restless officers who were casting uneasy glances at his frowning face. Our entrance broke into a complete silence. The General's keen eyes swept over our bedraggled appearances as he welcomed us with a charming simplicity of manner. "What happened?" he asked.

Joe explained that the car promised by Major Bacon failed to arrive, so we had walked. "General," he said, "you are well camouflaged, none of your soldiers would tell us where you lived."

"Splendid! Splendid!" the General repeated and addressing his staff observed, "They are learning to obey orders." Then turning towards me, he was sympathetic about my suit being soaked.

I said cheerfully that the cloth would soon dry, and we had finally found him, which was all that mattered to me, and I was hungry. General Harbord appeared relieved at my restored good humor, and General Pershing's smile, in remarking about my sporty behaviour, won me completely. As we moved together into the dining room, I thought him the perfect type for a commander-in-chief. He had a strong face, with a good mouth and a well-formed chin, stern eyes, and a manner suggesting a determination to attend to business and not waste time.

Joe and I were placed on either side of him, and there were eight officers at the table. As we were finishing soup, Major Bacon slipped into the vacant seat next to Joe and, to judge from Pershing's expression, he was about to say something in reprimand to his subordinate. "Please don't," I murmured. He hesitated the fraction of a second, then nodded acquiescence. I caught appreciation in Bacon's eye at this byplay, and surprise in Harbord's face that the General would yield to my plea. The General had been well briefed about Joe, as was evidenced when he referred to a Red Cross trip to Italy which Joe had made with Cornelius Bliss to have a look at the Italian army. He showed great interest when Joe informed him that they had left Gorizia only eighteen hours before the Germans broke through. When cross-examined about what he had noticed, Joe emphasized the amount of wood construction for comfort going on in the trenches and for the command.

The General remarked to Harbord that this was further proof that the attack on Gorizia had been a surprise. When he complimented Joe on his discerning eye as an artist, I was prompted to say Joe spoke Italian and talked with the men and young officers while Bliss was busy. Whereupon, being asked his opinion of the Italians' attitude towards the war, Joe spoke as his firm conviction, for what it was worth, he said modestly, that, in spite of Caporetto and Gorizia, the Italians would pull themselves together and do some effective fighting. This, regrettably, was a forecast never quite to be realized.

The Italian campaign turned the General's thoughts to the British, and he grew enthusiastic about their magnificent force, which he had just inspected at Cambrai. "An example to emulate," he called it. I responded to this theme by saying that, in a small way, Joe and I, with Mildred Bliss, had seen the mighty machinery of war in motion. To his amazed "Where?" I explained that for Joe's and my lectures in America, other people's experiences would not have gotten across to audiences. One needed to wedge in between accounts of the ruthlessness of the enemy towards civilians, and the courage of the latter in facing it, a few descriptions of the actual fighting.

A year ago, I told him, we had been on camouflaged military roads where bombing was frequent, when the French were moving a division through Toul, and we had continued on to Belfort. We had also gone through the British lines to reach the little strip of Belgium still in the possession of the Belgians. This past September we were in Rheims under a bombardment, and in Coucy le Chateau.

"All civilians were evacuated from Coucy two years ago," the General interjected.

"That's why we wanted to go there," I told him, and to his rather perplexed inquiry about our papers, I said casually, "A special pass issued at the request of the minister of war, and across it the words, 'generals to facilitate passage.' We were cautioned to use 'discretion' in travel on military roads."

Additional comments on our credentials were interrupted by the unexpected arrival of a colonel who was a Texan. During the ensuing conversation with him, the General, with a keen sense of humor, referred to meeting Dr. Anna Howard Shaw in Texas. He had been much impressed, he said, by a speech she made before two hundred women when he was one of only six men in the audience. It was at a time when woman suffrage was very unpopular in Texas, but she had persuaded him to give subsequently a short talk favoring it, and the audience had almost torn him limb from limb. He admitted with a contagious laugh that Dr. Shaw could have converted him to anything, because she knew all about the workings of a three-inch gun.

When the General gave me his attention again, I said I was reminded of a Massachusetts regiment I had recently been with, after it had reached the war zone from the Texas border. I mentioned the locality, and General Harbord, who was at my left, remarked to Pershing that "poor spirit" had been reported among them. This I denied indignantly and said I could prove it. With my eye on General Pershing I hurried on with my story. A hurricane was blowing at the time I was with this regiment, and fortunately a rain squall drove the men inside the "Y" hut in crowds, where I was alone, at my request to the secretary.

They were the finest type of New Englanders, I declared, but obviously something was bothering them. For about an hour I had moved about munching a sandwich and trying, in vain, to engage in conversation with the small groups I joined. Refusing to accept de-

305

feat, I changed my tactics, and mounting a small platform, I faced row on row of depressed, but not sullen, faces. "Too much mud and no tobacco, eh?" I said as a feeler, after a few preliminary remarks.

"No complaints on that score," they came back at me in a chorus.

I tried again. "Am I to think you don't want to fight?"

That did it! At once many voices shouted, "No soldiers ever wanted to get to France more than we did." And then the trouble exploded like a bomb. It seemed "some fellows," who turned up several weeks back, told them they had heard as a fact that these Massachusetts troops were sent over to France by mistake, and that they would be back on the Texas border before January.

"No fighting; isn't that enough to jar us, lady?" they exclaimed.

General Pershing and his dinner guests had heard me out.

"Trust a woman to get the truth," General Harbord put in drily.

I was waiting for Pershing's reactions. "I made these men a promise that they would receive official reassurance," I said earnestly, meeting his gaze squarely.

"They will, of course," he replied, adding that the episode was most illuminating as an example of failure to deal with enemy propaganda. He asked how many men I had been able to talk to in the same way. About two thousand, I told him, and that, at my suggestion, I had visited other "Y" huts where the men drifting in were supposed to be "difficult" or "uncommunicative."

"Have you other specific instances as revealing as that of the Massachusetts regiments?" was his next question. I assured him I had, and that I felt they should be remedied at the top level, "Meaning yourself," I asserted boldly.

To this he replied that, after dinner, General Harbord would go into his den with him and me for a further discussion of this topic. Meanwhile he wished my ideas on other phases of vital importance in the preparation of our soldiers for fighting. He assured me that although my experience was limited, it had the advantage to him of being an eyewitness account by the first woman he had seen after she herself had been among the troops in the forward area.

As a preamble, I told him that our procedure on the trip had worked. Joe and our escort dined with the local Y.M.C.A. staff and made the important speeches. I merely took a sandwich with me to the hut to which I was assigned, which gave me about two and one-half hours there. But in going to camps, we stayed together and allowed sufficient time to look around and visit with the men before sharing their mess.

General Pershing stated that, as he went through village after village and the men stood at attention, he longed to know what thoughts went on behind the salutes. But before he gave me a chance to tell him, at his request, what the men had talked about, he fired inquiries at me about conditions affecting their comfort, insisting that I be frank and omit none of the bad spots. Had the rolling kitchens arrived? Was the food well cooked and served hot? Were the billets as bad as reported in parts of the Gondrecourt district? How about the bunks in the barracks?

Thanks to a photographic memory for what interests me, I was able to answer each question categorically and concisely, always naming the place and unit. Our conversation did not carry beyond the ears of General Harbord when I mentioned the anxiety of mess cooks over shortage of food supplies. "Inadequate planning," Pershing declared. The prevalence of trench foot was a "hindrance to getting an army into fighting condition."

I warned him that a frank account of some conditions I saw in the Gondrecourt district would not be reassuring, in contrast to the majority of other areas where rolling kitchens, a good mess, and excellent barracks with warm bedding were the rule and not the exception. I said that rumors of a great deal of sickness had caused me to inspect three out of the five army hospitals. All were overcrowded and lacking in essentials, yet the army staff, I understood, constantly refused to let the Red Cross make up the deficiencies in supplies. I referred to oil for trench feet as an example, but pointed out that instruction in the care of the feet was even more needed than oil, and this was a responsibility, as I understood it, of the noncommissioned officers. I also informed him I had a list of supplies that were lacking, and that my statement could be verified.

The General said, with a grim set to his jaw, that he did not intend to wait for army red tape to "burn up from spontaneous combustion."

307

He listened attentively as I gave a picture of some billets in tumble-down houses with leaky roofs and broken floors, or over sheds containing pigs and other livestock. There were also instances when we had joined men at mess in damp shacks, insufficiently lighted, to be served poor food. Although none of them had complained, I voiced my severe criticism of a situation bad for the morale of the men affected, when contrasted with that of other Americans quartered nearby in Adrian barracks furnished by the French.

I countered the General's objections to requesting more barracks, when the French were very short of lumber for their own armies, by pointing out that it was only a fair exchange for the large sums contributed by Americans towards the support of the *foyer des soldats* for the French troops. "Why did not someone tell me that fact?" he asked, looking down the table. He added cheerfully that he would at once request additional barracks for Gondrecourt.

It became quite clear that no one was telling Pershing some of the things he needed to know, and that no one, equally, was telling plain soldiers many of the things they needed to know. My growing determination to help inform both was later to cause quite a stir at headquarters.

In another of his rapid transitions, he forced me to acknowledge reluctantly that I had seen a number of our men careless in keeping their uniforms and equipment in order, and many were unshaven, although every soldier's kit included a razor. If an opportunity offered, I had suggested tactfully to the kind of troopers he mentioned, that they should look all the time as though waiting for their best girls. A good way of putting it, the General interpolated. Then he said that too much depended on him personally in an insistence on neat uniform and well polished equipment, such as the British Army maintained, as essential in the training of Americans to fight. He had raised his voice and there was silence as he continued, "I am called a disciplinarian and I have to be."

In an attempt to turn his attention from the subject of negligence in the appearance of some of his soldiers, I told laughingly of a *poilu* who had confirmed the General's opinion of the smartness of a Tommy's uniform. It was when we had crossed the French lines on coming back from the British front. The *poilu* was seated by the roadside busily engaged in sewing a button on to his tunic. He explained his industry by telling me that "Monsieur" Tommy was always well dressed, and as he was about to go on duty with him and must be a credit to his own country, he was tidying up.

The General laughed so heartily that I ventured to report an anecdote about one of our boys whom I saw in his barracks snipping pieces of cloth from the bottom of his overcoat with small scissors. Seeing my bewildered gaze, the youngster said he had given up fighting the mud and was cutting it away. "I'll soon have only a peajacket, but it will be clean," he announced with pride.

"That's the best yet," the General declared with an engaging smile.

In the same vein he told of going to a guardhouse on an inspection tour, where he was much taken by a boy with an innocent face. "What are you in for?" the General asked.

"They accused me of stealing socks," the boy replied.

The General told me that, as the boy's eyes met his frankly, he was positive the accusation was false, and was only waiting for a denial before following up the case personally.

"Well, did you?" he asked.

"Yes, sir," the boy acknowledged.

Several times when Pershing became thoroughly engrossed with Joe, General Harbord's conversation with me disclosed the close bond between him and his Commander-in-Chief. "He's so human and simple," he said. With all his vast responsibilities, Pershing never lost sight of the fact that the machinery of war and the endless planning and desk work to build it up were only as effective, ultimately, as the men behind the guns. He was never "mentally bogged down," according to Harbord, who was kind enough to add that the General was obtaining from me pertinent information on situations that caused him constant anxiety. "Keep it up," he urged, before I was to be further interrogated.

I described a happy idea that came to me in the first hut, when some of the boys, on discovering that I would soon sail for home, begged me to communicate with their mothers on my arrival, to say

309

they were "doing fine and not to worry." I was handed odd little scraps of paper with names and addresses and often messages. I appealed to the secretary of the "Y" hut, who produced a good-sized notebook. Before the evening was over, there were well over a hundred names in it. I realized I must invent some way of recalling the boys by identifying the places I had seen them, without infringing on military regulations, I hastened to add, as I caught Harbord's watchful eye. This I did by a code invented by Joe and kept in a small book. Joe jotted the code down on a card, and Harbord, after a brief look at it, said it would pass.

General Pershing took fire at once at the task I had gotten myself into by promising to write to about nine hundred mothers from names contained in six books. "The best kind of propaganda," he termed it, and to my utter astonishment insisted he wished to receive sample replies from me. In order to have them reach him personally, he wrote down and handed to me the system of mailing letters used by his family.

Dessert was being served when Pershing brought up the subject of the German raid on the first Americans to face trench warfare. This was in the vicinity of Gondrecourt. Had I seen any of the company involved? he asked in a low tone, obviously much perturbed. About fifty at different places, I told him. To his question, what did I say to them, I repeated "Say to them? I just listened to an outpouring of deep humiliation." I gave him the tragic recital as it came to me. A number of the company showed me the newspaper account just arrived. It read, "Pershing issues first casualty list. Germans raid an American trench; kill eight, capture twelve."

The conversations were never consecutive and the men all talked at once, I said, but the substance was the same. "My, we're green," was a constant refrain through the narrative, coupled with gratitude that the facts had not been published. I was told that the Germans had come over about two in the morning, in a surprise attack, and that everyone was bewildered. The Germans knew exactly where the Americans were in trenches *alone*, and had to work fast, so as not to attract attention from the French in nearby trenches, where many Americans were billeted. No gun had been fired by a man in the company. They had cowardly allowed the enemy to kill a few and walk off with a dozen captured men, and not one of them had squawked an alarm. The agony of soul in their disillusionment about themselves was evidenced in white, drawn faces and haunted eyes. Talking freely with me seemed to have helped a little, and in saying good-by, they insisted that they would live down the disgrace and make good.

The General sighed. "That's the right spirit, but the men have so much to learn." Most of them carried cameras, he said, and had expected to photograph the Kaiser in captivity within a few months of landing.

My thoughts were still on the raid, and I said impulsively, "I suffered for each man in that company, and I know you did."

The General nodded. "Neither of us will ever forget this talk on that first German raid."

His gloom was noticeable and as a change in atmosphere I suggested that he ask Joe to tell a story our boys had enjoyed. Joe never had greater success with his famous "Yellow Dog," told in imitation Chinese, and the General made him repeat it. After dinner, Joe remained with the staff, and Pershing, Harbord, and I settled ourselves in comfortable leather armchairs in a businesslike den. General Harbord's reference to our boys getting on well with the French led to my recounting an incident in a *foyer des soldats*. I was chatting with an old *poilu* who told me of a German prisoner who had said to him that he had heard on reliable grounds that no Americans would ever come to France to fight, but that the British had put some of their men in uniforms to look like Americans. The *poilu*'s priceless comment on this was that "Even a German should know that no one on God's earth looked like an American."

It did me good to see Pershing's tension relax and hear him laugh. I also mentioned talks with *poilus* who had Americans brigaded with them in the trenches. They were enthusiastic about the *bon esprit* of Americans but said they were "too quick" and would never learn to keep their heads down in trenches. General Harbord concurred. "Our soldiers will always be restless in the stalemate of trench warfare," he said emphatically. I remarked upon the French troops seeming far more tired than in the previous year. Also, civilians in villages in the vicinity of Noyon, recently evacuated, after two years of occupation by the Germans, seemed nearer the breaking point. In moving about among troops in the war zone one heard much talk about depending on the American effort to counteract the harm done to Allied morale by General Nivelle's costly failure at Chemin des Dames.

The General said that even the appearance of the young, sturdy-looking American troops had such a heartening effect on French civilians that he sent regiments, on their arrival, through the villages. I told him I found this true of the *poilus*, who spoke confidently of the Americans' driving the Germans from the soil of France.

It was getting late, and since General Pershing and his staff had gained enough morale detail from an outspoken woman to last them for quite a time, Joe and I took our leave. In the weeks and months to come, however, I was to learn first hand that General Pershing was insistent upon the creation of the machinery and methods necessary to produce the small but vital changes I had discussed with him. Not since the Civil War had the United States been faced with a major responsibility for the building and maintenance of morale in thousands of troops—and never before in history had so many thousands been so far from home.

I can't quite recall the time, but it must not have been long after our first dinner meeting with General Pershing and his staff, when Joe and I were in Paris. Pershing called me on the phone and asked me to come in the early afternoon to his office in the city. He had come frequently to do this, and I was consequently little prepared for what I walked into when I arrived for the appointment.

Pershing was seated alone with Field Marshal Sir Douglas Haig. There were no aides to either commanding officer. After introducing me to Haig, he asked me to tell the British commander-in-chief why American troops could not be used in the war solely as reserves, an eventuality which could hardly be avoided if the United States did not achieve an independent front of its own.

Peculiarly, it was the British insistence, more, I think, from London than from military leadership there or overseas, which had placed the United States in this position almost from the outset. The French, on the other hand, genuinely favored an independent front for our troops and a consequent freeing of them from merely reserve status.

When I was apprised of the debate between the two military leaders, I knew why I had been called. Pershing realized that I was thoroughly in touch with American public opinion, from constant lecturing to audiences from coast to coast about the war. There was hardly anyone in civilian status—certainly no other woman except Mildred Bliss—who could speak with as much conviction and information as I could at that distance from American shores.

"The American public will never stand for such a role for our troops," I told Haig.

We did not discuss the subject for more than half an hour. But I think it is significant that the United States shortly achieved the position which Pershing and Newton D. Baker, the secretary of War, insisted it should have.

33

THE ROUGH ROAD TO PEACE

JOE REMAINED in France on an assignment "for the duration," or until our troops were to come home. The assignment was to organize a soldiers' development program under the auspices of the Y.M.C.A., but as a free lance, paying his own expenses, and with the co-operation of the army. This was at the instigation of Mrs. August Belmont, when she was in France on a Red Cross mission, and had General Pershing's personal endorsement.

My usefulness for the moment was at home, encouraging our workers at the garment centers, under the tireless leadership of Mrs.

Charles P. Howland of New York, and being constantly on the move, during the disheartening period of the Germans' steady advance beginning in March, 1918, lecturing not only in behalf of the Children of the Frontier, but in campaigns for the sale of war bonds and saving stamps, and in behalf of the Red Cross.

A significant incident occurred after a Red Cross meeting in Chicago in which I participated with an English officer, the main speaker, who had lost his leg at the front. He had been scheduled to talk also at a gathering of manufacturers and laborers.

But the chairman, on receiving advance information that strikers planned to break up the meeting, and fearing for the Englishman's safety, substituted me, since I was a woman. As the chairman stepped on the platform of a large hall, his voice could not be heard above the loud boos of a rabble. I, who was beside him, hurled back chairs thrown from the audience. I got well to the front and shouted, "You're crazy, and if you'll listen I'll tell you why!"

Then, in a sudden lull, I informed the strikers that it was not industrialists they were injuring but their own relatives, whom I had seen fighting gallantly in France, getting a dollar a day and offering no complaints.

"And your withholding supplies needed for their welfare by striking is absolutely crazy, in my opinion."

They listened to what I had to say about American troops. The attention became the kind a speaker prays for. The meeting achieved its purpose. After that I was called upon a number of times to lecture to strikers. Perhaps I had learned how!

An amusing episode in New York took place when I was walking up Fifth Avenue on St. Patrick's Day. The parade had temporarily halted opposite St. Patrick's Cathedral, when I saw and was infuriated by a banner on which was inscribed "Down with England."

I rushed into the street and, facing the bearer, cried out indignantly that I had seen the right kind of Irish in France, fighting beside the British and not against them. Whereupon a burly policeman warned me to stop my jawing. He was about to lay hands on me as a disturber of the peace when the temperamental Irish crowd, being for anyone in trouble with the law, applauded me lustily.

The parade proceeded according to plan, the offending banner now furled, and I a full-fledged participant, by invitation. Battles are rarely won by flight.

In late March, General Ferdinand Foch had been appointed Commander-in-Chief of the armies of the Allies. Disasters had reached their height with the fall of Coucy le Chateau. I received the news early one morning when I was in Cleveland for a number of speaking engagements arranged by my host, Samuel Mather.

I had been impressed by one of the garrison of Richard Coeur de Lion's fortress saying that, if Coucy was lost, the enemy forces would sweep over the valley of the Aisne for a distance of almost one hundred kilometers and reach the Marne, for the second time threatening Paris.

The Evening Transcript of Boston had been consistently generous in the space allotted to my war news. And my favorite reporter eagerly absorbed over the telephone the story I gave him on what was about to happen to the Allies.

Unfortunately, the head of the news room refused to permit quotation of what he termed surmise. Therefore the *Transcript* lost the opportunity for a scoop a dozen hours ahead of the headline news in every morning paper the next day.

By July 15, the emergency justifying the dispersal of American divisions had ended. With the counter-offensives by the Allies against the Marne salient late in July, and the Amiens salient in August, the situation was reversed.

In the early stages of the American fighting, the British had supplemented our supplies of arms and ammunition. We had been using British guns and British and French planes for a long time. It was not until August that the advance of an independent American army could be started. And now for the first time long-delayed American planes replaced British and French aircraft supporting our troops.

Starting with the reduction of the St.-Mihiel salient, the Meuse-Argonne offensive developed, and more and more German divisions were withdrawn from other fronts when the Americans broke the Hindenburg Line and threatened German communications with Germany itself.

In late October, in the third and final phase of the battle of the Argonne, which was the determining factor which caused the Germans to seek an armistice, I was on my way to France. We were to be at the Hotel Crillon, which was Jacacci's permanent home. Joe, on his brief visits to Paris, lived in a bedroom adjoining Jacacci's apartment.

The day after my arrival, as the clocks struck eleven on November 11, 1918, the roar of cannon in the Place de la Concorde, Paris, announced that the Germans had accepted the terms of the great Armistice. With a single impulse, the French, pushing aside other nationalities, surged forward until they surrounded the Strassbourg statue, and tore away black crepe which had enveloped it since 1871. Meanwhile the *Marseillaise*, sung by thousands of French voices, contested the reverberating echoes of thundering cannon.

After this historic moment, young America took over the celebration, shouting lustily. It was not a boastful noise for America's part in ending the long struggle, but sympathy for the French expressed in the American way.

Joe and I ran into General Pershing, who was no more in the mood for that kind of celebration than we were. The three of us had a quiet two hours in his apartments. With shining eyes and an eager rush of words, he burst out, "A year ago it was hope and faith, today it is realization!"

I mentioned a report, current among enlisted men, that he had been seen in the midst of artillery during the fighting in the Argonne.

"That's right," he said simply. In a voice of intense feeling, he went on to say, "I could not remain in the rear, the suffering was too great." It had been impossible for the supply transport to remain in contact with men plunging forward at a terrific pace without a pause. "The men were willing to pay the price," he reiterated proudly several times.

Then, in an abrupt change of mood, he said, "I fear that the Armistice is the day of illusion. How can it be otherwise with Americans shouting the refrain, 'The job's finished, home before Christmas.'"

With characteristic generosity he recalled with approval that Joe and his assistant, Tom Stevens, had given performances of a play, *Joan of Arc,* in the vicinity of Domremy, her birthplace, just behind the St.-Mihiel salient, while the fighting was in progress. It was a happy choice as a morale booster, he said.

He also said that Joe must accompany our army of occupation to the American bridgehead at Coblenz, and that distraction would be needed for months to come at recreation centers in the south of France, since the embarkation of the troops for home must inevitably be a slow process.

I had a French view of the situation that evening at the Crillon. I happened to be in the lift with Georges Clemenceau when it stuck between floors for some time. A French admiral who was with him remarked, "Je crains que la paix sera plus compliquée que la guerre."

For the next few weeks work was at a standstill. After Clemenceau had proclaimed in the Chamber of Deputies, "La France salue Alsace-Lorraine," Paris was in a state of suspended animation pending the opening of the Peace Conference and the arrival of President Wilson.

The Crillon had been taken over for the sessions of the Peace Conference and accommodations of the delegates. But Willard Straight, who was dangerously ill with flu, remained there and died. I had come down with the flu the day after the Armistice. Instead of being sent to the hospital, Jacacci and the Smiths were permitted to retain temporary possession of their rooms, a courtesy that continued for several months.

It was on the morning of December 14, 1918, that the President, seated alone, made his triumphal tour down the Champs Elysées.

Bishop Charles H. Brent in khaki was beside me in a window fronting the avenue. With the same realism he had shown in his long years of service in the Philippines, he was greatly perturbed by the general acclaim of the President as a saviour by the representatives of the Allied nations and the people of Paris. "This moment can't last," he said sadly.

Mrs. Jack Bonney, who had done splendid work for the committee from Columbus, Ohio, as headquarters, joined me in Paris several weeks after the Armistice. The plan was for us to go together

317

as far as Arras in the committee limousine driven by the faithful Dominick, the committee's chauffeur.

But the itinerary was rearranged because of a letter from Cardinal Mercier of Belgium to Jacacci. "Now that the Armistice has come," he wrote, "we must be responsible for looking after our children on the soil of Belgium at the earliest practicable moment." He requested that an emissary of our committee be sent to arrange with Belgian committees for the return of two hundred Belgian children, forced to flee from the convent of Ypres with the sisters at the time of the German attack, who had been under our care ever since.

Mr. Poland, of the Hoover Commission, covering northern France, warned Mrs. Bonney and me that we would be in the region where semi-starvation was still acute. The transport problem for the French Food Ministry had yet to be solved.

He further explained that an armistice on the old Hindenburg Line would have made it simple to reach the suffering civilians, but the Allied advance in the early fall of 1918 had perforce wrecked roads and isolated a number of towns and villages. Canals were damaged, with barges lacking and thousands of camions deliberately rendered useless for civilian needs by the Germans in retreat, who had also wrecked electric plants.

I was also informed that ours would be among the few non-military cars traveling north at this time, and we would be the first civilians not classed as officials to enter Belgium since the Armistice. André Tardieu of the French Commission issued our papers, and as on previous war-zone trips, the French and other military were to furnish us *essence* (gas). At Jacacci's suggestion, we took tins of sardines and bread for food, which proved adequate diet.

Cambrai, our first objective, was known to be in a desperate plight. This situation had resulted from Britain's failure to capture the town by a surprise tank attack in 1916. The constant Allied shelling had made it necessary for the inhabitants to flee eastward into that part of Belgium held by the Germans, but after the Armistice nothing could prevent them from flocking back daily to a region with no facilities for their care. Among them were families whose children had been in our care since the early part of the war.

The mayor received Marie Bonney and me in his office. There was something terrible in his steady repetition of the words, "Six thousand children under ten, and more arriving daily—no milk, not much food, and warehouses empty of children's garments." He ended by saying, "I can't face posting the news that bread rations have to be cut further."

I managed to get through on the telephone to the British Army transport at Mons. I briefly rehearsed the situation and he promised to have four lorries start at once for 77 rue d'Amsterdam, Paris.

I also reached Jacacci, who, as always, was lightning-quick in grasping a problem and equally prompt in action. He assured me on the telephone that a number of organizations would have supplies ready, including layettes for expected babies.

At this juncture, a curé and a doctor joined us, both well poised and friendly. They gave a quick look of relief at the mayor's cheerful expression, and during a quiet talk I accounted for the change by mentioning the recent telephone conversations.

I intended to exert every possible pressure through these important channels open to me to see that the camions, promised in the name of Foch himself for the relief of Cambrai, be immediately released from the army for that purpose. Before our departure, I gave the mayor a written request from Mr. Jacacci to keep him informed of the return to Cambrai of the families whose children were with us, leaving for his files the card index of the families concerned.

Progress to Valenciennes was slow as we were in the midst of old and young, with push carts, or bundles on their backs, and a stream of cows, goats, and other livestock following in their wake. In one high-wheeled cart, with men holding up a feeble horse between the shafts, sat an old woman with a crying baby in her arms. I caught a glimpse of a pile of grain, a sewing machine, feather beds, chickens, and a basket of eggs, all mixed together.

During an overnight stay at Valenciennes we inspected the emergency hospital being used for French civilians, as well as British and American soldiers coming back from the army of occupation of Germany in alarming numbers, ill with the flu. In a region of stark tragedy, it was heartening to see Tommies sharing their rations with

French children and old people, and to find British efficiency in handling the relief depot at such a high level.

We entered Brussels before dark, where much to my surprise, although motors were conspicuously absent, the streets were brilliantly lighted and shops displayed luxuries, including jewelry.

Brand Whitlock, the American ambassador, was at the hotel to greet us, and we spent the evening with him and the Vernon Kelloggs, who had been next in command to Herbert Hoover in Belgian relief. Whitlock summed up the present attitude by saying that the habit of enforced leisure acquired by the Belgians during the German occupation was now enemy number one.

Baron de Broqueville, who was in residence in Brussels, reintroduced us to members of Parliament. He urged us not to judge Belgian aristocrats by the affluent appearance of Brussels, and told us that many of them were doing a magnificent work in rehabilitation. But the people of Brussels insisted on gaiety and the first ball had been held the evening before. Moral deterioration, politically and socially, as a result of the lying and cunning developed to outwit the Germans, was difficult to contend with, he said. But he also referred to hopeful signs in the improved morale of the people and willingness to work since the return of Burgomaster Max, whom we met and talked with. Hollows under bloodshot eyes and an unnatural pallor were evidences of what he had gone through during four years in German dungeons, where he had suffered untold humiliations and even torture.

I delivered to Countess Van den Steen, one of the queen's ladies-in-waiting whom we had met at La Panne, a duplicate of the case histories of the children from the convent of Ypres who were with us, and arrangements were made between us for their return to Belgian soil. Also with her we met other Belgian aristocrats in charge of the rehabilitation committees. This accomplished the purpose of our coming to Brussels at the request of Cardinal Mercier, whom we motored to see at Malines.

On our arrival, we went directly to the Cardinal's palace. I appreciated instantly why he had succeeded in raising his people from the depths of despair through their long years of degrading captivity.

He spoke with earnest sympathy about the pride of Belgian aristocrats who had always kept a respectable looking garment for the
street. "Often when a Belgian lady came to see me," he said, "I did
not know whether it was to bring me a subscription for relief work
or to tell me she could no longer face existing conditions without
assistance." He confessed that his own body had often protested
when it had insufficient nourishment, but at such times he kept his
mind active by walking about saying prayers.

He commended the Bryce Report as accurate but considered that
he (Mercier) should have told the Hoover Commission less than
the truth, when interrogated by its members at the commencement
of the occupation, since it was obvious that his account of atrocities
perpetrated were believed to be exaggerated.

"The hunted look on my people's faces has disappeared since the
Armistice," he said with a sea of tenderness in his eyes. Then he
struck the same note as others in responsible positions. "To rebuild
morality is more difficult than to restore destroyed buildings," he
said.

He listened attentively to my account of the arrangements we had
made for the return of Belgian children.

At Lille we went directly to the headquarters of the Hoover Commission. A Lieutenant Wellington welcomed us cordially and said,
"We wish you to study our work, and since you have gas, we'll use
your limousine in field visits." We saw charts that silently told the
gruesome story of manpower of the region mostly killed off and the
women having suffered so much as to be of doubtful future economic
value. With the generation between sixteen and eighteen shattered,
"One must fight," a Belgian official said, "for the development of
children under twelve if the population of the north is to be saved."

At Woverin on Christmas eve, we paused to speak to an old couple.
The man was trying to rebuild a wall of his house with hands swol-
len from chilblains, the woman handing him the stones. Both looked
half-frozen as the cruel wind blew in violent gusts, but they were
smiling at each other, and in a window behind them was a white
muslin curtain, with a potted red geranium beyond. Madame Labbe,
who had accompanied us, threw a warm scarf across the woman's

shoulders with a gentle *Bon soir, Madame,* and handed the man a pair of woolen gloves.

Next day, Christmas, we were in Ypres, where even the sites of former buildings could no longer be identified. Without a Canadian officer, who subsequently returned to Paris with us, we would have missed the location of Vimy Ridge. As we stood on the ridge, where camouflaged screens were flapping dismally in the wind, he said, "The enemy possessed every height, and even the outskirts of Arras, but we Canadians held under constant fire—and conquered."

In Noyon there was only an arrow pointing to empty space, as if to say, "You cannot stay here."

On my return to Paris I had barely time to catch my breath before I was off again. This time, with Jacacci on a tour of inspection of many of the thirty children's colonies run by our committee, situated in the south of France and other areas of beautiful, peaceful country. In contrast with the break-up of family life I had seen, it was a particularly happy interlude to be planning for the future.

I scarcely recognized in these healthy, laughing children I was seeing daily by the hundreds the pitiful wrecks who had come to us too terror-stricken for speech. Now they were being trained by devoted sisters to become a part of a restored simple village community, or a former manufacturing center of the north.

After this heartening picture I returned to Paris and the Peace Conference. One evening that I spent with General Pershing and Bishop Brent, I started a conversation by remarking that they both looked as I felt.

Pershing was at his wits' end. "In war the pattern is strict discipline in a single high military command," he stated, and added that after the end of hostilities there was no unity in the civilian command taking over, and self interest was replacing self sacrifice. In speaking of the disastrous confusion he pointed out that in planning for the future practical measures needing immediate attention were ignored. He quoted as an example that he could get no action on ordering Bulgarians (a country without wheat) to transport grain from Roumania (a country without transportation) to starving civilians.

Bishop Brent spoke in the same vein. He said that in 1916, from the pulpit of St. Paul's Cathedral at a service attended by the King and Queen of England, he had stated with conviction that this was the war to end war. But now truth compelled him to say that this was the peace to end peace.

Burgomaster Max had said to me in Brussels, "Disillusionment will be used by many in every nation as an alibi for evading their responsibility in the building of a better world."

T. E. Lawrence of Arabia was at the Peace Conference, and gave violent harangues about broken promises to the Arabs to which no one listened. Whereas, Gertrude Bell, also present, with really constructive, workable ideas for the future of the Arabs, could get no hearing.

One of the most discouraged men I saw was Paderewski, with whom I lunched one day. His lament was the number of political parties fighting for supremacy in Poland. "As head of the government, I am helpless," he said despairingly.

Equally disquieting was an occasion when Jacacci, Ida Tarbell, and I were joined in a restaurant by an Englishman, close to Lloyd George, and a Frenchman who was in the confidence of Clemenceau.

Both were seemingly unaware of the fact that it was the United States Senate, and not the President, who had the authority to make peace. Bryce had written me that his was a voice howling in the wilderness on this same theme.

When our guests left, Ida Tarbell was very outspoken in saying that the President by his failure to bring over to Paris the Republican leaders in the Senate was rapidly losing the peace.

Some months later, Warrick Greene of Boston went at General Pershing's instigation on an official inspection trip to Middle Europe. He reported that former enemies must work together again promptly. In this way alone lay future security, among hungry, restless, idle populations was his plea.

"But back to a peacetime routine of work seems so obvious a solution that it is completely overlooked in Paris deliberations."

The only cheerful important man I talked with at that time was Admiral William S. Sims, U.S.N. He was full of enthusiasm about the complete cooperation in action that had existed between the British fleet and our own under his command. He praised the few American pilots in the North Bombing Squad, one of whom, John J. Schieffelin (later to become our son-in-law), was officially credited with having sunk an enemy submarine from the air.

Incidentally, in World War II he was selected to establish the naval training base at Quonset, Rhode Island. Later he was Flag Secretary of the Central Pacific Fleet, serving under Admiral Hoover, and also represented the navy, in the military government of Kyoto, Japan, with General Krueger in charge.

Jacacci wanted me to get an impression of Alsace which I did with Marguerite Shaw, of the American Fund for French wounded. We took a train to Nancy and from there motored into Alsace and back to Paris by way of Verdun.

During the days we were in Alsace, I constantly found myself evaluating impressions that did not vary much. In the villages especially, and even in the towns, the people were not unfriendly, but rather confused and in casual conversations I realized that Alsatians had a strong national spirit and tendencies. In spite of characteristics both in their stolid faces and *patois*, denoting a strong German influence, they had not become Germanized, and this in spite of the German language having been compulsory in education. On the other hand, Alsatians had even less in common with the French, and the administrative job facing their statesmen was delicate. The fact that the Germans had permitted parochial schools to function unmolested would make for another element of discord should the French forbid such a practice in accordance with the law of France.

In a little hamlet in an out of the way corner of Alsace we had reached by a detour, an aged man signalled us to stop. "Perhaps you can help me," he said, "in something I don't understand. The Germans tell us they won the war, but if that is so," he concluded, "why are French troops here in control?"

General Castelnau was using great tact in his civil administration of Alsace. He and members of his staff greeted us at *popotte* one evening in the salon of a large villa. A concert to be given after dinner explained the *grande tenue* of the company for which we had

324

been prepared and were in evening gowns. Red trousers, pale blue tail coats, white gloves in evidence made the occasion gay.

The General had given us a longhand letter to Commandant Sarot of Verdun, requesting him to put us up overnight at the citadelle. I had been asleep for some hours when aroused by a banging at my door. It was Commandant Sarot asking me if I would share my army cot with a woman. "Is she fat?" I asked.

"Judge for yourself," came back at me in a woman's voice that sounded familiar. I opened the door to face Evangeline Booth, of the Salvation Army. When summoned to breakfast we were still talking.

It was the Commandant himself who took us to the forts that had figured so prominently in the *communiqués*.

Later from the outside of Fort de Vaux as I stood gazing into the battle-wrecked land, Evangeline Booth pointed to a sprig of green growing out of a blackened tree trunk. "Spring will come even to Verdun," she said.

34

AMERICAN OCCUPATION
OF THE RHINELAND

WEDNESDAY AFTERNOON, February 12, 1919, at six o'clock, I was once again in Chaumont with General Pershing, seated in a small room of the chateau where Joe and I had first met him. It was bitterly cold and the General was making rather unsuccessful attempts to encourage the fire to burn more briskly in a huge stove. On a small table was a tray with a teapot and two cups and saucers. We were there to discuss plans for my trip the next day to Coblenz in a staff car, to talk to American soldiers.

Pershing wanted to learn through a woman's intuition how comforts were affecting American soldiers billeted in German homes in the Rhineland. He had found my judgment sound, he said, and therefore he was relying upon it again.

This late afternoon was the first time I had been alone with him since my arrival from Paris earlier in the day. As we both hugged the stove, the General drank three cups of very strong tea in rapid succession. He looked not so much physically exhausted as in mental distress, which was explained by his remark that he had just received word about the critical illness in Paris of Colonel Boyd, his principal aide.

He seemed discouraged and, with a very sad expression, remarked, "Never has an army come into a war with such ideals as ours brought—are our soldiers losing them, and is it my fault, bad leadership?"

"I believe that my trip will reassure you on both these points," I replied cheerfully to relieve his tension.

Abruptly he broached the subject of our boys billeted in villages back of the Rhine near Coblenz. He considered that in Coblenz itself the men were receiving plenty of attention. "Confine your activities to the out-of-the-way villages and towns difficult of access, and handle the boys as you did before—you'll get results, all right," he said optimistically.

This matter being settled, I suggested that only the corporal as chauffeur and soldiers familiar with local roads should be in the car with me, and that Captain Cooke, of the Visitors' Bureau, should remain in Coblenz. General Pershing concurred and said he would include this in his instructions. "It's important," he commented, "but not obvious to officers."

After that he devoted himself to instructions on what he wished me to cover in my talks, and also referred to facts I had written him of my relations with soldiers' families that showed a remarkable memory in recalling details. Our conversation was interrupted by the sound of approaching motors. A dinner party consisting of some twenty-odd visiting generals had arrived!

During the night General Pershing received word that Colonel Boyd had died and in the morning he sent me a message that he would see me later in the day before leaving for Paris. He turned up at lunch, obviously having passed a sleepless night, and I admired his gallant effort to be a good host in spite of his personal grief.

After lunch General Pershing excused himself to telephone and was gone a long time. There was a visible tension in the salon among a group of aides standing about of which I was fully aware. Their attitude toward me was one of suspicion, and rightly so, since I had been given no opportunity to explain to them my status at the chateau.

Adjutant General Davis, who had a humorous eye, drew up a chair and sat down beside me. He murmured *sotto voce*, "Is it because you saw red tape the length of the highway between Cologne and Lille that you selected that route?"

I explained to him that the idea of my going to Coblenz was General Pershing's not mine and that he had known I must be in Lille at a definite date.

General Davis gave me a keen glance and much to my relief said he would remind General Pershing that I had not yet received my permits. He was as good as his word, and soon came back with reassuring information.

As Captain Cooke and I went to General Pershing's office to receive our final instructions, the General handed me from his desk a round covered box made from a French shell. "My good-luck symbol," he said.

We spent the first night at Neufchateau, and by two the following afternoon were in Treves, now a part of the American occupation. We were having a bite of food when the commanding officer introduced me to Marshal Ferdinand Foch as a woman who had declined an invitation to dine with him that evening. "Doubtless preferring to be in a German village with American soldiers," he replied with a very winning manner and charming smile.

Good roads made our progress rapid and by 5:30 we reached a German village back of the Rhine with a jaw breaking name. While Captain Cooke was with officers, I wandered about chatting casually with soldiers drifting into the large hall where Gertrude Ely, of the Y.M.C.A. staff, was helping the get scenery in place for a show that evening. The fact that I was not in uniform aroused curiosity, and I explained about my work among French children from the invaded North, where I had been a good deal and knew conditions. They were tight-mouthed about their own fighting experiences, although many a face still showed the strain of battle, but communicative in expressing their views of Germany and Germans. Most of all they spoke of home.

I was appreciative of the conversational lead given by a sombre youngster who said with determination that hot water and cleanliness weren't everything, and he mentioned the surliness of German women and girls. Another agreed, "It's the Germans' fault, not ours that we are in their homes."

They seemed satisfied with the company of fellow Americans and told of long tramps to reach distant villages for get-togethers with them. Some of the older, better-educated boys, however, mentioned that when they spoke German themselves, or met Germans who knew English and seemed pleasant, it was difficult at times to obey regulations against fraternizing. Also the majority of them found it hard not to make friends with the children, as they had done everywhere in France.

When the subject changed abruptly to the rich farmlands all around, one delicate-looking, sad-eyed youngster informed me that the good crops awaiting harvest in the Rhineland made him "homesick for Iowa." This touched off others in the same vein about their states. There were many references to the laziness of Germans and high pay they demanded. This was contrasted with the French— old men and women, whom they had seen for themselves, working with great courage, from daybreak until dark, to reclaim destroyed fields.

Gertrude Ely, in introducing me for a short speech before the scheduled entertainment, said that General Pershing, himself, whom they would all soon see at Coblenz on a tour of inspection, had sent me into the Rhineland. I was going to villages with Americans in them which were the hardest to reach, because that was the kind of woman I was. They were to give me a hand and listen to what I had to say.

In accordance with General Pershing's wishes, I emphasized what the Germans had done in retreat to other people's homes and farm-lands, citing specific instances. I was constantly interrupted by perti-nent questions, which I had found by experience was the way to get points across to soldiers. I had to be informal and use an audience more or less as a study class, following its initiative, not my own.

They liked amusing anecdotes about our American troops, and of French children. In conclusion I paid a high tribute to the First Division, as "the first to arrive in Germany, the first to fight, and probably the last home." This last was received with a mock groan followed by a cheerful shout, "We'll take it."

I was determined, before going on to Coblenz, to make a surprise call on American troops in a locality seldom visited, because the roads to it were almost impassable. Very reluctantly Captain Cooke consented.

The roaring welcome I received from Americans rushing from all directions to the car, and increasing in number as the word got about, was sufficient reward for the effort.

I never found more response than from this isolated group of lonely youngsters where most of our conversation was about other Americans. During my talk I happened to mention troops I saw at St. Mihiel still living in trenches, and added, "Electricity has been installed."

"The bright light must be hard on *my* pet rat I had to leave be-hind me," yelled a red-haired youngster with a comical expression.

I did not get control of my audience again before it had listened with relish to some priceless far-fetched anecdotes of rats personally known in trench life.

Although it was nearing midnight when we reached Coblenz, General Dickman was awaiting us. He seemed stunned when General Pershing's guest refused to accept army hospitality, including that of the British High Command in Cologne. "Make my excuses, please," I said tersely, emphasizing that my limited time must be spent in fulfilling commitments outlined by General Pershing.

At my words, General Dickman promptly handed me an impos-ing document, which consisted of a daily schedule giving an itinerary and intersections on highways where soldier escorts would be picked up for each out-of-the-way selected village.

"Would I be ready to start by ten next morning?" he inquired.

He looked flabbergasted when I replied, "At eight sharp, and the following mornings seven o'clock." As I spoke I returned to him the document to have inserted on it a number of other villages, suggested by Gertrude Ely, which I had decided to include in the schedule.

Someone must have sat up most of the night, making the necessary changes, but I was off at eight, and I did get to the twenty localities indicated on the amended list, and without a hitch.

Arrangements were made for visits to the billets themselves, and plenty of time was allowed for me to be with the boys individually, and in assembled groups in nearby Y.M.C.A. centers, if any such existed. Otherwise I met them under army auspices.

Each experience was the same fundamentally and my welcome varied only in the method of expressing the same thought—"A lady from home, and no officer with her! Gee, that's fine!"

After the first day I sent a memorandum to General Pershing that read:

> Each appraisal of the American method of occupation intensifies my first conviction that it is being done with thoroughness and dignity. Our boys are never brutal but firm. . . . "Why let what the Germans offer under military compulsion knock us off our guard from gratitude?" was their attitude.

The General telegraphed in acknowledgment:

> Essential details lacking. Mail your longhand notes. Will return them.

From Cologne to Lille our route lay back into the interior for a while, and through some German villages where there was no army of occupation. Captain Cooke thought few, if any, Americans had been seen since the Armistice. He was very silent and obviously on the alert for trouble. A roar of voices greeted us in one of the more populous centers, where sullen groups of men blocked our passage, shaking fists angrily and shouting foul epithets.

As the limousine stalled, I threw aside Captain Cooke, who was protecting me with his body, and leapt to my feet. I addressed myself to the few women in the crowd in fluent German born of panic. "The war is over," I called out. "We are on the way to Lille to help French children." I felt their response and followed it up by pleading with them to make their men stop their attacks and let us pass.

After a slight hesitation the women seized the rocks from the men and pushed them away from the car. As we got through I waved my thanks. This was the only real manifestation of hatred we were to encounter.

Namur and Liege had put up no resistance to the German armies, and the intact manufacturing plants were ghost-like in their emptiness, with all the machinery taken off to Germany. Belgians in the streets, their faces lifeless, gave no reply to a friendly greeting. It was the same in all other Belgian industrial towns.

Vernon Kellogg was in Lille and awaiting me in the Commission for Belgian Relief office. He had just returned from Berlin and the interior of Germany. He said that the Germans insisted their defeat was brought about by the blockade and not by the Allied armies. Already some of us were beginning to ask ourselves, "Did we win the war after all?"

35

THE RECONSTRUCTION
OF INDUSTRIAL FRANCE

REBECCA, OUR DAUGHTER, had graduated from Westover School in the spring of 1920, and at that time Joe suggested that I take her on a trip to France. We had barely reached Paris when I found myself listening to Colonel Prangez, the head of the Bureau for the Reconstruction of Industry, who was expounding an astonishing proposition for which he had already made arrangements, including my departure in four days. He was sending me on a three-week trip to inspect the present status of two hundred factories in the ten invaded departments in the north of France. Later on, I was to go into Germany to obtain a picture of a contrasting industrial situation —for publicity in America. "I am only enlarging on your own original idea," he said, as though to propitiate me.

The idea to which he referred occurred in the fall of the preceding year, when Mrs. William Hill and I together had made a trip to the invaded north of France, in connection with the rehabilitation of the families to whom our committee had returned children. By chance I had noticed in Lille an enormous electric plant which had been deliberately wrecked by the Germans before their evacuation. Now, through French effort, it had been restored. Through the local *Dommage de Guerre* office, I had reached Prangez in Paris, to request photographs of this plant as destroyed and as reconstructed within the year. Also similar records of other factories.

These were the first official French government photographs of "before and after" brought to America, and, thanks to *The New York Times*, they had a good press throughout the country.

Prangez looked relieved when, instead of a protest at his highhanded treatment of me, I replied that my consent was contingent on our arriving at a plan. He told me that telephone, telegraph, and a secretary were available in his office, and at once. Shortly thereafter I was talking to Uncle Herbert Putnam in Washington, another fast thinker. He considered the proposed photographic exhibition well timed and agreed to be responsible for it. The first showing, with an accompanying pamphlet written by me, would be in the Library of Congress for invited guests. Then the exhibition would go on tour among civic centers and Chambers of Commerce in industrial districts of the United States.

Prangez gave me a background of the fundamentals I was to remember. First and foremost, in the region of destruction had been located one-third of all the industries of primary importance to France, such as steel, mining, and textiles, as well as nearly all the nation's resources in pit coal and iron ore.

Equally important in gauging the magnitude of the task was the fact that most of the factories, although far behind the battle zone in enemy occupied territory, were systematically wrecked. The machinery either had been carried into Germany or was rendered useless by dynamite, sledge hammer, or skillful removal by experts of vital parts, impossible to replace.

My attention was to be concentrated not on the bureau's achievements in general community rehabilitation, through the removal of destroyed buildings and the rebuilding of roads and bridges, but on its relations with the manufacturers. This consisted of direct loans advanced by the French government on expected indemnity payments from Germany. The funds were to be used for clearing rubbish from former factory sites, rebuilding plants, and getting them back into operation. He assured me that all were being reconstructed on modern lines, with up-to-date equipment and with electricity as the motive power. The plants allowed for expansion, yet with an eye to immediate production to provide for plant reinvestment.

The incredible industrial revival to date Prangez attributed to the spirit of the manufacturers, many of them beyond middle life, rich before the war and spending much time in Paris boulevard cafés. Now they were living in primitive quarters, supervising the rebuilding of their factories, and managing them personally when back in operation. Each and all took full advantage of the advice from his bureau's local technical sectors, including a staff of engineers and experts in the industries to be rebuilt.

Prangez had ready for me a questionnaire filled in, giving the source of machinery (stressing what was American-made), raw materials, and markets, before and after the war, as well as a detailed report on a factory, as a basis for my discussion with the manufacturer concerned. He provided a secretary to accompany me.

I dictated a brief letter for Prangez to get off to each manufacturer, stressing that I was not to be entertained by local officials, nor must I pay my respects to anyone unless he was actively participating in the reconstruction of industry. Factories were to be kept open after the closing hour on a short notification from me, and no meals or sleeping arrangements were to be made.

With the dynamic force of a Colonel Prangez at the planning level, a whiz of a secretary, and a chauffeur thoroughly skilled with a high-powered limousine, I found everything went like clockwork. The real factor in time-saving was that the three of us felt the need for food at identical odd moments. Our sleeping habits also fitted in, the secretary and I dozed together in between work on the road and after dark, and the chauffeur did the same during our inspection of factories. Therefore, we could travel far into the night without undue fatigue, and our starts were made very early. We shared a mutual satisfaction in having the daily progress reports I telephoned to Prangez indicate that we were keeping ahead of his schedule.

It made all the difference to be able to dictate data before the significant aspects of a factory restoration were dimmed. Even more essential was the opportunity to evaluate the information on neatly typed sheets the next day. Although the situation in every plant varied, as well as the presentation given by the individual owner, gradually a pattern began to take definite shape.

The French manufacturer had been classified in the past as an ultra-conservative, unable to compete with the steady advance of modernized industries of other nations. I found his character as remodeled as his plant, and he talked of trading with Germany as a matter of course. His methods were adapted to the challenge he was facing as, with confidence and courage, he began industrial life all over again. I saw for myself many examples of Prangez's organizing genius, notably in the success of his engineers and experts in promoting and guiding individual initiative to make it seem the manufacturer's own thought.

Everywhere we found a shortage of housing for miners and workmen, depleted building materials, and difficulty for industrialists in securing machinery. Although extremely short of tool-making facilities, the French were producing a surprising number of machines. It was a slow process to recover those stolen by the Germans. And in spite of American insistence on f.o.b. payments and exchange running against France, there were many machines bearing trademarks of British and American firms.

334

Industrial revival reflected the relative necessity of each industry restored. Tool shops were given a high priority. Particularly spectacular was the comeback of the mines, with Lens as a center. I had seen for myself, after the Armistice, that the town was completely wiped out during the fighting. The same was true in other parts of the Pas de Calais, with one hundred thousand miners rendered homeless. But the wrecking of the mines was deliberate destruction by the Germans, who had shattered the shafts with high explosives and filled them with water.

It seemed little short of a miracle that repaired mines were already producing close to a quarter of their former tonnage. The steel industry was also making firm strides towards recovery. Textiles, in which demolition had been appallingly thorough, were scarcely behind the others. The story of each factory was an epic in itself, but in retrospect two experiences linger in my memory. One concerned an enterprising, elderly steel manufacturer, and the other a tycoon in textile development, and as much of an individualist as Prangez was himself.

The steel manufacturer, an aristocrat, was before the war an absentee owner, with a racing stable in Paris, where he spent most of his time. He took me to a new and fairly large house, constructed for him by his workmen out of their own allotted building material. It was more prized, he said feelingly, than any property he had ever before possessed, and it provided an adequate home for his wife and daughter to join him. He was proud that the rebuilding of his factory was forging ahead, far beyond his expectations. "There's nothing to keep us back," he declared jubilantly.

The manufacturer's optimism apparently was contagious, as evidenced by one of his older workmen, who hobbled on one leg after me to the waiting car. He wanted to tell me, he said, that the Germans had a genius for destruction, "But fortunately we French have an even greater genius for reconstruction."

On our way to Lille we were intercepted by a communication from Prangez, telling me to disregard his previous instructions and go to Monsieur Monnet's house in Sedan, and be under his (Monnet's) orders. No auspices could have been better for obtaining an understanding of the intricacies of the textile industry, in which Monnet was the leading figure in France.

Our host was short and stout, with jet black hair and moustache and a square-featured face dominated by piercing dark eyes under bushy brows. Although I was a house guest in his enormous establishment the next four days, I was actually on the road with him in as strenuous a regime, inspecting textile factories, as I had been on the rest of the trip. I was able in this time to see for myself that 72 per cent of the industrial revival of the textile and other industries vital to France had already been accomplished.

The passes obtained by Colonel Prangez permitted us to go into the zones of Germany occupied by the Allies, and a German visa on our passports allowed entrance into unoccupied Germany.

We motored by way of Antwerp to The Hague, where we were the guests of our American Ambassador William Phillips and Caroline, his wife. A week later we were called for by M. le Cerf of the French Embassy's *Service Économique*, stationed in Berlin. En route to Cologne, he took us to Cleve by way of Düsseldorf, the headquarters of the Reds and profiteers near the Ruhr. There we were joined at lunch by an engineer of Prangez's bureau, in whose charge we were left by M. le Cerf. In his remarks he displayed the imagination and initiative which characterized the personnel of the technical sectors I had come across in northern France. This led to my inquiring about Prangez's instructions about our relative freedom of movement. He informed me they were flexible and were intended to fit in with what I myself thought important to the purposes of the trip. "What's on your mind?" he asked, after a searching glance.

I was wondering, I replied, whether it would be possible for me to get an impression of a few of the smaller towns and villages in unoccupied Germany, under conditions which would keep me from being conspicuous.

It was possible, he told me, through the services of a German. The engineer went on to explain that the German in question had not fought during the war, because of tuberculosis, but he was now well. Always a French sympathizer, he was working for France through Prangez's bureau, his disloyalty to Germany unsuspected. His special usefulness lay in locating machinery stolen from France, hidden in out-of-the-way districts. He was about to start on such a mission.

Within an hour, Rebecca and I were off with him in a car bearing a German license plate. After a two-day foraging expedition, we were to rejoin the engineer at Düsseldorf and be taken by him to Cologne, where General Henry T. Allen, the commander of U. S. Army occupation forces in Germany, was to meet us. The German was a Bavarian, and we had several German Egyptologist friends in common. He took us into a series of inaccessible, back-country villages, over lonely roads. Never will I forget our excitement when, in poking about in deserted buildings, the German's torch flashlight fell on the outlines of three huge French-made machines. After careful examination, he declared them intact and made a note of their whereabouts for later collection. He found a number of other machines in the next few days.

The German peasants were friendly and invited us into their homes. My ability to speak their language was a distinct advantage. I saw no evidence of serious privation beyond a shortage of milk. I constantly compared, in my mind's eye, the rosy-cheeked, decently clothed, well-shod German children with their pathetic counterparts in France. Some of the villagers we talked with casually had no realization of Germany's defeat.

I found visits to town markets illuminating. Shoppers were getting an adequate amount of food at noticeably high prices. In shops men and women were buying clothes, shoes, and other essentials, by no means cheap. We stayed overnight in a simple but clean hostel in a fair-sized town. The men who dropped in chatted with our German as one of themselves.

In the Ruhr, with the same German escort, I had several hasty but significant glimpses into industrial conditions and sampled the attitudes of the people there, as well as the Reds and profiteers of Düsseldorf. Later, when I compared notes with French Intelligence, I was pleased to have my fleeting bird's-eye impressions substantiated by those who knew the mentality of the Germans concerned.

General Allen, at Coblenz, offered to motor us along the Rhine to Wiesbaden by way of Bingen. I told him I could not adjust my mood to the enjoyment of a lovely German countryside, with untouched buildings. All I wanted was to find justification of the French claim for a large indemnity. He concurred wholeheartedly.

The General left us at Prangez's office at Wiesbaden. The staff there told me that, after our detour from Cleve, eighteen high-priced machines had been collected. I was given the details of the functioning of the office, then with another German in the pay of France as our escort, we visited German factories making iron products, cement, and electrical equipment. The workmen seemed sullen and uncommunicative, and, according to our escort, it was hard to get anything out of them.

The same German went with us to Frankfurt. On the way we stopped to inspect the enormous Bayer chemical plant. What struck me forcibly was that, although black bread, the nutritious staple of German diet, was furnished free, I saw none of it during the lunch hour, since the workmen were, without exception, eating white bread that cost them eight pfennings a loaf, and might under these circumstances have been considered on a par with champagne. We encountered the same thing at the enormous Krupp factory.

At Frankfurt, we devoted some attention to an exhibition of merchandise, where luxuries were conspicuously on display with people in line waiting to buy them. Even in the poorer quarters of towns in the vicinity, women wore furs, and always were well dressed. This I was also to see in shops in the poorest sections of Berlin. Profiteering in food stuffs and luxuries were as conspicuous in Frankfurt as in Düsseldorf.

Just before leaving Frankfurt I had need to telegraph to Metz. I wrote the message in French and handed it to the concierge of the hotel, who refused to send it except in German. "Metz is in France now," I declared. "It will not be for long," the concierge replied.

Prangez had decided we were to go to Berlin by train from Frankfurt. A Russian named Raoul Rabinerson and M. le Cerf again were to be in charge of us. By nine the following morning we were in a large hotel in the center of the German capital city, with but few strangers visible.

Germans I talked with, including members of the Reichstag,

338

seemed to think the people, under a republic, were like lost sheep. I was surprised to find that postcards of the Kaiser were still being sold in Berlin. I considered it worth noting that, in the Sieges-Allee in Berlin, among all the statues of the Hohenzollern family, there was not even a single nose broken, in spite of the revolution. On all sides I heard *ad nauseam* that Germans would not pay an indemnity to France.

It was a strange sensation to walk in the Unter den Linden, and an enjoyable one to be once again in the Kaiser Friedrich Museum, there to revel in the masterpieces of Velasquez, Leonardo da Vinci and Giorgione. Just as Rebecca and I were leaving the museum we ran into a German professor from Leipzig, who had been a fellow guest with Joe and me on our honeymoon visit to the castle of Baron Wendelstadt near Munich. "Can't we both forget the war for half an hour?" he asked. I shook my head and walked on.

That night we had no sleeper on our way to Metz, where M. Monnet was to meet us, and in motoring us to Paris was to show us sections of the Meurthe and the Moselle. Snoring Germans in an overcrowded compartment made sleep impossible. I read documents furnished me at Wiesbaden about the favorable industrial and economic conditions in Germany. They included the following published by Mr. Langsburgh, an important German financier, in June, 1919. "The means which our people in prominent positions in the state are using to prove that it is an impossibility to meet an indemnity of this kind [one hundred milliards of marks] cannot possibly deceive any man of affairs in the allied nations, and they are an insult to our own good sense."

Other official German reports proved that the government, although complaining that it could not find capital, was placing money and resources in outside countries, or lending it to neutrals. Several Germans I saw admitted to general speculation and illegitimate traffic in large volumes of stocks of every variety that remained in Germany at the time of the Armistice. Then, with my thoughts on the amount of stolen French machinery hidden away, I jotted a summary from my observations.

"There is a great deal of new building in the way of rather elaborate workmen's houses and factory development. For instance, in a large chemical factory I visited a laboratory which had been completed during the last two months, when by its side the laboratory formerly used for the same purpose, with modern appliances of every kind, was abandoned.

"It is evident vast sums are being expended on railway construction, roads, bridges, and in many up-to-date improvements. I cannot but ask myself whether a nation which owes what Germany owes should be allowed to spend quite so much on its own internal development."

The main reason my decision to spend a few weeks in England, after my German assignment, was a visit to Broadway, situated in beautiful country and interesting because of the number of noted artists who lived there. We were to be with Antonio de Navarro and his wife, formerly Mary Anderson, a beautiful American actress. She had left the stage at the height of a brilliant career to marry the rich Spaniard. His principal interest was in early pewter, his collection having been built around pieces salvaged from sunken ships of the Spanish Armada.

Rebecca and I were at Claridge's in London, talking to Tony de Navarro when, to my surprise, a strange man stopped to ask whether I was Mrs. Joseph Lindon Smith. When he got an affirmative answer, he produced credentials as a special writer for *The London Times*. It seemed the editor of *Le Temps* had telephoned from Paris advising an interview about my recent trips in France and Germany.

"You can't," Tony protested, and at my reply that "I must," with a disgusted look at me, he took Rebecca sightseeing.

I was still dictating when they returned. That afternoon I had a conference, arranged at Prangez's request after I had sent a cable to Paul Cravath, with John Maynard Keynes, the author of *The Economic Consequences of the Peace*.

Keynes' premise was that to crush Germany industrially would destroy world economy. He seemed to turn a deaf ear to the future of France, which was dependent on reimbursement by Germany for loans advanced by the French government to her manufacturers.

The first consequence to me of a two-column interview in *The*

Times the next morning was an invitation from Lord Robert Cecil to lunch with him in the City. He was kind enough to say, "Your material is interesting from the point of view of facts assembled from close observation."

When a steady demand for interviews poured in, Tony de Navarro went on strike. "Your daughter and I are leaving for Broadway tomorrow morning at ten," he said stiffly. I went with them.

36

SOME ASPECTS
OF PACIFIC PROBLEMS

ARTHUR JAMES had invited Joe and me to go on a cruise in the far Pacific on his yacht *Aloha*, starting from the port of New York on September 15, 1921. Incidentally, this would be the first American yacht to be in these waters since World War I.

I was ill at the time of departure, so an arrangement had to be made for us to join the party later. We sailed from San Francisco on November 4, which would allow Joe three weeks of painting at the Temple of Borobudur in Java, before the scheduled arrival of the *Aloha* at the port of Batavia. We could also have a stopover at the Philippine Islands before going on to Borobudur.

As I have said earlier, I had been indoctrinated by Brooks Adams and John Hay about the importance of the Philippine Islands in carrying out the Open-door Policy of America, which had assumed responsibility in the Pacific through active participation in trade as a deterrent to Asiatic aggression.

After William Howard Taft's departure from the Philippines in 1904 to become secretary of War, President Theodore Roosevelt appointed W. Cameron Forbes to serve on the Philippine Commission. His career there had lasted until 1913, and during the four final years he was governor general of the islands.

Forbes combined vision and a gift for sound administration with an instinct for business, inherited from ancestors who made the family fortune by trade in clipper ships between the Orient and New England ports.

He was a convinced believer in the advantage to Filipinos and American businessmen alike of making Manila a trade center, through a strong American merchant marine, as advocated by both Hay and Brooks Adams. The results were to be brought about by the development of rich resources on scattered groups of islands inhabited by primitive tribes with no common language, in exchange for American manufactured products. The question of our relations with the Philippines on a trade basis had been a controversial political issue in the United States. Free entry of cane sugar from the islands was opposed by the strongly entrenched western U. S. sugar industry.

Another conflict in interests was cigars made by Filipinos, which competed with those manufactured from Virginia tobacco.

I found in government papers which I had been permitted to examine in Washington a recurrent theme which appealed to American idealism. This was the adventure of establishing a democratic form of government similar to our own among widely scattered tribes in an out-of-the-way region of the Pacific.

When President Wilson took office in 1913, he was determined to grant to the Filipinos the independence they so "honorably coveted."

Filipino patriots had strengthened the position of the well-organized Anti-imperialist League, and under Francis Burton Harrison as governor general the Filipinazation policy had gone on apace.

But President Warren G. Harding reversed his predecessor's policy. In the spring of 1921 Cameron Forbes had returned to the islands on a special mission headed by Major General Leonard Wood, to make a thorough survey as a basis for what was to be known as the Wood-Forbes Report, and Wood was now governor general.

General Pershing had given me another interest in the Philippines in talking about the Moros on the Island of Zamboanga, among whom he had had many years of service as military governor. He described the primitive, warlike Moros, who had been converted to Islam by Moslem missionaries during the sixteenth century, as "amoral but not immoral." Pershing told me that the character of the Moros differed fundamentally from that of Christianized, civilized, political-minded Filipinos. His procedure had been to guide rather than break the spirit of proud Moro individualists.

As an example of his success, he said that, when lawlessness and the murder of foreigners became rampant, he had accomplished the disarming of the Moros by persuasion. Voluntarily, they had brought in to the military thousands of javelins, krises, and other primitive weapons. He also said that the Moros had never accepted the suzerainty of Spain. Their dislike of Christians, however, was confined to Filipinos, and they referred to the American flag as theirs and confidently awaited annexation to the United States.

During Pershing's administration, he had replaced a Spanish dungeon by a modern prison at San Ramon, where Moros serving life sentences for murder had for the first time come in contact with our civilization and liked it. In adopting the trusty system, permitting inmates to live in cottages with their families, Pershing had followed the plan initiated by Forbes among the Filipinos, but he had omitted a period of strict disciplinary servitude.

Incidentally, Pershing's constructive approach to the treatment of convicts, unexpected in a military executive, was responsible many years later for my doing some prison work under Lewis Lawes, a leader with similar ideas.

In an age when the public looks to jets for the elimination of space, it will be hard for readers to appreciate that five hundred miles of sea between Manila and Zamboanga required five days by sea in the ordinary passenger service. The problem was solved for us when Lawrence Benton, the collector of customs on the Island of Zamboanga arranged for us, on the day we landed at Manila, to be included on a tour of American businessmen on a fast Japanese steamer.

Benton managed to devote a good deal of time to Joe and me. He praised Forbes's administration for its construction of good roads on Zamboanga and the other isolated islands in the Mindanao group.

343

He spoke highly of the promotion of rubber and many other tropical crops. He told us that the trusties on the penal farm were furnished free land, tools, and animals. They received one-half of the production of their individual holdings, and still there was a good profit, enabling the prison to be almost self-supporting. "It shows what good soil can do," he said.

In the cool of an early morning, we started off by car for the prison. On the way, Benton took us into several homes of friendly Moros, where the interior walls of bamboo structures consisted of ingeniously braided ribbons of the nipa palm. Joe found the craftsmanship of the Moros in the making of brass of a high order, artistically.

After an inspection of the prison plant, we entered an assembly hall, where about thirty of the trusties looked rather lost in the huge space. As each was presented by name and came forward to shake hands, I noted their distinctive faces and an arresting self-reliance. They had clipped hair but were not in prison stripes.

One of the oldest, after eying me intently, unexpectedly smiled. With this encouragement, I unostentatiously opened a Koran I had brought with me. He peered at the Arabic script then reached over and took possession of the, to him, sacred book. I watched the Koran pass from hand to hand in unmistakable reverence. When the same friendly convict brought it back to me he touched his mouth. This gesture and what he said, Benton interpreted as meaning that the Moros wanted to know whether the words were on my lips and, if so, for me to repeat them. At the sound of my rhythmic intoning in the fashion of sheikhs, these Moro lifers crowded close to me and stood in motionless silence. In their faces was the religious concentration of all Moslems when listening to the words of the Koran.

The next afternoon I was back at the penal farm reservation on the invitation of the same trusties. It was gratifying to observe the pride of possession of the owners in their homes, with their children clinging to them affectionately, as in any happy family. The wives kept the cottages clean and neat and a few had small flower gardens. I also wandered about in plantations where convicts were hard at work without supervision.

344

We were barely settled in the hotel in Manila before we received an invitation from Governor Leonard Wood to dine with him. Thanks to Cameron Forbes's introduction, he agreed to my reading the report of the Wood-Forbes Special Mission. It was not yet printed but available in typewritten form, and a copy was lent me late the following afternoon, on the understanding it would be called for at eight the next morning.

Daylight surprised me as I pondered the adverse changes and uncertainties brought about by the Wilson administration. In Secretary of War Weeks's instructions to the mission (March 23, 1921), considerable stress was laid on finding out how the Philippine government was handling justice, health, agriculture, and finance.

The report brought out the facts of demoralization in every government department. It also contained a pertinent reminder that, even with extensive transfers of responsibility to Filipinos, the Americans maintained decisive control, because the preceding Congress had not acted on President Wilson's plea for independence. It stated that the great majority of Filipinos wanted independence, but under the protection of the United States.

The first of four recommendations of the report read:

"We recommend that the present general status of the Philippine islands continue, until the people have had time to absorb, and thoroughly master, the powers already in their hands."

Through Colonel Frank R. McCoy, the chief of staff to the mission, and Captain Robert C. Candee, who had been active on the inspection trips, I obtained authoritative information as they took me about and arranged interviews. The governmental situation was complex, to say the least, with news still by word of mouth in remote provinces, and with eight different languages and eighty-seven dialects spoken on the islands.

There were but few Japanese living in the Philippines, because they found the climate unhealthful. The ownership of real estate was largely, and evenly, distributed between a fairly heavy Chinese population and the Catholic orders, which had thrived since the days of Spanish overlordship.

Businessmen were the most discouraged Americans I met in Ma-

345

nila. Their argument in support of Cameron Forbes's policy was that the United States, the greatest consumer of tropical products in the world, had every tropical crop it required awaiting development in the Philippine Islands. But Americans purchased such crops mainly from British colonies or from regions controlled by Japan. Our imports of this character were shipped to us in British or Japanese bottoms and were insured by English and Japanese companies. An American merchant marine was practically an impossibility, with the steadily increasing wage scales paid American seamen, and with inadequate government subsidies for trade-carrying vessels.

I was disappointed that no one was able to locate Emilio Aguinaldo, about whom I had heard much from John Bass, the leading American newspaper correspondent accredited to the Philippines during the war with Spain.

A real experience was a long talk with Sergio Osmeña, the first speaker of the Philippine Assembly, established by William Howard Taft during his regime, and now speaker of the House of Representatives. Osmeña was a Filipino with some Chinese blood and according to all accounts a fine character and co-operative with American officials. He had a sad face, but a responsive smile, and altogether he seemed to be the right man in the right place for the good of his people.

But Manuel Quezon, the president of the Senate and leader of the Nationalists, looked what he was, a wily politician. Although small in stature, this adroit diplomat of mixed Spanish and Chinese blood had an eloquence in public statements which made him a formidable adversary. He talked to us fluently in well-modulated English but said little of note.

Colonel McCoy related an amusing episode connected with baseball. In 1911, Cameron Forbes, accompanied by General Pershing, had gone to a remote island to settle a violent dispute. While strolling about between negotiations, which were getting nowhere, they saw some of the Filipinos who were involved in the dispute making a feeble attempt at baseball.

Forbes rounded up all the available Americans, who laid out a proper field. Then the Americans, led by the governor general and

346

Pershing, gave a demonstration of baseball. Shortly thereafter, nine Americans and nine Filipinos were battling it out on the baseball field, the dispute entirely forgotten.

As we headed for Singapore on the *Granite State,* the fact that the status quo in the Pacific had been shaken as an aftermath of the war seemed clear from conversations I overheard on shipboard. The only travelers were businessmen seeking contracts in the Far East.

The economic supremacy of the British, with Singapore as their base, was no longer taken for granted. And quite significant was the number of first-class Chinese passengers, who looked extremely prosperous and rather ruthless. They kept to themselves, in the midst of a general camaraderie among French, Belgians, Italians, Japanese, and a few Americans.

I made friends with an American named Hood, who was on his way to Bangkok to present a bid for the building of a bridge. The British had offered to do the job on the basis of a small down-payment with final settlement some years hence, the French offered equally favorable terms, while the Italian and Belgian firms were prepared to pay a large cash premium for getting the contract.

Hood told me that the Siamese preferred the Americans, so I persuaded him to cable his firm to find out what it could do about a delayed payment. He received in reply a message which read: "Cannot meet terms of competitors because American steel companies demand f.o.b. on delivery."

My unforgettable first impression of Singapore was of the mixture of races, colorfully costumed, drifting past the statue of Sir Stamford Raffles, who early in the nineteenth century had acquired the island for England from the Sultan of Johore. Skin colors varied from the pallor of Europeans through the yellows of Japanese and Chinese, the clear browns of Malays and Javanese, to the darkness of Indians. The inky black body of a single *Tamil,* nearly naked, leaning against the pedestal of the statue, was the oddest imaginable contrast to Sir Stamford's stolid British self-assurance, expressed in every line of his figure and face.

An opportunity to gain knowledge of the economic and political activities in a foreign country has always proved irresistible to me.

So it was now. After we were settled at Raffles Hotel, another American fellow-passenger invited me to see some rubber plantations with a group of Americans who were in Singapore on business for a tire syndicate in Ohio.

We rose to a high elevation above the ocean before we reached country where there was literally nothing but rubber plantations. The only things to see for miles in every direction were small trees, set out with even spaces between them. Close up, the sound of sap dripping into the containers encircling each tree was a monotonous refrain. On stopping for a hasty bite at the house of an English director of one of the plantations, we learned from him that the majority of these plantations, as well as the sugar plantations in another direction, were owned by wealthy Chinese.

These aggressive people had made fortunes in real estate transactions in Singapore and other towns of the Malay Peninsula. They even controlled the capital in most of the far eastern steamship companies, including the British Blue Funnel Line. "Englishmen who are doing business in these parts," he said ruefully, "realize only too well that the Chinese have become the backbone of the East, a fact not yet acknowledged in England."

On the return trip to Singapore, we had passed through a popular summer resort close to the ocean, where long avenues of attractive trees led to villas of every conceivable type of architecture, many painted in vivid colors. They were Chinese-owned, for the most part, and my curiosity was aroused as to what an interior would be like. Therefore, when a Japanese whom we had liked on the steamer asked Joe and me to go with him to call on a rich Chinese family, we accepted with alacrity.

We turned in to a wide driveway leading to the largest of these villas, much overplanted with a blaze of exotic blooms of ill-assorted colors. The hostess was a large woman with friendly eyes. It looked as though a good deal of the family wealth was carried on her person in the form of valuable jewels, an incongruous note on her beautifully embroidered Chinese garments. The furniture and interior decoration were a combination of the worst in oriental design and vulgar, rococo, expensive European.

348

Neighbors came shuffling in, wearing lovely Chinese clothes and a number of huge precious stones. The men stood apart and silent, but the women frankly stared at us, chatting Chinese in shrill voices. Our hostess talked to us in well-modulated English, as politeness compelled us to taste deadly looking sweets and syrups brought in on great silver trays.

The experiences of the day had provided an advance showing of the coming era, which held rather terrifying potentialities for the Western World.

37

A YACHT AND PRIVATE CARS

ON LANDING at the port of Batavia in Java, we went directly to Borobudur, where Joe was to paint figures in high relief in this largest and most magnificent of the many temples in the Far East dedicated to Gautama Buddha.

During Joe's long hours of work, I studied the story of Gautama's life, as recorded on the many terraces in an endless series of reliefs in which men, animals, and trees were rendering homage to him as the Buddha.

From what Sturgis Bigelow had told me, I recognized the meaning of the varied attitudes of the enshrined Buddhas which typified the five steps which Gautama took to reach Nirvana.

The unfinished unseen Buddha seated within the *dagoba* at the summit meant to the initiated that the higher one rose towards the understanding of Gautama's teaching the less necessary the outward symbols of perfection associated with inactivity and contemplation.

Delightful interruptions were the visits from Dutch friends of Aunt Ruth's accompanied by Javanese wives. Dutch officials also brought Javanese colleagues, who told me that Javanese held all except the top positions in the government of Java under a Dutch governor general. Anyone who knew the administrative structure of these possessions, however, realized how tight Dutch control actually was.

Three weeks later the *Aloha* party joined us. The James's guests were Miss Florence Sullivan, Williams Matheson, Peter Alvord, and a Dr. Vogel. Before returning to Batavia, we motored through a country with very rich soil, which was being intensively cultivated by industrious Javanese.

In Java, as in the Philippines and at Singapore, the Chinese were in evidence—more particularly, in a large and very active colony located near a sleepy town where we stopped to pay our respects to the governor general.

No thinking person could be in the far Pacific at that time without grave concern. World War I would have been a stalemate without America's intervention. Now, just as surely, Great Britain's and Holland's control of the Pacific against Asiatic aggression was a losing battle without American collaboration as an Asiatic power. Japan was on the verge of declaring war on China. And yet, during President Warren G. Harding's administration and that of Calvin Coolidge, political emphasis centered on the unprecedented prosperity throughout the United States.

I had gained an economic picture of the Philippines, and now at Singapore and other ports harbor masters' invoices gave me a realistic, even if incomplete, sampling of trade movements in the Pacific. Among these invoices, only a few were for American cargoes, and the American flag was on none of the ships coming from the other side of the Pacific.

In Calcutta the unanswered question was whether British administration could win out against endless delays to European traffic caused by sacred cows wandering through the thoroughfares. To me, the Hindu religion, with its caste system and untouchables, was repellent. I was reminded, as countless others must be reminded today, that color is no warranty against outmoded social systems, and that inequality can as readily be perpetuated under religious and social auspices in the Far East as in any other quarter of the globe. E. F.

Carritt used to tell Oxford philosophy students that there is scarcely anything ridiculous that has not "somewhere been considered a duty, though somewhere else a crime." Nevertheless, the panorama at Benares, of the devout bathing in the sacred Ganges against a backdrop of wailing mourners gathered about the funeral pyres, could only feebly awake in me that tolerance with which one should approach the most deeply held articles of faith exhibited by others.

The climax of our experiences in India occurred at Delhi, the capital under the Mogul emperors. One of the best-known English architects showed us his plans for a new Delhi. The all powerful Hindus were enthusiastic about the revival of a former magnificence, even if it had to be created under alien rule.

Joe and I had an introduction to Lord Reading, the viceroy, even as Arthur James did. I found at the Residency, when we were entertained by Lord and Lady Reading, an atmosphere of uncertainty among British officials. There was dismay at the (to them) unexpected uproar over the recent imprisonment of Mahatma Gandhi by the British, and anxiety because of the constant threat to the safety of the Prince of Wales, then on a tour of India. The persistent undercurrent of dissatisfaction among the Hindus, under the leadership of the Brahmins, was frankly admitted. Altogether, it was impossible to ignore an intimation of drastic changes in India, in which the terms would be dictated to Great Britain.

But I felt confident that, in the probable future control of government by Indians, they would have too much sense to discontinue the smoothly functioning, long-established administration based on British principles of law. Also, an army organized on British ideas of discipline and training seemed likely. Both of these surmises have proved correct.

At Bombay, where we rejoined the *Aloha*, the restlessness of the Hindus was being kept in check by George A. Lloyd, who later was to be the last strong Englishman in Egypt.

A final impression of the British Empire was gained by us in Ceylon, where, unlike the situation fostered by Dutch in Java, the people governed had no say and there was no social contact between them and the British. It was Little England again, in a country

351

where, in motoring to reach great temples, we passed through jungles with monkeys mocking us.

38

ACROSS THE BIG
CYPRESS SWAMP

When the *Aloha* reached Ceylon, I found myself seriously ill. It accordingly became necessary for Joe and me to return to Boston by the first available steamer. Back home, after a series of illnesses culminating in pulmonary trouble, I made the sudden decision to flee even the X rays which were, in a matter of hours, to tell me and my doctors how really bad off I was.

Gathering up my now grown daughters, Frances and Lois, and taking Jennie, our housekeeper, and her husband, Sidney, who was our chauffeur, I prepared to leave for Florida. For reasons of my health, I added Laura Loughery, a young Canadian nurse who was soon to prove the best of friends as well. The island of Boca Grande on the Florida west coast was our destination. Joe and our other daughter, Rebecca, had meantime gone to Cambodia to paint, unaware of my decision.

Ten years of unremitting work in Europe during and after the war had left me drained. There was no cause which I wished to espouse—I seemed to have had my fill of such responsibility. But I was shortly to run into another cause which, as events proved, I could not dodge, and it is only fair to say that it is with me still—the work which has since become canalized in the American Association on Indian Affairs. The years since I have designated my "working career" with Indians, public health, narcotics, and penal administration.

Within a few days of our arrival on Boca Grande, I hired a guide and his electric launch. Within a few weeks I was beginning to feel my old self again. When my half-brother Palmer Putnam joined us, we departed in the launch for Fort Meyers on the mainland, planning to go on a narrow canal to Lake Okeechobee.

The first night on the canal, we put up at a lodging place at Labelle, a village situated on the edge of the prairie. A regional map on the wall of the dining room, with "Indian Reservation" marked on it, attracted our attention. The landlady informed us that the reservation was only two hundred miles away and that her two brothers were constantly on it. Dick, the elder, taking hunting parties from the North, and the younger Winton, because he liked Indians, spoke their language, and was the only white man they trusted.

At my request, both men were located on a cattle range, and within forty-eight hours we were off, with the brothers driving us in two cars, and with food supplies and camp outfit in two trucks driven by a cook named Tom and a boy named George.

By noon we were south of shacks and a road and shortly came to a district known as the "Devil's Garden." Winton called my attention to tomato plants growing wild as evidence of what this rich soil had produced when the area was a part of the good fields the Indians had worked twenty years ago, when they grew sugar cane, corn, and other profitable crops. Then whites came along, stole their belongings, and finally drove them away. Indians could make a living like other industrious men, he said, but to clear land for a garden, get cattle and hogs started, and be forced to abandon everything would discourage anyone's incentive to work.

This group had consented to move to a federal reservation on the assurance that the government would give each family five hundred dollars' worth of supplies and two dollars a day in cash until the members of the family were on their feet from hard work. "They got nothing and they don't like to see U.S. on a car," Winton ended bitterly.

We pitched camp that first night in a delightful pine "hammock" on a height. Here the Indians named Winchester Rifle and Henry Clay met us with venison for supper.

353

The camp was astir by sunrise: Dick, Palmer and George, accompanied by Dick's dogs, going with the Indian hunters to hunt a panther that had eluded the Indians and was rapidly destroying their livestock. The rest of us, with Sidney at the wheel of George's truck, and Frances driving Dick's Ford, headed for the site prepared for our reservation visit by the Indians.

The reservation was situated along the edge of the Everglades in land that was mostly sand sloughs and swamps. According to Winton, the Indian hogs had to be raised too close to the favorite haunts of panthers to be secure, while suitable ground to which panthers never penetrated was pre-empted for hogs owned by the superintendent of the reservation. His cattle roamed the only good pasture nearby.

Because Winton was with us, we received a smiling welcome in Seminole homes, which consisted of wide, square platforms about three feet above ground and floored with smooth planks. A broad overhang from the roof afforded shade. The only furniture consisted of several movable benches.

The garments enveloping the stately, long-boned figures of the women, reminiscent of mid-Victorian modesty, were period costumes of arresting beauty. A Seminole dress consisted of an extremely full calico skirt, made of small, bright-colored pieces stitched together effectively. The skirt covered the feet. Above was a fichu-like black cotton cape, popular among Southern women in the Civil War period, its tightness emphasized by the width of a ruffle of the same brilliant pieces reaching to the waist at both back and front.

To make up for a lack of adornment on her hair, which was piled high in a knot on top of the head, an Indian woman wore graduated strings of heavy beads, fitting her neck like a stiff collar and extending as far as her shoulder blades.

After our introduction to these shy people, we were served a delicious supper of wild turkey stew mixed with buds of cabbage palmettos. Two Indians then guided us to our camp site, which was already prepared.

At sunrise all of us, with the exception of Laura and Winton, who departed for a series of clinics under the auspices of a white medicine woman, resumed the search for the panther who was destroying the Indians' hogs.

Soon we left the truck and tracked the animal on foot over parched prairie. Then for several hours we tramped through the same hammock in different directions, into swamps and bogs often in the kind of jungle called "thick-eye." No sunlight penetrated its depths, and unpleasant insects dropped on to our bare necks from branches above. If the supposed root of a tree on the surface of the ground moved, it was a moccasin.

Unexpectedly we found the panther's footprints near a pond quite close to the reservation. He had entered the adjacent jungle with the intention of making a second killing of Indian hogs at dawn. Finding fresh tracks at dusk always meant getting a panther in his overnight hideout, Dick said jubilantly. We would go back to camp, have a good hot meal, a few hours' sleep, and then return to the hunt.

None of the hardships encountered during the long day had reduced our high spirits. But on re-entering camp, I took in at a glance the fact that our modest baggage had been searched and the camp outfit generally was in confusion. Laura handed me a scrawled note. I read aloud: "You folks have until sunup to be off the reservation as undesired visitors—or else jail at Fort Meyers.—Superintendent."

It was Dick who found his speech. "This order must be obeyed," he said firmly, and as though to combat dissent. And he went on to say that publicity would be unfortunate for all concerned, particularly for the Indians, and might destroy Winton's usefulness among them. "And they need his friendship so much," he concluded with grave earnestness.

Dick's premise was unanswerable, and just as the sun rose, our cavalcade on wheels entered the agency grounds. The superintendent was seated on a porch. He neither rose nor took his feet from the rail. I thought he looked surprised as his eyes fell on Frances, Lois, and me in the first car with Dick, who returned his "Good morning." I did not.

Upon returning to Boca Grande after our ignominious expulsion from an Indian reservation, I marked time almost unconsciously for something even more sensational to happen. I was not really surprised, therefore, on hearing Winton's voice one day on the telephone, informing me that I was to be the first white woman to enter the Big Cypress Swamp, on the invitation of his friend José Billy, the chief of the Miccosukee tribe of Seminoles, as a protest against the government's treatment of guests of the Indians. I had been greatly interested by what Winton had already told me about this proud, independent, small tribe who, rather than make peace on terms dictated by the United States, had withdrawn from civilization.

The last day of March, we were again in Labelle to start off with the same guides and through the same country, but transformed during the previous month. A profusion of sweet-scented blossoms greeted us on a prairie carpeted with fresh grass, where frisky newborn calves and yearlings were playing. The Devil's Garden was a riot of color, with herons, white egrets, meadowlarks, and other song birds visible.

At a particularly desolate spot, Winton stopped the car as we sighted a thin column of smoke. This was the guiding signal for our entrance into the Big Cypress Swamp, where waiting Miccosukees had cut for us a narrow opening through the treacherous terrain. In time we emerged in a grove of palmettos. The flaming reds and yellows of exotic blooms contrasted with delicate shades of wild orchids, against the varied greens of high ferns and waving grasses.

Into this wonderland came a single Indian, wearing a one-piece cotton garment ending in a short skirt, colorful without being gay. A tall white egret feather adorning the top of his head added to his stature and dignity, and the perfect English in which I was welcomed to the Big Cypress Swamp by Chief José Billy, our Miccosukee host, somehow increased my sense of unreality in these surroundings.

Three Miccosukees named Charlie Cypress, Jim Tiger, and Ingram Billy stood near a cheering fire. A long line of quail on an improvised table were promptly turned by our Tommy into supper served on palmetto leaves. The Miccosukees had a self-reliance that inspired an instant respect and they were friendly without being aggressive. They took for granted something that was unusual among Indians—the forming of one group when eating.

356

While Winton was kept busy gratifying a natural curiosity about strangers, José and I had drawn slightly apart. He explained his English had been taught him at a white man's school, and on his rare trips among whites, he knew from their talk against Indians how bad they were. His response to my enthusiasm about the marvels of spring was to define the season poetically as a time for "renewal of the spirit." Soon I was mentioning having witnessed the annual revival of nature commemorated by a festival at the height of the June sowing of crops by races not white. This loosened his tongue, as it was intended to do, and he told me in some detail of the Miccosukee green-corn dance, held during the first week of June. "Tribal affairs are settled then for the year," he said. After a brief silence, he startled me by asking if I would like to learn a Miccosukee secret. At my nod of assent, he told me that the Miccosukee men, during the period they were assembled, talked for one period of twenty-four hours about Jesus Christ without stopping for food or drink.

"What do you do about him the rest of the time?" I asked with eager interest.

My blank look at his reply, "Nothing," caused him to question me. Did I know, he asked, any Christians who devoted twenty-four hours a year to talking about Jesus Christ?

In the early morning, we struck a trail that took us through sugar cane of a coarse red variety and brought us to a human power mill. Four young boys walked in a wide circle pushing on a pole, the grinding force required for this ingeniously contrived machine. With peals of merry laughter, a group of half-grown girls seated nearby were throwing ferns and sprigs into the boys' faces as they went round the grinder. When Winton got out of the car for a word with them, I followed, to watch the flow of liquid into a rough container carved out of a tree trunk.

Suddenly, becoming conscious of my presence, the girls crowded round me, one of them so close I felt her breath on my cheek as she talked excitedly to the others. With difficulty, Winton rescued me and explained her remarks. It seemed that once in a paper, which José Billy had brought from Miami, she saw a picture of a white woman wearing a beautiful trailing gown and jewels. But the picture lied, she declared, and it was they, the Indian girls, who had the beautiful dresses and jewels, and what a white woman wore was very ugly.

"It makes her happy," he said grinning.

In the days that followed, the Miccosukees and our party became fast friends, and as I found myself feeling more keenly our indebtedness to them, it occurred to me that a council or feast, given by us whites, might be in order. At first, when I proposed a barbecue to José Billy, the chief had misgivings. After a great feed, and after we were gone, there could only be discontent. But in the end he agreed to my proposal.

It turned out a jolly affair, and as the Miccosukees departed in little groups, carrying away with them all of the food they could conveniently bear, José Billy said for them, "We Miccosukee will never forget the woman with truth in her face, our name for you."

This farewell touched me, and it and the forced retreat from the reservation earlier stuck in my mind and ultimately set my purpose. I would make it my business to work in some capacity for Indian welfare, when my health and the necessary time would permit it.

When we returned to civilization at Labelle, we were greeted by Thomas A. Edison and Henry Ford, both of whom congratulated me for my "courage in risking my life among savages." Thus did Americans think of Indians a short forty years ago.

But my chance to help right the balance between those who first discovered America and those who followed after Columbus came rather swiftly. A few weeks later, at a dinner in Washington given by the undersecretary of State, I mentioned both my expulsion from the Florida reservation and my pleasant experiences with the forgotten and despoiled Miccosukees.

Next morning, I received a telephone call from the secretary of the Interior, whose office was responsible for Indian administration throughout the United States. He was commanding rather than inviting me to come and discuss with him the plight of the Miccosukees. After considerable discussion, the secretary expressed his intention to do something constructive for these self-reliant Americans. But when he did carry through in the ensuing months, I knew that, although I surely was not looking for a cause, the Indians of our country must ultimately become a major responsibility in my working career.

The winter of 1924 was the first of many visits in New Mexico, among the people of the pueblos and in isolated Spanish-American villages. These were a totally different people from the Seminoles of the Florida swamps, but they had these things in common with the latter: they knew the measure of friendship and they needed a protecting hand, quite independent of the government, if they were to achieve what they so justly deserved.

39

LONDON AND ENGLAND
REVISITED

As WE NEARED the close of our stay in New Mexico in 1924, Rebecca, who had been presented at Court the year before, when she and Joe had returned from Cambodia, wondered if it wouldn't be only fair for Frances to have the same experience in England. I was by this time ready for a renewal of the life I had known there, and we made the voyage shortly after returning to Boston.

At the enormous mansion of the Earl of Stafford, whose two daughters had visited us some time before in Boston, we early fell into the hubbub of the season and the conversation about the coming Derby and its likely winner. It was at luncheon, in fact, before we were to depart for the Derby. The Earl was complaining that an ancestor had gambled away the family fortune in the age of Charles I. At this point Lady Elizabeth, his daughter, urged that no one should go to the races without placing a bet. What was my choice of winner? I declared Salsovino the Smith choice, partly because he was the entry of Lord Derby. The fact that the house of Derby had not won in more than a century didn't help the odds, which were long in our favor.

"It's time a Lord Derby horse did win," Rebecca called down the table.

The words were scarcely out of her mouth when an odd-looking man invaded the dining room. Instantly, luncheon was interrupted as the entire household flocked to place bets.

The running of the Derby is a familiar picture by now, and there is no need of describing it. But I can never forget the sight of Salsovino thundering to the finish more than a length and a half ahead of his nearest challenger. The Smiths were among the few whose faces were smiling and happy as the great crowd left the race track that day.

The next morning, I was aroused from a sound slumber by a voice on the telephone saying, "This is Margot Asquith. Will you dine with me next Thursday at 8:30?"

"I don't know?" I replied sleepily.

"Anyone knows whether she can dine or not. Get out your engagement book," she retorted sharply.

I pulled myself together, paused a few moments, then said, "I'll be delighted."

Paul Cravath had written she was to be nice to me, and that's a command, she told me, thus enlightening me as to how she knew anything about me.

I was soon to discover that being on Lady Asquith's social list meant acceptance by a much publicized group in London known as the "Souls," noted for both originality and unconventional thinking, in which Beatrice and Sidney Webb had been leaders.

This first taste of a London society not restricted to the literary giants I had known was quite an experience. Lady Asquith's long, hard face and abrupt manner indicated a determination to have her own way, but there was about her an unquestioned fascination. At the table, in a company of twelve, she took the lead in a general conversation which was provokingly argumentative and brilliantly carried on in a light vein.

I sat next to Herbert Asquith who appeared to have resigned himself to a life of least resistance since his retirement from the political arena after having been prime minister at the beginning of the Great War. He struck me as rather pathetic: his face was an unhealthy red, his eyes tired, he had become stout and flabby, and his manner was listless.

He took no part in the general conversation and his talk with me was desultory. Several times I caught him staring at me, as though searching his memory. Suddenly he remarked abruptly, "We met long years ago at a garden party and I told you my ideals."

I was still pondering the meaning of his deep sigh when we ladies were signalled to leave the table.

I will always feel grateful to Margot Asquith for adding materially to my varied impressions by inviting me to drop in to lunch any week day on notification to the butler. I did so several times, to find about ten at the table, men, for the most part, and in the public eye.

It was an object lesson to me of the English mind in action to listen to a good-natured, quick-witted exchange of conflicting opinions representing opposed political parties.

Lady Cunard, the wife of the head of the Cunard Line, was a hostess of a very different calibre, but she had her following. She was a favorite of my friend Charles Coffin of General Electric and had responded generously to his request to give me a good time. She was lively and amusing but seemed rather volatile in character, and I could not understand Lord Balfour's presence at her parties, where the guests offered principally conversational chit-chat. He would appear, sit half an hour, talking with Lady Cunard alone, then slip away. The first time I saw him, he was about to depart, when I heard Lady Cunard say she wanted him to meet Mrs. Smith, a special friend.

I noticed how tall and stately Lord Balfour was as he dutifully sat down beside me. His personality was surcharged with intellect and a magnetic charm, almost contradicted by a cold eye. F. E. Smith, the Earl of Birkenhead, was later to describe him as a "rapier in an umbrella."

I mentioned Jacacci, a possible conversational link. Since on his recent Boston visit to us, he had seen quite a little of Andrew Mellon, the secretary of the Treasury, in Washington at the time of the Balfour Mission. Jacacci had been full of the subject after meeting Lord Balfour with Mellon. England had lent ten billion dollars to keep small nations in the war on the Allied side, and the mission had come to America to propose that our government assume a part of the indebtedness, in the form of long-term loans to the countries concerned, to be used towards the re-establishment of normal world trade.

Lord Balfour did remember Jacacci and referred to him as a man with an "instinctive wisdom."

His praise emboldened me to repeat Jacacci's account of Mellon's personal reaction to the purpose of the Mission. It was a sound solution, Mellon had said, according to Jacacci, but it would be dismissed without serious consideration by our government. This was exactly what happened.

Lord Balfour's expression of interest in my conversation was at once replaced by an obvious suspicion that I was attempting to draw him out on the subject of a mission that had failed. His relief was amusing when I tactfully said I had to leave.

A few evenings later I was included in a large dinner party given by a family my father knew well. To my amazement, the hostess said I was to sit next to Winston Churchill.

He was slim in those days, and without the inevitable cigar. I had met him casually and been taken to his studio, where I was able to judge for myself that his talent as an artist was far beyond amateur rating. His landscapes showed originality, brilliant handling of color, and a technique that at least approached Sargent's.

During dinner, when we were talking about art and Egypt, he casually mentioned he was to speak in Parliament the following morning on future world problems England would be called upon to face soon. "Nothing I'd like better than to be in the Visitor's Gallery!" I exclaimed impulsively, adding that, of course, obtaining a seat at this late date would be out of the question.

Whereupon Winston Churchill, promising to send me a seat, said modestly there would be only a few in the gallery to hear him. Furthermore, the vast majority of the members of Parliament, if present, would be relaxed, with their feet up, reading newspapers.

I could hardly believe my eyes when both prophecies were proved quite literally true at one of the epoch-making speeches of modern times. After this episode, I gave up trying to understand the English mind.

He would have to live much longer politically before overcoming the long public after-taste of the Dardanelles Campaign, for which he had been responsible in World War I, and the London docks strike before the war, which had been his undoing as home secretary.

It was very evident that the people did not regard royalty as merely a symbol of government. The spontaneous enthusiasm voiced in the streets at their sight in passing was from a firm conviction that King George V, his Queen and members of the royal family, belonged to them personally. Therein lay the strength of the British throne.

I was fortunate to be present at a royal garden party. Queen Mary was tall, with a superb figure, and her face, with classical features, was still beautiful. The King and Queen walked through the garden and then disappeared, leaving the Duke and Duchess of York to do the honors. Mrs. Bowes-Lyon, the mother of the Duchess, remembered me from our having been fellow house guests at the Antonio de Navarros at Broadway in 1920 and presented me to the Duchess.

Lord William Cecil, the King's chamberlain, joined us at a supper given by Lord Birkenhead, after Frances' presentation at Court.

It seems that in the instructions given her by Mrs. Kellogg, the wife of the American Ambassador, Frances was not told that when it came her turn to be presented she was to make a low curtsey and pass on. Therefore she had remained in her curtsey waiting to be recognized by the King. She had caught the King's eye, and he had smiled at her, which, according to Lord William, was a triumph.

In other places, as well as at the palace, the past was delightfully the present. For instance, at Grey's Inn among barristers. Also, see-

363

ing the city and the Tower of London under the auspices of Philip Burne Jones (who recalled my having met his father) was like turning the pages of early English history at random.

I touched many different circles of friends and acquaintances of my father's, as well as Joe's and mine, who formed a pleasant habit of dropping in.

One afternoon, reminiscences with several Egyptologists was interrupted by the appearance of Sir Almroth Wright, a scientist I had met in Paris through Dr. Harvey Cushing during the war.

He had with him Alexander Fleming, a younger scientist whom he insisted on bringing into the limelight. When Sir Almroth said he had come in the hope that I would go with them to his laboratory, I deserted the Egyptologists and went.

Sir Almroth discussed important contributions to research made in that laboratory, but I remember most vividly his saying that his younger colleague, Fleming, would eventually discover something new—which he did, in penicillin.

From science I jumped to law. I had known Lord Birkenhead when, as F. E. Smith, he was on an American lecture tour and Paul Cravath had motored him to Dublin. Also, Joe and I had visited Cravath on his Long Island place when Smith was his guest. Lord Birkenhead had brought to the position of Lord Chancellor of England an amazing brain, an unsurpassed wit, and an intellectual incisiveness which was the despair of his contemporaries. The legends he had built, and was to build, were legion in a country which unqualifiedly admired brilliance, joined with human attributes such as his—liquor and larks and high affairs, all rolled into one life—a life which began with the prosecution of Irish patriots in rebellion against England and was to end in his sudden death and bankruptcy.

Lady Birkenhead was charming and entertained delightfully, and their daughter Lady Eleanor became a friend of my girls. Under their roof I met some of the great legal minds of England, and also laughed more there than in any other English home. Lady Birkenhead told me her husband had just returned from a mission to Ireland, where his life had been in constant danger. It was only the Irish respect for his courage that had saved him from physical attack, she said.

364

It was Lord Birkenhead who reminded me seriously that Frances, having been born in London, must renounce her allegiance to the Crown, now that she was of age. He cut the red tape for her in a procedure that was rather complicated.

One afternoon when Lord Birkenhead dropped in on me at Claridge's, and the subject of the press came up, his opinions were as illuminating and decisive as his utterances on the law.

He shared my enthusiasm for Henry Wickham Steed, who became editor of the London *Times*, and whom Joe and I saw something of in Rome during the winter of 1903, when he was a correspondent. A few years later Steed arranged an interesting dinner in England where we met a small group of other high minded newspapermen. I described it to Lord Birkenhead as a notable occasion for an exchange of views, and that it had given me the comfortable feeling that public opinion would be safe when guided by such correspondents, who believed in ethics and responsibility in the handling of news.

Naturally, the Northcliffe Press and what it stood for came to mind in a strong contrast. The personal dislike he aroused in me on meeting him in Paris had been strengthened, I said, when, in 1922, in a temple at Bangkok, Northcliffe had scrawled his name across two pages of the visitors' book.

Lord Birkenhead had laughed but suggested that I must begin to accustom myself to a press which subscribed to lowered ethics and sensationalism. It was, he said, a trend that was here to stay.

I mentioned that my girls knew Lord Beaverbrook's son and daughter and that we had been invited to spend a weekend in the country with them. Whereupon he advised me not to miss the opportunity of meeting this Canadian who was a more and more powerful factor in the newspaper world. His only further comment was that Lord Beaverbrook had been an excellent minister of information during the war.

The large Beaverbrook estate was English countryside at its best. Lady Beaverbrook was lovely to look at and her height, which she tried to minimize by wearing shoes without heels and flat hats, made her husband's stature even more insignificant.

I thought that his attitude of mastery towards people and surroundings was the consequence of that tendency in short-statured people towards assertiveness. His face was shrewd, with a wary expression in small eyes.

We arrived at lunch time for an informal meal with several other guests. Hardly were we seated before Lord Beaverbrook ordered the butler to place a radio on the table. He mistook his wife's mild protest and turned it on still louder. Lady Beaverbrook's reaction when I decisively shut off the sound, saying that I preferred conversation, was a look of concern lest her husband should be discourteous to a guest. His reaction, on the contrary, was to tell the butler to remove the radio.

He seemed to respect me for the unexpected spirit I had shown, and during the rest of our stay he was a good deal with me. His presence kept me mentally stirred up.

He obviously was proud of both his wife and his children, and he indicated it in many ways, while they obviously were devoted to him. His magnetism and certainty of himself were great. He had moreover an ability to cause a casual remark to be news. I felt that even a simple statement, such as that a hen had crossed the road, would be dramatic.

It seemed to me that Beaverbrook would be a formidable opponent, and a compromise reached would certainly be on his terms. There was about him an originality and determination that made him a man to be reckoned with, as something new in the influence exerted by the press. Altogether, I found him an intriguing study at a number of later London meetings, arranged at his initiative. I have come to the conclusion in recent years that the old "press lords," exemplified by Beaverbrook, Northcliffe, and William Randolph Hearst, would find it somewhat more difficult to thrive nowadays. The media of public opinion are vastly greater, and the control which a single powerful newspaper publisher once could exercise now is dissipated—I might add, for the better. But it is difficult to avoid the conviction that powerful television networks may have assumed the same kind of domination.

40

POSTWAR FOCUS IN NEW YORK

By 1926 both Rebecca and Frances were eager to move to New York. Joe considered he could carry on his Boston Museum responsibilities from New York as headquarters and I was glad of the opportunity to live near my father.

The farewell Boston dinner given us has lingered in my memory. Brooks Adams was our host. In an amusing speech, he said it was inevitable that I, being a New Yorker, would eventually feel the urge to return. Then he recalled Joe's amazing adaptability, having been aptly described by Judge Robert Grant as "the best housebroken Bohemian who ever lived in Boston." He went on to say, "I'm positive Joe will compel New Yorkers to accept him on his terms, not theirs."

The role that New York was called upon to play just past the middle twenties was not unlike that thrust upon North America in relation to Europe in the post-Renaissance period. It was the focal point for what amounted to a world reorientation after the Great War. Anyone who has read Walter Prescott Webb's *The Great Frontier* will understand the implications I am suggesting.

The city had become the point of departure for men from overseas who were on important missions seeking financial aid, trade concessions, and, perhaps most important, certain diplomatic alignments for their own home countries.

And much stranger than all this, at least to Bostonians, whose literary and intellectual culture had been dominant for so long, New York was by now a receptive metropolis for experiments, offering a world of new art, not always understandable but new, a world of F. Scott Fitzgerald, George Gershwin, and Sinclair Lewis.

I saw the beginnings of new trends in the novel, in verse, and criticism, the latter most strongly represented by George Jean Nathan, H. L. Mencken, and Burton Rascoe, who were to point the way to American literary dominance in the nineteen-fifties. It is hardly necessary to evaluate the new music which captured the imagination of people everywhere, for it is still with us.

Between the rash post-war feeling of many that only the new was worth cultivating and Albert Guérard's temperate statement that "not everything in the past deserves to be loved," there was a middle ground which Joe and I could accept and be happy with. Perhaps history will find it acceptable too. It consisted in the frank realization that the New York of the period from the turn of the century to World War I had disappeared, if not without a trace, then certainly without promise of any future resurgence. We knew that the new values were speedily replacing the old, and those that deserved to be perpetuated probably would be.

Among the unacceptable new attitudes was the one universally referred to as the "disillusionment." Agnes Repplier, whom I knew well, described it a few years later (in 1937) in a now famous essay she wrote on Horace: "No word in our language has been so misused in the past nineteen years as the word disillusionment. . . . Men still are deeply resentful . . . that the world peace was not a highway to Utopia . . . every crime and every folly have been excused on this ground. . . ."

This phenomenon was at the core not only of the political and cultural mood of the era, but continued to have a profound effect upon American policy as a whole for the entire period from the close of World War I to the opening of new hostilities in 1939. It was anomalous in an America which, for perhaps the first time in a century, had found in its idealism a sure ground for national unity and an ambitious scheme for improving the lot of the entire world. But there it was. And there were political reasons for its deep-running quality among our people. They had begun as early as 1919 to see that the peace might be frittered away. And there was nothing in the ensuing eight years to disabuse them of the fear of this eventuality. Wilson's program had been lost. The Washington Naval Conference had been held—with already discernible results adverse, once more, to that idealism which was at once a virtue and a pitfall for America. Materialism, grown from individual acquisitiveness to a social disease, was everywhere. And, finally, there was Prohibition liquor!

Conversation concentrated on the steady rise in prices on the stock market, with shares feverishly changing hands. Prosperity was not just around the corner but here; it was expected to be permanent; and a spending orgy based on easy money was reflected in the social life of the city.

Psychologically it is difficult for me to make a necessary connection between disillusion and the rising materialism, but the two were clearly parallel developments.

The emphasis on liquor in entertainment shocked me. I had associated vintage wines with pleasant occasions when groups of friends gathered together for an exchange of ideas and had ideas worth exchanging. A drink played a dignified part but was not an end in itself, as it was at the all-pervasive cocktail hour. The alternative was "bathtub" gin or whisky of doubtful ancestry on the one hand, or being offered safe liquor secured from a hijacker with a Park Avenue address at a high price, on the other.

Ethics took a further downward plunge when, in a popular Broadway production, the sympathy of the audience was supposed to be directed to a bootlegger. His liquor had been stolen from him by a hijacker, the actual robbery taking place on the stage. My escort on this occasion was the assistant to New York's famous District Attorney Jerome, who in his day carried on a dramatic fight against crime.

I am reminded of former President William Howard Taft's views on the adoption of prohibition, conveyed to me when I sat next to him at a dinner in St. Louis. His words positively tumbled over one another. The fact that the law was "unenforceable" and individuals would "frankly evade it" was "overlooked in an emotional campaign to keep our returned soldier boys out of saloons." To disobey a law from a "personal decision that it was unreasonable" would prove to be a "dangerous precedent." Gradually, everyone at the table was listening, as, with a voice of authority, he went into prophetic details of the inevitable consequences, every one of which were to be realized.

It is quite impossible for a city as large and as sensitive to social change as New York is to escape a certain sharpening or hardening of the tendencies of an era. Joe felt a "cruelty" in New York towards those who could not, or did not wish to, adjust themselves to its now frantic pace. The world of New York tended to drop those who found themselves at odds with its tempo.

In his first reaction of withdrawal, he found relaxation in rambles far down town, poking about through crooked, narrow streets and alleys in districts containing what Al Smith called the "sidewalks of New York." It was exciting to come across an arch, a bit of a cornice, a doorway or column as part of a low building dating to a much earlier city, soon, alas, to be under an auctioneer's hammer, marked for destruction. These were details that no one would have the interest to preserve, save Joe, who paused to reproduce them with his brush.

Joe's nature was not one of withdrawal, and soon he was responding to the city's endless opportunities, within the grasp of every individual of initiative and intellect. He looked up friends among sculptors, artists, actors, and museum people, and was himself again. One of his impulsive decisions was to give a Smith party, of the kind Bostonians had liked. We consulted a New Yorker experienced in social matters about the proportion of acceptances to expect for a play in his studio at ten in the evening. An estimate of about a half being considered rather on the high side regulated our procedure for a floor space that, with a stage, would seat seventy-five comfortably.

The party was an unusual one in social New York: a play in a studio, invitations sent in verse, with answers requested also in verse, judges appointed in advance for the selection of the best replies, the winners to be read aloud to the audience, and prizes to follow. Royal Cortissoz was to be the chairman of the judges, and apparently the party was being "talked about." Next, I heard that some planned to bring dinner guests, but since no hostess had mentioned the fact to me, I discounted the rumor.

When the evening of the party arrived, it was soon obvious, in theatre parlance, that we were to have a capacity house—and then some! People poured in until every crevice was filled with hastily gathered chairs. Still the crowds came! There were rows of standees, and some guests were pushed out into the street, or took refuge in quarters next door. A rush order was put in for more food and drinks. The caterer afterwards declared he had served over two hundred, and I saw no reason to doubt his statement. Later, on expressing surprise that guests had been brought without advance warning to the hostess, I was told a studio was considered different from a house, and if word got about that a party would be good, people just turned up.

That first New York season Joe was frequently on the move, as were his museum-owned paintings, on loan exhibitions. His schedule included a small pageant in the West, lectures in several cities, and in February, 1927, he went down to Guatemala with Sylvanus G. Morley to paint for the Peabody Museum at Harvard.

We frequently went to Condé Nast's fabulous studio, where we met a good many intellectuals. Well-known personalities contributed to special occasions—Alexander Woollcott, who had recently won a large audience for himself, and Robert Benchley, writing for *Life*. Also Brooks Atkinson of the *New York Times* and John Mason Brown of the *Evening Post*.

At one of these entertainments I met H. L. Mencken for the first time. I liked his reference to my father as having a "mind not dated," as revealed in his ability to keep pace with the new literary genres, which bore no resemblance to the old. He demands a "purpose but does not insist on form," Mencken told me. He had been greatly impressed by a lecture my father gave on the subject.

Mencken and I became friends, and I enjoyed his mind in action, always searching for something different.

The Frederic R. Couderts' house was also a stimulating center of social life, with an emphasis on French guests. It was in their delightful library that I saw Joffre on his first trip to America. Surrounded by books, he seemed happily relaxed.

I next met him at an official dinner at Washington given in his

371

honor. Mrs. Crozier, the wife of the General William Crozier, who headed ordnance, was on one side of him. I was within earshot of him when she said, "General Joffre, in the final military analysis, what stopped the Germans at the Marne?"

He opened wide a pair of very blue eyes, evidently astonished that there might be any doubt on the subject, tapped his chest proudly, and replied, "I did!"

Frank Crowninshield made Joe a member of the Coffee House and also arranged for him the courtesies of the Players Club. Both included guest privileges for ladies, and we met writers, press editors, dramatic critics, and distinguished actors. Joe found much in common with both producers and actors, who accepted him as one of themselves. Some of the older producers who remembered his introduction of the dome lighting system to the American stage consulted him as a lighting expert.

Crowninshield gave us a few glimpses of the parties which have since been the trademark of the twenties. One evening centered around Tallulah Bankhead, whose energy, on and off the stage, was imitated by many but never equalled. Meeting her at close range, in action at a party, I found rather frightening. But what was even more unforgettable was the presence of Irving Berlin. He had with him some of the well-known singers of his topical songs. The resulting enthusiasm of the guests inspired one of them to improvise a parody of a rival composer. The evening ended with Ernest Schelling playing the piano by running two oranges over the keys. This exploit was followed by Joe, who picked up a guitar to accompany a song in pretended Chinese.

It was the era of Marc Connelly's *Green Pastures*, which appeared on the stage early in 1930. Joe and I, by chance, were with Marc immediately after the final dress rehearsal. He told us he knew he must intervene, soon after the start, since the acting was going from bad to worse. While he was groping for a means of handling the situation, the superb Negro, symbolizing the Divinity, raised his hand and broke into Joseph's lines. "Brethren and sisters," he said, "let us kneel and ask for divine guidance." He proceeded to lead the cast in prayer for about ten minutes. Then the rehearsal was re-

372

sumed and the acting "actually was inspired, as it had to be," according to Connelly.

The first notable break from the strongly entrenched, standardized productions of the London stage, with their increasing emphasis on magnificence, was introduced by H. Granville Barker, whom we had known. His stage settings created the mood for such plays as those by Euripides, Maeterlinck, and Yeats, and as manager he saw to it that the actors conformed to character, by losing their own personalities and conforming to the roles they were portraying.

Joe always responded enthusiastically to praise of Barker, but he insisted that America had Winthrop Ames. Ames had a special gift for recognizing potential talent, often with complete disregard for previous parts taken by actors. This was noticeably true in his choice of Leslie Howard for the lead in John Galsworthy's *Escape*. Joe had renewed a former Boston intimacy with Ames connected with theatricals, and was always welcome in his New York theatre, as an observer of his production methods. He watched several rehearsals done by Howard alone, as the escaped prisoner, when Ames's suggestions brought out an unknown power in his range of acting.

William Gillette's appearances in New York were always a treat. A critic once said of his acting that he could dramatize a postage stamp.

Through Paul Cravath, as president of the Metropolitan Opera, Joe and I knew the Opera Guild at its start. It was established by the creative civic genius of Mrs. August Belmont, who, before her marriage as Eleanor Robeson, had been one of the most popular of theatre stars. The purpose of the guild was to help meet the enormous annual deficit of the Metropolitan. Its continuance today is a monument to Mrs. Belmont's efforts.

Joe always enjoyed himself when Royal Cortissoz dropped in for a late afternoon chat. He was a witty and brilliant conversationalist, steeped in the meaning of art as Joe knew it. The fact that Joe had known St. Gaudens well, and had seen John La Farge a number of times in his Newport studio, generally with Sargent, made for a close bond between him and Cortissoz, who had written lives of both men.

373

Barry Faulkner's visits were in this same refreshing category. He was a popular painter of murals in public buildings, notable for his designs and colors. Although his own work was not dated, in general he shared Cortissoz' and Joe's view of art.

A real art treat lay in the nearby Manship studio on 72nd Street. Eric Gugler alone among architects could have created an adequate background for the personalities of Paul Manship and his incomparable wife Isabel. The studio was built on the ground level and opened into a charming garden. The living quarters on the second floor were notable architecturally. People of artistic taste, society as such, and fellow sculptors and painters flocked to the Manship studio, where guests were surrounded by Paul's sculpture in every stage of completion. The first informal showing of Joe's paintings on his return from abroad was in the Manship studio, and in New York was the counterpart of what Sargent had done for Joe in London.

The late 1920's proved an eventful period for other members of the Smith family. Early in January, 1927, Rebecca had her first New York exhibition at the Feragil Gallery. It consisted of portrait heads done in pencil or sangrene crayon. In addition to those lent by owners, she had some heads of models for sale. The show got off to a good start when Royal Cortissoz wrote a very favorable review and Sir Joseph Duveen bought two heads of models.

Rebecca had already had a London exhibition of Indians in the spring of 1925. That winter, she had been with me in New Mexico, and it was during a short trip abroad, before Joe's and Frances' return from a painting trip to Egypt, that the exhibition took place. It was arranged through Lady Cunard, who brought the head of the Guypil Gallery to an informal showing of Rebecca's Indian paintings at Claridge's. There was an immediate offer of an exhibition from the Guypil Gallery, but proper advertising for it was out of the question, because of time.

Rebecca solved that problem by having sandwich men carry notices of the exhibition at the entrance to Lords at the time of the Eton-Harrow cricket match, which was attended by all social London.

Lord Allenby, who remembered meeting Rebecca in Egypt, was among the first visitors. And it enhanced the success of the exhibition

374

to have Sir Joseph Duveen buy one of the Indians for the Huntington Library in Pasadena.

I felt very proud of Rebecca's and Frances' artistic careers as girls. Both had Egyptian paintings with their father's collection in the Boston Museum. The Guimet Museum in Paris owned one of Rebecca's Ankhor Wat pictures, as well as Joe's.

It was in February, 1927, that I shared an experience with my father. Logan Hay, the president of the Abraham Lincoln Society, had invited him to stay at his house at Springfield, Illinois, and be the speaker at the banquet on the anniversary of Lincoln's birth.

The evening of the banquet, my father and I followed Hay to a raised platform in a hall where about three hundred guests were already seated. When the meal was finished, Hay rose and asked anyone who had seen Lincoln to stand. Four tottering old women, the strings of their small bonnets tied under their chins, and two even feebler men struggled to their feet. Once up, each took a firm grip on the back of his chair. Hay's "Thank you" and a kindly caution to take their time in reseating themselves proved far more dramatic than an attempt at identification.

There was a buzz of excitement when, upon being introduced, my father told the audience that as a boy of sixteen he had heard Lincoln's address given at the Cooper Union, New York, on February 27, 1860.

George Palmer Putnam, his father, a Whig, had collaborated with William Cullen Bryant, a free-soil Democrat, in planning that historic meeting, called for the purpose of finding a leader for a new political party, whom they believed they had discovered in Abraham Lincoln.

Father referred to the significance of the Lincoln-Douglas debates in the 1858 election campaign for U.S. senator from Illinois. Apparently Lincoln's adversary had every advantage. Stephen A. Douglas, the "little giant," was a popular figure in both his state and the nation, having already served two terms as senator, whereas Lincoln, despite a term in Congress and his great speech at Peoria four years before, was not yet a national leader and did not have a firm grip on the electorate of Illinois.

But Lincoln's rare knowledge of constitutional law, quick wit, logic, and shrewdness never let Douglas get away with generalities. Above all, he was inspired by a sense of human rights and divine justice.

These were the qualities, Father said, that got Douglas into a fix, because his replies to questions adroitly put satisfied neither the northern nor the southern Democrats. Although Douglas won the senate post, Lincoln was marked for future national leadership.

My eyes had been on a very old man seated directly facing me on the floor level. He was completely bald and his head shook slightly as he held his right hand cupped over his ear, his gaze never leaving my father's face. At these words about Douglas, he created an interruption by getting up and saying, "I was a cub reporter on the *Independent* at the time of the debates. The speaker of the evening has convinced me that both the paper and I were wrong in having believed Douglas was better than Abe."

When my father's voice could be heard above the hubbub, he said laughingly that he felt he had been justified in his evaluation of the two men.

I cannot be sure, but I should guess that this was one of the last occasions when men of mature memory could recall Abraham Lincoln in action.

To the New York of my readoption, I am indebted for the opportunity it gave me to know a great scientist, Dr. Alexis Carrel, winner of a Nobel prize in medicine and physiology and a member from 1912 to 1939 of the Rockefeller Institute for Medical Research. He would invite me to his laboratory, where he was conducting research on digestion. He was giving the same diet to three generations of mice. He knew them all by name and pointed out to me their different characteristics.

Several years later, when Joe and I were about to go abroad, Dr. Carrel telephoned before sailing time, requesting me to stay where I was because he needed me for at least three hours. On his arrival at our apartment, he produced the manuscript of *Man, the Unknown*. He explained that it was ready for the printer and that he wanted my opinion of the text. Reading parts of it aloud, he paused frequently to question me about scientific statements. I felt flattered until he told me that he wished to find out whether his premises and conclusions would be understood by a layman of average intelligence. Satisfied, he said, "They will," and took his departure.

When we did not have to be overseas on Joe's various commissions, we had the opportunity to renew an old friendship with General Pershing. He visited us twice at Dublin, and I, accompanied by my Aunt Fanny Putnam, was his guest several times at his Chevy Chase residence near Washington. On my first visit, he gave me a bound copy of his report on the war in France, inscribing it, "To Mrs. Joseph Lindon Smith with cordial esteem and high regards. Also with vivid recollections of her splendid services among us soldiers during the World War. Sincerely. — John J. Pershing."

During World War II, I saw General Pershing at Walter Reed Hospital, where he lived the final years of his life. On one of several occasions when General George C. Marshall came in, General Pershing referred to the years when, after his retirement, he was in charge of the American military cemeteries in France. He said that, on his last trip, he had been shocked by the commercialism which had crept into the administration of the cemeteries. He had detailed Colonel Dwight D. Eisenhower to go to France to restore dignity to these resting places. This Eisenhower had accomplished effectively and without unpleasant publicity.

Both generals had considered Eisenhower extremely promising as a colonel because of his unusual ability in conducting maneuvers, and had urged his appointment as commander-in-chief in World War II.

But to return to the chronology of the late 1920's, the first of the weddings of our children occurred in May, 1927, when Rebecca married William Ambrose Taylor, Jr., a nephew of Mrs. Edward S. Harkness. In January, 1928, Frances married Raymond Otis, the son of Joseph E. Otis of Chicago. Both weddings were in New York.

Notwithstanding the financial panic of November, 1929, Rebecca, by now an established young New York matron, planned a party in Lois's honor which may have made her the most talked about debutante of the season. It was a large affair built around the idea of "gobble and go," with a number of groups criss-crossing across town to the various restaurants and night spots. When it was over, the *New York Times* society and news columns had reported it rather fully. Other newspapers and magazines picked it up, and some months later we even saw it in the *Egyptian Gazette* in Cairo.

Early in January, 1930, Joe and I were on our way to Egypt. We had barely arrived at Harvard Camp, where he was to paint, when I received a cable from my stepmother saying that my father was seriously ill and constantly asked for me. I returned home at once.

My father's final illness was in character with his entire life. At my stepmother's request, I attended to his mail, which comprised correspondence with a number of civic enterprises in which he was still active. He was also president of the Copyright League, which retained a lawyer in Washington to look after copyright matters in Congress.

A delayed letter to my father from the lawyer for the Copyright League stated that a dangerous clause had been introduced as a rider to the appropriations bill, which was to be acted upon by the House the following morning at eleven o'clock. Time, therefore, was a factor, and I had only the lawyer's office address.

By this time my father was alarmingly ill. When I approached him with the letter in my hand, he was seated with his head slumped forward and his eyes closed. But as I briefly stated the copyright crisis, he rallied and dictated to me a clear memorandum of instructions. Four hours later he was in a final coma and died during the night of February 27.

By nine the next morning, I telephoned to the lawyer the contents of the memorandum, which he used at the Congressional hearing. The pernicious clause was defeated.

The final family wedding in New York, that of Lois to John J. Schieffelin, took place in March of the crucial 1932 election year.

After Franklin Delano Roosevelt was sworn in as president on March 4, 1933, his declared bank holiday was the first of remedial measures with which he met the business crisis which had steadily grown worse since the stock market crash of 1929.

Not soon afterwards I dined with Robert Lamont, Secretary of

378

Commerce in the Hoover administration. He dismissed as an interlude the principles of government initiated by President Roosevelt.

The John D. Rockefellers, Jr., were far truer prophets of the future. They adjusted themselves speedily to new conditions, in which the staffing of an immense establishment would not be possible. They were the first prominent New Yorkers to move into an apartment. Society generally began to follow suit. A mushroom growth of large apartment houses sprang up on streets and avenues formerly made attractive by open space and well-landscaped mansions.

The Smiths were considered peculiar for not availing themselves of the prevalent buying on installment, financed by bank loans. We paid cash or went without. We were glad we had rented instead of owning our apartment for there were many casualties among those who owned.

Movers packed our furniture into a huge van and Joe fitted his carefully protected antiquities among our other belongings. I gave one final glance around the empty rooms, which symbolized the end of the New York saga. Then I got into the car with Joe, followed by our faithful retainers, and Sidney, our chauffeur, at the wheel, led the van on the long trek to Dublin.

41

EGYPT AND ARABIA

FROM REISNER'S OFFICE

George A. Reisner was the head of the joint expedition of the Boston Museum and Harvard University located at the pyramids of Giza in Egypt and known as Harvard Camp. Between the years 1928 and 1939 I was with Joe on his annual trips to this center of archaeological activity. While he painted in the ancient tombs and temples, I stayed with Reisner in his office. To offset his steadily failing eyesight, Reisner's work and writing were aided by Evelyn Perkins, his devoted secretary.

It was amazing how Reisner managed to conduct archaeologists and special visitors over a dig. He was so thoroughly familiar with his excavations that, from memory, he could interpret the significance of the scenes depicted on the walls of the tombs. My function was to guide his steps over the rough approaches to temple or tomb enclosures. I was with him when he took a Greek archaeologist to see the Sphinx. At the expense of romance and mystery, which had persisted since remote antiquity, Reisner said he had solved the riddle of the weather-beaten face appearing on the crest of a rocky ledge above a mass of yellow sand. His excavations had disclosed below the face an outstretched massive lion body and awkward paws. A discovery of Reisner's at the pyramid Temple of Mycerinus furnished the clue which identified the Sphinx as a portrait head of Cephren, the son of Cheops, and a part of his funerary complex.

Reisner enjoyed having Clinton Crane, a leading American engineer, examine with him the construction of the great pyramid of Cheops. Crane studied carefully the enormous smooth blocks of stone, evenly fitted together without mortar. Reisner explained to him that granite blocks from the Mokattam Hill quarries reached successive levels by being dragged up sandbanks set against an inner core of rough stone. When all were in place, the edges that jutted out were smoothed from the top down. Crane and I crawled inside the pyramid, where the construction was even more remarkable, and Reisner showed us the simple tools the Egyptians had used. "It couldn't have been done," said Crane.

Reisner had the great gift of being able to interest himself in the present as well as in the past of Egypt. Since he and Joe were professionally occupied with archaeology and I was not, I found his insights into Near and Middle Eastern life and politics very interesting and valuable.

With Russell Pasha, the commandant of the Cairo police, he was able to reflect the basic human failures which had beset the Egyptian economy at both the ancient and the modern poles. In the period of

Cheops (beginning 2656 B.C.), for three generations agricultural labor was drained in order to build monuments to members of the royal family. In the decade after 1928, as Russell Pasha witnessed it, the comparable economic failure of the country could be traced to the opium traffic. In both cases, the result was something approaching national economic collapse.

Reisner had given me a very good background for an understanding of the Arab lands when Joe, in early December, 1928, decided to cut short his working season in Egypt and go on an expedition to paint the rock-cut temple of Petra in an isolated part of Trans-Jordan. I welcomed the opportunity to go along.

Russell Pasha had arranged with Peake Pasha, the British head of the Arab Legion, to have a visitor's camp at Petra which closed because of disturbances among tribesmen reopened and placed at our disposal, with a guard from the Arab Legion for our protection. He also arranged for a Sheikh Isa to look after us. The Sheikh spoke English as well as the dialects of many tribes.

Reisner, before our departure, was enthusiastic about our being the guests of the Arab Legion, and even more so at the prospect of my meeting Ibn Saud, on an introduction given me by Charles R. Crane, who was a friend of my father's.

Sheikh Isa met our train at the Jerusalem station. He was stout and middle-aged, and had a quiet dignity. He wore European clothes, except for a native headdress, and I noticed he carried a Koran on his person.

We changed more than countries when we passed in a car over the frontier of Palestine into Amman, the seat of the Arab government of Trans-Jordan under a British mandate. Here Peake Pasha welcomed us. His dashing manner and strong, handsome face gave him the outward characteristics that a romantic hero should have. Thanks to Peake Pasha, we made the all-day train journey to Ma'an, the station for Petra, with the prime minister of Trans-Jordan in his private car. He held the train to greet two thousand tribesmen who were assembled in his honor. The Minister kept Joe and me at his side while he spoke to the head of each tribe. He told them through Sheikh Isa as interpreter that we were friends of Peake Pasha, who expected to see us in Amman after three weeks. Later Sheikh Isa explained the tribesmen knew that the Prime Minister meant *alive*. "News travels fast in the desert," he said.

The riding part of the trip, made under the escort of four Arab legionnaires who were to remain with us, ended in a narrow gorge hemmed in by high peaks. Soon we had reached a temple, which, like Abu Simbel in Egypt, was rock-hewn in the side of a cliff. But here at Petra the stone was rose colored.

This was the fabled temple known as *el-Khuzneh* (the Treasury), built at the time of the Emperor Hadrian, when Petra was on a main caravan route, later to be by-passed in favor of Palmyra. The façade, with alcoves and columns of Graeco-Roman character, came up to Joe's highest expectations as an artist.

Every afternoon, after Joe had finished painting, we entertained. Our guests consisted of tribesmen who dropped down from steep mountain slopes. They also emerged from caves dotted over the face of nearby cliffs, once lived in by the Edomites, who were supposed to be the earliest inhabitants of Petra.

After we left Petra, we had the novel experience of being for five days guests of the British Air Force at headquarters high above Amman. This was a return courtesy to us for entertaining the commandant and others of the force at Petra, when they were salvaging one of their planes after it had crashed in a nearby valley.

Members of the British Air Force were unanimous in telling me that Lawrence of Arabia had greatly overestimated the strength of Hussain, and had not realized that Ibn Saud was the master-mind among the Arabs of Arabia. All spoke of Ibn Saud with awe and respect and believed that his political leadership as Caliph of Islam would bring a sorely needed solidarity not only to Arabia, but be a factor towards peace among Moslems in other countries.

I looked forward to meeting this man, whose power Reisner had described to me before we left Egypt for Petra. The alignment in the Moslem countries had been fundamentally disturbed by World War I, and most particularly the power and influence of two peoples whose outlook expressed fundamentally different philosophies of government. In Turkey, which before the war had been dominant in the Near and Middle East, the post-war drift had been towards democratic concepts and ideals, looking towards the West. In Arabia, on the other hand, the attempt was being made to adapt tradition and the strength of Islam to modern civilization.

As a result of Abdul Hamid's success in stirring up Moslem fanatics to kill Young Turks, an army led by Mustapha Kemal took over the government of Turkey in 1908. Abdul Hamid was deposed by a *fetwa* of the Sacred Court of Islam and a younger brother became Sultan Caliph as Mejid II.

In the fall of 1923 Mustapha Kemal summoned a constitutional assembly, which elected him first president of the Turkish Republic. He took the name of Ataturk and Constantinople became Istanbul. In 1928, it was no longer a question of putting an end to the Turkish Caliphate, which was already dead, but of abolishing Islam as the state religion of the republic. This was the issue which faced Ataturk among his own people.

The political situation in Arabia had been influenced in quite another direction. When Turkey's protection of the sacred cities of the Hedjaz, Mecca and Madina, was challenged by the advance of the British armies in 1916, Hussain, the shereef of Mecca, acting on the advice of T. E. Lawrence, went over to the Allied cause. Consequently, in the redistribution of territory formerly controlled by the Turks, Hussain remained shereef, and his son Feisal was established in the newly made kingdom of Iraq, while other sons became the rulers of Trans-Jordan and Syria.

Meanwhile, a Moslem leader had arisen in the hills of Saudi Arabia in the person of Abdul Aziz Ibn Saud. His initial success had begun as early as 1902, in the renewal of the old-time influence of the Wahhabi, fierce tribesmen fanatically dedicated to the precepts of primitive Islam. Ibn Saud formed these desert warriors into an *ikhwan* (brotherhood), maintained a strict discipline among them, and attempted to bring his dependencies economically up-to-date.

By 1924, Hussain's political strength as king of the Hedjaz had greatly lessened, and Ibn Saud, without warning, took possession of Mecca and Madina. The foreign powers did not intervene, and Hussain gave up the Hedjaz without a struggle and disappeared.

383

By 1928, the Arab Federation was making front-page headlines in the Arabic press of Cairo and Alexandria. Articles gave picturesque accounts of Ibn Saud, who was described as a great Moslem, descended, like the Prophet of Islam, from the tribe of the Koraish, and, also like the Prophet, gradually uniting all Arabia. It was intimated that Ibn Saud was favorably regarded as a candidate for Caliph of Islam, even in some of the conservative circles of the el-Azhar University at Cairo.

When Ibn Saud received us, he stood alone in a rather small room. Even without the Bedouin garment and the *kaftan* which fell over his shoulders, his desert origin would have been obvious. It showed in every line of his body, in the deep lines of his heavily bearded face, and in eyes that were far seeing and shadowed from constant exposure to the sun. I sensed his magnetism as he bent far down from his great height to meet my direct gaze.

Because of Charles Crane's recommendation, Ibn Saud welcomed us as friends. He spoke of an impasse reached in transacting business by his Wahhabi, who cut the wires each time he had a telephone installed in his office, claiming it was the voice of the *shaitan* (devil) coming over the wire. Exasperated, he finally summoned leaders among them to hear the words they were accustomed to hear in the mosque, but coming from a loud-speaker. "The Koran!" they exclaimed. Ibn Saud had asked them whether the *shaitan* could repeat sacred words. All of them said he could not. After this, his Wahhabi came to the office with their religious sheikhs to listen to the Koran.

The communal bowl was brought in and we seated ourselves on cushions placed around it on the floor. Before breaking bread, Ibn Saud performed the Moslem ritual of repeating the *fatah* in the loudest voice imaginable. I joined in, and his comment on the amount of sound I made was that "It is surprising Allah has given you, a Christian, so big a voice in so small a body." Then he honored me by producing from among the substances in the communal bowl a sheep's eye. "Because we have repeated the Koran together," he said.

With the assistance of Sheikh Isa, I was able to live up to my end of a conversation in Arabic. Ibn Saud was obviously pleased when I

384

told him of Peake Pasha's having said that Ibn Saud was modifying the ideas of his intractable Wahhabi warriors to fit into modern life, while he himself was building up a strength and cohesion throughout Arabia.

He responded to the Prime Minister's statement to me that Ibn Saud as Caliph would respect the territory of the present Hashemite rulers by saying earnestly, "That should be a conclusive argument in the decision."

He expressed gratification at our friendly interest in the desert tribes surrounding Petra, and listened attentively to an incident I told him connected with three half-starved Bedouins accused of being camel thieves. Two of our legionnaires brought them into camp for food before they were handed over to the owner of the camels for the "Koran test" in the nearest Mosque.

Ibn Saud's comment was that even an ignorant Moslem would tell the truth with his hand on the Koran. "There is no political substitute for Islam," he declared, with fire in his eye.

But he thoroughly disapproved of the amount of food we had given the tribesmen. "They will have only the memory of mutton to live on," he said sadly.

We had been with him almost two hours when voices outside the building seemed like delegations waiting for him to appear. But Ibn Saud began now to talk more as though he were thinking aloud than addressing me.

He talked of the poverty of Arabs living in the relentless desert of sweeping sands, inured to untold hardships since childhood, scantily clad, with insufficient food, seeing children die of starvation, women old before their time. Their only comfort was the thought of what Allah, in their daily communion with him, promised them in Paradise—abundant food, rivers flowing with milk and honey, and wives who would remain perpetually young.

He found a new hope in the rumored expectations of finding oil deposits in the barren wastes occupied by some of his followers. With money from oil, Ibn Saud said, his Arabs would not have to wait until eternity for the good things of life which other people, mostly those in the West, were enjoying. His eyes had become burning

385

coals of fire as though he was seeing a vision. His voice ceased abruptly. He rose. We did the same. The interview was at an end.

In 1933 an American oil company struck oil in Ibn Saud's territory. Six years later, when rich deposits were being developed, I saw Ibn Saud in Egypt. The oil company was improving the living conditions of the desert tribesmen within its oil concession. But Ibn Saud had lost his vision. Had he been elected Caliph of Islam, he might have withstood the temptation of luxurious living and shared his great wealth with his fellow Arabs. But in this he had failed.

42

ATATURK'S TURKEY

IMMEDIATELY AFTER CHRISTMAS, 1931, when Joe had put in two months of painting at Giza, he decided to visit the excavations at Ur of the Chaldees being carried on by Leonard C. Woolley. He wanted also to accept an invitation from Nicholas Roosevelt, our recently appointed Minister to Hungary, to stay with him in Budapest. After the stopover in Turkey, he planned to see the Persian exhibition in London. Reisner was again enthusiastic at the opportunity offered for me to get an idea about what kind of dictator Ataturk was.

At a Cairo dinner given soon after our return to Harvard Camp in the fall of 1930, I had sat next to Prince Mehemet Ali, the heir to the throne of Egypt until the birth of Prince Farouk. He talked to me about a recent trip he had made to Turkey. He spoke of Ataturk as a great fighter in repelling the British attack against the Turkish positions at Gallipoli. He also spoke of Ataturk's success in preventing the Allies from driving the Young Turks from the peninsula of Anatolia.

After the defeat of Greek armies in Asia Minor, and following the exchange of Greek and Turkish nationalists there, Turkey had the advantage of a homogeneous population in Asia Minor, it held a small slice of Europe (Thrace); and occupied the immediate vicinity of Constantinople. Ataturk was now in a position to create a new Turkey, different in every particular from that of the Ottoman Empire, which had been regarded by the European powers as territory to be divided among themselves.

Ataturk was an avowed agnostic, and the Young Turks in power with him were violently antagonistic to Islam. Therefore, Ataturk decided to end recognition of the religion which had guided the thoughts, actions, and form of government of the people of Turkey for the past twelve hundred years, as incompatible with the progress of a new Turkish state he was creating with his eyes to the West. "How effectively," Prince Mehemet Ali said, "you will be able to judge for yourself from introductions I am giving you."

But our first destination was Ur, to which we proceeded by a variety of means after we left Harvard Camp. There Leonard Woolley's vivid imagination recreated for us, out of the extant crumbling mud-brick ruins the glories that had once been Ur of the Chaldees. After that we had a few days in Baghdad, as the guests of Reisner's old friend, Paul Knabenschuhe, whose consular post and excellent linguistic accomplishments made him an invaluable interpreter of the Moslem world. His apprehensions concerned the pervasive poverty and exploitation of Near Eastern populations, ruled by kings without vision.

From the patriarch of the Assyrians, we heard the story of twenty thousand panic-stricken Assyrians fleeing the Turkish armies advancing into their homeland. They had caught up with British troops who did what they could to care for the sick and the old and provide all the refugees with food they could hardly spare themselves.

The most interesting personality I met was Nuri as-Saad, the prime minister of Iraq. He was reputed to be a practical leader who had sought to reconcile the passionate idealism of the Arab awakening with the hard facts of economic and political survival in a world of greater powers. He expressed the belief that peace in the New East would continue as long as there was a popular hero like Peake

Pasha at the head of the Arab Legion, and British officers in the Frontier Force.

On our departure from Baghdad, we looked forward to revisiting Istanbul. The old wooden structure of the Galata Bridge had been replaced by one of steel and concrete, and in the streets over modern buildings were the names of firms known in European cities.

Joe and I went at once to Sancta Sofia, in a confident search for something familiar, but nowhere else could I have obtained a more instant realization of an entirely different Turkey than the one I had seen thirty years before. Gone from the great entrance court were the turbaned scribes in long flowing robes, squatted on the ground, writing with narrow quill pens. In their place were smartly dressed, Europeanized, unveiled young Turkish women, seated at tables, clicking away on typewriters for those who came to them with business to transact. Inside Sancta Sofia, the change was even more startling. The imposing platform, where the Sultan, as Caliph, led prayers, still remained. It was meaningless, however, with the beautiful stations of the first four successors to Muhammad dislodged and turned backside.

The noise and confusion, caused by workmen rushing about obeying orders, had replaced the sonorous intoning of the Koran reverberating through the columns. In accordance with the interdict of Islam against portraying an image of Allah, angel, or man, a thin coating of colored plaster had covered, and thereby preserved, Byzantine mosaics through the centuries. Now, in what Thomas Whittemore had liked to refer to as a "litany of light," Christian murals of saints and angels emerged over vast expanses of wall.

I had kept in touch with the emancipation of women movement in Turkey through correspondence with Leyla, Hamdy Bey's daughter, who became a part of it. I had also met Turkish feminists, who from time to time had visited Egypt, where the women were not yet active in an organized effort of the kind. Most important of all, I had seen outside of Turkey Madame Halide Edib and followed the principal role she had played in furthering the revolution by active participation with the party of Ataturk in the early days of his political power.

Being with Joseph C. Grew, our American ambassador, gave us an opportunity to evaluate the fast-moving events in Ataturk's Turkey, from the non-Moslem point of view. The more he discussed various phases of Ataturk's meteoric career, the more I found their counterparts in Akhenaten's. The resemblance was indeed striking. He, like the Egyptian king who lived some three thousand years earlier, had made no attempt to hold on to a crumbling empire. Both had changed their names and capitals, and had created from barren wastelands new cities notable for their beauty.

Akhenaten had gone back to a precedent established in the pyramid age and lost under later Pharoahs. In statues Nefertete, his queen, was seated beside him and was of equal size. Ataturk had encouraged emancipation of women, made use of their leadership to aid his political fortunes, and recently had given them the right not only to vote but to hold municipal office.

Their greatest similarity was in action against religious tradition: Akhenaten, in doing away with an entrenched priesthood, which was succeeding in combining the authority of church and state; Ataturk, in his successful struggle with the *ulema* representing the political power of religion over the government, with a sultan who was also caliph of Islam.

In one important particular, there was a complete contrast between the two. Akhenaten was a pacifist. Ataturk, on the other hand, was a military genius who had achieved his position by force of arms.

The fact that Ataturk was of Anatolian peasant stock doubtless influenced his choice of Ankara for the capital. A further advantage was that the vast majority of the National Assembly, over which he presided, were, like himself, Anatolians. I learned that the Young Turks who surrounded Ataturk in key positions were "attuned to the goal he set, to have Turkey let alone to work out its own destiny."

Ataturk had assumed personal responsibility for stamping out illiteracy and in an educational campaign he replaced Arabic with the international Latin script. To ensure a complete break with Moslem tradition, he abolished the *sharia*, God-made law, and adopted a code resembling that of Switzerland. And he discarded the Moslem lunar calendar, based on the *Hegira* (flight of the Prophet from Mecca).

Ataturk also emphasized the need for culture and encouraged its development with the creation of additional museums. The Turks were never a creative people and their art was unimpressive. Joe visited museums of the new regime with the director who had replaced Hamdy Bey at his death. He described as rather pathetic the discovery that Ataturk's enthusiasm for stressing Turkish art had resulted in instructions to have some splendid early Persian examples relabeled Turkish.

I asked a number of well-informed Turkish women whether they believed the *sharshaf* (native dress) and heavy black face veil had disappeared for good. The general opinion expressed was, that when the peasants from nearby country districts began to get about more, the streets would begin to look like those of former days. As one lively old Turkish lady put it emphatically, "Tradition cannot be banished by legislation, only by a *fetwa* of the sacred court of Islam, and that no longer exists."

One particularly intelligent woman who had co-operated closely with Madame Edib helped me in many ways, primarily by introducing me to a scholarly Turk who had been employed by the government to translate the Koran into Turkish. During our brief stay in Istanbul members of the diplomatic corps constantly reiterated that official recognition of Islam had ended and that Sancta Sofia was in process of becoming a museum.

Prince Mehemet Ali's choice of a Turk to show me Islam in action in Istanbul proved to be a highly educated man, capable of speaking both French and English. A serenity about him suggested a religious mystic. His introductory remark was, "I am fortunate. Ataturk trusts me even though I am a devout Moslem." I soon discovered he was well versed in classical Arabic and in the traditional literature of Islam.

In the few days available, he took me to fifty out of the two hundred odd mosques in Istanbul. We visited important mosques in the heart of the business center, unpretentious ones in out-of-the-way districts inhabited by poverty-stricken people, and a number that were between these two extremes.

This gave me an excellent cross-section. Each experience was different, yet retaining two fundamentals. There was a general sad need of repairs, since Ataturk permitted no government expenditures for the upkeep of religious buildings. And all the Turks I saw in mosques were in communion with Allah. They took no notice of my presence, and after praying, departed, in silent reverence, to go their various ways.

To wear a fez was a prison offense. Islam required a Moslem to keep his head covered while praying, but the bare forehead must touch the ground in frequent prostrations. Turkish Moslems obeyed Ataturk's edict to wear a visor cap in public, but accomplished the double purpose of the forbidden fez by turning the cap around during prayers.

Ataturk accepted no compromise with religion. He believed that, to fit his people to hold their own in the modern world, the past must bow to authority legally vested in him. He offered his people education and a better standard of living as a substitute for tradition. The business center of Istanbul had been remodeled. In the poor districts, school buildings had been erected, homes improved, and even attempts at hygiene made. Mosques were falling apart from the normal processes of neglect, not by wanton destruction.

Ataturk's adherence to the concept of the rights of the individual argued well for Turkey's contribution, under his leadership, to peace in the Near East. But whether Turkey could succeed by ignoring the strength of Islam among its Moslem citizens was, to me, an unanswered question.

43

FINAL YEARS
AT HARVARD CAMP

ALTHOUGH REISNER'S SIGHT was almost gone after 1933, his mental faculties were unimpaired, and Harvard Camp remained an intellectual and political center. Students of Egyptology from many nations were as welcome as eminent scholars. But the fine humanity in Reisner caused him to keep his study door always open to his Qufti workmen, who brought to him for solution their family and other problems.

Notables, who, from a long experience, understood the increasing complexities of the Near East, were among those who sought Reisner's advice. In Egypt he had the confidence equally of British and Egyptian officials. He kept himself informed on every phase of current events by having either Evelyn Perkins or me read to him *el Ahram*, an Arabic daily newspaper, as well as the *Egyptian Gazette*.

During the many years of Reisner's excavations, when he had lived mainly in villages, he interpreted the Koran to the timid, densely ignorant, and superstitious *fellaheen*. He encouraged my studies in Arabic literature and on Islam, and at his instigation I started what was to become a fairly comprehensive library on Islam, which eventually I was to give to the International School of the Middle East Institute in Washington.

In our daily exercise on the terrace, Reisner frequently contrasted the administrative firmness of Lord Lloyd with that of his predecessor, Field Marshal Lord Allenby, who had continued to make concessions to the Egyptians after the disorders of 1919. Irresponsible followers of Zaghlul, the then national leader, killed British military and civil servants and several Egyptian ministers because they had shown friendly leanings towards England. But in the fall of 1924, the murder of Sir Lee Stack, Sirdar of the Sudan, on a Cairo visit brought matters to a crisis and Lord Lloyd replaced Lord Allenby.

Reisner believed that unless a Labor government returned to office in England, a peaceful settlement would come from Lloyd's skill and firmness in his dealings with both the palace and Nahas, the recognized leader of the people after Zaghlul's death.

The most interesting official Egyptian I met with Reisner was Mohamed Mahmud Pasha. He was early in character, as a graduate of Balliol College, Oxford, to have attained, as his first position in Egypt, the secretaryship to the British adviser of the Interior Department in the Cromer regime. These formative years, when Mahmud was in close touch with British inspectors in the provinces, gave him an insight into the problems and hardships of the *fellaheen*.

As prime minister, Mahmud launched reforms aimed at getting more land into the ownership of the *fellaheen*, and giving them justice in water distribution, in which King Fuad was taking a personal interest.

But unfortunately, when all promised well for long-overdue economic reforms under a strong prime minister, and with the support of Lord Lloyd, the Labor party gained control of the British Parliament. Ramsay MacDonald headed the government. He dismissed Lord Lloyd, and Nahas became prime minister of Egypt. The long British administration of Egypt finally ended with the signing of a treaty in 1936. It seemed an anachronism to have a people's government in both England and Egypt bring about an abandonment of Mahmud's program to benefit the *fellaheen*.

Reisner often insisted that I accompany Joe on his brief absences from Harvard Camp. Several of them were to Chicago House in Luxor, as James H. Breasted's Oriental Institute headquarters were called. Once Harold Nelson, the head of the expedition, took us by car across the almost trackless desert to the Red Sea, over the route used in the days of ancient Egypt.

After steam had replaced sailing *dahabiehs*, *felukas* were still in evidence on the Nile and the essential life of villagers was not affected. But I heard a forecast of the fundamental changes about to be introduced by the motorcar and the bus from an old sheikh. He had not formerly left his home district, but when I went this time to pay my respects, he was gone. Later on, he told me he had made a trip in a passing "quick-cart with an engine in it." He said, "Now we villagers will be like the Inglesi [English], making big dust going nowhere."

Joe and I spent the spring of 1935 at Persepolis in Iran, living in the restored hareem of Darius while Joe painted reliefs for the Oriental Institute in Chicago. We shared with villagers the traditional celebration of *Noruz*, the Persian New Year, in a land of "roses and poetry." We watched a fire balloon rise into the sky, while villagers jumped through flames below, just as their ancestors had done through the centuries.

Back in Egypt we visited with Edward Quibell in Saqqarah, where he was engaged in handling archaeologically a bewildering amount of alabaster found in a passage of the Step Pyramid. And occasionally we stayed a few consecutive nights in Cairo with Russell Pasha and Dorothea, his wife.

In 1938 we occupied for a few weeks the expedition house of the Egypt Exploration Fund at Araba el Madfuna, so that Joe could paint in the beautiful temple of Abydos built by Seti I (1313–1292 B.C.). A year later, on April 2, 1939, on our return from a second visit to Abydos, Joe's paintings were exhibited at Harvard Camp. This annual event was organized by Mrs. Reisner and her daughter Mary. The guests, who included many Egyptian dignitaries, had caught Reisner's mood. Momentarily the approaching war was forgotten while homage was paid to the glories of ancient Egypt.

The final morning in 1939, before Joe and I were to sail, the early sun and I were alone on the terrace together. As my eyes swept over the familiar horizon, with the pyramids emerging far and near above the mist, the beauty of the scene served ironically to deepen my depression, which was occasioned by Reisner's condition. The doctors had told Joe and me it was alarming. Should war come, Reisner would remain in Egypt, but we would be in America.

Reisner, Joe, and I had tea in Reisner's office. "I don't feel like being read to," he said bluntly. After a few turns on the terrace, the three of us sat on a bench. Suddenly he cheered up as he reminisced about interesting visitors to Harvard Camp whom he remembered.

He recalled that Bernard Shaw's enthusiasm for Hetepheres II, whom he termed the first red-haired trouble maker in history, was matched at the other end of the scale by his objections to the pyramids. "Don't they obstruct your view?"

Noel Coward had defined the pyramids as "Big and out of my line." The same idea was expressed differently by John Drinkwater. He had looked at the three great pyramids of Giza with a rapt expression, then murmured, as though to himself, "What a stage setting, but who could write the script?"

I referred to a call from Vincent Sheean and his attractive wife. It was after he had written some articles on Iran that he informed Reisner he was about to do a feature sketch on village life in Egypt. In response to Reisner's surprised expression, he said with disarming truthfulness, "I bring a virgin mind to the subject."

Reisner recalled the unexpected arrival of the crown prince and princess of Sweden one time at Harvard Camp. The crown prince explained that they managed to leave the palace at Cairo, where they were guests, by a back entrance and found a waiting taxi, thus getting the chance to see Reisner's excavations and to talk to Joe about Persepolis, where he had been recently.

The crown prince had talked like an expert about Reisner's dig. The prince's manifest pride in a prehistoric collection in the Stockholm Museum, which he had personally excavated at Mesa Verde in Colorado, convinced Reisner that his royal highness may have regretted having to become a king, at the expense of a life which could otherwise be devoted to archaeology.

Time flew and we had to rush to get dressed for a farewell Harvard Camp dinner. It was Reisner who dominated the conversation at a gathering of old friends at a long table. His humor was as strong as his incredible courage in ignoring physical handicaps. Encouraged by Evelyn Perkins, he told a series of inimitable anecdotes about village personalities and family feuds, which Russell Pasha capped with equally amusing experiences.

Dessert had been served and the champagne glasses were refilled.

Percival Elgood, an authority on the Ptolemaic period, witty as ever, spoke with an apt turn of phrase. He was followed by Douglas Derry, who, in a light vein, discussed some of the mummies he had met. And Bryan Emery had a few words to say about his recent discoveries at Saqqarah.

There was a pause as Reisner slowly got to his feet. He held up his glass of champagne in a steady hand. Looking from one end of the table to the other, with evident pleasure at having so many intimate friends with him, he said in a low and penetrating voice, "Each one of you here has seen the slate pair and knows what it means to me to have that great treasure in Boston." He hesitated a split second, then added, "And each of you also knows that Joe and Corinna mean more to me than the slate pair."

44

INDIANS, PUBLIC HEALTH, AND THE LAW

It is perhaps anomalous to speak of my "working career," since obviously I had been a fairly hard worker all of my life, up to and including the time I discovered in the Miccosukees of Florida a people who needed help. But the years since 1924 have given me an active working interest in the Indians of the United States as a whole, an opportunity to participate actively in public-health programs, a small role in the national and international effort to control narcotics, and, in between, a brush with one of the most difficult problems of penal administration, the rehabilitation of discharged women prisoners. Such has been my "working career."

If the Miccosukees were not a clincher to my determination, my experiences in New Mexico with the pueblo groups were bound to settle the matter. I had attended the meetings of the Santa Fe, New Mexico Association, at the insistence of Alice Corbin Henderson.

This group was working among the Indians of the Southwest beginning in the 1920's. Encouragement was given to Southwestern Indian weaving and pottery making. Miss Elizabeth White, one of the founders of the Eastern Association, with headquarters in New York, was beginning to look to national programs for Indian betterment.

Rather rapidly, a good many things began to fall into place—perhaps because of the sudden activity of a great many people. Miss White organized an exhibition of Southwestern Indian work in New York. At Joe's instigation, the Fogg Museum at Harvard began showing Indian work as art. John D. Rockefeller created in Santa Fe, from a plan drawn by Kenneth Chapman and presented by Gus Nussbaum and Joe, a laboratory for Indian research. And not least of all, Miss Mary C. Wheelwright of Boston created at Santa Fe the Museum of Navajo Ceremonial Art.

By 1926, I was a member of the Executive Committee of the Eastern Association and represented it and the New Mexico Association in furthering the enactment of Congressional legislation relating to Indians. I enjoyed the responsibility in an entirely new field in which I had the cooperation of Louis C. Crampton, the chairman of the powerful subcommittee on appropriations.

Two years later, I enlarged the scope of my work with Indians by accepting appointment as national chairman of Indian Welfare of the General Federation of Women's Clubs. I was soon to find the bonds between the general and state federations excellent both for reaching Indians in their home surroundings and for the enactment of legislation.

In North Dakota, I found on the reservations a shocking lack of amenities and a complete lack of hygiene in Indian homes. On subsequent trips west, I spent much time in Montana as the guest of Mrs. Henrietta Crockett, who had been the first public health nurse in the state's employ. During her long career as secretary of the Montana Tuberculosis Society, she remained the dominant factor in all matters pertaining to Indians. She and I organized in Montana, and in several neighboring states, clubs composed of Indian women living on reservations which were accepted by the state federations of Women's Clubs as member groups.

At the request of Charles J. Rhoads, Indian commissioner during the Herbert Hoover administration, Mrs. Henrietta K. Burton, the head of Home extension for the Indian Bureau, and I organized an Indian Home Care program on reservations.

The first effort of this kind was for the women on the Crow reservation in Montana. On my next visit to the state Dr. William G. Cogswell, the able executive secretary of the Montana Board of Health, said that Mrs. Crockett and I had better find out locally the reason for the flood of protests made against the program by the tribal council and Indian leaders.

I decided to seek the advice of Chief Plenty Coups of the Crows en route to the reservation. He was now blind and feeble but still spoke to the Crows with a voice of authority. I had met him at Arlington Cemetery, when, at the unveiling of the Tomb of the Unknown Soldier, Plenty Coups, as the chosen representative of the Indian nations, in laying a wreath on the Tomb, had made the widely published statement that "Maybe the Unknown Soldier was an Indian."

Plenty Coups listened attentively to the dilemma I presented, then offered to send an Indian to deliver his message to a conference called by Crow women which the tribal council was supposed to attend.

Mrs. Crockett and I entered the hall under the escort of a large delegation of Indian women. The sullen faces of a group of men standing well to the back was explained by one of the women, who admitted to me that she had told the tribal council that three million white women believed that the Crow women, and not the men, should represent the tribe at Washington.

The meeting was called to order by the secretary, and Plenty Coups' message, addressed to the tribal council, was read. It was to the effect that he had seen white men drive their buffaloes from the range, take the Crows' land from them, and cause other calamities. But these changes were as nothing compared to those about to be brought about by the organization of their own women.

After a dazed silence from the men, I suggested that they be seated and let me tell them about the Indian Home Care program for which I was responsible. I said its purpose was to persuade Indian housewives to look after their children, make their homes attractive, cultivate vegetable gardens and—but before I could go on I was interrupted by the head of the tribal council, all smiles. "That's what we want them to do," he said.

The reservation clubs and the Indian Home Care program became increasingly useful in bridging the gap between state and federal field units and tribal councils. Moreover, I was delighted to find that contact with civic-minded white women at state conventions was arousing in Indian women leaders a faint glimmering of their rights and responsibilities as citizens.

The Eastern Association had meantime become the Association on American Indian Affairs. Two of its most productive thinkers through the years have been Oliver La Farge, of Santa Fe, and Miss LaVerne Madigan, of New York. Mr. La Farge has served as president, and Miss Madigan as executive director. Under Mr. La Farge's presidency in 1958, the concept entitled "We Shake Hands," developed by Miss Madigan, was launched in a limited scale, soon to become general.

It was based on the premise of the Indians' need to preserve pride of identity in the process of adjusting themselves to the ways of nearby white communities. A small group of Omahas at Macy, Nebraska, were the first to adopt "We Shake Hands," which functions under an Indian field staff with Miss Madigan as supervisor. Soon these Omahas were publishing a news sheet, and the boys had organized a club and, upon their own initiative, had acquired a building, where they entertained recently made white friends.

Tribes in the Dakotas and Montana were the next to undertake "We Shake Hands," and the association continues to receive requests from tribes throughout the Indian country to participate in it. It gives me satisfaction to collaborate with Miss Madigan in what has become a major Association project.

You don't have to be an Indian to work effectively with Indian groups, but it helps. I must always think of Will Rogers as one of the most effective voices for the Indian, and as a Cherokee from Oklahoma he had both the insights into Indian problems and the knowledge of trouble spots. He told me early that he could not concern himself too much with Indians made wealthy from oil production. He accordingly took me to poverty-stricken and neglected small groups living in isolated regions.

In those days hard-surfaced roads were few and far between in many districts. A car fought mud a great deal of the time. Fortunately Will was as expert with a spade as with a rope, and he never stopped telling amusing anecdotes when digging a car out of a mud hole.

Will's pride in his Cherokee inheritance was a great asset to the Indian cause. Whenever any of us sent him a telegram about a crisis which affected Indians in any part of the country, he replied with a statement which was bound to be treated as headline news by the newspapers. Prompt and favorable official action followed in Washington.

Indians afforded me my first enterprise in the field of public health. The immediate problem was trachoma, an eye disease which often terminated in partial or complete blindness. It was known in Egypt as early as 1500 B.C. Crusaders brought it into Europe from the Near East, and it finally reached America, where Indians became its principal victims. The number of cases I saw among Navajos and other Indians in New Mexico and Arizona, most strikingly their children, resulted in my going into action.

With the hearty approval of Dr. Simon Flexner of the Rockefeller Institute, I got Dr. Francis Proctor, a retired Boston oculist living in Santa Fe, to provide the money for an Indian Bureau physician to go to Vienna for an intensive course in the treatment of trachoma. Upon his return, this doctor provided instruction for other doctors who were detailed to work among Indians in many parts of the country. Trachoma, although not cured, was soon under control.

For some years now, trachoma studies have been going on in Saudi Arabia, under the supervision of Dr. John C. Snyder, dean of the faculty of the Harvard School of Public Health, in co-operation with Aramco, the Arabian American Oil Company. According to Dr. Snyder, the discovery of a safe and effective vaccine for the control of trachoma appears "reasonably hopeful." This is a result of tests being made in the research wing of the medical department of Aramco in Saudi Arabia, and by Dr. Snyder in his Boston laboratory. Curative measures are still needed among the Indians of the Southwest, where trachoma is again a major health problem.

An invitation to combat spotted fever came when I witnessed in Montana the terrible sight of a young boy in the final stage before death. National action was justified by the rapid spread of the disease from the Rocky Mountain states, until cases had been diagnosed in thirty-four states, even including a few along the Atlantic seacoast. In January, 1931, upon the recommendation of Dr. Cogswell, bills were introduced in both the Senate and the House for the purchase by the federal government of the Montana spotted-fever laboratory located at Hamilton.

I was just returning to New York from a trip to Egypt, and had barely landed when Dr. Cogswell called me on the telephone. He said he had received information that Congressmen, harassed by many urgent depression problems, were in no mood to consider a bill to buy a Western laboratory engaged in research on what was, to members of Congress, an unknown disease.

In this emergency, I appealed to each Federation chairman of Public Welfare in the forty-eight states to wire her senators and representatives, giving the number of spotted-fever cases in the state. If there were none, she was to mention the number of cases in the nearest neighboring state, and to stress that spotted fever was deadly and on the move.

Congress apparently panicked from fear of catching spotted fever, and the appropriation was passed.

When the State and Territorial Health Authorities Conference met in Washington in the autumn of 1930, Dr. Cogswell asked me to prepare data on Indians and their health problems. After he had presented this report, I was asked to stand questioning by the delegates. This experience led, I think, to my acceptance by Dr. Albert J. Chesley, the executive director of the Minnesota Department of Health and permanent secretary of the conference. From that point, health was the undercurrent of my Indian activities, and was so to continue even after Dr. Chesley's death in 1955.

Dr. Chesley's colleague was Dr. Haven Emerson, who had been health commissioner for the city of New York and had taught a course in public health at Columbia University. It was a liberal education for me to travel with them into the Indian country and meet with tribal councils. Dr. Chesley's health programs were usually adopted, and members of the various Indian councils would seek his advice about making their people understand the importance of health measures. His leadership was also vital to the medical care undertaken for Indians by state, federal, and county health units.

Among Dr. Chesley's major health achievements was the effort to control tuberculosis among Indians. He devised the scheme of having an Indian wing built onto a well-equipped state sanitarium whenever possible. Minnesota was the first state to adopt this policy. Montana soon followed, and I was able to assist its program to fruition by working for a federal appropriation to supplement state funds in the construction of the Indian wing, dedicated to Henrietta Crockett, of the Montana State Sanitarium at Galen.

Our association today co-operates with health authorities, at all levels on their work among Indians, through a National Indian Health Committee, of which Dr. Carl Muschenheim is chairman and I am a member. One of the best analyses of the future of Indians was recently given by Oliver La Farge. "This country is full of men of good will. We can match brotherhood with determination, pair understanding with courage, and have high hopes that in the end the innate feelings of America will respond and that our Indians, like all other Americans, will be free to choose their mode of life, to keep what they want to keep, discard what they wish to discard, and find in modern America nourishment not only for their bodies but for their spirits."

Indians and public health may seem to have no necessary connection with the control of narcotics, but prevention is common to two of them. As early as 1941, as the war came on, Mrs. Sara Whitehurst, the president of the General Federation of Women's Clubs, inducted me into narcotics work. I have never had any regrets. On the contrary, I think of this as one of my most fruitful activities.

Mrs. Whitehurst invited me to Washington to discuss the broad subject of the Federation's program in this field. On my arrival, she spoke of my familiarity with the international control of narcotic drugs through long association with Russell Pasha in Egypt. Therefore she had appointed me adviser on narcotic drugs to the General Federation's Public Welfare Department. I was to re-establish the General Federation's influence in the international field.

She told me that the agreement for the limitation of the manufacture of narcotic drugs at the 1931 Geneva Convention was prepared by our American delegates. She added that it was the General Federation's leadership which had stimulated ratification of the agreement by the Senate. But since then the Federation had confined its activities to securing passage of a uniform narcotic drug act in all the states.

War was known from long experience to increase drug addiction. The Federation must consequently be ready for prompt action, Mrs. Whitehurst told me.

I expressed gratitude for an assignment which, to me, was a personal memorial, in a sense, to Theodore Roosevelt, who as president had closed the opium dens and shops in the Philippine Islands. "Our American people must never get revenue from opium monopolies!" he had thundered at me, banging his fists on a table. He had enlisted the assistance of Bishop Charles H. Brent, who knew of the disastrous effects of opium on the native populations in the islands.

Soon after William Howard Taft became president in 1909, the first international opium conference was held at Shanghai, on the initiative of Theodore Roosevelt and Bishop Brent. Its purpose was to establish the principle that the only way to prevent illicit traffic in opium was to restrict its production. Incidentally, this procedure was advocated by American delegates to The Hague in 1912 and at all future international drug conferences.

After Theodore Roosevelt's death in 1919, Bishop Brent, for the final ten years of his life, continued what was he told me a losing battle against the enormous profits involved. He considered that England and the Netherlands were the worst offenders.

With this background, I accompanied Mrs. Whitehurst to an

interview with Herbert J. Anslinger, the commissioner on narcotics, an office which functioned within the Treasury Department.

"I've waited some years for your visit," Anslinger said in welcome to me, after expressing his appreciation to Mrs. Whitehurst for coming.

He was a heavy-set man with a strong-featured face. He gave the impression of wasting neither his own nor other busy people's time. He and Mrs. Whitehurst disposed of formalities quickly. Then he asked her, with a courteous bluntness that I was to find characteristic, how far the General Federation was prepared to go in a crisis that would be controversial.

"Tell Mrs. Smith what you wish done and I believe you will be satisfied," she said and departed.

Russell's written recommendation of me in a personal letter made Anslinger take for granted both my knowledge and discretion, he told me. His face was stern as he spoke of the vigilance that was necessary to prevent amendments to existing narcotic laws that would nullify their effectiveness. The crisis with which we were all faced was an amendment to the Harrison Act, to be introduced at the next session of Congress. The suggested amendment had to do with the tiny black seeds of the opium plant used to decorate bakery products. They were harmless in themselves but war had cut off Czecho-Slovakia as a source of supply.

Every dram of crude opium obtained from the opium plant on arrival at an American port was kept locked up in the Treasury vaults. It could only be released under a warrant by Anslinger, after which it was channeled through medical practice to the patients legitimately requesting it. But commercial growth of the poppy in the United States, legalized to please housewives, would be disastrous, Anslinger said. The bootlegging of crude opium would result in an enforcement problem with which law-enforcement agencies were not equipped to cope.

I reported back to Mrs. Whitehurst that Anslinger was depending on the General Federation to defeat the amendment.

She warned me, as my assignment was outlined, that clubwomen loved the tasty opium seeds.

404

At the next board meeting of the General Federation, a number of women spoke in favor of the amendment for the commercial growth of the poppy. On noticing that they were all thin, I addressed myself to the stout, reminding them that fattening bakery delicacies would be less tempting without the attractive seeds. Apparently many of those present were on a diet, and Anslinger's request for support for defeating the measure was endorsed.

The next step came with my presenting the matter to Dr. Frederick Stricker, the health officer for Oregon. He was also chairman of the Opium Committee of the State and Territorial Health Authorities Conference. He promptly made me consultant of his committee and authorized me to oppose the amendment.

Senator Charles L. McNary of Oregon looked rather grim as I faced him in his office and outlined the organized campaign by two powerful bodies to defeat the amendment. I told him that the attack would be aimed against the attorney general of Oregon, who had strongly advocated the growth of poppy seed for commercial purposes. There was no criticism of the Senator, who had introduced the measure by request. He looked decidedly relieved and said that he was confident that he could kill the amendment in committee. And he did.

Again in 1942 there was need for concerted action. Anslinger felt that, should the war be protracted, the opium reserves in the Treasury vaults might be depleted. There had been serious thefts from our stocks overseas, held for the medical use of our fighting forces. As a precaution, he wanted Congress to pass permissive legislation authorizing the Commissioner of Narcotics to issue licenses for the growth of the opium poppy in restricted areas under Treasury supervision, if such action became advisable. This Opium Control Act passed the House on the unanimous consent calendar. But it unexpectedly struck a snag in the Senate Committee, of which Senator George of Georgia was chairman.

Anslinger telephoned me at Dublin, requesting me to talk with Senator Walter F. George. I appealed to a woman high in the General Federation who was a fellow-citizen of the Senator's in Georgia and had worked with him closely. Consequently, in the early morning after my arrival in Washington, I was with Senator George in his office. Upon my presentation of a confidential memorandum to him from Anslinger, Senator George was entirely co-operative. He succeeded in killing the amendment.

A real test in the narcotics campaign came in the spring of 1943, when I opened a letter with the postmark of Shiraz, Iran. I read over the signature of an American admiral I had known in the Near East an account of narcotic drugs being made available to Americans bringing lend-lease goods to Iran for trans-shipment to Russia.

I was soon in Washington again to see Anslinger. He told me that in India and other countries of the Far East, opium was being sold in government licensed shops. Obviously our country had no control over this traffic, but in other situations it did. In other words, international control was still very weak.

There was to be another friendship in Dr. Walter H. Judd, a representative to Congress from Minnesota. For many years he had been a medical missionary in China, and like Bishop Brent, he knew the need for drastic action to control the traffic in narcotic drugs among native populations. He was responsible for Joint Resolution 241, known as the Judd Resolution, introduced into Congress and passed into law in 1944. It gave to the president of the United States the task of urging "upon the countries where the cultivation of opium poppy exists the necessity of limiting the production to the amount required for strictly medical and scientific purposes . . ."

Our own narcotics laws were strengthened the following year by legislation requiring strict inspection and examination of ships' crews, cargoes, and passengers, to reduce or eliminate the amount of opium being smuggled into the United States.

In half a century, world-wide acceptance has gradually been won for the American opium policy advocated by Theodore Roosevelt in 1909. A great deal of voluntary effort has gone into the result, but all of us who have had a share in it know that the time we have spent has been well repaid.

But narcotics were not my only concern in the interesting zone of human rehabilitation. Lewis E. Lawes, famous for his earlier activities in New York state prison reform, when he was warden of Sing Sing, was now engaged in a war phase of the prison problem.

When I came for an appointment, I found him alone in a small room off one of the busy offices in the Empire State Building. He told me that our mutual friend, Ruth Bryan Owen, had recommended me for a difficult job on a volunteer basis.

"Whatever it is, I can't take it," I told him firmly.

His quiet, "You can and you will," startled me. Then he gave me the background of what he had in mind. Women prisoners needed a second chance on the completion of their sentences—a goal which he considered practically impossible in their home towns. Attempted rehabilitation would be defeated locally, with a return to prison inevitable, unless friendly hands were outstretched in new home surroundings.

Lawes said he would give me a month's notice to find a civic-minded, kindly disposed woman in each community to which a released prisoner was sent for a definite job. That woman alone would know of her prison past, and it would be her responsibility to build up a small circle of local friends for the former prisoner. Lawes and I were to work out together any problems that arose, and I would be expected to keep in touch by correspondence with each prisoner.

This was a Thursday, and he expected me to leave for Alderson Federal Reformatory for Women in West Virginia the following Monday. I was to stay a week to study the administration and the psychology of women prisoners.

The word Alderson recalled an unforgettable evening I had spent with Miss Mary Harris. She had created this prison, which was studied as a model by those interested in prison reform in many countries. A significant departure was that Miss Harris had been permitted to train her successor, a Miss Helen Hironimus (then in charge), who had served for some years as her assistant.

"Shall I tell your husband or will you break the news?" Lawes asked abruptly.

I replied that Joe was accustomed to my having causes thrust upon me. He expected only that they be worthy ones.

Lawes promised to get me detailed data. Then he handed me

three letters he said were from prisoners. I was to get my answers back to him before my departure Monday. With two of them I found no difficulty, but the third had me stumped. I put a notation on it to that effect, returning it by messenger with my other two replies. Whereupon Lawes telephoned me to say that, in the future, I could mail my answers direct to the prisoners. The third letter was a fake and had served as a test of my gullibility.

On approaching Alderson, I found there was nothing to suggest a prison. There were no high surrounding walls nor bars on the windows and doors of the few large buildings. Scattered about were cottages like those one might expect in a real-estate development for people of good taste but modest means. The entrance gates stood wide open, and there was no guard. Splendid trees were growing on well-kept grounds, where color showed in the late blooms of flower beds. The women who could be seen moving about the paths looked cheerful and were not in prison stripes. Yet my strongest first impression was one of intangible discipline.

On the steps of a cottage I was welcomed by a tall, slim, dark-haired woman, with an agreeable manner but determined eyes. She introduced herself as Miss Hironimus. She explained that the enormous filing cases, which literally furnished the room allotted to me, contained records of the prisoners. Mr. Lawes had thought this was the simplest way for me to become familiar with them, she said.

We had supper together and, at about seven, joined most of the prisoners in a large assembly hall, where an orchestra was playing. Even some of the older women were dancing and, in spite of the absence of men, everyone seemed to be having a good time. I joined in. My partners discussed the topics of the day or particular interests which they were developing. A number of them said they would arrange with Miss Hironimus about entertaining me in their cottages. It seemed incredible that these well-groomed, courteous women, many of them under thirty, were paying the penalty for criminal acts.

Early the following morning, breakfast was served in my room by a smiling blond of about thirty-five, wearing a nurse's uniform. "Don't ever become a drug addict," she advised, as a preamble to

408

telling me her own history. Overwork in a hospital and taking drugs to keep going on a hard case were the original sources of her trouble. When drug addiction became the dominant factor in her life, traffickers began charging her more and more for the next dose. "Finally I became a trafficker myself and here I am," she said.

She was a pitiable sight as she stood there, clinging to my hand in wide-eyed terror because she was about to be released. Two years, she thought, was insufficient time to build up resistance, and once the protection of Alderson was withdrawn, she dreaded a relapse.

The distracted nurse left the room as Miss Hironimus entered, soon expressing to me her pessimism about approval of a recommendation she had made through official channels for an extension of two years' in the prisoner's stay. She suggested that I speak to Lawes.

Lawes listened to me attentively on the telephone but warned me that he was doubtful of success. "You must succeed during my stay," I insisted. Longer sentences in drug addiction cases were something for organized women to fight for, he said before hanging up.

As I tackled prisoners' records, I was favorably impressed by many of the questions and answers appearing in the dossiers. For instance, "List special interests. If none, what do you think you would like to develop?" Also "Plans for the future?"

When Miss Hironimus was ready for a round of visits to prisoners, she found me reading the record of a thoroughly debased old woman who had been in and out of state prisons many times, as a prostitute and a keeper of bawdy houses. Her late ambition was to study music and become a piano teacher. I learned that she had served only two years of a ten-year sentence and had made a promising start as a pianist. I abandoned the records to accompany Miss Hironimus, who wished me to talk with another inmate.

She knocked on the door of a room in one of a group of isolated cottages. In response to her query whether the inmate would like visitors, a bright-eyed little old woman opened the door. She was wearing a white lace cap and ruffles around a simple, dark brown dress. She was delicate in appearance and somehow possessed an air of refinement. She raised a finger for silence as she led us towards a large bird cage. Two fluffy canaries had recently broken through their shells.

"I love the tender yellow creatures," she whispered. The ensuing conversation was a monologue about her pets.

"Surely that charming old lady didn't do anything really bad," I exclaimed when the interview was over and we were walking down the path. On learning her identity, I involuntarily shuddered in horror. She was serving a life sentence for the kidnapping and death of a child, a case that for weeks had occupied the front pages of newspapers because of its stark brutality.

We next visited a nearby greenhouse, where I was shown around by an intelligent, kindly looking young woman. She emphasized that it was the seedlings she particularly enjoyed caring for, because they were so helpless. I was again shocked to hear after we had left that she was serving a life sentence as the old lady's assistant in the kidnapping. Miss Hironimus told me that practically all prison experts were as misled about the characters of these two women as I had been. I was not much longer learning that you can't gain much insight from conversations with prisoners.

As we walked over the prison, Miss Hironimus's lucid explanation of each function soon began to provide a picture of the whole. She told me that classroom studies were supplemented by long hours in workshops, where the inmates were learning the trades of sewing, carpentry, machine operation, and many others. Interludes of reading in the library and early evening entertainment in individual cottages or at general gatherings completed the daily routine. Gradually, lost self-respect was regained and characters rebuilt. "We've had no attempted escapes or second sentences," Miss Hironimus said.

I managed to digest the thousand records deposited in my room at odd moments. For me, lunch was a working meal. My afternoons were devoted to visits to prisoners, and my evenings to early suppers cooked for me in various cottages.

Three prisoners lived in each cottage apartment. They seemed congenial and took pleasure in having a guest. The food was excellent and well served. After the dishes were cleared, neighbors came in.

We all sat on the floor, and I took my new-found friends with me on adventures I had experienced, in and out of tombs and temples in Egypt and elsewhere, across the trackless desert, and to England, France, and Italy. Their responsive faces and intelligent questions offered confirmation of what both the librarian and Miss Hironimus had said about the prisoners' absorption in new ideas on worth-while subjects. By nine each evening I was left at my cottage by my hostesses, to whom I had made a promise to correspond. Each one said she would furnish me with a new address when she moved. They always spoke of moving, not their ultimate discharge.

A special occasion was an informal piano recital for me by the old madam. As she struck the keys her coarse face became transfigured. She even attempted a Chopin sonata with fair success. When she discovered that I had actually known Paderewski and other great musicians, she eagerly plied me with inquiries about them. On parting, I volunteered to send her some piano scores.

The opportunity to be present at a ceremony for a released prisoner was one I should remember for a long time. I was informed that a small but adequate wardrobe was being furnished her from the large stock of material in the prison, and made to order from the prisoner's own selection. It was a kind of trousseau—for leaving, not for marriage.

This prisoner was in her late twenties. She had on a dark brown suit, a blouse, a hat with a touch of color, and a top coat. She took out of a large valise and showed those of us standing about several dresses, lingerie, and extra pairs of shoes and slippers.

As she turned to enter a motor, she looked rather appalled at the prospect of becoming again a part of the outside world. But I had confidence she was both mentally and morally equipped to make a go of it.

The real thrill of my stay occurred just before my departure from Alderson, when I received a telegram from Lewis Lawes which read: "Extension of prison term has been granted."

My activities with Lawes continued. Between us, satisfactory community contacts were made for released prisoners. And in a surprisingly short time, many of these women could return to their home towns. My correspondence with other prisoners also flourished.

An event of exceptional significance occurred when Lawes telephoned me to say that he had arranged for a released prisoner to dine with me at my New York club. On hearing her name, I remembered her case.

Her parents were gentle folk who had become seriously ill. Both were too sensitive for hospital care in wards containing many beds. Soon their young daughter had exhausted her savings, caring for them in private rooms. She held a position of trust in a Federal Reserve bank and took funds to meet her personal deficit at home. Her withdrawals continued for three years without discovery. Then her parents died.

Up to this point, one could sympathize with the woman's dilemma, which prompted her financial dishonesty, even though one could not condone it. But after her parents died, she continued to get easy money for several years before being found out and sentenced to Alderson.

Lawes had insisted that her wrongdoing was an accident. On the completion of her prison term, he secured for her another position of trust, this time in a New York bank. A commercial company had bonded the woman, but only on condition that Lawes sign the bond. She was very beautiful, with large blue eyes and jet-black hair and a charming manner. At once she referred to Alderson and her prison friends, with whom I was corresponding. She was unusually intelligent and an amusing conversationalist. Her ultimate career fully justified Lawes' faith. She married a successful businessman who knew of her prison record. She became a leader in her community and was known for her ultra-conservatism and the exacting standards she employed in judging the behavior of others. I kept in touch with her for some years. Several times, as a house guest, I got to know her family, whom she was bringing up according to strict principles of right and wrong.

I cherished my meetings with Lawes whenever I chanced to be

in New York. They generally took place in his home. I had an appointment with him at his office on what turned out to be V-J Day. My son-in-law, Jay Schieffelin, told me that no engagements would be kept that memorable day. But Lawes had not forgotten my meeting with him.

The enormous lobby in his building was deserted and but a single elevator was running. I got out of the elevator and walked down a long empty corridor to reach the small room where I had first met Lawes.

"I knew you'd come," he said.

For more than two hours we sat and quietly talked. I was away when illness caused him to retire. He died in the spring of 1947, at his home at Garrison-on-Hudson.

45

JOE AND EGYPT

FOR THE EGYPTIANS

THE EGYPT of American and British archaeologists that Joe and I knew so well, belonged to an era that closed after World War II. Reisner had died in 1942, and Harvard Camp was to be handed back to the Egyptian government. The Metropolitan Museum Expedition at Thebes had also closed.

Egypt seemed of the distant past when on October 11, 1946, the Dublin community celebrated Joe's eighty-fourth birthday. He had reached a time of life when supposedly a man took fewer chances with the uncertainties of travel. But an encouraging cable from Bryan Emery, saying that he and his attractive wife Molly were again expecting us to stay with them at Saqqarah, turned the scale in favor of Egypt as usual.

When Emery met us at the Cairo station, he told us that he had resigned from the employ of the Egyptian government after the completion of his excavations at the Archaic Cemetery, which had produced such sensational finds, and where he had been profession-ally occupied since 1935.

He was now in British Security, but he would continue to have possession of the government house, where Molly would be with Joe and me while he lived in a Cairo flat, coming to Saqqarah for weekends.

Our nearest neighbor at Saqqarah was Abd' Essalam, an engineer of international reputation as well as an architect. He was directing the government work both at Saqqarah and Dashur, and under him was a group of well-trained young Egyptians. His attractive house, built on a high ledge overlooking the cultivated areas below, had become the same cultured center that Harvard Camp had been. Englishmen and Americans met there with Egyptian officials inter-ested in archaeology. And Joe and I were warmly accepted.

Joe's Egypt had remained the same: a land of ancient tombs and temples, of brilliant sunshine and simple existence, which he shared with villagers, rising with the sun, painting long hours, and going to bed soon after darkness fell.

Some years before, at Cecil M. Firth's suggestion, Joe and I had penetrated far into the interior of King Zoser's Step Pyramid, dat-ing back to Dynasty III (2780–2680 B.C.), so he could paint a fig-ure of the King. We had plunged down a narrow passageway in a stooping position, because of the lowness of the roof, with its jagged rocks, until we reached some stone steps where we could stand erect before entering a small room. I got a general impression of blue faïence tiles lining the walls and a small false door of stone, the surface of which was in bad condition. A spirited figure of King Zoser was carved in low relief on the door. Above his head were the outspread wings of a vulture, and blue tiles were on either side of him. Joe had painted with great difficulty, as there was no air in the room.

Now, years later, by an even more perilous descent, we reached the room. The false door lay in fragments over on the floor, the tiles, loosened from the plaster which had held them in place, were scattered over the floor, and the figure of King Zoser was forever lost.

This catastrophe aroused Joe's determination not to devote his entire time to the great tombs of Saqqarah, where he had so often worked, but to paint some of the new finds made by Egyptian archaeologists which ultimately might not be preserved by being removed to the Cairo Museum.

Fortuitously, Joe also was chosen to paint some of the wonderful new discoveries made at Karnak. Pierre Lacau, who had for many years been head of the Egyptian Antiquity Service, had returned to Egypt from retirement in Paris to publish on the early Egyptian shrines. The materials of all of the latter had been found intact in blocks used in building a much later pylon, under archaeological repair in World War II. Lacau summoned Joe to make studies of some of the details.

It was good to be staying again at Chicago House in Luxor. And we were proud to have in the Oriental Institute of the University of Chicago the only expedition continuing to function under American auspices. The staff was busily engaged in the continuing research for the many volumes on Medinet Habu, the temple of Rameses III on the Theban Plain.

In addition, members of the staff were playing an important role in the new era by collaborating with such distinguished Egyptian archaeologists as Labib Habachi, Ahmad Fakhri, Zaki Saad and others. They were also assisting young Egyptians who had replaced British officials in the Antiquity Service. And Egyptian scholars and Egyptologists were making good use of the comprehensive library at Chicago House.

Esa, our general factotum, was a genius at the art of stretching a simple meal, thus permitting us to entertain both British officials and American diplomats, glad for a reprieve from the political dissensions, riots, and bombing outrages in Cairo. Egyptian statesmen urged Parliament to ameliorate the deplorable conditions among the *fellaheen*, if only as a matter of political expediency. But the landlords had the ear of both government officials and the palace.

It was not from guests, but from our villagers that we heard of events of significance. Members of the large staff of the Soviet Embassy distributed food personally to *fellaheen* in their villages, supposedly combining their acts of charity with the spreading of Russian propaganda. I had confirmation of what was transpiring from one of our villagers. All cordiality was gone when he said to me that he and his fellow villagers had been told by good new friends that Americans were bad because they killed black people. And he proceeded to repeat the gruesome details of many lynchings that had taken place in Southern states during the past twenty years.

An even more significant episode occurred at a luncheon given by our American ambassador, Pinckney Tuck, which Joe and I attended. Among the guests were the American designer of fighting planes we had furnished the Russians as allies during the late war and a member of the staff of the Soviet Embassy, beside whom I was seated.

As we talked, I found the Soviet Embassy official agreeable, with an air of sincerity about him. Suddenly, he interrupted himself in the midst of a sentence. I saw that his attention was focused on a conversation across the table between the American designer and an expert on plane manufacture to whom he was explaining the details of the planes delivered to Russia.

"Excuse me," the Russian said firmly. "I distributed the planes in question, which were made in Russia by Russians."

A dead silence around the table was broken by the American designer's saying he could furnish evidence that the planes were of American manufacture.

We returned home in the spring of 1947, but were back in Egypt in the fall. The Antiquity Service again permitted us to occupy the Saqqarah government house. Here we were to stay for the next two years. We lived a quiet life, pursuing our ways entirely apart from the increasing political chaos. One day I went into Cairo, seated beside the driver of a government truck, to buy some much-needed paints for Joe. On reaching Opera Square, we found progress was blocked by a shrieking, fanatic crowd. Soldiers were emerging from a tank. As I tried to reach the paint shop on foot, I asked a nice-looking Egyptian what had happened. He told me that when a bomb exploded, the police had "dismissed themselves from duty."

After buying the paints, I managed to reach the truck. I dragged the terrified driver from under the seat, pushed him onto it, and said, "Put your trust in Allah but keep your hands on the wheel." My carefully articulated Arabic caught the favorable attention of the crowd who cleared a way for the truck.

Since Russell Pasha's retirement and his able Egyptian assistant had been killed by a mob, the police force had deteriorated. The same was true of the Egyptian army and Sphinx Pasha, who had created a loyal, efficient force. The palace, instead of combatting corruption, was known to be sharing in it. The leaders of the Nationalist party had become equally venal, and the *fellaheen* continued to be exploited.

At a time when it had become increasingly apparent that only a drastic change could restore a stable government, real progress was being made by the establishment of trade schools under the auspices of Cairo ladies. *Fellaheen* were gradually included in committees of village civic centers and contributed to the expense of improvements.

At a Cairo reception given by the wife of the prime minister, five ministers were compelled to listen to details of clinics and other welfare projects presented by enthusiastic lady participants, who emphasized the need for additional government appropriations.

Towards the end of our stay in Egypt, two delegates of the United Nations told me they had recently been in Turkey, Greece, and elsewhere to make a study of economic conditions. They declared they had not seen in any country of the Near East women as determined and well organized as these Cairo ladies.

Young Egyptians were meantime rising to their responsibilities. A number who had studied in America or England called an evening meeting of students and had Joe as their guest of honor. The topic discussed under an able chairman was students' responsibility toward the *fellaheen*. It was based on the premise that diversified, small industries had become a necessary supplement to agriculture, in view of an alarming annual increase in the population of Egyptian villages. The consensus among the students present favored such a program, to be put into effect by American technicians.

Our experiences with Egyptians reached a happy climax when H. E. Sanhoury Pasha, the minister of education, came to call. He touched the hand of a life-size painting by Joe of Mereruka (2600 B.C.) hanging on the wall and said, "I can't believe it isn't stone."

He asked Joe if he would be willing to teach his painting techniques to several selected Egyptian graduates of the Government School of Higher Art at Cairo. The Minister wished them to be trained to paint a government-owned series of their own traditional art. He also wanted Joe to exhibit his season's paintings in the entrance rotunda of the Cairo Museum among the treasures of Ancient Egypt.

Joe accepted both propositions enthusiastically, and shortly thereafter Abbas Shohdy, his first pupil, came to Saqqarah. Joe was delighted with Shohdy's draftsmanship, but found that his pupil had to unlearn the French method in which he had been trained. During the two subsequent painting seasons in Saqqarah, Abbas Shohdy developed into a worthy disciple of Joe's technique.

In the spring of 1949, the dean of Arabic inspectors of the Ministry of Education wrote a pamphlet about Joe and his paintings. It was entitled *Joseph Lindon Smith: The Artist and the Man*. At the time of our departure, thousands of copies were being distributed in Arabic and in English at Near East cultural displays, carried out with the active assistance of the cultural attaché of the American Embassy in Cairo.

Altogether, Joe was in a happy mood of continued usefulness when, on September 18, 1949, our golden wedding anniversary was celebrated in Dublin. We had returned to Loon Point from Egypt, for here and here alone could we renew with our children and our friends the half century of our life together.

There was something rare about it, quite aside from the time which had elapsed since our wedding and the rather furious pace of our adventures around the globe. It was a rare occurrence in America to have a father's and a son's fiftieth anniversaries celebrated in the same house, in the same community, with the same families represented. Dublin was little changed. The lake remained unspoiled. Even the newcomers to these "sacred groves," where, like Vergil, we had so often returned to the things we loved, were so much a part of the gentle tradition of the community that they were indistinguishable in spirit from the oldest settlers.

We gave a rather large dinner on Loon Point. Then the neighbors took over, with the late Lyneham Crocker acting as master of ceremonies. He also served as historian and produced a charming account entitled *A Happy Road and a Golden Milestone.*

Our Rebecca, who had come from Switzerland, staged a play which depicted in witty fashion the record of our married life, as culled from diaries and letters in trunks stored in the attic. Our daughters played their parts well: Joe and I recognized all of the amusing take-offs of their parents.

This was followed by a ballet that symbolized our special interests, with Harmony as the keynote. Her attendants first brought in a large vase inscribed with the words "Archaeology" and "Arabic," to which Knowledge danced. Art and Drama on another vase were interpreted by Beauty. The final vase was Laughter. This versatile dancer handled with dexterity many balloons, large and lovely in colors, and on the balloons were names of Joe's endless amusing stories.

Our young grandson, Johnny Schieffelin, dressed as a dog, trotting behind Laughter, was the hit of the show. "Joe's yellow dog story!" exclaimed the audience. This, his most popular story, he told in pretended Chinese, about a courtroom scene where the verdict depended on the identity of a dog, described differently by a variety of Chinese witnesses.

The reception for us was at the home of the elder Catlins, now owned by their daughter, Mrs. Frederic W. Allen. The celebration ended when Dan Catlin, her brother, conferred jointly on Joe and me an honorary degree of Master of the Art of Living.

Lyneham Crocker's final words in summing up the events were, "Surely it was with such people in mind as Joe and Corinna that Browning wrote, 'The best is yet to come.'" Prophetic indeed, in view of what the next year held in store for Joe!

He had received a letter from the Egyptian government saying that the house in Saqqarah was again at his disposal and, as in previous years, Egyptian pupils were awaiting instruction in the methods of reproducing their own ancient art.

During the summer of 1949, Abd' Essalam spent two weeks with us in Dublin to recuperate from a slight illness which he had suffered in Washington. He seemed completely recovered when he left for important business on the Pacific Coast. We were totally unprepared for the news we shortly received from the Egyptian Embassy that Abd' Essalam had died in the Mayo Clinic after a minor operation.

Again the Cairo Museum gave an exhibition in the spring of 1950. At its close an article appeared in an Arabic newspaper under the heading, "Joseph Lindon Smith—Egypt's Cultural Project." What pleased Joe was the statement that Mr. Smith's paintings had stimulated the interest of many Egyptians to go and see for themselves the wonderful monuments of their own country, and to take pride in their great traditional art.

During the winter of 1950, Joe had been on his feet each day, painting hours on end in inaccessible niches and before reliefs and statues from Saqqarah and Theban tombs, among them many recent discoveries. Never had his undefeatable energy been more noticeable than on this trip, nor his enthusiasm.

After the golden wedding anniversary, Joe's Egyptian paintings had been on view in the Art Gallery of the Century Association, the club having waived the regulation of allowing a member to have a one-man show only once. This was Joe's third. An even greater honor was accorded him by the Smithsonian Institution of Washington in breaking a strictly-adhered-to precedent of never exhibiting the works of a living artist, by having Joe's Egyptian paintings shown during June, 1950.

An added recognition was the collaboration of the government of Egypt, at the request of the Egyptian ambassador, who at the time was arranging a traveling exhibit of Joe's Egyptian work through art centers of the United States.

At my instigation, wives of all members of the Egyptian Embassy staff were present at the opening, when the gathering remained standing near a small platform during brief speeches. These charming, shy little ladies gravitated to me, frequently murmuring excitedly, "It was wonderful we Egyptians had gotten out so many Americans."

I like to remember Joe in this his final public appearance away from home, standing with the American flag on one side of him, and on the other, that of Egypt, a country which had adopted him.

I am glad that his final illness was in his own bed and that he saw his great grandson, the child of Jessie and her husband, the Reverend Samuel W. Hale, Jr.

He often spoke during the last days of Amelia Earhart and of her solo flight years before across the Atlantic. He had found in the courage of this kinswoman of ours by marriage a salient fact of life. And perhaps he knew what she had once written in a letter to me: "A heart and soul wide open to each new opportunity, defying the onrush of years in his zest for living—to me that's Joe."

46

PRESERVING WHAT REMAINS

A COMMONPLACE of human existence is the transitory character of all that we are and all that we achieve. The freshness and vitality of a moment of high achievement is its own reward. The arts of the stage, the dance, and musical performance are especially notable in this respect. The arts of painting, sculpture, and musical composition, on the other hand, are imperishable if good. They need none of what Samuel Taylor Coleridge called "theatrical illusion"—that moment of creativity in which the artist, his actors, and the audience all perform together—to make them come alive. But only the memory of those of us who saw them can recall some of the great performing artists of the past.

I had occasion to be reminded of these facts in 1953, when, in the early summer, a cursory examination of our "treasure chest," consisting of the attic and many downstairs rooms in the "Old House," which Joe and I had first occupied in Dublin after our marriage, revealed that insects had been thorough in their destruction of the contents of the attic trunks, possibly even other belongings in other parts of the house. The "New House," fifty yards away on the same grounds, our home for more than fifty years, was undisturbed by the invaders.

I sent immediately for an insect exterminator, whose verdict was that practically everything in the attic would have to be disposed of. Carpenter ants and buffalo beetles were the worst offenders, he said, and their progress, once started, was rapid. Silverfish also had eaten big holes in garments and draperies. He predicted that very little could be saved of the costumes, stuff on the walls, and scenery.

Here, marked for destruction of a more systematic kind, were the appurtenances of countless plays, pageants, masques, and musical events in which Joe had participated, all of which had been created by him. I tell of them now, not to evoke personal memories but to touch briefly upon stages in a civilization and a culture which segments of American society developed from the 1890's until our own day. But what was must first be destroyed, a bit at a time, before we can recall what, in fact, was.

Windows were removed from the largest attic room, fronting the lawn, a truck was stationed directly below to catch things thrown out. The insect exterminator told me that, after the attic was completed, there must be a careful examination of the downstair rooms. He mentioned, as particularly vulnerable, woven material, deer skin, and buffalo hide in the Indian collection, and draperies, canvas in paintings, parchment, leather bindings, and books. Looking over each object would be a slow process, and until it was done, it was useless for him to come back for a personal checkup before fumigating the premises.

"We'll start with the costumes," I said to the village woman who came to assist. I seated myself before the first of an endless number of trunks with lids raised. As a hand lifted out and held for my inspection tattered remnants of silk, with colors, original form, and design still identifiable, I forgot the present catastrophe as I remembered the costume on Ruth St. Denis, then at the beginning of her brilliant career.

I remembered meeting her with Joe at the Lenox Library, where she so often read about the Orient. He inquired whether she would be interested in creating an East Indian nautch dance, as *the* feature in an Egyptian festival he was producing for Louis Tiffany. She caught fire at once as he expounded his ideas, and when he asked whom she wanted for her partner, she replied, "You, Mr. Smith."

The ravaging insects, aided by squirrels, had eaten great chunks out of Joe's special trunk containing costumes he had worn as a dancer. I pushed aside some of the mass of accumulated sawdust and found a small fragment of East Indian cloth, which had been part of a short skirt worn by Joe in that spirited dance long ago with Ruth St. Denis.

In another scrap I was able to identify a Neptune costume, in which Joe had made a leap from a standing position on a white horse, to join as Neptune his Queen Aphrodite. The part was taken by an acknowledged star of rhythmic expression in dancing. She had done in this Newport show a series of sensational barefoot dances, in and out of a pool, that had staggered the imagination of the entranced audience.

During supper, after the performance, she had broken away from an admiring group to talk to me about Joe. It took someone of her special kind of professional training, she told me, to appreciate how extraordinary were my husband's feats, as a dancer, perfect in timing and rhythm, and she added earnestly, "He does things with his body that can't be done."

A pair of undamaged oriental slippers, under a loosened board in the lid of the trunk, recalled vividly a musical adaptation around the character of Aladdin. This was a charity benefit in a Boston theatre that Winthrop Ames had agreed to produce, provided Joe would be Aladdin. For nearly two hours he had been almost constantly on the stage, dancing with endless variations.

A rabbit's white ear switched my thoughts to Joe as the White Rabbit in a performance of *Alice in Wonderland*, performed in a

Boston theatre, which had caught the attention of a Broadway producer. He had gone to Joe in his dressing room after the show to tell him he actually had been a rabbit. "Also," he said, "your incidental dancing has what it takes, Mr. Smith." Before he left, he proposed that Joe join his company.

Each stirring up of the mass of costumery revealed something. For instance, several hard lumps were part of the horns and hoofs worn by Joe as a faun, which was one of his famous characterizations.

A glittering bit of silver fabric fell to pieces as I handled it, but not before I identified it as a fish costume Joe had worn at a Submarine Ball which he had given as a benefit for the Children's Art Center in Boston. Mildred Bliss, with her usual vision, had created the center, which an architect friend of hers had designed for the grounds belonging to the Music School Settlement. The idea was to give children of all races living in the slums of Boston a chance to come in direct contact with art, not least of all so that potential talents might be discovered and trained intensively.

Tangled threads mixed with the sawdust were too persistent to deny having once been a costume of Jack Frost, in a play which, from the improvised affair in Dublin, had developed into a symphonic poem. The first formal appearance was in Chicago, where the music of an inexperienced composer was performed by a first-rate American symphony orchestra, for a production in the Opera House.

As I watched the trunk now being hurled from the window into the truck, the words, "Please examine the toad, Mrs. Smith," interrupted my trend of thought. I crossed the room to a platform on which the toad had sat for almost fifty years, when not on the road. A glance told the sad story. One leg, all but severed, the body riddled with holes, the back of the head gone, and glass eyes on the floor because there was nothing left to hold them in place.

In spite of Walt Disney's genius with animals, this was the only toad to have hopped across a stage to music played by a symphony orchestra.

In October, 1907, Joe had accepted a proposal to do *Jack Frost* as a benefit for the pension fund of the Chicago Symphony Orchestra. It was easy to recapture Joe's and my first conference with Frederick August Stock, conductor of the orchestra, in the Dublin studio. I saw at a glance that Stock was unusually temperamental, even for a musician, quick tempered, worn out by a hard trip, during which he had missed a train connection, and rather resentful of the committee which had sent him to Dublin to complete the final production arrangements.

Joe had wasted no time in explaining his plot and the principal actors in a pantomime dance: Jack Frost, a large toad, and—

Stock could not contain himself, "A toad?" he stammered despairingly.

At this unpropitious start I had intervened, "As a musician, you will find the scenario abounds in elaborate suggestions which cannot fail to evoke response to orchestral effect," I said soothingly.

Stock apologized for his interruption, and to my relief, I saw from his expression, as he listened to the story, that he had grasped the orchestral possibilities of this "dream fancy," as he called it, borrowing from his German and his newly acquired English.

"I must begin to think over the music," he said with restrained enthusiasm. A further and greater shock than the toad awaited him. The music was by an unknown at the time.

"You expect my orchestra to be a laboratory in which to test experimental music?" Stock shouted explosively, on hearing that my cousin Edward Burlingame Hill was the composer, and that this was his first orchestration.

"Please, calm yourself, Mr. Stock," I said firmly.

With a supreme effort, the conductor of the orchestra managed a feeble smile, "I'm supposed to co-operate—"

I took advantage of this admission to say that I was confident he would find Mr. Hill's musical score as full of interpretative meaning as he had found the story. "Both are worthy of your orchestra," I insisted.

That evening, Stock was beaming as Ned Hill rose from the piano. "Your masterly performance convinces me of the merits of this composition," he said. "What fun we will have."

In Chicago, the excitement was tremendous, when, immediately

425

before the rehearsal, at a back entrance to the stage, the toad's enormous back emerged from a huge packing case marked "Fragile." The members of the assembling orchestra deserted their instruments, fascinated as they watched Joe crawl inside and manipulate the toad's movements from within. Stock, meantime, was in the conductor's box, rapping for attention without getting it.

At last, the première arrived. The performance was a success, but it was the toad who took repeated curtain calls, to the thunderous applause of the audience, as he sat with a strong spotlight bringing out the brilliance of his blinking eyes.

And the composer was honored as well as the toad. Professor Walter R. Spalding, the head of the Musical Department of Harvard University was in the audience purely by accident when the Boston Symphony Orchestra repeated the performance in a charity benefit. At the time he was looking for a substitute during a forthcoming leave of absence. The performance caused him to offer it to Ned Hill, who ended up by spending the next thirty-two years in the Musical Department of Harvard.

Now, forty-five years later, the toad of the Chicago and Boston triumphs was destined for the Dublin dump.

Bits of a costume worn by Henry VIII were reminders of one of the early plays given in the large Greek Amphitheatre, built in 1921 on a long curve of the lake shore after the community had outgrown the seating capacity of our Teatro Bambino.

The title of this play was *Birds of a Feather*. The scene was in paradise where Henry VIII, Muhammad the Arabian Prophet, and Joseph Smith the Mormon, discussed together the charms of their respective lady friends on earth who obligingly materialized on the stage and in the pit.

Remnants of costumes recalled gnomes, wood sprites, and fairies who dropped from tree tops or came up from underground to fly into the limitless realms of the sky following Amelia Earhart. This was in a play given in her honor, at the edge of Dark Pond on the Brewster Estate, on her visit to us at Dublin in 1934, after her solo flight across the Atlantic.

Hour after hour, I inspected the contents of attic trunks, precious moments spent in conjuring up past associations, to compensate for having to accept a relentless present. Occasionally I found myself staring at a completely untouched garment, an anomaly in the center of ruins. In a few trunks sufficient material was left to suggest the vast numbers of actors, amateur and professional, who had become Italian or French court ladies and courtiers, Greeks, Hindus, Chinese, Mayas, Persians, Egyptians, Mexicans, and many other stage nationalities, as well as American Indians.

Titles and plots of plays rushed upon me in a steady stream, and incidents connected with the performances.

Joe's wooden model, for the making of an enormous figure of Cahokia, who was to speak as an oracle from high up in the sky, was too much eaten to be preserved, but it evoked a flood of recollections connected with the Pageant and Masque of St. Louis. Joe had been given a site in Forest Park for the largest stage ever used for a theatrical performance, with over seven thousand in the cast and an amphitheatre that seated one hundred thousand people.

Instead of the expected loss, the production had shown a credit balance of thirty thousand dollars, which formed a nucleus for the founding of a civic theatre in the park. One critic wrote: "All the city was there! It was a great demonstration of democracy's idealism, of its passion for an art that it could understand, of its love for the home town, its past and its future."

After supper on the third and final day of the last clearance, I walked about the now empty rooms with a lantern in my hand. Shadows engulfed me amidst the strange emptiness of bare walls. I particularly missed an American bald eagle, which had been suspended high in a corner of the studio and was associated with fanciful journeys the children had taken in its claws, from bedtime stories told them by their father.

Then I was in the attic, in the largest of the rooms, with forbidding empty eaves, and raised lids of trunks, also empty. The outward symbols of the past had vanished from this room which Joe and I occupied after our marriage. The gay posters and scenarios which had occupied the walls around the room, an unobtrusive bit of scenery or other stage accessory which in other years I saw the first thing

427

in the morning, lit up as the sun streamed in, had now vanished, and with my consent.

In a sudden panic, I doubted whether memory could stand the strain of keeping the past, faced with nothing tangible of all that had occupied this room—these rooms. In this moment of pessimism and defeat, I heard a step mounting the stairs, then a voice. The bug exterminator was back.

"I didn't think you'd have the courage to do it," he said, "But what a playroom remains for your great grandchildren!"

47

HOW TO BE USEFUL
OVER EIGHTY

"To have expressed all that is latent in us," was George Santayana's description of the reward of old age. He had one of the most brilliant minds of his day, but he was content to spend his final declining years in a withdrawal from the world. My contention is that a person never has discharged all that is latent as long as the mind functions.

Today there is much scientific research and planning for fruitful activity for people of advanced years, in order to extend the period of their independence. I am convinced, however, that independence for the elderly lies within the reach of each individual. My premise is simple and workable: Never stop being useful! At the same time, gradually acquire the skill to set up a scale of priorities, eliminating nonessentials.

I was fortunate in my inheritance from hard-working, clear-thinking forebears, who contributed much to the times in which they lived. From their example and that of my parents, I early acquired as a *modus vivendi* the habit of being useful, to which I have adhered in spite of serious and persistent physical setbacks. Youth finds it difficult to understand the struggle against feebleness and loneliness, which are the twin enemies of the old.

Chronic and increasing feebleness are inevitable. But loneliness can be combatted by engaging in a phase of work for which long experience can be an asset. The test of your success should be sought from others, not yourself as an interested party. For you must constantly re-evaluate your experience in order to make certain that it is up to date, that it meets the requirements of changing conditions. Otherwise your further usefulness may automatically come to an end.

An Arab proverb written in 800 A.D. says that "He who has knowledge and does not succeed in passing it on to others has failed in achieving the purpose of knowledge."

This is what I call keeping experience at work. And one must remember that the mind, like everything else, never remains static: it usually advances, but it can retrogress. The way to prevent it from slipping backwards is to use it to the height of one's ability. In my own case, with an inherited Putnam obstinacy, I have not scattered my interests but have kept to a continuity of effort in the same specialized fields. Narcotics and my connection with prisoners were temporary assignments, but work with Indians and in Public Health, which started in each case with a touch of the dramatic, have remained integral parts of my life.

For many years I have participated in the various Indian programs, at the invitation of officials at the top level. I believe my usefulness can be accounted for by a habit which I have adhered to throughout a fairly lively career. This consists in withdrawal at will from the artificial pace of modern existence, to devote myself to reading and quiet thought. And during these intervals at a mental oasis, as it were, I have firmly refused to allow the interruptions produced by the telephone, to which most Americans have become slaves. I have tried always to get and put into systematic order the information on pending issues in which I am involved. This reduces both effort and frustration. Equally, I have tried to be quite precise in conveying to others information and judgment necessary to group or executive action. It all fits under the simple heading, "Be Prepared."

An essential factor throughout my active life, interrupted by frequent illnesses, has been my attempt to maintain satisfactory relations with the medical profession. I have always been successful in conveying to medical consultants what I expected to do, in spite of illness, and they have managed to make it possible. A doctor's job, at least in part, is to make continued action possible for his patient.

The strength of one's interests, and one's willingness to pursue them as long as life permits, constitute the sustaining force of both youth and old age. Charles Eliot Norton's snub of long ago unwittingly set the stage for my life-long interest not simply in the Arabic language but the progress of the peoples of the Near and Middle East. Today, when nothing seems certain except uncertainty, I continue strongly my attachment, not unmixed with delight, to the frequent break-throughs of these peoples in political, industrial, and cultural matters. And of abiding importance is the renewed recognition in these lands of the contributions which may be made now, as well as those which were made half a century and more ago.

In Egypt, the French Institute has been allowed to return to property which was confiscated by the Egyptian government following the attack on Suez in 1956. The German Institute in Egypt has also been re-established.

In the early days, excavations in Egypt were carried on under concessions from the Egyptian government, which permitted approximately one-half of the finds to be exported by the excavator. In this way, objects of undoubted authenticity and of known provenance were acquired by the foreign museums concerned. Not only did this procedure bring to America outstanding collections but it supplied essential training in Egyptology to young men who today staff the museums and universities of our country.

It was the realization of the importance to scholarship of the Nile Valley which led to the formation of the American Research Center in Egypt, incorporated under the laws of Massachusetts in 1950, having as its headquarters the Museum of Fine Arts, Boston. The center provides in a modest way an opportunity for the kind of study at Cairo in Egyptology and Islam that is available in the classical field in the long-established American School at Athens.

My fears about the ultimate future of Ataturk's Turkey, a nation which almost too quickly removed the Islamic underpinning of an entire political structure, reoriented towards democracy, were not unfounded. But fortunately the re-evaluation of Islam in relation to the future of democracy in that land is getting serious, constructive attention.

I am fascinated by the growing insights the Near and Middle East is demonstrating in the Communist drive for dominance. Arabic speaking peoples, mostly adherents of Islam, have a genius for detecting double-talk, and a corresponding genius for admiring simple honesty. The Communist plan for selling oil at cut-rate prices throughout the world means only one thing to the Eastern peoples who are producing this commodity in such vast amounts: the destruction of their own price structure and their income. The United States has clearly revealed an opposite course, which they admire. A development of signal importance, moreover, in combatting the spread of communism in the Near and Middle East has been the American-Arab Federation for Commerce and Industry, with headquarters in New York.

To bring the peoples of the Islamic world and the newly created nation of Israel into a more just and harmonious relationship may not be possible in my time, but the solvent of new political and social concepts must ultimately erode away the attitudes produced by centuries of religious difference.

A genuine compensation nearer home, for having outlived my contemporaries, is the developing strength of welfare among Indians and in public health programs. The contributions of the Eisenhower and Kennedy administrations to these long-delayed objectives have been magnificent. It seems to me that President Kennedy's appointment of Philleo Nash guarantees a commissioner who genuinely understands the needs of our first citizens.

Being useful over eighty consists of these things, I think. But there is an even more fundamental need. To me, it consists in keeping one's eyes turned towards tomorrow, not towards long-distant school days. In fact, I have a good deal of trouble understanding women who insist that the years of school and college were the happiest times of their lives. What is a life for, anyway?

And when there are no more tomorrows, may it not be that, because of the events I have seen, the people I have known, and the record I have set down, slight though it may be in the history of man, I too may take comfort in Horace's hope:

Non omnis moriar.

INDEX

Abbey, Edwin: 60, 125

Abdalla, helps sail boat: 224, 229

Abd' Essalam: as neighbor, 414; in Dublin, 420; death of, 420

Abdul Aziz Ibn Saud: 383

Abdul Hamid II, Sultan of Turkey: and killing of gardner, 105; description of, 108; attends prayer, 108; visit to, 109; and spies, 112; stirs up Moslems, 383

Abdul Rahman: 224

Abdul Wahed: as guide to *Khutmeh*, 230–40; on Koran recital, 231; mother of, 234

Abraham: 99

Abraham Lincoln: 66

Abraham Lincoln Society: 375

Abukir, pyramid of: 230

Abu Simbel: 92ff., 382

Abu Simbel (dahabieh): 205, 212

Abydos, temple of: 394

Académie Julien: 102

Adams, Brooks: name on guest book, 187; friendship with, 265–67; on Philippines and Open-door, 341; on Manila as trade center, 342; farewell dinner of, 367

Adams, Henry: and Mrs. Gardner, 155, 166; name on guest book, 187; and brother, 265f.

Adams, John Quincy: 265

Afreet (evil spirits): 222f.

Agassiz, Alexander, identifies trout: 186

Aguinaldo, Emilio: 346

Aisne River: 296, 315

Akhenaten: 227f., 389

Alban Hills: 198

Albanians, as guards: 109

Alban Mount: 181

Albert, Prince: 42

Alcoholism: 61–62

Alderson Federal Reformatory for Women: 407; visit to, 408ff.

Alexander, George: 65

Alexander the Great, sarcophagus of: 100ff., 112–13

Alexandria, Egypt: 95, 210

Algonquin, sinking of: 288

Ali (reis): temper of, 220–21; and crew desert, 222

Alice in Wonderland: and Lewis Carroll, 58; white rabbit in, 423

Alid party: 109

Allah: 107, 384; in Moslem tradition, 99; implored, 223; in Paradise, 229; communion with, 391; *see also* Moslems

Allen, Mrs. Frederic W.: 184, 419

Allen, Gen. Henry T.: 337

Allenby, Field Marshal Lord: 374, 392

Aloha (yacht): 256, 258, 341, 350ff.

Alsace-Lorraine: 317, 324

Altman, Benjamin: 150

Alvord, Peter: 350

American-Arab Federation for Commerce and Industry: 431

American Association of Indian Affairs: 352

American College at Beirut: 101

American Expeditionary Force, headquarters of: 302

American Red Cross: 272; *see also* Red Cross

American Research Center: 430

American School of Classical Studies (Athens): 431

Ames, Winthrop: 373, 423

Amiens salient: 315

433

434

439

446

Index

Van Cortland Park: 39–40
Van den Steen, Countess: 280, 320
Vanderbilt, William H.: 29
Van Eyck, Jan: 149
Vatican: 174
Vaughan, Henry G.: 135
Velasquez, Diego Rodríguez de Silva: 166
Venice, Italy: 114, 123
Verdun, France: 302, 324f.
Victor Emmanuel III: 178
Villa d'Este: 199
Vimy Ridge: 322
Vogel, Dr.: 350

Wahhabi: 383ff.
Walker, Howard: 138
Walter Reed Hospital: 377
Warner, Margaret: 64
Warner, Susan: 38
Washington, D. C.: art collections in, 144; experiences in, 214–19
Washington Heights: 18–19
Washington Monument: 51
Washington Naval Conference: 368–69
Webb, Beatrice: 360
Webb, Sidney: 360
Webb, Walter Prescott: 367
Weber and Field's Variety Show: 44
Weeks, John W.: 345
Weigall, Arthur: 240
Wellington, Lieutenant: 321
Wendell, Barrett: 131, 133ff.
"We Shake Hands": 399
Wessex, England: 77
Westchester County: 34
Westminster Abbey: 68, 244
Westover School: 331
West Palm Beach, Fla.: 268
Wharton, Edith: 132–33
Wheelwright, Mary C.: 397
Whistler, James: 124; etchings of, 142; paintings in Freer Gallery, 145; meeting with Mrs. Gardner, 156; Mrs. Gardner's collection of, 166
White, Elizabeth: 397
White, William Allen: 283ff.; co-

operation of, 285; and war activities, 289
White House, reception in: 214–15
Whitehurst, Mrs. Sara: 402ff.
Whitlock, Brand: 320
Whitman, Mrs. Henry: 135
Whittemore, Thomas: 388
Whittier, John Greenleaf: 269
Widener, Joseph: 146
Wiesbaden, Germany: 337f.
Wiggin, Mrs. Kate Douglas: 34–35
Wiley, John: 5
Wiley and Long: 4
Wiley and Putnam: 4–5, 39
Williams, Dr. Linsly R.: 293
Willkie, Wendell: 37
Wilson, Woodrow: 7; neutrality policy of, 6, 273, 275, 281; at Dublin, 196; election of, 217; distrust of Spring-Rice, 287; and state of war, 288; interview with, 289–90; arrival in Paris, 317; and Peace Conference, 323; on Philippines, 342, 345; program lost, 368
Windsor Hotel, fire in: 40
Wings of the Dove, The: 125
Winton (Florida guide): 353ff.
Wister, Owen: 252–53
Woman's Order of the Chefckat: 109
Woman suffrage: 305
Wood, Leonard: 342, 345
Wood-Forbes Report: 342, 345
Woollcott, Alexander: 371
Woolley, Leonard C.: 386f.
Worcester High School: 31
World War I: and archaeological activities, 271; activities in, 271–313 *passim;* Gen. Giraud on, 274–75; "Children of Frontier" activities in, 277, 290–300; Red Cross in, 290–93, 307, 313; trips to war zones, 293–300; morale in, 301–302, 306, 312, 320; and Gen. Pershing, 301–330 *passim;* and Peace Conference, 322ff.; Dardanelles campaign in, 363; and social changes, 382f.
Woverin: 321

Interesting People has been set on the Linotype in 11½-point Caslon Old Face, with 1½ points of space between each line. A development of eighteenth-century England, the Caslon type face was soon transplanted to the American colonies, where it achieved widespread popularity. It remains to this day the most enduring element in American typography. Because of its historical link with American printing, Caslon is especially well suited to this account by a member of one of the country's great publishing families.

UNIVERSITY OF OKLAHOMA PRESS

NORMAN

B SMITH, J.
Smith, Corinna Haven
(Putnam)
Interesting people; eighty
years with the great and
near-great,

		DATE DUE